THE HELL OF IT ALL

Charlie Brooker

The Hell of it All

faber and faber
guardianbooks

First published in 2009
by Faber and Faber Ltd
Bloomsbury House
74–77 Great Russell Street
London WC1B 3DA
on behalf of Guardian Books
Guardian Books is an imprint of Guardian Newspapers Ltd

Typeset by Faber and Faber Ltd
Printed in the UK by CPI Mackays, Chatham ME5 8TD

A CIP record for this book
is available from the British Library

ISBN 978–0–571–22957–4

10 9 8 7 6 5 4 3

CONTENTS

INTRODUCTION

Hello, reader, and welcome to another collection of scrawled gibberish, scraped from the pages of the *Guardian* and fashioned into the unassuming paper brick you currently hold in your hands. I hope you enjoy the majority of what you're about to absorb. If not, well, sorry. Use the book for something else. Like security: you could probably club a burglar unconscious with it, if you swing it forcefully enough and angle the spine just right, so it connects with the bridge of their nose. Or just rip it up, make a papier-mâché shield out of it, and go fight dragons. It's your book. Go crazy.

Just like my previous anthology, *Dawn of the Dumb*, the columns here are assembled into chapters, alternating between Screen Burn TV review columns written for the *Guardian Guide* and more wide-ranging (some might say random) pieces tackling any subject under the sun, scribbled for the *Guardian*'s G2 section. The contents are rather arbitrarily presented in chronological order, although you can read the individual articles in any order you like. Like I said earlier, it's your book. Honestly. You own this.

Eagle-eyed readers may spot the occasional word or turn of phrase that didn't appear in print. That's because I've gone back and dug out the 'uncensored' versions of a few of the columns, where it was possible to do so. In a couple of other places I've simply rewritten something slightly to amuse myself. Usually, I've made things more childish. God I hate me.

Thanks are due to many people for their help and assistance in getting this all together: Julian Loose, Liz May Brice, Annabel Jones, Lisa Darnell and Lucinda Chua. Also Malik Meer and Kathy Sweeney at the *Guide*, and Emily Wilson and Mike Herd at G2. The largest, belated thanks are due to Tim Lusher at the *Guardian*, who gave me my first real 'break' with the paper. Apologies to anyone I've missed out. I'm forgetful, not to mention an absolute shit.

Anyway, stop reading this now and go enjoy your book. *YOUR BOOK.*

CHAPTER ONE

In which nightclubs are derided, spiders are feared, and the vast majority of people inexplicably fail to blow their own heads off

The hell of nightclubs [13 August 2007]

I went to a fashionable London nightclub on Saturday. Not the sort of sentence I get to write very often, because I enjoy nightclubs less than I enjoy eating wool. But a glamorous friend of mine was there to 'do a PA', and she'd invited me and some curious friends along because we wanted to see precisely what 'doing a PA' consists of. Turns out doing a public appearance largely entails sitting around drinking free champagne and generally just 'being here'.

Obviously, at 36, I was more than a decade older than almost everyone else, and subsequently may as well have been smeared head to toe with pus. People regarded me with a combination of pity and disgust. To complete the circuit, I spent the night wearing the expression of a man waking up to Christmas in a prison cell.

'I'm too old to enjoy this,' I thought. And then remembered I've always felt this way about clubs. And I mean all clubs – from the cheesiest downmarket sickbucket to the coolest cutting-edge hark-at-us poncehole. I hated them when I was 19 and I hate them today. I just don't have to pretend any more.

I'm convinced no one actually likes clubs. It's a conspiracy. We've been told they're cool and fun; that only 'saddoes' dislike them. And no one in our pathetic little pre-apocalyptic timebubble wants to be labelled 'sad' – it's like being officially declared worthless by the state. So we muster a grin and go out on the town in our millions.

Clubs are despicable. Cramped, overpriced furnaces with sticky walls and the latest idiot theme tunes thumping through the humid air so loud you can't hold a conversation, just bellow inanities at megaphone-level. And since the smoking ban, the masking aroma of cigarette smoke has been replaced by the over-bearing stench of crotch sweat and hair wax.

Clubs are such insufferable dungeons of misery, the inmates have to take mood-altering substances to make their ordeal seem halfway tolerable. This leads them to believe they 'enjoy' clubbing. They don't. No one does. They just enjoy drugs.

Drugs render location meaningless. Neck enough ketamine and you could have the best night of your life squatting in a shed rolling corks across the floor. And no one's going to search you on the way in. Why bother with clubs?

'Because you might get a shag,' is the usual response. Really? If that's the only way you can find a partner – preening and jigging about like a desperate animal – you shouldn't be attempting to breed in the first place. What's your next trick? Inventing fire? People like you are going to spin civilisation into reverse. You're a moron, and so is that haircut you're trying to impress. Any offspring you eventually blast out should be drowned in a pan before they can do any harm. Or open any more nightclubs.

Even if you somehow avoid reproducing, isn't it a lot of hard work for very little reward? Seven hours hopping about in a hellish, reverberating bunker in exchange for sharing 64 febrile, panting pelvic thrusts with someone who'll snore and dribble into your pillow till 11 o'clock in the morning, before waking up beside you with their hair in a mess, blinking like a dizzy cat and smelling vaguely like a ham baguette? Really, why bother? Why not just stay at home punching yourself in the face? Invite a few friends round and make a night of it. It'll be more fun than a club.

Anyway, back to Saturday night, and apart from the age gap, two other things struck me. Firstly, everyone had clearly spent far too long perfecting their appearance. I used to feel intimidated by people like this; now I see them as walking insecurity beacons, slaves to the perceived judgement of others, trapped within a self-perpetuating circle of crushing status anxiety. I'd still secretly like to be them, of course, but at least these days I can temporarily erect a veneer of defensive, sneering superiority. I've progressed that far.

The second thing that struck me was frightening. They were all photographing themselves. In fact, that's all they seemed to be doing. Standing around in expensive clothes, snapping away with phones and cameras. One pose after another, as though they needed to prove their own existence, right there, in the moment. Crucially, this seemed to be the reason they were there in the first place. There was very little dancing. Just pouting and flashbulbs.

Surely this is a new development. Clubs have always been vapid and awful and boring and blah – but I can't remember clubbers documenting their every moment before. Not to this demented extent. It's not enough to pretend you're having fun in the club any more – you've got to pretend you're having fun in your Flickr gallery, and your friends' Flickr galleries. An unending exhibition in which a million terrified, try-too-hard imbeciles attempt to out-cool each other.

Mind you, since in about 20 years' time these same people will be standing waist-deep in skeletons, in an arid post-nuclear wasteland, clubbing each other to death in a fight for the last remaining glass of water, perhaps they're wise to enjoy these care-free moments while they last. Even if they're only pretending.

Think of a number   [20 August 2007]

I was queuing for a ticket at Clapham Junction when it happened. The train was leaving any minute from a platform at the other end of the station, so I was tense. To add to my woes, the person in front of me using the machine was one of those professional ditherers the Sod's Law Corporation apparently employs to arrive in your life at the most infuriating moments.

As time drained away, he gawped at the screen like a medieval serf trying to comprehend helicopter controls, confounded by one simple question after another – questions such as where he was going, and how many of him there were. His hand hovered over the touch screen, afraid to choose, like a man deciding whether to stroke a sleeping wolf. Meanwhile I ground my teeth to chalk dust.

Finally the prick was done, and once I'd waited for him to collect his tickets and his bloody receipt, it was my turn. Having no change, I opted to pay by card. But just as my hand moved towards the keypad to enter my pin, a voice in my head whispered: 'You don't know what it is.' And it was right. I didn't. I scanned my head, but nope: my pin had vanished. It had gone.

I tried inputting something that seemed about right. INCOR-RECT PIN said the screen. I slowed my breathing to clear my head. Rested my hand on the keypad a second time. Tried to fall back on muscle memory. Performed a finger dance. INCORRECT PIN.

I became aware of the snaking, sighing queue behind me. Now I was the ditherer. A third bum guess would swallow the card, so I snapped it back into my wallet, turned on my heel and walked off, past the eyes of everyone in the queue, trying vainly to look as though not buying a ticket had been my plan all along, and everything was going smoothly, thanks for asking. Annoyed, I went outside and hailed a taxi.

As I sat in the back, I examined the contents of my head. The number had to be in there somewhere. After all, I've only got one card. One pin to remember. And I use it all the time, every day; in supermarkets, cafes, cashpoints, stations . . . everywhere. I realised that I'd better remember it soon or I wouldn't be able to function in modern society. Yet the harder I thought, the more elusive the number became. The only thing I knew for certain was that it didn't have a letter J in it. And that wasn't much of a clue. My brain had deleted it for no reason whatsoever.

I asked friends for advice. One told me to close my eyes and visualise my fingers on the keypad. Trouble is, I'm so scared of thieves peeking over my shoulder, I've perfected the art of making my hand look like it's entering a different pin to the one it's actually entering. When I try to picture it in my mind's eye, I can't actually see what I'm doing. I've managed to fool myself within my own head.

Someone else told me the key was to stop worrying about it and go Zen. Next time you're passing a cashpoint, relax: it'll just come to you, they said. But I couldn't relax. If you forget your pin, you have two guesses at an ATM, and two guesses in a shop. A third incorrect guess incurs a block, and isn't worth risking. Fail on your first two tries and you have to wait till the following day, when your guess tally is reset. All of which makes each attempt pretty nerve-racking – like using an unforgiving and incredibly irritating pub trivia machine.

Over the past few days I've approached cashpoints with misplaced confidence, only to suffer last-minute performance anxiety. It's like trying to go at a crowded urinal, when you're wedged between two men with penises the size of curtain rods, pissing away like horses. Just as a shy bladder refuses to wee, my brain refuses to dislodge the number. It won't come out. Not a drop. I'm impotent.

This morning I gave in and called the bank, ashamed. Sensibly, they wouldn't read my pin out over the phone, but offered to post a reminder. But because they're a bank, and banks work to an infuriating Twilight Zone calendar in which any task that would normally take five minutes in our dimension suddenly takes five to ten 'working days', I'm currently operating in that unsettling limbo familiar to anyone who's lost a wallet; you become a social outcast, carrying ID into your home branch and begging for some old-fashioned banknotes to tide you over.

Inconvenience aside, what's creeped me out is the thudding blank hole in my head where the number used to live. It can't be possible to completely forget something so familiar. Perhaps it was stolen. Perhaps someone hacked into my mind while I was dreaming and sucked it away through a pipe. Or perhaps this is stage one of my inevitable descent into thrashing, bewildered madness. What am I going to forget next? How to chew food?

In the meantime, if anyone's got any hints on lost-memory retrieval, pass them on. I've tried everything from getting drunk to lucid dreaming, and the little bastard is still hiding in the bushes, looking on and laughing. I can sense it. But I can't see it.

Whippersnapper TV   [27 August 2007]

Young people today are nothing but trouble. They slouch. They're lawless. They tote knives and flob on the ground. Look into their eyes: there's no gratitude there. Just blank-eyed nihilism and belching. Although the belching's coming from lower down, from the mouth bit. Young people undermine society. They come over here, into our present, downloading our ring tones. Would you want your daughter marrying one? Young people think they own the place. Well, they don't. Yet.

But what can be done? The softly-softly approach is as much use as a Plasticine ladder or a glass trampoline. Take a group of youths hanging out by the local bus stop, intimidating innocent pedestrians with their 21st-century patois. Now approach them. Try to point out where they're going wrong. Be patient. Take your time. Use diagrams. Will they listen? Will they heck. They won't even look you in the eye. While you politely set them straight, they stare at their shoes and snort, because you're old and dull and they hate you. That's how their minds work. They've got no respect for their superiors.

You can't win with young people. But you can punish them. The older male generation loves dreaming up punishments for the young. It's the only thing that still gets them aroused. Last week, moon-faced political letdown and professional idiot David Cameron suggested a new kind of penalty.

'I'd like to see judges and magistrates tell a 15-year-old boy convicted of buying alcohol or causing a disturbance that the next time he appears in court he'll have his driving licence delayed,' he said, through his fat failing mouth, adding, 'And then I'd like that boy to tell his friends what the judge said.'

Dribbling gump though he is, Cameron's on to something here. And that bit where the crook-boy has to tell his mates what happened is the key.

In the mind of a young person, being told off is cool. An asbo, therefore, is like a badge of honour: a sort of alternative Victoria Cross. What's required is a form of punishment that genuinely humiliates the offender.

Every so often a comedy judge in America will sentence someone to some kind of embarrassing public penance: walking down the street in a chicken suit, and so on. We need to go one better, by establishing a dedicated 24-hour digital TV channel on which young offenders humble and debase themselves.

Here's how it works. Let's say a 16-year-old called Ryan has stolen a shopping trolley and spun it round and round in the town centre while screaming abuse at horrified passers-by. He's arrested and charged and hauled into court. The judge sentences Ryan to five hours' community service on Channel Loser.

As part of his punishment, Ryan has to hand over his mobile

phone, so the police can search through his address book and text all his friends, telling them what time to tune in. Let's say it's 4 p.m. As the clock strikes four, Ryan's friends flop down on the sofa, switch on the box, and this is what they see.

Ryan is wearing nothing but a pair of bikini bottoms. 'Hello,' he says, reading slowly from the autocue. 'My name's Ryan Daniels and I stole a trolley.' Then the *Thomas the Tank Engine* theme music starts playing and Ryan has to dance to it. When the tune comes to an end, it instantly skips back to the beginning and Ryan has to start again. This sequence is repeated until he bursts into tears.

Then Ryan's mum walks in, spits on a bit of tissue, and wipes his face with it. Then she produces a bag of his laundry and goes through every item in it one by one, complaining bitterly about the state of his underpants and so on.

Once she's gone, Ryan climbs into a paddling pool filled with ice-cold water and sits down until his genitals have shrivelled to squinting point. Then he has to stand up and pull down his bikini bottoms, at which point a girl from *Hollyoaks* walks in, points and laughs in his face for 10 minutes.

Then Ryan has to push his face into a cow's backside. The sole concession to his personal dignity is a bucket on the floor to be sick in. Finally, there's a three-hour interactive section where the audience at home texts in phrases that Ryan has to read aloud. This, the simplest section, is also the most entertaining. Picture it.

Come the end of his punishment, Ryan will never re-offend and probably won't even go outside again. Problem solved. What's more, we've all been entertained. Everybody wins. Cameron, if you're reading – you can have this idea for free.

Next week: solving climate change with kites.

Planet of the spiders [3 September 2007]

Forget rainy April or snowblown February – early September is the very worst time of year, for one simple reason: it's spider season. Every year, right about now, thousands of the godless eight-legged bastards emerge from the bowels of hell (or the garden, which-ever's nearest) with the sole intention of tormenting humankind. To a committed arachnophobe like me, spider season is like a live-action version of the videogame Doom. My flat is briefly trans-formed into a sort of white-knuckle ghost house in which dropping your guard, even for a moment, can have terrible consequences. The other night, for instance, I awoke at 4 a.m. for a dozy late-night trip to the lavatory. As I sat there, blearily performing the neces-saries, a spider the size of a small dog unexpectedly crawled out from behind the toilet and scampered across my bare right foot. I reacted like I'd been blasted in the coccyx with a taser gun. Blind panic took control of my body before the need to stop 'going' had registered in my brain. You can imagine the aftermath. It's like a dirty protest in there. I may need to move house.

What's the point of spiders anyway? They're just mobile night-mare units put on the Earth to eat flies and frighten people by scuttling out from under the TV stand and lolloping crazily toward you. Non-arachnophobes just don't get it. Fear of spiders isn't a choice, but a residual evolutionary trait that some people have and some don't, just as some people can fold their tongues and others can't. When I see a spider, I'm across the room before I know what's happened, like an animal running from an explosion. It's not learned behaviour, you patronising idiots. It's automatic code, hardwired into the brain. Some brains. My brain.

Once, when I was a student, I was preparing a meal in a hall of residence kitchen when some japester ran in carrying a huge spider he'd found outside. Having made a couple of girls scream, he decided to lunge in my direction. Without even thinking, I swiped at his belly with a kitchen knife in a desperate bid to stave him off. The blade narrowly missed him, which was a shame, because it meant I had to spend the next half-hour listening to him self-righteously bleating about how I must be crazy and he was only having a laugh. I just shrugged. Don't startle someone with a knife in their hand unless you're prepared to face the conse-quences, moron. Next time I'll go for the eyes.

But like I say, non-arachnophobes don't understand. Too lacking in imagination and/or basic human empathy to comprehend the instinctive primal reaction spiders provoke in genuine sufferers, they blather idiotic platitudes like 'It's more scared of you than you are of it', which is absurd since (a) spiders aren't gripped with hypnotic dread at the sight of people, and (b) the spider's primitive brain doesn't have any concept of fear, in much the same way it doesn't have any concept of what the *Police Academy* movies are.

Spiders are so resolutely horrible, they don't even have to exist to be scary. A few weeks into a bumper spider season, I find I'm often as frightened of spiders that aren't there as ones that are: terrified to pick up a shoe in case there's a spider in it, for example.

This is because spiders have precisely the same modus operandi as terrorists: they target innocent civilians at random, strike unexpectedly, and cause widespread disproportionate fear. Oh, and they often die as a result of their actions, or at least they do if I've got a rolled-up newspaper to hand. Spiders don't videotape their own suicide notes before embarking on their death campaigns, but that's only because they're too thick to operate the controls.

All of which prompts the question of why the military doesn't get involved. Think about it: if the army fought the War on Spiders instead of the War on Terror, it would be (a) winnable, (b) cheaper, (c) popular, and (d) justifiable in the eyes of God. I'd certainly slumber more soundly in my bed if I knew Our Lads were available on 24-hour call-out; a dedicated anti-arachnid task force that would turn up at your home in the dead of night and splatter that absolute whopper that ran under the cupboard an hour ago and has left you unable to sleep ever since. Oh, and please note I'm suggesting the use of lethal force as a default. None of this fannying around with pint glasses and sheets of paper and 'putting him outside'. He'll just crawl in again, stupid. If a murderer climbed through your window you wouldn't just 'put him in the garden'. You wouldn't rest until you saw his brains sloshed up the wall. It's the same with spiders. If it's not been reduced to a gritty, twitching smear, it's not been dealt with at all.

Actually, since this is a liberal paper, I suppose arrest and detention might be acceptable. The army could take care of that: scoop the bastards up and whisk them away to spider prison. The cells would need impossibly tiny bars, mind. Anyway, that's what this country needs: an armed response to the arachnid menace. That this hasn't happened is the greatest tragedy of our age.

– The above column on spiders was written at the last minute as a replacement to the following article, which was spiked prior to publication on for being slightly too bleak for Monday morning Guardian *readers to countenance . . .*

Pointlessness abounds   [intended for 3 September 2007]

Here's a sentence rarely used to open newspaper columns: why don't the vast majority of people just blow their own heads off? You, with the coffee cup. You, with the shoes. Why are you bothering? What's the point? Is there a point? And has anyone written it down in an easily-digestible form? With pictures? Like a *Mr Men* book? If you think that sounds a touch depressing, you're wrong. Pointlessness is liberating. But we'll get onto that in a minute. First, let's consider life: the case against.

OK. I live in London, a city where it's hard not to look around and think, 'Christ, so it's come to this?' on a daily basis. Cities are one of human civilisation's most significant creations, and London is supposed to be one of the finest cities in the world. But it's horrible. It's cold, cramped, and ringing with sirens. Visually, it's an unending collage of immense grey boxes squatting beneath immense grey clouds, surrounded by thick grey-tasting air. Your best chance of seeing a splash of colour in London is to stare at a billboard or spew on the pavement. Coincidentally, those two activities also represent the finest entertainment the city has to offer.

But it's not just London that's awful. You are too. And by 'you', I mean 'us'. Humankind. After all, we clearly peaked about 40 years ago, and it's been downhill ever since. For all this talk of the dazzling modern age, the two biggest advances of the past decade are Wi-Fi and Nando's. That's the best we can do. Meanwhile the environment's crashing, fundamentalists and morons are at each other's throats, God's so disappointed he's wished himself out of existence, and the rest of us are merely pottering around, distracting ourselves by fiddling with our iPod settings.

Ooh look I've changed the menu screen wallpaper. Ooh look I've changed it back. Ooh look I've – oh. A mushroom cloud. That's annoying. How am I going to power my iPod now? The charger's just melted. As have my hands. And I'm thinking these thoughts with a boiling molten brain bubbling through a fissure in my freshly carbonised skull. Oh well. Night night.

And even assuming the world doesn't come to an end while you're standing in it, the sheer scale of creation renders most existences futile. The universe is so timelessly immense, absolutely anything you say or do is meaningless by comparison. In the grand scheme of things, even mankind's brightest stars – yer Beethovens and Shakespeares and Einsteins – are fleeting pixels, gone in the blink of a mosquito's eye. And most of us don't achieve anything like as much as them. In fact most of us achieve less than, say, Daniel Bedingfield.

So, to return to my opening question, why don't the vast majority of people just blow their own heads off? The answer, presumably, is that life's inherent meaninglessness is precisely the thing that gives it meaning in the first place. If Jesus Christ turned up tomorrow on CNN to officially announce what the point of existence was, it would ruin everything. What if it turned out to be 'collecting teacups'? By that reckoning, most of us are failures. As it stands, none of us are. In the absence of any formal rules, the only thing required of us is basic human survival. And we might as well be upbeat about it.

Daniel Bedingfield, incidentally, worked this out some time ago and wrote a catchy, cathartic song about it – 'Gotta Get Thru This' – which went to number one. If he'd called it 'Might As Well Blow My Own Head Off' it wouldn't have had half as much airplay. We can all learn from that. We can all learn from Daniel Bedingfield. Now there's a sentence rarely used to close newspaper columns.

CHAPTER TWO

In which lies are told by everyone except Simon Cowell, Jamie Oliver cooks tomatoes, and the 24-hour news networks look for Madeleine McCann

Like, totally psychotic   [14 July 2007]

You know what I miss? Fray Bentos steak and ale pies. I haven't had one in years. But as a student, I ate them constantly. I thought they represented grown-up cooking. After all, this wasn't your average takeaway slop. No. A Fray Bentos supper required preparation and patience. You had to shear the lid off with a tin opener, and chuck the pie in the oven for half an hour. The end result was sublime. Except it wasn't. Having wolfed down better, fresher meals since then, I now realise that what I was eating tasted like dog food boiled in a stomach lining by comparison. At the time I just didn't know any better. Now I couldn't face one. I've been spoiled. You can't go home again.

I'm starting to wonder if obsessively watching *The Wire* has similarly spoiled me in terms of TV drama. By now, the sound of yet another person blasting on about how good *The Wire* is probably makes you want to yawn your soul apart, but really: it's so absorbing, so labyrinthine and bloody-minded, it makes almost everything else seem a bit . . . well, a bit Fray Bentos.

Take *Dexter*. I'd heard a lot of positive things about it. Beyond positive, in fact: people queued up to give it a blowjob. And tickle its balls. And look it in the eye while they did so. These were people I trusted. And then I sit down to actually watch it and discover my head's been so warped by Wirey goodness, *Dexter* simply gets on my wick.

The premise is as dumb as a dodgem full of monkeys. Anti-hero Dexter is a blood-spatter expert working for the Miami police department. He's also a serial killer. But that's okay, because he's managed to channel and control his murderous tendencies by indulging in vaguely justifiable slayings – i.e. he only kills other serial killers.

Preposterous, yes, but there's nothing wrong with a preposterous set-up *per se*. Unfortunately the show ping-pongs between quirky, tasteless comedy and what it seems to earnestly believe is a compelling study of the psychopathic mindset. It's a bit like watching an episode of *Scooby-Doo* in which the lighthouse keeper who's

17

disguised himself as a sea monster in order to scare people away from his gold spends half his screen time mulling over the philosophical meaning of masks. And then stabs Shaggy in the eye with a toasting fork.

What's more, the show depends on the viewer finding Dexter himself curiously charming despite the fact that he enjoys strapping his victims to a gurney and torturing them with a drill. The easiest way to achieve this is to make said victims 'worse' than he is. Implausibly worse. This week, for instance, Dexter's stalking a hit-and-run drunk driver – which means he can't be just any old drunk driver, but a serial offender who's apparently ploughed through an orphan in every state, repeatedly beaten the rap, and then shrugged it off as no big deal.

They might as well cut to a shot of him dancing on a grave with a bottle of champagne in his hand. Enter Dexter stage left with his power drill. Cue cheering. Cut to ad break. Phew, this show is, like, intense, man. It totally toys with your sense of moral justice and shit. Awesome!

Add to that a bunch of mono-dimensional cops working alongside Dexter (including his sister, whose sole character trait is a potty mouth), an irritating voiceover that's about one-tenth as wry as it thinks it is, and a smattering of unbelievably bad yet apparently earnest flashback sequences in which young Dexter is schooled in the art of anger management by his FBI-profiler dad, and you're left with a weird, offensively simplified mulch which only an idiot could truly refer to as 'dark'.

Which isn't to say it's utterly terrible; I'm curious enough to try the next episode. But don't be fooled into thinking it's any more sophisticated than *The A-Team*. It's gorier, that's all.

Death to the liars [21 July 2007]

Shriek! Panic! Kick the neighbours awake and tell them the truth! Your TV is deceiving you! The Queen didn't storm out! Gordon Ramsay didn't catch that fish! And that animated 3D map the weatherman stands in front of ISN'T REALLY THERE! It's all a lie!

A disgusting, despicable lie! HANG THEM! HANG THE LIARS! On live, un-manipulated television – pure and truthful, the way it used to be.

Yes, for months now the papers have been behaving like hairless pod people who've just pulled the tube pumping hallucinatory Matrix code into their brains and stood up, truly awake for the first time in their lives, squinting and blinking at the world as it is, rather than the cartoon fib they've been fed. And now they're bravely running round town knocking on doors, alerting the dreaming populace to the cold hard truth, goddammit.

Revelations about premium-rate phone-in lines and misleading news reports are one thing, but come on – Gordon Ramsay didn't catch a fish? Frankly, I'd be surprised if he was on the boat in the first place. Most of it's blue-screen trickery anyway. When you see him chopping onions, those aren't actually his hands – they're CGI simulations. He's not even a real man. He's a bear in a rubber mask. And a violent, angry bear at that. They just edit out the bits where he attacks people and steals picnic baskets, dub someone saying 'fuck' over the top, and hide subliminal messages in the accompanying musical bed, commanding you not to question the verisimilitude of what you're seeing.

Yes, television routinely tells fibs, and should always be approached with a healthy degree of scepticism, and any big lies it tells deserve to be exposed – but to hear the tabloids bang on about it, you'd have thought they were fearless campaigners for truth who'd never, say, take 25 photos of a celebrity emerging from a nightclub, select one in which their eyes are in mid-blink and their gob's half-open (probably because they're telling the photographer to piss off), then run it to illustrate a story about how drunk they are, because look, look, you can see it – those drooping eyelids, that dangling jaw.

'We're all worried sick about him – he's on the fast track to an early grave,' said a source close to the star (who can't be named for reality-based reasons). Massaged reality is all around us. Although of course, since I work in both newspapers and television, you shouldn't believe anything I say anyway. These aren't even real words. I filmed the individual letters two years ago, then edited them out of sequence to give the impression of an article.

Right now, for example, I'm pretending to write about *Heroes*, which starts this week on vanilla terrestrial television following a wildly successful run on the Sci Fi channel earlier this year, and which I'd somehow managed to miss until now. In fact I know so many people who've already seen it – downloading it here, burning it onto a DVD there – I've sometimes felt like a Victorian gentleman who's somehow beamed himself into the future and discovered himself to be a walking anachronism.

And now, finally, I understand what the fuss was all about. *Heroes* is great: a sassy modern take on comic-book superheroes, clearly influenced by Alan Moore's *Watchmen*. Nonsense, maybe, but hugely entertaining nonsense. Surprisingly grisly too.

If you're one of the three people who hasn't already watched the entire first season on an iPhone or something, I won't spoil any of it for you. But for pity's sake do tune in, because it's a beautifully assembled piece of popcorn fun – even though none of the actors have real superpowers, and apparently the words they're saying are all scripted in advance, and they just turn up on set (yes 'on set' – those aren't their real homes) and read the scripts out and pull faces that make it look like they're experiencing real emotions and then it all gets edited together into a 'story', which the public buy hook, line and sinker. Man, it's a devious world.

– *Despite my kind words here, the dumb-but-fun* Heroes *went all to shit in its second season. That's life.*

Charley Hoarse [28 July 2007]

And on the 55th day, God sent a flood to destroy all of Britainkind. And Oxfordshire sank. And Gloucestershire sank. And the Vale of Evesham became a stagnant puddle with a few bits of roof poking out of it. And Sky News did sadly gaze upon the scene, running a Breaking News caption each time a lilypad floateth past, and there was much wailing and gnashing of teeth, for even though this was the most boring natural disaster of all time, there was much ruining of carpet and wine cellar, and the people were greatly upset. And eventually God appeareth at a hastily-arranged press conferenceth and said, 'lo, I missed.' And God wenteth on to admitteth he'd been aiming for Borehamwood in a desperate bid to silence Charley off *Big Brother 8* who, God explaineth, gets right on God's tits with her constant bloody jawing, like.

Deities aside, it's hard to imagine anything that could shut Charley up. She's the most boring housemate in the programme's history – far more boring than the ones who spend their time moping silently in the background, like Thingytits from year two and Whatsisarse from year four, because she's pro-actively boring. Unstoppably so. She'd cross a lake of fire to babble into your ear about herself for 17 solid hours.

Charley's name is fitting, because listening to her ceaseless self-centred rambling is PRECISELY like listening to a dreary cokehead chewing your ear off at 3 a.m. with a punishing soliloquy about what they're like and what they think and what the really great thing about them is. Frighteningly, Charley's not on coke. Can you IMAGINE what she'd be like if she was?

Actually, there's no point imagining. She'd never get hooked in the first place. Pass her a mirror with a white line on it, and she'd automatically blow it out of the way to get a better look at herself. She can't strut past any vaguely reflective surface without compulsively pouting and checking her hair. Stand Charley in front of a weeping widow at a funeral, and she'd command her to keep still while she checked her reflection in the teardrops.

Maybe she'll be out by the time you read this; it's possible, although I've given up assuming. She's been stuck in there so long, and against so many odds, she feels like a ghost that's been haunting the building for centuries. Chances are she'll steadily eat herself alive – courtesy of that weird hand-chewing thing she constantly does – rather than be evicted.

With weeks still to go, rumours abound that yet another twist is in the offing. After the All-Girl Opening twist, the Prize Money twist, the Fake Eviction twist and the Unconvincing Australian twist, loyal viewers suffering repetitive twist fatigue must be praying for a Not a Twist at All twist in which precisely nothing unusual happens. Although if there MUST be a twist, I'd welcome one in which the twins have to run out of the nearest fire exit and keep going until they're 10,000 miles from the nearest camera or microphone.

Incidentally, is it me, or are they not 'identical' any more? One's getting thinner, and the other one's swelling like an ankle. It'd be interesting to see if she's put on precisely the same amount of weight as the other one's lost. In fact it might even make the show seem like a valid 'experiment' after all. Hey, what'll happen if we feed one of them nothing but baking soda for a week? Let's find out! Cool!

Speaking of experiments, Brian is now my favourite to win. Under-educated rather than stupid, and with a voice so low and slow it sounds like the electronically disguised intonations of a silhouetted whistleblower in a hard-hitting documentary, Brian's so inherently sweet-natured he's impossible to fully dislike, even if you strain your hate cells.

You know how you can always cheer up an upset toddler by hiding your face behind your hands, then parting them quickly and saying 'peek-a-boo'? And you know that dopey gurgling smile that spreads across its face when you do that? Well, that's Brian basically. And that's why he should win.

The endearing Jamie Oliver   [4 August 2007]

Jamie Oliver. Now there's a man who provokes a reaction. On the one hand, he's a cheeky, knockabout TV chef. And on the other, there's *Jamie Oliver's Cookin'*: Music to Cook By.

In case you'd repressed this particular abuse memory, *Jamie Oliver's Cookin'* was a compilation CD released (and heavily advertised) in the year 2000. 'A good blast of these tunes, a nice bit of tukka and some good company is the recipe for a nice time. Happy days!' said Jamie in the accompanying blurb. Yet track one is 'Dancing in the Moonlight' by Toploader: the sort of song that comes on the car radio while you're gassing yourself with a hose, and merely serves to reinforce your decision.

The TV ad featured Jamie on drums, bashing out a pukka rhythm and wearing a gummy open-mouthed grin, like a drunk who's just kicked his own teeth out and thinks it's hilarious. It caused many to regard Mr Oliver with a level of contempt normally reserved for war criminals.

I didn't make up my mind until I caught wind of the outpouring of middle-class smug-o-wank surrounding his *School Dinners* series, which gave despicable 4x4-driving parents something to feel all superior about: they could tut at the McNugget-wolfing pauper kids while simultaneously shovelling chargrilled asparagus and parmesan shavings down their own spoilt shitbag children's throats.

It was then I decided Jamie Oliver was worse than Satan – which wasn't really fair, since all he'd done was spruce up a school menu or two. He didn't hypnotise the audience into nodding along in unison. Now he's back with a pared-down series called *Jamie At Home*, in which he simply enthuses about food each week for half an hour. It's endearing. It is. Shut up. It is.

This week: tomatoes. Jamie walks around his massive garden showing us some tomatoes he's grown. Try not to notice how massive and posh his garden is, because you'll want to hit him, and instead focus on the tomatoes. Look! He's slicing them up into a salad! And it looks bloody delicious. A plateful of juicy homegrown tomatoes drizzled with olive oil and herbs and tiny shards of chilli, with a few blobs of mozzarella beside it, glistening in the sun and . . .

Hang on. The credits list no fewer than four 'food stylists'. One 'senior food stylist', three regular 'food stylists', and one 'assistant food stylist'. Which presumably explains why those tomatoes looked so nice. Four people stood around doing that salad's hair. Somehow, I feel cheated. But mainly bewildered. And a bit scared. I mean 'food stylist'? What kind of modern hell are we living in here? How do you get into it? Where do you train? Can you get a food styling degree? Do food stylists have their own trade magazine? 'Strawberry Hat – the Food Stylist's bible'. As ridiculous career choices go, it's up there with 'bee dentist'. This world is doomed.

Straight after *Jamie At Home* comes *Cook Yourself Thin*. Each week 'four cool cooks' take a flabby prole and teach her to cook slimline versions of her favourite recipes. That's the idea. It's flawed. For one thing, the moment the voiceover calls them 'cool cooks', you want everyone involved to pack up and go home. What's more, they're plainly too plump to be hosting a show called *Cook Yourself Thin*. One's got arms like a fat scout's thighs, for Christ's sake.

Worst of all, the cookery's a swizz. This week, a woman who likes roast beef dinners is told to drop Yorkshire pudding, use chicken not beef, and swap the big, golden, crispy roast spuds for weasly new potatoes in their skins. That's shit! It's not the same.

At the end, having eaten their recipes for six weeks, she's dropped two dress sizes! Amazing! Unless you pay attention to the large onscreen caption which explains she's also been 'encouraged to exercise', that is. Perhaps, in the new TV spirit of truth and honesty, it should be renamed 'Cook Completely Different Things and Jog Yourself Thin' instead. Or maybe just 'Bullshit'.

Pfff. This country.

A weatherbeaten Richard Hammond
[18 August 2007]

Hey kids! And by 'kids' I mean you, even though you don't look like a kid any more. Jesus, the ageing process has kicked your arse worse than ebola, hasn't it? Those jowls are practically down to your elbows. Ergh.

Anyway, hey kids! Here's a fun new game for you! Tune in to Bruce Parry's amazing adventures in *Tribe* and try to guess precisely how long you'd last in the same environment before suffering a breakdown, clawing at the lens and begging to be taken home to your coffee table and your pillows and your central heating and TV. This week, I managed about 38 seconds, which is an improvement of 20 seconds over the last series. I must be toughening up, like a great big grimacing hard man.

In case you're not familiar with the series, here's how it works: each week, former Royal Marine Bruce Parry – who vaguely resembles a rugged, more weatherbeaten Richard Hammond – visits a remote tribe in order to experience their way of life. Which might sound a bit worthy and dull until you see exactly what 'experiencing their way of life' entails.

Parry doesn't stand around aloofly watching the natives and making wry asides to camera: he rolls his sleeves up and joins in. If the tribe goes hunting, he goes hunting. If the tribe get dirty, he gets dirty. And if the tribe indulge in a bewildering array of sado-masochistic rituals from flagellation to deliberate self-poisoning, he . . . well, you get the idea.

Those sado-masochistic rituals form the centrepiece of this week's instalment, in which Parry immerses himself in the life and culture of the Matis, a tribe of hunters from the Brazilian rainforest. The Matis were only 'discovered' by the outside world in the 1970s: within a few years we'd introduced them to T-shirts and rifles and – oops – hundreds of diseases they'd built up no immunity against. Lots of them died, so they're understandably wary about letting outsiders back into their midst, and even warier about outsiders with cameras. Interestingly, they complain that previous film crews had ordered them around; told them to strip off and pretend they didn't wear clothes to make for a racier documentary. Seems the ongoing TV fakery scandal has now reached as far as the Amazon.

Parry wins their trust by undergoing four excruciating trials that wouldn't look out of place in one of the *Jackass* movies. First, they squeeze some incredibly bitter fruit juice directly into his eye. Then they whip him. The fourth and final trial (being stung all over with some vicious form of nettle) looks unpleasant, but it's not a patch on the third, which involves having a powerful frog poison smeared directly into a fresh wound on his arm. Before long Parry's on all fours, spewing stomach contents with the force of a broken pump. (Thankfully, the camera doesn't capture the next bit, where he runs behind a bush and virtually blasts his own pelvis through his arse during a spectacular anal evacuation.)

Occasionally you suspect the Matis might simply be fucking with our Bruce, having a laugh at his expense – at one point they teach him some local phrases and stand around howling as he repeats them, parrot-style (naturally, they've taught him a load of obscenities). Suddenly I imagined a show in which a foreign reporter befriends a 'tribe' of 'authentic' Glaswegian teenagers, and enthusiastically participates in a series of 'rituals' they insist are genuine – drinking a pint of phlegm and sewing a ribbon on his bollocks.

It's a testament to Parry's skill as a gung-ho, immersive presenter that even as a viewer, you quickly acclimatise to the tribe's way of life, truly seeing them as people rather than exotic aliens. And there's plenty we could learn from them. The Matis have a regular ceremony in which men disguised as 'spirits of the forest' dance into the camp and mercilessly thrash all the children with canes – for no particular reason, it seems, other than to shut them up. If that's not the work of a truly utopian society, I don't know what is.

A moody shot of an inanimate object
[25 August 2007]

As the overlong, overcomplex, ratings-challenged *Big Brother 8* enters its final week, it's time to roll out the red carpet and introduce the annual Screen Burn Housemate Awards – coming to you live from a laptop in London's glittering south end. Fanfares, golden envelopes, and a host of stars from stage and screen – none of these will be featuring. It's just me, typing with an achy elbow. Whoopie doo.

Anyway, let's kick off by doling out the Biggest Waste of Space Ever to Enter That Godforsaken Building Award – which goes to Billi, the insignificant monotone gonk who drifted across your screen for about 10 minutes, mumbling about hair straighteners like the world's most tedious ghost. You know how every so often the *Big Brother* editors like to open a section with a moody shot of an inanimate object – an outdoor chair with dew glistening on it, or a spoon on the sideboard – as though they're constructing an arthouse masterpiece? Well each time Billi appeared on screen, I hoped it would cut to one of those. Just to liven things up.

The Cheesiest Git award goes to Ziggy, the lipless human shrug.

Obsessed with preserving his nice-guy image, he spent decades tirelessly explaining what a reasonable and tolerant human being he was, accompanying each monologue with a series of open-palmed, eyebrow-raising 'honesty' tics that made him look absolutely mental on fast forward. As a result of these incessant hey-I'm-one-of-the-good-guys routines, Ziggy wrinkled his forehead so often it developed an alarmingly deep set of lines, like isobars on a weather map drawn in charcoal. In fact by the end of the series, his forehead was so weird and furrowed I kept mistaking him for one of those rubbish aliens that used to turn up on shows like *Deep Space Nine*, indistinguishable from a human apart from some kind of zany prosthetic brow.

As narcissistic as Ziggy appeared, he wasn't a patch on the Most Psychotically Self-Obsessed Housemate In History – Charley. Or Hurricane Charley, to use her full name. Apparently suffering from some kind of OCD compulsion to repetitively flick her hair and pout at the nearest mirror, Charley wasn't content to be the centre of her own universe, and tried to impinge on everyone else's. The mildest perceived slight would cause her to launch into a feverishly gabbled diatribe, often so absurdly one-sided and abusive it scarcely made sense. Arguing seemed to give her purpose in life; locked alone in a shed for six days, Charley would pick fights with her own thumb for entertainment.

The Best Lookalike Award is always a hotly contested category, and this year was provided a bumper crop. Almost everybody looked like somebody famous. We'll overlook some of the glaring doppelgängers (Ziggy = Christian Bale, Chanelle = Posh Spice), and subtler similarities (Charley = Charlie Williams, David = Ray Liotta), and present the award to Jonty, for his startling quasi-resemblance to Mark Lawson – not the closest lookalike ever, but close enough to make it vaguely possible that some day soon Lawson will be walking down the street only to find himself suddenly surrounded by squealing teenage *Big Brother* fans jumping up and down and taking his photo, while a van driver zooms past parping his horn and bellowing 'Jontyyyyyy you fuckahhhh!' out the window and then we zoom in on Lawson's face and he's absolutely fuming and

IT'S FUNNY TO THINK ABOUT THAT. Which is why Jonty wins.

Finally, the Let Brian Win award goes to Brian, on the grounds that Brian should win. He's possibly the most thoroughly good-natured housemate in the programme's history, and deserves the prize money simply for being so nice. At the time of writing, the creepy twins are his closest competition, but they'd only waste the cash on nonsense. So will Brian, of course, but at least he'll guffaw like a baritone cartoon bear as he does so. BRI 2 WIN!!!!!!

– Brian did, indeed, win.

'What you see is what happened . . .'
[1 September 2007]

If the ratings are to be believed, almost everyone in the country has been watching *The X Factor*. Last week, 500 million people tuned in: a whopping 654% audience share. It almost won its slot, but was narrowly pipped to the post by a repeat showing of *Rockliffe's Babies* on UKTV Gold 2 +1 (a brilliant episode, to be fair – it was the one where they caught a man doing a thing and then some stuff happened and then it was the end).

We're clearly still not sick of Cowell and co just yet. In fact it seems we're content to watch what is essentially the same series year in, year out; the broadcast equivalent of a recurring dream. Rather than forming an angry mob and storming the ITV building armed with cudgels and staves, we sit and dribble and clap our hands, gurgling 'again! again!' like toddlers enjoying the repetition on *Teletubbies*. Well, I do anyway.

These bumper ratings have come in the middle of an interesting time for TV, as the industry suffers a collective nervous breakdown, gazing up its own arse and wondering whether the turds lodged within are real or fake. At last week's Edinburgh TV festival, there was much agonised discussion about a 'crisis of trust', and a fault line developing in the 'relationship with the viewer'. Since *The X Factor* got swept up into the ongoing fakery argument too, it seems audience figures are largely unaffected by the 'crisis', provided you serve up enough desperate losers for them to point and laugh at.

But since ITV are, hilariously, promising 'zero tolerance' for any and all forms of telly fakery, it's worth asking just how real the show is. Early press reports, for instance, suggested the first episode included footage in which Cowell pulled an executive producer aside to discuss the return of Louis Walsh, which turned out to be a 'pick-up shot' rather than an actual record of events. Unless I blinked for an unusually long time, it had been removed from the broadcast version. But why? Walsh's return seemed so thumpingly false anyway, the whole thing might as well have been an animated sequence. And no one gives a shit, because this is only wrestling, and not a real sport.

Yet despite this – despite NO ONE GIVING A SHIT – Cowell said, 'What you see is what happened. We don't try to censor this show. I've always said we will allow viewers to look through the keyhole and that's what we do. It's raw and we don't censor. It's not a sanitised, make-believe show.'

I had no idea *The X Factor* was part of the Dogme 95 movement, but there you go. Since it's year zero for authenticity, I look forward to watching the following sequences over the coming weeks:

1. The scene where the producers 'pre-audition' the hopefuls, filtering out the merely 'average' ones and selecting the 'good' and 'bad' ones to be seen by the celebrity judging panel.

2. One of those post-audition sequences in which a singer is shown returning to their proletarian workplace, where their colleagues are nervously lined up 'awaiting the news', except instead of shouting 'I got through!' and everyone running in to give them a hug, they mumble 'I failed' and everyone weeps and wails and rubs it in their face with dismay.

3. Currently, only the good singers are allowed to have tragic back stories. I'm waiting to see one of the comically ugly or dreadful singers recount a heart-rending tale about how their dad died, or their best friend died, or they got leukaemia of the voice and barely pulled through, before walking into the audition room to be humiliated by the sniggering judges. The show must have amassed a staggering archive containing hour upon hour of boss-eyed fatsos with voices

like harpooned gnus blubbering into camera about how they're entering *The X Factor* in honour of a dead relative – none of which makes it into the edit because it doesn't suit the 'story'.

Well, come on. Apparently this isn't a 'sanitised, make-believe show'. So let's see it. Cough up.

The madding crowd   [15 September 2007]

It's an ongoing, fast-moving story, and events may have drastically changed between the time of writing (Tuesday morning) and the time you read this (Now O'Clock), but nevertheless, I've got to discuss the rolling news coverage of the Madeleine McCann case, because I've scarcely seen anything else.

Here is a story that's been granted saturation coverage through-out the slow 'silly season' despite, for most of that time, a lack of any concrete developments. For the news channels, it's perfect: an emotive, unfolding, open-ended human interest drama with regular interest 'spikes' each time a celebrity endorses the search campaign or a suspect is named. The news-slingers thrive on these spikes, like junkies clawing at crack rocks.

When Robert Murat popped up, Sky News could scarcely contain their glee. Breaking news! Breaking, breaking news! Here's video of the man police are talking to. That's him on the right. Here's one of his former schoolfriends. Here's his villa, live from the Sky Copter. Martin Brunt is on the scene. Martin Brunt is on the scene. Martin Brunt is on the scene.

When that trail cooled off, the coverage degraded into mawkish reports marking 'one more day' and occasional shrieks accompanying false sightings. And then, last weekend, the McCanns became suspects and things went totally insane.

We were treated to hours of live coverage of a police station door. On BBC *News 24*, reporter Jane Hill stood amongst the throng, expressing her amazement at the size of the crowd gathered there, who seemed to have come merely to catch a glimpse of the McCanns. She described how uncomfortable it all was, as though she wasn't there merely to catch a glimpse herself; as though we weren't tuning in merely to catch a glimpse of her glimpsing it. On Sky News, Ian Woods was doing the same thing. Look at all these locals, they kept saying. They've come to stand and stare. Look at them looking at this door. Now keep looking at it.

And then they split the screen in two while the newsreader back in London spoke to someone else in the studio, leaving one half of the screen streaming live footage of the door, so our view of it went uninterrupted; so we wouldn't miss a nanosecond of door-opening action if and when it occurred. Unlike the backward, ghoulish crowds, we sophisticates could sit on our comfy sofas eating peanuts, looking at the door on our plasma screens.

On Sunday the McCanns headed home. We saw live footage of them leaving the villa. Live footage of the drive to the airport. Live footage of anchors standing outside the airport interviewing their own correspondents about the drive to the airport. You could watch a motorbike drive behind Jane Hill on *News 24*, then flip over to Sky in time to see it pass behind Kay Burley. Sky's Ian Woods was booked to fly on the McCann's plane; he conducted interviews with fellow passengers inside the airport. What do you think? And what do you think? Kay Burley spoke to him live on the phone as he described the seating layout prior to take off.

During the flight itself, Adam Boulton's Sunday morning show was also split in two; one half streaming live footage of the McCann's home in Rothley, where nothing was happening because they were still several hours away, sitting in the sky, with Sky sitting behind them. It was like an episode of *24* in which all the action was paused. Yet you can't look away. It's live. It's hypnotic. Something might happen. Here is the airport. Here is the house. Here is a relative. Here is looped footage of the car journey. Here is the view from the chopper. Here is East Midlands airport. Here is the news.

At the scene of accidents, Police traditionally wave back rubber-neckers by saying 'move along now, there's nothing to see'. Sorry, officer. Can't hear you. 24-Hour News Entertainment has wedged its fingers in our ears. And it's going 'nyahhh nyahhh nyahhh' so loudly it's completely drowned you out.

The infested   [29 September 2007]

I had a rat once. Not as a pet, you understand – I'm not that cool and alternative and lawless and hard – but as an invader. I was living in a shared house near Clapham Junction, and one day my flatmate heard a noise coming from a kitchen drawer, pulled it open and got rat in his face. It had been nesting there for some time; it was the drawer where all of our overdue bills were kept, and it had gnawed these up into tiny strips of bedding.

Anyway, we cornered said rat in the bathroom, shutting the door so it couldn't get out, and pondered our next move. We tried chasing it out with a broom – but that didn't work because every time we opened the door it leapt into a small hole in the wall behind the sink. Instead, a lengthy face-off began. I'd heard that poison is a bad idea, as you end up with a decomposing rat under your floorboards, and the subsequent reek can spoil the mood if you're trying to get off with someone, so instead we went to the local pound shop and bought some rat traps, slid them gingerly into the bathroom and waited. And waited. And finally, after 24 hours, we heard death arrive with a loud SNAP.

Except it wasn't death. The trap had simply torn one of the rat's ears off. A trail of ratty blood led from the trap to the hole. I felt sad and sick and mournful, but re-set the trap with a sense of duty – the next snap would surely finish the poor thing off. This was now a mercy killing. Another day passed, and then SNAP.

This time it had lost part of its face. More blood, but still no body. Clearly, this wasn't a rat trap. It was a rat whittling machine. We were inadvertently subjecting the rat to the sort of torture you'd see in one of the *Saw* movies. That's what you get for using pound shops. Unable to bear the guilt, I went out and bought a deluxe top-of-the-range trap called something like RatFuck 2000. It looked like it could slaughter a bear.

Instead it ripped its tail off. I quivered with shame; shouted apologies down the hole, like a concentration camp guard appalled by his own actions. There was no option now but to repeat the process of tearfully setting and re-setting the trap, until finally, on the third day, Mr Rat went to heaven. He was huge and probably deserved a decent burial, but we didn't know what to do with him so instead we wrapped him in a carrier bag and, in the dead of night, threw him in a bin across the road, feeling like Dennis Nielsen.

All of which is an overlong and indulgent introduction to what will now be a brief review of *Help Me Anthea, I'm Infested!*, a bizarre little show in which Turner teams up with a cheery/chubby exterminator and sets about ridding folk's houses of rats, fleas, ants, cockroaches, lice and probably wolves. Normally I'd watch this sort of thing with one side of my face sneering and the other chortling. But thanks to my harrowing rat experience, I found it uncharacteristically hypnotic. Despite her image as a kind of walking, talking doily, Anthea turns out to be a hard, judgemental piece of work who spends most of her time haranguing the human inhabitants for living in filth. The end result is a strange psychodrama in which the punters are caught between unfeeling vermin on one side, and an unfeeling former Blue Peter presenter on the other. And in the background, millions of insects being turned into corpses by the exterminator. There's shrieking and wailing and gnashing of teeth, and then, finally, salvation. In the first show, a woman whose flat had been cleared of an ant infestation described it as a 'life-changing experience'.

It's empowerment through genocide, essentially. Yes. Empowerment through genocide. Great name for a band. Odd concept for a series.

They walk and they don't smile [6 October 2007]

'They walk and they don't smile. I wonder where this lifestyle is taking them.' As succinct a summary of commuters as you'll find, and it comes from a Tanna tribesman crossing Waterloo Bridge, walking against the flow of grim-faced drones scurrying toward another day pulling metaphorical levers in the office.

It's an encounter which pretty much sums up *Meet The Natives*, Channel 4's quirky anthropology in reverse show in which the aforementioned Chief Yapa and four of his buddies (Albi, Posen, Joel and JJ) visit Britain to mingle with some tribes of our own – the working class, the middle class and the upper class.

In these wearying, we're-so-good-at-telly times, I'd assumed *Meet The Natives* was going to be a fairly hateful laugh-and-point sniggerfest in which a bunch of hilarious primitives were manipulated by producers into making arsing great tits of themselves. And I wasn't alone. Before it had even aired, an article for the website of this newspaper sniffily described it as 'part of TV's new cultural voyeurism', which made it sound a bit like *Big Brother* in grass skirts. But in practice, it's far more charming. Downright heart-warming in fact. That's a phrase I don't get to type very often. Mainly because I don't know what it means. I don't have a heart. I have an unbeating onyx cricket ball. And stone-cold marble eyes. And a brain woven from tangled wisps of cynicism. I'm a miserable robot. Pity me.

Anyway, there are a few suspiciously manufactured moments – we see the gang enthusiastically trying on suits in a branch of Asda, for instance – but on the whole, whenever there's a joke, we're the butt of it. The tribesmen aren't portrayed as naive simpletons or noble savages, but regular people from a different background – thanks mainly to the savvy decision to give them their own cameras and provide their own narration. In this way, we see our world through their eyes – or at least feel like we do. It's one of the strangest, most fascinating examinations of our own culture I've seen in years.

This week, they're hanging with the upper classes, which involves witnessing a fox hunt (which they dismiss as 'crazy'), swilling champagne and staying at Chillingham Castle as guests of the impossibly posh Lord Humphrey. This perked the interest of my hate cells, because the upper classes always come across as uniquely hateful on TV. I borrowed a loudhailer and prepared to scream at the box. But no. Wrongfooted again. Humph and co turn out to be so gracious and welcoming and spellbound and non-patronising, you can practically warm your hands on the goodwill pouring off the screen. When the Tanna men crew don traditional black tie outfits and sit down to dinner it feels less like they're being dressed up for comic effect, like kittens made to wear top hats for a demeaning poster, and more like they're gamely sampling some of our cultural quirks first-hand. Because they are. At one point Humph talks them through the ins and outs of ritual cutlery use – starting with the knives and forks on the outside, moving inward as you head for dessert, and they look on in polite fascination, admiring the poshos for 'living according to the ancient ways of their ancestors, like we do'.

After dinner, they change back into their native dress and perform a ceremonial dance designed to promote 'peace and unity', inviting the blue bloods to join in if they want. And they do, laughing and singing. It's so lovely and life-affirming, you want to crawl in through the aerial socket and hug everyone on screen. There's another sentence I rarely get to type.

By the time Chief Yapa and co are gleefully frolicking in the snow (which they've never seen before), you'll probably be watching them through a haze of joyful tears. If TV manages to broadcast anything as simultaneously thought-provoking and charming this year, I'll be dumbstruck. And I'll probably have to switch the set off for good. I tune in to hate, dammit. Stop being so nice.

Henry VIII on a jetski   [13 October 2007]

I've got nothing against well-educated people, but it's hard to behave naturally in their presence. Often, when I'm talking to someone terribly clever, I find I'm concentrating so vehemently on disguising my own ignorance, I can scarcely hear them. My brain's worried that they're about to refer to some book I've never read, or use terms I don't understand, and I'm going to have to go into 'nodding mode', because the alternative – screwing up my face and going 'buh?' like a farmyard animal – is too humiliating to contemplate.

None the less, I'm going to attempt something foolhardy here, by taking a little public journey into the depths of my own stupidity. I'm going to list every fact about King Henry VIII I can think of, off the top of my head, without resorting to Wikipedia. Ready? Let's go. Um. Henry the Eighth was a fat Tudor king with a beard. He composed 'Greensleeves'. He had six wives: Catherine of Aragon, Anne Boleyn, er, Lady Jane Something (?), another one called Anne (I think), one called Catherine, and another one. He was either involved in the Wars of the Roses or he wasn't, and he reigned from 15-something to 15-something-else.

That's about it. History isn't my strong point. Try me on theme tunes. Anyway, as you can see, I'm hardly qualified to point at *The Tudors* and chortle derisively about how inaccurate it is, which is a pity because everyone else seems to be doing it. The other day I heard someone snorting that they couldn't take any of it seriously because they'd amalgamated two of Henry's sisters into one single character. Well whoopee-doo! I didn't know he had ONE sister, let alone a pair of them.

This probably makes the whole thing easier to watch. Historians are doubtless chewing their fists with frustration every time they spot an anachronistic shoe buckle, whereas from my perspective, they could lob in a scene where Henry invents the gramophone or has a holiday in Jamaica or plays Trivial Pursuit with Lloyd George – in fact, virtually anything – and I'd take it at face value.

Even I, however, am unconvinced by a few things. For starters, Henry appears to be using some sort of hair gel. And he looks distractingly like Malcolm McDowell's Alex in *A Clockwork Orange*, to the point where, in my head, the whole thing has become a bizarre medieval spin-off from the motion picture.

The similarities are legion: Henry, like Alex, is a spoilt, selfish brat who enjoys ultra-violence and plenty of the old in-out, in-out. He's moody, prone to boredrom, and has a hair-trigger temper. And he's surrounded by a small coterie of droogs (one of whom appears to be played by Chris Martin from Coldplay, so with any luck he'll get his head lopped off at some point in the next few weeks). The only thing that's missing is the spacey Moog soundtrack. Maybe next week Henry will invent the synthesiser and perform an impromptu space jam. I probably wouldn't notice anything wrong.

Unlike Alex, however, Henry doesn't have a sense of humour. Or much charisma. In fact, he's wholly unlikable. All he does is strop around like he owns the place (which, to be fair, he does), scowling at underlings and screwing anything that moves. In short, he's a massive arsehole, and as such it's impossible to care about him.

In last night's episode he discovered he'd fathered an illegitimate child, and was so overjoyed to have finally proven his spunk worked well enough to produce male offspring, he rode around on a horse bellowing 'I have a son, God! I have a son!' at the sky.

This may or may not be historically accurate, but it definitely makes him a twat. Not a fascinating villain, or even just a flawed human being, but a twat. I'm giving him two more episodes to show some redeeming qualities. Or even just mildly interesting ones. And if he can't manage that, he can sod off back to Tudor-land. Or wherever it was King Henry came from.

Smartarse kitchen [20 October 2007]

Sometimes you don't know what you've got till it's gone. Taste buds for one. As I write, I'm suffering from a heavy cold; in fact, I'm having to pause SHNORRFF every few moments to SHLORRRP blow my SSCCCHHHPORFFFF nose.

I don't know why I typed those sound effects in; sympathy probably. This stinking virus has turned my taste receptors down to a barely functioning minimum, to the point where everything I eat tastes of chewy oxygen and not much else. You could grind a dog's head and a shoe together into a paste and spoon-feed it to me, and I'd probably think it was chicken liver pâté, provided I kept my eyes closed, and provided you plucked all the dog hair out beforehand, and provided you'd managed to find a pestle and mortar big enough to mash it all up in, and provided – look, it wouldn't be worth it. I'm just saying I can't taste anything. There's no need to get carried away. What's the matter with you? You're an idiot.

Still, in my current taste-budless state, I'm probably ideally equipped to look at *Heston Blumenthal: In Search of Perfection*; I'll never get to taste any of the things he cooks in the series anyway, so I'm not missing out. Each week, Heston, who really ought to buy a new pair of glasses because the ones he has are completely the wrong shape for his face, and the lenses are so thick his eyes resemble a pair of olives hovering somewhere behind his head, possibly in another dimension, and it all makes him look a bit like a mad German doctor performing experiments in a horror movie . . . each week, Heston takes a classic dish (chicken tikka masala last week; hamburgers this week) and decides to create the 'perfect' version of it. Which involves travelling round the world to try out all the existing variations, then returning home to recreate it under laboratory conditions.

For the uninitiated, Heston's a renowned chef who specialises in ker-azy scientific cooking. He's best known for serving things like snail porridge and egg-and-bacon ice cream. He could probably make you a cloud sandwich if you asked. Or a blancmange made of numbers. He can do anything, basically. Which leads me to my first complaint about this programme: instead of *Heston Blumenthal: In Search of Perfection*, they should've called it Mister Impossible's Smartarse Kitchen. As titles go, it'd be both more interesting and more accurate.

Not that I'm saying the show's rubbish, no. It's quite interesting, especially if you like watching a man peering at food, and picking at food, and massaging and injecting food, and putting food in a centrifuge. This week Mister Impossible is creating the perfect burger, so he starts by studying the molecular structure of meat. We see lots of CGI recreations of the tissue structure as he explains how the way in which the beef is cut affects its texture. It's all a bit CSI: Dewhurst's.

Eventually he chooses three different cuts of beef and blends them together. Then he spends about 10 years perfecting a home-made bun. And another 10 years creating his own slices of processed cheese. He even makes his own ketchup. And then, just before he slaps the whole lot together and shoves it down his cake-hole, he picks up a bottle of common-or-garden supermarket mustard and squirts it all over the bun, which seems a bit rash after all the trouble he's gone to.

The end result looks suspiciously like a Burger King Whopper, albeit at 50 times the cost. It probably tastes 50 times better too, but I'd be astonished if a single viewer follows the recipe to the letter. Building your own nuclear warhead would be simpler, and once you'd made it you could terrorise millions into cooking you as many burgers as you wanted, home-made cheese slices and all.

Still, it's fun to watch Mister Impossible doing his experiments. It's nice to know he's out there, even if you'll never taste the results. It's a pointless job, but somebody's got to do it.

Like a gay Terminator   [27 October 2007]

What time is it? Time to swivel our eyes in the direction of the computerised *X Factor* mothership, which has entered stage three – live singathon mode – and is currently hovering over the Saturday night schedules like a brooding cloud; not so much entertaining the nation as inflicting itself on the populace. And either it's my imagination, or this year's collection of hopefuls are the feeblest in the show's history. Last week's live show lasted eight hours and felt like a tour of a black museum.

Now, obviously these programmes rely on a strange collective hallucination taking place, a nationwide mind-shift which makes substandard performances seem acceptable because they're part of some important cultural 'event' – how else do you explain the almighty success of *Britain's Got Talent*, in which a man whose act consisted of a puppet monkey waggling its backside made it through to the final – but I can't imagine the illusion's going to sustain itself this time round. I fear somewhere around week three, the public's going to suddenly blink and rub their eyes and splutter, 'but . . . but this is RUBBISH' as one. And then they'll start questioning everything, and before you know it we've got an uprising on our hands. The producers are going to have to start embedding subliminal hypnotic swirls on the screen if this country's going to survive until Christmas.

It doesn't help that there are more categories for processing than ever this year. The Girls (14–24) are unremarkable, as are the over-25s and the groups (although creepy brother-sister duo Same

Difference, two smiling pod people who look like they're about to hand you a religious pamphlet, warrant a mention for sheer shudder value alone).

The Boys (14–24) consist of Andy, Leon and Rhydian, only one of whom stands out. Both Andy and Leon look meek and terrified, like small boys at a circus trying to hide behind their mum's legs whenever the clown comes near. Consequently, Andy invested his performance with all the surging emotion of a graphic designer selecting a typeface from a drop-down window, whereas Leon, lumbered with an appalling big-band arrangement of 'Can't Buy Me Love' which sounded like a musical approximation of the hiccups played by an avant garde jazz outfit on a violently yawing ship, looked downright apologetic. There was deep confusion in those tiny eyes: confusion and pleading; the precise look of a human guinea pig who, while dosed beyond reason during a secret military LSD experiment, has just been handed a colouring-in book by one of the overseers and commanded to fill in the blanks with an imaginary pen.

Rhydian, however, is a star, and quite the most bizarre Saturday night spectacle in years. Prior to the live show he'd already wound the nation up by spouting egomaniacal bilge in his VT segments – although it's worth bearing in mind that he may have been the victim of a standard telly trick, whereby you switch the camera on and ask someone a question like 'would you like to be bigger than Michael Jackson?' and they say 'yes', and you say 'sorry, could you say that again, but this time phrase it as a complete sentence?', and they say 'I'd like to be bigger than Michael Jackson', and you isolate that soundbite and edit it into a sequence designed to make them look like the most deluded self-important twat in the universe.

Anyway. Rhydian. Styled and dressed precisely like a gay Terminator (or, if you're a nerd, Paul Phoenix from *Tekken*), he stomped around the stage howling notes like a terrifying robotic early warning system created by a lunatic. It's the sort of act you imagine is massively popular in Eastern Europe, or onboard intergalactic cruisers in the year 3400, shortly before they crash into the sun. Or in perverts' heads while they slice up their victims. Rhydian's a tit, obviously, but he's also the only entertaining act in the entire show. For God's sake let him win.

– Rhydian didn't win. Leon won, and disappeared.

The Excretion Bin   [3 November 2007]

'Three centuries ago the great English scientist Sir Isaac Newton wrote, "I seem to have been like a boy playing on the seashore whilst the great ocean of truth lay undiscovered before me." Today once again we are like children playing on the seashore but the ocean of truth is no longer undiscovered . . . we have unlocked the secrets of matter, the atom; we have unlocked the molecule of life, DNA; and we have created a form of artificial intelligence, the computer . . . we are making the transition from the age of scientific discovery to the age of scientific mastery.'

So begins *Visions of the Future*, a series in which theoretical physicist Dr Michio Kaku squints into tomorrow and describes what it looks like, accompanied by plinky-plonky popular science music and the occasional burst of portentous strings.

It must be nerve-racking making a 'things to come' show like this, because (a) it's hard enough to predict tomorrow's weather, let alone what kind of tinfoil hat you'll be wearing in 2029, and (b) the archives are cluttered with inadvertently funny 'ooh, look at the future' shows from yesteryear which got it hilariously wrong, proudly depicting the family of tomorrow enjoying picnics on the moon and having their bums wiped by kindly pipe-smoking robots with twirling antennae on their boxy metal heads.

In fact, it seems safest to limit your predictions to the assertion that your film about predictions will end up being used in a future documentary series as ironic archive footage illustrating how wrong past predictions used to be – especially if you depicted said future documentary being broadcast in 4D on a magic floating screen in an automated Mars penthouse.

Anyway, Dr Kaku isn't fazed by any of that. He steams straight in. Programme one concerns computers and artificial intelligence, and before long he's confidently claiming that within our lifetimes we'll be fitted with brain-enhancing microchips, which means every morning you'll see the Microsoft Windows start-up screen in your head while you're brushing your teeth, and instead of whistling in the shower you'll download a ringtone and play it in full Dolby Digital 5.1 surround sound through a ring of tiny speakers embedded in your neck. And instead of having a poo, you'll select a folder marked Stomach Contents and drag it to the Excretion Bin.

Actually, he doesn't quite go as far as that. But that's definitely what's going to happen.

Kaku's essentially an optimist, which means the show makes a nice change from the usual bleak futurologist's warnings about how we'll all be scrabbling around an irradiated wasteland desperately sucking the marrow from polar bear skeletons to survive. Nonetheless, there are a few hairy moments. Things get alarming when he nonchalantly describes how robots will soon be out-braining humans and experiencing emotions. A few talking-head interviewees earnestly discuss the prospect of our new metal chums losing their rags and using us as squishy, screaming batteries, just like they did in *The Matrix*. Kaku's personal take on the potential Rise of the Machines is characteristically upbeat: he reckons we'll still be able to control their thirst for vengeance, presumably by ticking the 'Benevolent Mode' option on a drop-down menu before they bludgeon us to death.

I'm not so confident. I think the revolution started several months ago, except rather than physically oppressing us with lasers and giant metal fists, the machines are slowly driving us mad by crashing every 10 minutes, forcing us to install drivers at whim, and limiting our power to communicate to typing a humorous one-line 'status update' into Facebook. We're at their beck and call already.

Still, I'd rather be ruled by Emperor GX4000 and his army of USB-compatible stormtroopers than, say, David Cameron. So it's not all bad.

Nobody knows anything [10 November 2007]

There's a famous showbiz maxim, coined by William Goldman: 'nobody knows anything.'

Nobody knows what's going to be a hit; nobody even knows whether what they're working on is any good. Books, movies, TV shows . . . they all exist in a quantum state of undefined quality until an audience actually receives them, at which point an opinion is formed. But sometimes it's more complicated still. This week, for instance, I've watched two completely different programmes from beginning to end, yet I still can't tell you if they're great or awful. That's because I'm not a proper critic. Proper critics are aloof and high-minded, whereas I'm a buffoon who peppers his copy with unnecessary bum jokes.

Anyway, programme number one is Stephen Poliakoff's *Capturing Mary*, a sumptuous drama about nostalgia and regret with a vaguely supernatural hue, which stars Maggie Smith and, bizarrely, David Walliams. Everything about it screams SNIVEL BEFORE ME, MERE HUMANS, FOR I AM TELEVISION OF QUALITY – which means if you get bored, you assume it's your fault and not the programme's. Because it's a genius and you're a pleb.

I can't work out whether it's actually any good. For every plus, there's a negative – so while it looks a million dollars, and Maggie Smith is great, and the story holds your attention, it's also stagy and pretentious and uses an irritating framing device whereby Maggie Smith's character wanders around an empty posh old house recounting all the events from her past to a simple working-class black guy called Joe, who has to chip in every so often to ask things like 'so wot 'appened next – dincha tell him to fuck off or nuffin?' like a faintly implausible character from *EastEnders*.

Presumably Joe represents some kind of metaphor for something (as does every other character, and the house itself, and probably even the cutlery) but I'm far too dim to tell you what it might be. This is precisely the sort of thing that makes me hurl poncy contemporary fiction across the room with annoyance, feeling vaguely guilty and stupid as I do so, wondering if I'm essentially behaving like a monkey pissed-off by Sudoku, or merely enraged by pretension.

Still, I watched to the end, then rolled it all around in my head for several hours afterwards, and even went to sleep still mentally chewing it over, as though *The Late Review* were taking place in my head, so ultimately it won. (Although I mainly kept marvelling that they'd somehow made Maggie Smith look a bit like Rod Hull, which was a comfortingly cruel and stupid thing to think, and precisely the kind of thought that keeps me sane.)

Immediately after *Capturing Mary*, I watched a DVD of the bizarre *Food Poker*. It's all poles apart round my house. *Food Poker* skilfully combines the public's ceaseless appetite for TV cookery with the poker craze that peaked two years ago. It's a bit like *Ready Steady Cook*, but better, because it's even more contrived.

In each edition, four celebrity chefs draw cards with random ingredients on them, then try to whip up meals using said items against the clock, in order to impress a jury of food-loving members of the public. It's got absolutely nothing to do with poker, obviously, but you've got to admire them for insisting it does despite crushing evidence to the contrary.

But why stop at poker? How about Food Cluedo, in which four celebrity chefs have to create edible murder weapons, try to bludgeon someone to death with them, then eat the evidence before the police arrive? ITV should look into it immediately.

The *Food Poker* format is so stupid, it sort of works. On one level it's annoying, and on the other it's quite good. It's the *Capturing Mary* of daytime cookery shows. Now there's a quote for their next press release.

Wedding balls   [17 November 2007]

Do you want to die alone? Of course not. But you will. Ha! In your face!

Yes, no matter how happily married you are or how huge your harem is, ultimately, at the precise moment of shutdown, no one else is shooting through that tunnel of light beside you. You're on your lonesome, into infinity. Unless perchance you're a Siamese twin. I'm not sure what happens to you then, but chances are there's no relief from your conjoined torment, even in death. There you'll be, sipping cocktails with Einstein and Monroe in the afterlife, still joined at the waist and chest to Blinky Bo-Bo, your drooling, underdeveloped sidekick. Nightmare.

But I digress. Back to dying alone, which scares people so much they resort to desperate means to avoid it, like getting married. They actually look at someone and think 'Yeah, out of all the people in all the world, I'll spend the rest of my life with you. Each morning for the next 50-odd years I'll see your face, and your arse, and that weird bumpy little mole on your lower back. That'll greet my eyes every single day. And I'll hear your voice; hear it talking about what you'd like for lunch, or who's annoying you at work, or arguing with me about towels. I'll go to the supermarket with you, week in, week out, staring at the side of your head as item after item goes through the scanner. Beep, beep, beep, beep. What did you get that for? We've got loads of those in the cupboard. Never mind. You're my life partner. From here to eternity. And we're stuffing these carrier bags together. Woo-hoo. Yee-hah. Beep. Beep. Beep.'

It's not easy, selecting a cellmate. Generally speaking, the ones you want don't stick around, and the ones you don't want – well, when you finally quit trying, that's your future spouse, right there. I'm sure you'll be very happy together. At the checkout.

But assuming you haven't simply thrown your hands up with despair and married the nearest bit of background filler, there are countless ways to meet Mr or Mrs Right. Fix-ups from friends, internet dating sites, and now *Arrange Me a Marriage*, in which 'matchmaker' Aneela Rahman attempts to pair off on-the-shelf Brits in a traditional Indian styl-ee. For the purposes of the show, this boils down to (a) getting someone's friends and family to choose a partner for them, (b) concentrating on suitors of 'appropriate' class and family background, and (c) not letting your intended couple meet until you've organised a big daytime house party where they'll clap eyes on each other for the first time, while you all stand around grinning at them, presumably in the hope they'll start shagging out of sheer discomfort.

Aneela's first 'mark' is a high-flying London company director called Lexi, who's 33, unmarried, and starting to feel the bite from her under-deployed ovaries. Like every single woman in the world, Lexi insists on meeting a tall man. I feel sorry for shortarsed men. Women are unbelievably shallow on this issue. I've never heard a man insist his wife must have big tits, but I've heard countless women complain about a man's height. What do you want, you whining harridans? A ladder in a hat?

Anyway, at the risk of being a big Mr Blabbermouth McSpoiler, it's fair to say that despite feeling as clinical and controlled as a scientific investigation into renewable energy sources, Aneela's matchmaking appears to succeed (although that might be down to the fact that if you can find two people prepared to consider hooking up on a TV show, chances are they'll be pretty compatible).

But it's all so slow, and meticulous, and devoid of emotion, it feels like selecting cattle for breeding. Call me old-fashioned, but some smothered, cornered speck in my being still believes in the random joy of romance, and I just can't see that flourishing in a system that runs like software. Which is worse: dying alone, or having the alternative defined by committee? Answers on a Valentine's card to the usual address.

CHAPTER THREE

In which David Cameron loses weight, neighbours fight for their right to party, and someone from Five appears

Smell the weight come off   [8 October 2007]

Has David Cameron lost weight? I've only caught glimpses of him out of the corner of my eye over the past week, and either the TV's set to the wrong aspect ratio or he's shed a bit of face flab. Presumably this means that whenever he puts his top hat on (i.e. the second the cameras stop rolling), he looks less like a chortling chubby-cheeked toff and more like an angular, dashing Fred Astaire type.

Cunning move. I smell a focus group. Research has probably shown he's become 15% more electable thanks to his leaner face alone. No one wants a prime minister who looks like he'd steal chips off your plate when your back's turned. He's doubtless had advisers following him round for months, slapping sausage rolls out of his hands every 10 minutes. Maybe he'll go the whole hog and strip off for a calendar, like Putin. Yeah. That'll work.

Of course, it's possible he's simply done it for his own sense of wellbeing. Although I doubt it. He probably consults an image analyst each time he wipes his arse, just to check he's using the brand of bog roll with the highest voter approval rating. And instead of leaving the bathroom and theatrically wafting a hand under his nose and saying, 'Pherrrrrgghh, I'd give it 10 minutes if I were you,' he blames Gordon Brown for using it before him, then promises to reduce future emissions by a factor of 10 within six months.

That'll be difficult if he's been taking the slimming pill Alli, which I read about the other week in this very newspaper. Alli, currently available in the US, is a weight-loss wonder drug that works by 'limiting fat absorption' in the body. And apparently it works pretty well, if you're prepared to overlook some of the side effects, which include producing bassoon-like farts and walking around with hot slicks of oily excrement leaking out of your backside.

The manufacturers actually advise people taking the pill to 'wear dark pants and bring a change of clothes with you to work'. That or get used to leaving a damp brown trail behind you, like an incontinent slug. It's not ideal, really. Presumably many of the people buying Alli do so in order to make themselves more attractive to potential sexual partners. Which is fine until you're in the bedroom, and they're ripping your clothes off in a lust-crazed frenzy, only to discover molten shit running down your thighs. As passion-killers go, that's worse than overhearing a police press conference about a missing child on the radio during intercourse.

Pity, because like many people I find the notion of an instant slimming pill pretty tempting. My physique's wired up all wrong. Even if I sit indoors eating deep-fried cake for a month, my arms and legs stay skinny, while my neck and face bloat like wet dough. And my head's too big for my body anyway. In fact, I'm built like a novelty Pez dispenser. A disappointing one. The last one left in the shop, after all the Donald Ducks and Popeyes and even Geoff Hoons have gone.

Thankfully, women are able to overlook such physical defects and see the person within. Or at least they can if it's a potential partner they're looking at. When they stand in front of a mirror, all that pent-up criticism comes rushing back and their brain reinterprets the image until all they can see is a flabby, unlovable sea cow staring back at them.

(Not all women, OK? I'm not generalising. Just describing what 99% of women think, and doing so in crushingly authoritative terms.)

It's demented, because even though men are shallow and fussy, we're also desperate. And this blinds us to much of this perceived blubber. Besides, extreme skinniness is horrendous. Ever had sex with an incredibly skinny person? It's like fighting a deckchair. They could have your eye out with one of those elbows. That's not sexy. That's terrifying. If the lights are off, you have to keep kissing them just so you can tell where their head is. Actually, if they've been taking Alli, that's probably dangerous in itself. One minute you think they've got saliva running down their chin, and the next you suddenly realise it's not their chin at all. And it's definitely not saliva. Best to keep the lights on and remain certain. And the next day, hide the pills and buy them a cake. Heck, you can share a few slices together. Now that's romantic.

Shut up shut up shut up   [15 October 2007]

Earlier this year I was watching *The Seven Ages of Rock*, and during the episode on indie music they showed a clip from a home video (by a Libertines fan) in which Pete Doherty and Carl Barat were holding an impromptu late-night gig in their own home. Swooning followers were sardined into the living room as the celebrated duo entertained them with their distinctive blend of clunking pub rock and self-regarding pretension.

Suddenly, the concert of the decade was interrupted by a distraught middle-aged neighbour pleading with them to shut up because she had to go to work in the morning. The crowd jeeringly dismissed her, and eventually the police arrived, at which point Barat and Doherty heroically launched into a rendition of 'Guns of Brixton', thereby well and truly sticking it to the man.

As I watched, I found myself wishing we lived in a ruthless police state. I wanted that party broken up by stormtroopers. I wanted them to beat Barat unconscious with his stupid guitar and ram a sparking 250,000-volt Taser into Doherty's gormless Stay-Puft Marshmallow Man face. Because it reminded me of the first time I lost it with a neighbour.

Now, this may surprise regular readers, but in 'real life' I'm actually pretty tolerant. Or maybe just cowardly. I don't like open confrontation, so if my neighbours hold a party, it needs to be very loud, and very late, and very unrelenting, to make me complain about the noise. But even I have my limits. A few years ago, I lived in a flat beneath a large group of rowdy Australians. Now, it doesn't matter that they were Australian . . . except it absolutely does. At night, the Australian accent becomes uniquely intrusive. It's bony and piercing. It sounds like a violin complaining to an angle grinder. It's not conducive to a sound night's sleep.

Anyway, the Aussies regularly drank and jabbered and stomped around into the wee small hours. They drove my girlfriend at the time insane, but since she didn't actually live or pay rent in my flat, she felt I should complain on her behalf. But my fear of being the boring, petty, fusty guy from downstairs who moaned about the noise was so acute, I'd brush off her demands, saying things like, 'They're not bothering me,' and 'Let them have their fun,' and so on and so on, like a sap.

And then one day they bought a karaoke machine. And installed it over my bedroom. And stayed up until 4 a.m. every night for a week, blasting out cover versions of 'Rebel Yell' and 'Girls Just Wanna Have Fun' through an amplifier. And downstairs, in the dark, on the fifth straight night of this, I finally discovered my breaking point. For the first time in my life, I grabbed a broom and start thrashing wildly at the ceiling, screaming and wailing, like a mad aunt trying to stop a war. And when that didn't work, I called the police and sat boiling with dark satisfaction as I heard them arrive and start remonstrating with the despicable bastards upstairs.

That was then. This is now. And in an apparent bid to test my capacity for xenophobia, a fresh group of Australians has just moved in next door and started using their roof terrace as an occasional al fresco debating society and drinking club. Which is fine and everything, except, y'know, it's kinda right outside my bedroom window, so when they kinda carry on late into the night, it kinda stops me from like, sleeping and stuff? But thanks to my in-built aversion to being the 'boring fusty guy', I said nothing for weeks, until last Wednesday, at 2.30 a.m., when I meekly popped my head out of the window and asked if they'd mind moving inside. And thankfully they did so, and were very polite and charming about it – except for one of them, a woman, whose knee-jerk reaction was to glower at me and snap, 'We pay rent here! We've got a right to talk!' as though I were the walking embodiment of an oppressive fascist regime clamping down on the flower children.

So from now on, every time I enter or leave my flat, I know she's going to be looking at me and thinking, 'There goes the petty uptight guy,' or 'I hate you,' or 'I pay rent here! I've got a right to talk!'

And I know how she feels because I once felt precisely the same about another neighbour I had, one who used to moan about my incessant talking. Not the volume of it, but the content. For instance, one night I was entertaining a friend by describing an imaginary scenario in which he was forced at gunpoint to have sex with an incontinent horse. I got quite into it, and my voice grew louder and louder, the details more explicit and unnecessary, until suddenly I was interrupted by a plaintive, disgusted cry from downstairs. In my head, I snorted at the small-minded sniveltude of my fusty, boring neighbour, because I knew with 100% conviction that I was right and he was wrong; that I was cool and brilliant, and I'd never be like him. Ever.

That's the sort of thing I reminisce about sometimes. Late at night. When I can't sleep. Can't sleep because she pays rent there, and she's got a right to talk.

Mood music   [22 October 2007]

If I was compiling a list of things I wouldn't want to happen to me, 'losing my ears in an accident' would rank pretty highly, just below 'accidentally coating my own eyeballs with hot melted cheese' and three slots above 'sharing a sleeping bag with Piers Morgan' (which comes one place higher than 'being force-fed live mice').

I don't know what you'd have to do in order to actually lose both ears – over-enthusiastically push your face through some railings to gawp at a nudist, perhaps – and I'm not sure it would actually affect your hearing that much, what with most of the listening mechanisms being housed deep inside your head. But I'm guessing that since the external ear-shaped part catches all the sounds and funnels them toward your brain, removing it would drastically reduce your field of hearing, so you'd have to twist your head sideways until the exposed hole was directly facing whatever it was you wanted to listen to, which would turn any attempt at conducting a romantic conversation over dinner into a bleak farce.

And obviously you'd stand out, especially if you also needed glasses, and the only way to keep them in place was to continually press them against the bridge of your nose with your knee (because you'd also lost your hands in the accident – I forgot to mention that earlier). And local kids would torment you by running up from behind (where you couldn't hear them) and suddenly blowing across the hole, so your head whistled like an ocarina.

Anyway, all things considered, I'd miss my ears, partly because it'd rob me of my favourite pastime, which is trudging through London with a Walkman on. (It isn't a Walkman, OK – I'm not 500 years old – but it isn't an iPod either: it's another brand of MP3 player, but calling it 'an MP3 player' is an awkward mouthful and, besides, you know what I mean).

Pounding along in a musical bubble is fantastic for the following reasons: (1) you get to ignore everybody else; (2) you feel like you're in a movie so if you, say, tread in some dogshit, it seems less like the everyday misery of treading in dogshit and more like a magical interlude from an epic adventure; (3) you're oblivious to the car horns and screaming and intermittent volleys of gunfire that make city life more stressful than it need be.

Your choice of soundtrack is vital. I was reminded of this the other day. One of the most overtly 'fun' (and deceptively vital) aspects of making a TV show is choosing the accompanying music, and I often download potential backing tracks almost at random from Napster, then walk around listening to them on headphones, thinking about which bits of the show they'd go well with. Which is all well and good until you find yourself trying to choose the music for a 'suspenseful' scene, as I was the other day. In practice, this meant sitting alone on my sofa at 3 a.m. with a load of horror-movie music on heavy rotation.

It was terrifying. In fact, I'd recommend it to thrill-junkies: fuck the latest Alton Towers terror-coaster – just whack the *Halloween* soundtrack on to your iPod and listen to it while walking around your own house in the dead of night. Try it tonight. It's great.

All of which makes me wonder why they haven't invented an intelligent mood-complementing MP3 player yet. They've got ones for joggers that deliberately select fast-paced tracks when they're running quickly, but why should they have all the fun? When are we going to get a music player that can tell, say, that you're melancholy (maybe by measuring the level of moisture on your face and working out whether you're crying or not), and demonstrate its sympathy by playing some welling, mournful strings? Or perhaps do the opposite, and try to cheer you up with a stirring burst of 'Oops Upside Your Head' (although if you're sad because you've just lost your ears in an accident, that last choice could be construed as tactless).

And it wouldn't just detect obvious moods, like joy or sorrow. It's the future, you cunt. It'd clearly be far more sensitive and advanced than that. If you were in the mood for a biscuit, for instance, it wouldn't only see it coming a mile off and select the perfect piece to get you in a biscuit-eatin' frame of mind, but time its cue perfectly so that great bit with the drums would kick in just as you took your first bite.

In fact, the only thing it might have trouble with is choosing a piece of music that goes nicely with the feeling you get when you're sick of having music chosen for you by a smartarsed machine. That'd be too self-reflexive. It'd overheat and explode and unfortunately, since the mood-detecting chip is made out of uranium (yes, uranium), the blast would devastate an area twice the size of Asia and millions would perish screaming in flames and it'd all be your despicable fault. But that's technology for you. It's risky.

Loves me, loves me not   [29 October 2007]

Friends occasionally come to me for advice, which is odd, because one glance at my shambling semi-existence should be enough to convince them I'm in no position to offer guidance on anything. I wouldn't trust myself to tell someone which end of a mug to drink from.

But still they come. The other day, a friend wanted to know if a colleague of hers was (a) flirting with her or (b) not flirting with her, and (c) how she should proceed, bearing in mind she didn't know the answers to (a) or (b) yet.

I like it when female friends ask for advice about men, because it gives me a chance to slag off my entire sex with as much authority as I can muster. So I said, 'Duhhh – he's a man! Of course he was flirting.'

'What if he's just being friendly?' she wondered.

I snorted like she'd asked whether horses have gills, and shook my head, which was pointless because we were on the phone.

'Look. All men, without exception, are shallow, priapic skunks. A man would fuck a ham sandwich if no one was looking. Sex is all men care about. It's the only thing. There's literally nothing else going on in our minds. Remove those thoughts and our skulls would cave in. And any man who says otherwise is lying – lying in the hope that his wheedling little lies will lull you into a false sense of security, and he can have his way with you. Up against a bin, if need be. He doesn't care. He's a man. At the end of the day he's just a quasi-sentient jizzing machine. A cum dispenser. That's the soft-ware he runs on. That's what makes his eyes blink and his limbs move. He's a dick and a larynx and absolutely nothing else. Hello. Hello? Hello?'

She hadn't hung up. Just fallen silent. I'd gone overboard a bit, and was befouling her harmless romantic daydreams, robbing her world of magic. I felt bad, as if I'd just told a six-year-old that not only does Santa not exist, but only an idiot would think he does. Worse still, this was an ex I was talking to.

'Is that what you thought when you met me, then?' she asked.

'What? Nooooo! Of course not! Don't be daft. Look, I'm joking. Ignore everything I just said. He's probably lovely.'

I managed to make the about-turn sound convincing, although part of my brain was still thinking, 'Yeah, but come on, he is a man.' It gets easily disgruntled, that bit of brain, and ought to learn when to shut up.

Anyway, the key to working out her next step was to decide whether said man had been genuinely flirting or not. Which wasn't simple. With flirting, there are more variables than Stephen Hawking could handle. It's as complex as poker, but with far higher stakes: potential life-enhancing happiness or crushing humilia-tion, not piffling financial loss.

Body language doesn't always help. What if one minute they're playing with their hair and touching your knee, and the next they've got their arms folded? What if they are flirting, but only for their own detached amusement? Worst of all, what if they're already taken, and deeply in love, thanks for asking? How do you subtly find out? You can't ask outright: that drops your guard and the answer might leave you not knowing what to do with your face for a good 10 minutes.

So you drop casual prompts . . . but don't get a straight answer. Now what? You're in limbo. You're no longer even yourself. On the outside you're a picture of amused, confident nonchalance, while on the inside your brain is gnawing itself to shreds, assessing odds, crunching integers. Above all, you want to avoid The Sudden Look of Horror, and the awful, awkward vacuum that envelops the pair of you when it transpires that You Misread The Situation Like An Idiot.

Infuriatingly, you won't get anywhere without risking exposure to that Sudden Look. And nothing's worse than discovering later that you didn't misread the signs, but now something's come up and sorry, but see ya. Years ago, on a night out with a girl I was slowly going crazy for, the sheer weight of mental calculation left me unable to make any sort of move. We shared a cab together, and after it dropped her home, she sent a text message saying: 'I wanted you to kiss me.' But the moment had gone. A week later she met the love of her life and that was that. It happens to everyone at some stage, obviously. But this was worse because it happened to me.

Anyway, we discussed all of this, my friend and I, and ultimately my advice boiled down to this: all you can do is prepare to go mad for a while. Maybe there's a sunbeam at the end, and maybe there isn't. But it's out of your hands. To quote Abba: 'The gods will throw the dice/ Their minds as cold as ice/ And someone way down here/ Might wind up sucking the cock of despair.'

If you'll excuse the crude paraphrasing.

Abroad at home   [5 November 2007]

Technically, you're not reading this, because technically, I'm on holiday. Except I'm not. Instead, I'm basking on the glamorous sun-drenched beaches of my living room, having failed to book a holiday for the millionth time in a row. My last proper holiday was three years ago (OK, there was a week in Spain two years ago, but it doesn't count because it was a relationship-break-up trip, and therefore the polar opposite of fun and relaxation).

I'm useless at every single aspect of holidays. Timing them for one thing. I tend to exist in a permanent work-bubble, fighting off deadlines with my bare fists. Then, when there's an eventual lull, I think, 'Wow, I really need a holiday', but by then it's too late. What's more, I'm single. How, as a tragic singleton, are you meant to go on holiday anyway? I know from experience what couples do on holiday: they argue. But I'm not a couple. Who am I supposed to slowly fall out of love with? I can't slowly poison my relationship with myself. Or can I?

I know several people who regularly go on holiday alone, including one whose idea of a rejuvenating break was a week on the Trans-Siberian railway, where he read books and stared out of the window into a landscape of unending nothingness, until he wound up drinking vodka just to get it over with quicker. He considered this a life-enriching experience. Another friend urged me to simply jet off somewhere alone because it gives you an unparalleled sense of freedom. 'Just stick a pin in a map of the world and fly somewhere,' was her advice, and it was such a stirring notion I was about to fire up Google Earth and do just that (I'm modern, see), when she added a small caveat. 'Just don't go for more than a week, because you end up talking to yourself.'

'Huh?'

'Well, it's the evenings, you see. It's fine during the day, because you can just lie on the beach or walk round museums with an iPod on, but in the evenings there's not much you can do except eat alone in restaurants or sit alone in bars. If you're a woman it's not so bad, because you get chatted up now and then, which can be amusing, but you're not a woman so you'll probably have to sit there reading a book or something. And eventually you'll get so lonely you'll start talking to yourself. I went for a week and started talking to myself on the last day. Go for a fortnight and you'll totally lose your mind somewhere around day 10.'

There are other options, of course. Activity holidays for one, although the idea fills me with revulsion. I don't want to go trekking with a bunch of disgusting strangers. What if a really annoying jabbering, bearded bloke latches on to me on the first day and decides I'm his best mate and won't leave me alone, and I'm stuck with him in some Arizonian wilderness and the sun's beating down and he's talking and talking and farting for comic effect and eating sandwiches and walking around with egg mayonnaise round his mouth until I want to grab the nearest rock and stove his skull in, and carry on smashing and smashing and roaring at the sky until the others dash over to pull me off him, but by then I've gone totally feral and start coming at them with the rock, which by now is all matted with gore and brain and beard hair, and I manage to clock one of them hard in the temple and they're flat on the ground, limbs jerking like an electrocuted dog, but as I swing for the next one some self-appointed hero rugby-tackles me, but I'm still putting up a fight so in desperation they all stamp on my neck until they're certain I'm dead, then throw my body in the river and make a lifelong pact to tell no one the truth of what happened that day? What sort of holiday is that?

The final option is to go somewhere with a group of friends, but that requires a degree of planning and forethought which is, frankly, beyond me. So I'm doing what I always do: arranging a week off and spending it at home. The closest I've got to visiting a far-off land is playing Half-Life 2 on my Xbox 360, and that's set in a dystopian future filled with nightmarish monsters that shriek in your face as they tear you to shreds with their claws. It does at least have a level set on a beach, which makes me feel approximately 0.1% as though I'm on holiday, except rather than relaxing on a sun lounger, I'm machine-gunning commandos and splattering insectoid beasts with my jeep. And this is my way of unwinding? I'm an idiot.

I'm going to go on holiday somewhere, somehow, before the end of the year. I just don't have a clue where or how. Answers on a postcard please. But preferably not a picture postcard from somewhere sunny. That'll only enhance my crushing sense of failure.

Rough in the jungle   [12 November 2007]

I'm a Celebrity . . . Get Me Out of Here! – ITV's star-studded 're-imag-ining' of *Cannibal Holocaust* – starts again tonight, and I can't wait. Actually, that's a lie – I can wait. For ages. In fact I'll Sky Plus it so I can skip all the ad breaks and boring bits. With judicious fast-for-warding you can pack an hour of the show into less than 15 min-utes.

If you enjoy this sort of thing, it's best to watch it on your own, like pornography. There's no point tuning in if you live with a gen-teel aesthete or snooty John Humphrys type: their appalled, dis-gruntled huffing tends to drown out all the screaming and eyeball-munching. But viewed alone, it's ideal background wall-paper; something pointless to glance at while checking your emails.

I just wish the technology would hurry up so I could watch it in a little inset box in the corner of the screen while simultaneously playing a videogame. That kind of demented convergence isn't far off – a few months ago I was playing a 3D murderthon called Prey or Bludgeon or Sociopath or something, and was startled to discov-er that the levels were peppered with TV sets spooling old movies such as *To Kill a Mockingbird* in their entirety, which meant if you fancied a break from the relentless slaughter you could sit down and watch Gregory Peck gently plead for tolerance for a few min-utes, then turn round and blast someone's jaw off with a shotgun. That's the future of entertainment, right there.

Weirdly, for a programme based around the relentless humilia-tion of desperate K-listers, *I'm a Celebrity* has a fairly solid track record of relaunching careers (far better than, say, the now defunct *Celebrity Big Brother*, which, in the fame stakes, surely ranks 10 steps below releasing an internet sex tape starring yourself and a microwaveable ready meal for one). Joe Pasquale did OK out of *I'm a Celeb*. So did Tara Palmer-Tomkinson. And Peter Andre. And Jor-dan. Modern deities, one and all. When Myleene Klass entered, she was a washed-up former pop singer. By the time she left, she was the most desirable woman in Britain. M&S put her on massive bill-boards, just so the grey, trudging populace below could glance heavenwards, between guttural sobs of despair, and gaze upon a bikini-clad example of all they should aspire to be. Not bad for a show that forces its contestants to eat boiled kangaroo anuses.

Tonight's line-up is headed by profoundly irritating self-declared 'inventor of punk' Malcolm McLaren, who's presumably taking part in the hope that it will further his reputation as a shocking icono-clast, although since that reputation exists only in the minds of two or three idiots, one of whom is McLaren himself, this seems unlikely. Besides, Johnny Rotten did it a few years back and almost certainly won't be beaten. If he hadn't walked out, he'd have won.

Also present are Rodney Marsh, 'legendary PR guru' Lynne Franks and Michelin-starred chef John Burton Race (who perpetu-ally resembles a cross between Victor Meldrew and Droopy). There's also former *EastEnder* Marc Bannerman, aka Gianni, the dopey-looking Di Marco, who somehow always looked as though he was on the verge of gurgling for birthday cake like a four-year-old. He decided to take part after pal Dean Gaffney (tortured to the brink of madness on the show last year) advised him to 'go for it'. 'I trust his judgment – he's a shrewd fella,' says Marc, exhibiting a tear-jerking degree of gormless blind faith in the wisdom of friends.

Then there's someone from *Five*. There's always someone from *Five* in these things. There's no way there's only five of them. They just keep reappearing, like ceaseless waves of enemies emerging from a spawn point in an old-school videogame. This one's called J, which implies that instead of giving them proper names, the cen-tral processing unit is merely assigning them a random letter the moment they materialise, presumably in order to conserve pro-cessing power for the gigantic end-of-level boss, who's scheduled to arrive some time midway through 2014, once we've blasted our way through 26 of his minions.

The most surprising inclusion is erstwhile Catatonia front-woman Cerys Matthews. The news that she was taking part was accompanied by gasps of pity and mild despair from almost every-one I know. 'Why?' they all said. 'Why? What a shame.' It's a bit like when Kirsty MacColl died.

Completing the pack are former *Changing Rooms* decorator Anna Ryder Richardson, 200-year-old supermodel Janice Dickinson (played by Steve Tyler from Aerosmith) and ex-*Hollyoaks* star Gemma Atkinson (a major figure in the *Nuts*/*Zoo* Axis of Wanking). Disappointingly, there's as yet no sign of ruddy-cheeked *Apprentice* psychopath Katie Hopkins, who was rumoured to be appearing, but since they always lob a few more contestants in the moment things start getting boring (i.e. somewhere around day three), there's still plenty of time for her to show up and gnaw the eyes out of a wombat's face or something as part of a Bushtucker Trial.
If past series are anything to go by, one or more of these people can expect to be hosting their own gameshow this time next year. And whoever it is, good luck to them. Unless it's Malcolm McLaren.

– In the event Malcolm McLaren pulled out before the first episode had even aired, the pussy.

CHAPTER FOUR

In which Cerys Matthews romances a baby, Peter Andre and Jordan cause bafflement, and total sensory deprivation is attempted.

Pineapple Prawn Dippers [24 November 2007]

As you read this, *I'm a Celebrity. . . Get Me Out of Here!* should be just past the halfway stage. Not that you can tell, because it's the most repetitive reality show in history. Each series looks the same. The same jungle backdrop. The same bodywarmers with numbers on the back. The celebrities' names change year-on-year, but their personality types remain more or less consistent. There's always a Quiet Pretty One, a Bitchy One, a Dopey Bloke and a pair of Will-They-Won't-Theys.

The chief innovation this year is the inclusion of not one, but three Gnarled Grumpy Ones – Rodney Marsh, Lynne Franks and John Burton Race. Out of everyone, the latter is my favourite. While others gurn or whoop or cross their eyes, Burton Race remains steadfastly deadpan. In fact at times his face literally resembles a dead pan. With the remains of Tutankhamun floating in it. What I'm saying is he looks like a recently reanimated corpse.

When he smiles, which isn't often, it resembles a pained grimace, as though someone's just plunged another electrode into his balls to keep his heart ticking over. If that face appeared unexpectedly at your bedroom window, you'd scream for six months straight, until your brain couldn't hear itself think any more and all sense of reason evaporated like escaping steam. Eventually, they'd have to lock you in an isolated cell and stuff towels down your throat to stop your relentless howling upsetting the other patients. He deserves to win, if only so next year Iceland feel obliged to include him in their sponsorship stings, where he can glide between platters of Pineapple Prawn Dippers and Chicken Lasagne Squircles looking like the ghost of frozen ready meals past.

The rest are a pretty average bunch. Janice Dickinson (played by an undernourished waxwork of Sandra Bullock carved by inmates in a hurry) simply squawks her way round camp like Ruby Wax with a stubbed toe. Lynne Franks (who I'm assuming has been voted out by the time you read this) seems like a menopausal owl. Rodney Marsh talks to everyone as though they're sitting in the back of his cab. Katie Hopkins has thus far disappointed millions by failing to act like the mumsy viper we came to know and fear from *The Apprentice*, and instead adopted a sort of cheerfully-game jolly-hockey-sticks persona, which isn't half as much fun.

Christopher Biggins, the ultimate jolly old uncle, doesn't appear to be capable of experiencing negative emotions, and would probably guffaw at a bus crash. Anna Ryder-Richardson has said and done nothing, and Gemma Atkinson has somehow managed to do even less, as though she's so painfully aware she's been chosen to participate simply on account of her tits and bum, there's no point even trying to display even the most rudimentary semblance of a persona.

The most depressing spectacle is the sight of Marc Bannerman repeatedly dribbling over Cerys from Catatonia, who seems to be playing along out of confusion. This is disappointing because Cerys is quite sweet, while Bannerman looks and sounds monu-mentally gormless. It's like watching a well-intentioned student nurse letting a brain-damaged adult baby get too close for comfort. Lord knows what Bannerman's 'oh-face' looks like, although I fear we're about to find out. My guess is that at the point of climax he merely looks confused, gawping at the hot yop spurting from the tip of his funpole in cowed amazement, like a dog trying to follow a card trick.

If the contestants feel familiar, the Bushtucker Trials feel like outright repeats. There's only so many testicle-chewings you can watch before all sense of novelty vanishes. Time for a revamp. Instead of humiliating the stars by showering them with fish gunk and maggots, they should simply command them to strip naked and perform increasingly grotesque sexual acts. Preferably on themselves. It might sound extreme, but we're currently subjected to live cockroach-eating, and the thrill is starting to pall. So come on, ITV. It's Bannerman's 'oh-face' or bust.

Specialist, arcane idiocy   [1 December 2007]

Hooray for us humans. We've made the modern world so frighten-ing and twisted, merely contemplating it leaves you profoundly depressed. Global warming, terrorism, bird flu, peak oil, gun crime, David Cameron. Horrifying developments all. And it's too much to take.

But rather than standing up and fixing things, we've created something to take our minds off it: a celebrity culture complex that requires your full concentration just to keep up. Unless you put the time in, sorting your Jodie Marshes from your Alicia Douvalls, staying on top of the Ziggy/Chanelle split, and memorising the names of everyone from Girls Aloud, the whole thing slips from your grasp, and before you know it, you don't know who or what anyone on TV is talking about.

Katie & Peter Unleashed is a specialist programme for hardcore nerds. Presumably designed with populism in mind, it's actually only of interest or use to the 0.2% of the population who could pass a trash culture exam with honours. A documentary about German tractors would cost less and have equal demographic appeal, but shhh: don't tell anyone in telly. They'll have a breakdown.

It's hosted by Peter Andre and Jordan. The pair met a few years ago on *I'm a Celebrity*, and subsequently married. This is entry-level knowledge which the programme assumes you're equipped with in advance. If you're not, it might as well be broadcast in Gaelic.

Just to complicate matters further, it's part chatshow, and part behind-the-scenes documentary about the making of a chatshow, which means your brain's constantly struggling to work out which element is the most boring. The behind-the-scenes bits generally consist of Peter and Jordan moaning and bickering about the content of the show while various members of the production team look on, trying not to openly snigger while mentally congratulating themselves for being part of such a brilliant human endeavour.

The star couple don't seem especially happy. Jordan, for instance, spends most of her time putting Peter down in a flat monotone voice. There's something supernaturally loud and inhuman about her intonation. She sounds like a cardboard box that's learned to bark, even while whispering. Peter regularly gets dragged into the whirlpool of joyless sniping, but otherwise remains scarily upbeat, like a barman cheerfully ignoring a death in the corner of his pub.

Just as you've got the hang of the behind-the-scenes stuff ('ah, I see: we're supposed to laugh at how stupid and banal they are – ho ho ho'), the chatshow proper kicks in, and it's difficult to know how to react. Is it supposed to be awful, or is the awfulness entirely incidental? What's my irony level here? Throw me a fact sheet, you fuckers.

Last week, their guests were Jermaine Jackson (from *Celebrity Big Brother*), Jacqueline Gold (from *Fortune*), and Vanessa Feltz and her partner Thingybobs (from *Celebrity Wife Swap*). Since they were all drawn from other reality programmes, most of the discussion revolved around things they'd said and done on their respective shows, which left the whole thing feeling like a conversation between people who'd been trapped together at the same cocktail party for the past 58 years. Disappointingly, they failed to hatch an escape plan.

Then there's a silly 'format point', such as a 'topical' staged mudfight between two vague celeb lookalikes. Last week, it was Prince Harry and Chelsy, because they've just split up, see? Again, anyone who doesn't read *Heat* magazine like a divine screed sent from God would come away baffled.

Then there's more behind-the-scenes stuff, and more chatty bits, and more format points, and it goes on and on and on until it's over. By the time the credits roll, you've ignored the outside world for an hour, yet experienced nothing. You haven't even been entertained. Just vaguely distracted, like a cow gazing idly at a washing machine. Hooray for us humans. Hooray for what we do.

To Do List   [29 December 2007]

It's the time of year when, looking back over 12 months of disappointment and failure, people make new year's resolutions in a desperate attempt at self-improvement. Stop drinking, stop smoking, stop shovelling butter down your gullet till your gut presses against your belt like a balloon full of mud . . . you name it, we'll swear to forgo it. And we'll succeed until January 3, then flip the autopilot back on and continue to make pigs of ourselves. Not that that's going to stop me drawing up a list of resolutions for our dear friend television, however . . .

1. No more talent shows: 2007 largely consisted of one big talent show broken up by depressing news bulletins and the occasional shot of Fearne Cotton. Dancing, singing, circus tricks, novelty acts . . . it's hard to think of a single endeavour that wasn't tested by the hoary combo of a live performance and a row of pantomime judges. What next? Strictly Come Woodwork? Belching on Ice? Britain's Got Dentists? We could do with a break, and judging by the overall quality of this year's *X Factor* contestants, we're wringing the nation dry as it is. Let's have a six-month moratorium, minimum.

2. Exploit the writers' strike: The ongoing writers' strike means we'll have to wait longer to see new seasons of hit shows like *24*, *Battlestar Galactica*, *Ugly Betty* and so on. So let's make our own versions. Let's save up that money we didn't spend, and make a homegrown *24* in which Adrian Chiles (Jack Bauer) has to stop Gloucestershire flooding again by kicking individual raindrops back into the sky. Or a series of *Prison Break* starring the surviving cast members of *Porridge*. Or *CSI: Droitwich*, with all the CGI biology bits done on an old Amiga. Come on, Britain. Let's make it happen.

3. More fakery: Television spent most of 2007 with its head in its hands, whining that the audience didn't love it any more because it had been making stuff up. But only a moron would believe anything they saw on TV in the first place – telly is the equivalent of an excitable toddler claiming to have seen fairies at the bottom of the garden, after all. Instead of vowing to bin noddy shots and solemnly promising some kind of editing year zero, show some balls and stride purposefully in the opposite direction. Fake everything. Replace George Alagiah with an animated horse and recreate breaking news stories with puppets. Produce a travel show in which Michael Palin falls through a portal in his own soul and spends six weeks exploring his dreams. Have God show up at the end of *Songs of Praise*. Bill in *The Night Garden* as a documentary.

And if anyone phones up to complain, stubbornly insist you've broadcast nothing but the truth until they believe you.

4. Put the late-night sign language interpreters on the red button: Simple one, this. The other day I tuned into Sky Movies to catch a post-midnight showing of *Manhattan*. No offence to my deaf brethren, but it would've worked better without the bloke in the lower-right corner flapping his arms around like a man signalling for help on a burning oil rig. He wasn't even in black-and-white to match the film. Never mind all this interactive news nonsense – use the red button to make sign-language an optional extra at all times of day, not just in the dead of night. That way everyone's happy.

5. Promote quality programmes: Contrary to popular belief, the networks DO make quality programmes. They just don't tell anyone about them. It's like they're embarrassed. Do you really need a break bumper every five seconds reminding you that *The X Factor* exists? No. Besides, crap sells itself. Rechannelling those insane marketing budgets into enthusiastically promoting the pearls among the slop might raise viewing figures, and perhaps more importantly, improve TV's reputation. Even if no one watches, at least they know you tried.

6. Stop squashing end credits and shouting over them: I'm going to keep banging on about this until it happens. Which it won't. But I like a fruitless yell at the void, me.

LOL IM BONKERZ!!! [12 January 2008]

It must be great being a rock star. Never mind the money and the drugs, what about all the blowjobs? Fans queue up, open-mouthed, shuffling slowly forward on their knees, dumbly pointing at their own lips and pleading with their eyes, like they've been poisoned and your balls are full of antidote. That's not empty conjecture – that happens. It's happened to every rock star ever, with the possible exception of Chris De Burgh, although I dare say there's been the odd moment when his monobrow's arched with grubby ecstasy backstage.

No wonder so many people try and fail to be rock stars. Once upon a time, you had to be talented or pretty or lucky to succeed. Not any more. Not since the advent of *Bedroom TV* – the music station that shows nothing but members of the public miming to their favourite songs in homemade videos. Like YouTube, but somehow slightly better, because it's on proper telly. Albeit only just.

Anyway, against the odds, it's fascinating. I watched it for four solid hours this evening. It's on in the background as I type these words. I can't switch it off. I've laughed out loud several times. Not at the 'wacky' videos made by LOL IM BONKERZ!!!! types (who, naturally, are well represented), but the overtly sincere ones. You can spot these a mile off: their creators tend to shoot them in black-and-white for extra sincerity. There's one for 'You Lost That Lovin' Feelin'' which consists of a wide, single locked-off shot of a stocky balding bloke lip-synching in his living room wearing his best suit and sunglasses. A few minutes later, he turns up again, this time in colour, sitting at a table opening and closing his gob to '1973' by James Blunt like he really means it. I can't get enough of it.

My favourites are the ones who love themselves to death and back and seriously believe the viewer will be impressed by their MAD SKILLZ. One mammoth idiot mimes to a sultry dance number with his shirt off, exposing his six-pack, pulling earnest come-to-bed faces and demonstrating the occasional martial arts move. Nothing Kanye West wouldn't do, except Kanye West probably wouldn't make a video by holding the camera in one hand and pointing vaguely toward his face, glancing awkwardly at the pop-out LCD viewfinder throughout. And he definitely wouldn't shoot it in a cramped upstairs bedroom at his parents' house.

Then there are the people who've edited their videos in Windows Movie Maker, added a few hideous visual effects, and decided the resulting masterwork requires full opening and closing titles, replete with credits like 'A Brian Films Presentation/ Concept: Brian/ Cameraman: Brian/ Produced and Directed by Brian'. Sometimes they even chuck a copyright notice on the end, presumably in case someone at Paramount tunes in, steals their idea, and turns it into a summer blockbuster.

Most of the videos are simple clean fun, however: there's loads of teenagers mucking about and giggling, performing interpretative dances to Kate Nash, and a fair few endearingly unsexy people gamely wobbling around to sexy songs. One of the more prolific contributors, a bloke called Ian, specialises in dressing up as a girl and looking moody; he's weirdly good at it. In one video, he simply sits on the floor by a bin, disconsolately miming 'Torn' by Natalie Imbruglia. Somehow it's better than the original.

And when someone nondescript comes on and mimes a nondescript song, you can simply look over their shoulder, inspect the state of their home and wonder why they bought that *Shrek* poster, or what's in that binbag on top of the cupboard. Keep your eye on the background and you see a lot of things you don't usually see in music videos, like infrared burglar alarm sensors, *Firefly* box sets and multi-bag sacks of Walker's French Fries. This automatically makes it vastly superior to MTV. At least until the novelty permanently wears off, some time around March.

– At the time of writing, Bedroom TV *appears to have disappeared from the Sky EPG altogether.*

All by myself   [19 January 2008]

Hey sugar. I'm stimulating you. Right now. Can you feel it? No, really: when you're reading, your brain's constantly stimulated. And it'll continue to be stimulated when you put this down and do something else. Even if all you do is gawp listlessly at a tea towel, the information keeps flowing in, and your brain keeps chewing it up.

And that's a good thing, because left to its own devices, the brain gets fidgety. Switch the lights off, deprive it of stimuli, and after a while it starts daydreaming. And if the lights never come back on, those daydreams become reality.

Your brain transforms into the ultimate unreliable narrator and soon you'll believe all manner of disjointed oddness. One minute you hear the theme from *Hollyoaks* playing from nowhere, then you're INSIDE the theme from *Hollyoaks*, which by now is full of colours, and they're grinning at you, and then you realise you're one of them: you're a grinning blob of colour that lives inside the theme from *Hollyoaks*. Or maybe you're a mile-wide pool of pork-flavoured honey with a bus and a hook for a face. Either way, you've gone bonkers.

That's the basis for this week's creepy *Horizon* special on sensory deprivation, in which six volunteers get slammed up in the dark for 48 hours. How creepy? Way creepy. The experiment takes place in a disused nuclear bunker; one of the men running it can't be shown on camera 'for security reasons', and we're told research like this was abandoned 40 years ago when the scientists conducting it decided it was 'too cruel'. It's the Fact Ents equivalent of a horror movie.

Three of the guinea pigs are simply kept in dark rooms, while the rest are made to wear eye masks that reduce the world to a grey blur, headphones that pump a continual white noise drone into their ears, and gigantic foam mittens so they can't even scratch their bums for entertainment.

Meanwhile, a psychotherapist with an unnerving omnipresent grin monitors their progress using night vision cameras, taking notes each time they pace up and down, talk to themselves, or hallucinate. One sits on the end of the bed watching snakes and cars and the occasional human visitor; another (the comedian Adam Bloom, oddly enough) strolls round a non-existent pile of empty oyster shells.

These laugh-a-minute sequences are interspersed with talking-head testimony from former victims of sensory deprivation: a guy called Parris who was locked in solitary for years for a crime he didn't commit, and former hostage Brian Keenan. Parris invented a fantasy world, then couldn't escape it; Brian was tormented by imaginary music that wouldn't stop playing unless he bashed his head against the wall.

It took them months to go that mad, mind. I reckon I'd get there quicker. Lock me in there and within five minutes I'd be running screaming round the room, pursued by a giant version of Joe Pasquale's face on wheels.

Fortunately, the experiment isn't simply being performed for entertainment. The show has a point to make.

After their ordeal, the volunteers are tested to see how susceptible to suggestion they've become – and surprise, surprise, they're highly malleable. The point being, any confession made by someone who's spent the past few days swatting invisible monsters is likely to be worthless. Nonetheless, sensory deprivation techniques are being used around the world right now, at Guantanamo for example. It may not technically be classed as torture, but the programme leaves you in no doubt whatsoever that anyone sanctioning such treatment on a fellow human being is a hateful pig of the lowest order.

Rumsfeld's retired. I wonder if he sleeps at night, and if not – and I pray not – what self-made horrors he visualises as he lies in the dark? Here's hoping they chase him through this night and the next. From now until never o'clock.

CHAPTER FIVE

In which George Clooney becomes a coffee ambassador, all-out war is declared on reality, and Lulu has a wonderful dream

1,000 Things to Ignore Before You Die

[19 November 2007]

Oh Christ. They're back again. Those lists. Lists of Things to Do Before You Die. Fifty Movies to See Before You Die; 200 Recipes to Cook Before You Die; 908 Items of Flat-Pack Furniture to Assemble Before You Die, and so on. And so on. And so on.

The *Guardian*'s currently running a list of 1,000 Albums to Hear Before You Die. Since the advent of CDs, the average album is about an hour long. So that's 1,000 hours of my life I've been commanded to give up, just like that. 1,000 hours. That's 42 whole days. Factor in sleeping time and it's more like three months. That's not a list. That's a sabbatical.

The worst 'before you die' lists are the ones aimed at middle-class tourists. These are infuriating for several reasons. First, the writers use them as an excuse to show off about how cultured and well-travelled they are, so there you get lots of entries like: 'No 23: Eat Spicy Malaysian Street Food While Watching the Sun Set Over Tioman Island in the Company of Some of Your Brilliantly Successful Novelist Friends.' The conceited worms are recounting incidents from their own lives and holding them up as aspirational examples for us all. At first this strikes you as smug. Then you realise it's merely desperate. Who are they trying to impress, precisely? The Joneses? They're prancing around in front of an invisible mass of readers, nonchalantly cooing about how wonderful they are. It's 50 times more snivelling and undignified than any Z-list celebrity you care to mention stripping naked and inseminating a cow on a Bravo reality show. At least that's unpretentious.

Presumably the aspirational list writers are engaging in a last-ditch attempt to stave off their own gnawing sense of pointlessness. What's that? You swam with dolphins? Hiked round Machu Picchu? Swigged cocktails in Vegas? Wow. Thanks for sharing. Now shut up and tie your noose.

Thing is, for all their faults, the lists work. It's hard not to get drawn in. There's so much crud and shod surrounding us on a daily basis, so many fair-to-middling fartclouds of 'content' and 'lifestyle choice', we're all desperate to get our hands on something actually, authentically good. And that's what the lists promise: a handy cut-out-and-keep guide to what's worth bothering with. In practice, however, they merely inspire feelings of inadequacy. No matter how cynical or detached you are, you can't help experiencing a pang of shame at not having seen Venice for yourself, even when the writer boasting about it is clearly a prick of the grandest magnitude.

As a result, it's hard not to walk around in a permanent state of guilt. Right now, I'm feeling vaguely guilty for not having seen *The Sopranos* beyond season two. I watched the first season, then fell behind and never caught up. The other week, as luck would have it, a PR company promoting the box sets sent me all six seasons in their entirety. Hark at me. Now they're sitting on my shelf, making me feel bad for not having watched them yet. And what about all those books I haven't read, meals I haven't eaten, countries I've never visited? How am I going to have time to fit all this stuff in? I can scarcely get it together long enough to perform the simplest of household chores, never mind all this extracurricular homework set by our cultural arbiters.

Besides, the more someone tells you how incredible something is, the more disappointing the reality turns out to be, largely because of the drum roll that preceded it.

Take the Grand Canyon. I visited the Grand Canyon in my mid-20s. Hark at me (again). I stood on a ridge and gazed out and waited to have my mind blown. All I experienced was yet more guilt. I'd heard that it was breathtaking. I'd read florid descriptions of its life-altering majesty. But it was these descriptions, not the canyon itself, that were at the forefront of my mind as I stared at it.

'Come on, you shallow idiot,' I said to myself. 'You're supposed to be feeling something here. What's the matter with you?'

Then I went back to the car, ate crisps and fiddled with the air-con, feeling box-empty inside. Call me shallow, but I've had more impressive trips to the toilet.

March of the Pods [26 November 2007]

Not long ago, I bought a coffee machine. You pop in a cute little metallic coffee pod, push a button and hey presto: you've made an espresso without having to faff around spooning coffee powder into a receptacle and banging it about and getting grit all over the sideboard and shouting like a sailor in a thunderstorm, which is what baristas do. It's made by Nestlé. I'm dimly aware they're supposed to be monstrously evil . . . but look, I hadn't made the connection at the time, and besides, I need my coffee, OK? I'm a heartless monster.

Annoyingly, you can't just walk into a shop and buy the special pods. You have to order them online, via an impossibly snooty website full of blah about the 'subtle alchemy' of coffee and so on. On handing over your details, you're inducted into a mysterious 'club', the consequences of which were lost on me until this week, when a glossy magazine plopped through my door. Turns out that by buying a coffee machine, I'd inadvertently subscribed to a 'lifestyle', and this magazine would regularly arrive to congratulate me.

I like free magazines because they're hilariously desperate, and the classier they purport to be, the more desperate they are. *Nespresso* magazine is the most acute example I've ever seen. It's as hateful as *Tatler*, but with an overbearing and whorish emphasis on coffee pods bunged in for good measure. Let's take a walk through the latest issue. The cover is a black-and-white photo of official 'Nespresso ambassador' George Clooney sitting at a table with a couple of coffee pods on it. They're tastefully out of focus, so you don't notice them at first. But they're still there. Inside, there's another huge photo of George balancing four coffee pods on top of each other.

The contents page is broken up with little colour photos of coffee pods, and snapshots of the contributors, including 'legendary star photographer Michel Comte' (posing pretentiously with his hands on his chin). Best known for snapping superstars, Comte has recently 'taken a humanitarian bent' by covering 'war-torn locations such as Iraq, Chechnya and Afghanistan'. But this week he 'joined George Clooney for a coffee and the latest Nespresso campaign'. Beneath Comte's photo is a bright blue coffee pod. Next, several pages showcasing the latest Nespresso coffee machines, which are intensely coloured because 'intense colours are the rule on the catwalks of the season'. Another inspiration is 'rock legend David Bowie, whose alter ego Ziggy Stardust defined both glam rock and its look in the 1970s'. To underline how fashionable the machines are, they're accompanied by photos of Louis Vuitton shoes, Chanel bags, the Bilbao Guggenheim museum, and some coffee pods.

Then, a series of full-page Q&A sessions with five 'Nespresso Coffee Experts', each posing with a cup of coffee and spouting bumwash. (Sample: 'Q: What elements or setting do you need for your own personal coffee moment or ritual? A: An open mind and sharpened senses.') Coffee pods in this section: nine. Now we've arrived at the George Clooney profile proper. 'My parents brought me up to read and to ask questions, and to constantly question authority,' he reveals. 'Because authority unchecked, without exception, corrupts. Always.' Something to contemplate there, while you gaze at more photos of George and the pods.

Next, a guide to festive entertaining 'dos and don'ts', in which the letter o in the word *dos* is replaced by a photograph of a coffee pod, upended and shot from above. By now, I'm actively enjoying this relentless pod barrage.

Pages 32–37: a piece on the Keralan coastline, accompanied by exotic photos of natives (and coffee pods). Page 38: upmarket ski destinations (and a coffee pod).

Page 40: a profile of the mastermind behind Swiss watchmakers Chopard. 'A true epicurean, Karl-Friedrich Scheufele's passion drives him to pursue excellence in all aspects of life,' reads a caption beside a photo of Karl, his hot wife Christine, and three more coffee pods.

Page 42: a feature on milk. Real milk, you understand, not that powdered formula gunk people in the developing world mix with unclean water and bottlefeed to babies, causing diarrhoea and vomiting. For some mad reason, that's not mentioned at all. No pods, either: a double oversight.

Pages 46–51: Indian recipes inspired 'by the flavours of the Nespresso Grand Crus'. Coffee pods next to the food and, in one case, balanced on the edge of a plate. Brilliant.

Pages 54–59: fashion spread starring a man who looks about 50 and a sexy woman who looks about 25. Cups, machines and Nespresso logos are visible. But boo: no coffee pods.

The unexpected pod drought continues throughout a feature on ghastly overpriced crud to put on your coffee table, a guffy peep about yachting, an advert for Chopard watches, and a self-celebratory piece on sustainable farming practices in Costa Rica, the last page of which is suddenly improved immensely – at last – by a minuscule photo of a coffee pod in the lower right-hand corner, serving as a full stop at the end of the article. Finally, the home straight: several pages of chinaware from the Nespresso range, a deluge of coffee pods and an order form. And that's it.

I went back and counted. In total, there were 281 visible coffee pods – 281 tiny bullet-shaped reminders of the bizarre, anxious banality of marketing. On the one hand, it's a pointless free mag. On the other, it's the by-product of an entire industry peopled exclusively by desperate, snivelling lunatics. And most damning of all, it's put me off my coffee.

Everyone's talking about . . .   [3 December 2007]

Heat magazine – the tittering idiot's lunchbreak-pamphlet-of-choice – has caused a bad stink by printing a collection of comedy stickers in its latest issue. Said stickers are clearly designed to be stuck round the fringes of computer monitors by the magazine's bovine readership in a desperate bid to transform their veal-fattening workstation pen into a miniature Chuckle Kingdom and thereby momentarily distract them from the bleak futility of their wasted, *Heat*-reading lives.

Most of the stickers are baffling to anyone who isn't a regular reader – there's one of Will Young sporting a digitally extended chin, a shot of a man's head on a crab's body accompanied by the words 'Roy Gave Me Crabs', and a photo of the editor looking a bit like a monk. So far, so hilarious.

But one consists of a shot of Jordan's disabled five-year-old son Harvey, with the words 'Harvey wants to eat me!' printed next to his mouth. In other words, we're supposed to find Harvey's face intrinsically mirthful and/or frightening. Ha ha, *Heat*! Ha ha!

Jordan herself is on the cover of the same issue, as part of a montage depicting Stars Who Hate Their Bodies ('Jordan: SAGGY BOOBS'), so chances are she wasn't in an especially upbeat frame of mind when she later stumbled across the snickering point-and-chortle demolition of her blameless disabled son nestling in the centre pages. She immediately lodged a complaint with the PCC. Personally, I'd have caught a cab to their offices, kicked the editor firmly in the balls, taken a photo of his stunned, wheezing, watering face and blown it up and hung it on my wall, to be contemplated every morning over breakfast.

Of course, *Heat*'s always had a psychotically confused relationship with celebrities. On the one hand, it elevates them to the status of minor deities, and on the other, it prints clinical close-ups of their thighs with a big red ring circling any visible atoms of cellulite beside a caption reading 'Ugh! Sickening!' This is what the misanthropic serial killer in *Se7en* would've done if he'd been running a magazine instead of keeping a diary.

This might seem a bit rich coming from someone (i.e. me) who regularly says cruel things about public figures for comic effect. Eagle-eyed readers may have noticed I scrawled some fairly abusive things about Jordan myself in a recent *Screen Burn* column in the Guide, for instance. Isn't *Heat* effectively doing the same thing, only with more gusto, not to mention photos?

Good question. Thanks for asking. My defence, in as much as I've worked it out, runs like this: people on TV aren't real people. They're flickering, two-dimensional representations of people, behaving unnaturally and often edited to the point of caricature. They're fictional characters and it's easy to hate them. Everybody hates someone on TV. But you never really hate them the way you'd hate, say, a rapist. Because they're not really there, and with one or two exceptions (TV psychics, say), they're ultimately harmless. Put Vernon Kay on my screen and I'll gleefully spit venom at him. Sit me next to him at a dinner party and I'll probably find him quite charming, unless he does something appalling. That's not hypocritical, it's rational.

In fact, in my limited experience, the more unpalatable you find someone's TV persona, the nicer they turn out to be in real life. Recently I was walking down the street when someone I'd written something nasty about suddenly darted across the road and introduced himself. Almost immediately, I started apologising for the article, explaining (as above) that people on TV aren't real people and so on. At which point he looked faintly crestfallen. He hadn't read the piece at all, but he'd seen a TV thing I'd done and just wanted to say how much he enjoyed it. Then he asked what it was I'd said that was so bad, so I found myself sheepishly repeating it while staring at the ground. There was an uncomfortable pause. And then he laughed and said it was all fair game and not to worry. And I thought, who's the dickhead in this scenario? Because it sure as hell wasn't him. I'm the dickhead. I'm always the dickhead: always have been, always will be.

Even so, and speaking as a dickhead, there's surely a world of difference between tipping cartoon buckets of shit over someone's TV persona, and paying a paparazzo to hide behind a bush to take photos of their arse as they stroll down the beach in real life, so you can make your readers feel momentarily better about themselves because ha-ha her bumcheeks are flabby and ho-ho he's bald and tee-hee she's sobbing. And even if you accept that degree of intrusion, on the basis that these people rely on the media and yadda yadda yadda, how insanely superior and removed from reality do you have to be to invite your readers to laugh at a photograph of a small disabled boy whose only 'crime' is (a) being disabled and (b) having a famous mum with 'SAGGY BOOBS'?

Each week, *Heat* opens with a featurette called 'Everyone's Talking About . . .' detailing the latest showbiz scandal. Last week, it was 'Everyone's Talking About . . . Marc Bannerman'. This week it ought to read 'Everyone's Talking About . . . What Total Cunts We Are'. And maybe it will. We shall see.

The Axis of Real Stuff [10 December 2007]

So let's get this straight. A US intelligence report decides that Iran isn't as big a threat as once feared, and Bush decides this proves that, actually guys, I think you'll find it is. You've got to admire his steadfast refusal to acknowledge anything that doesn't complement his monochromatic world view. He's a true tunnel visionary. Awkward facts simply ricochet off him, like peashooter pellets bouncing harmlessly from an elephant's hide. He knows what he wants to believe, and he'll carry on believing it until it kills him. Or us. Preferably us. He can always recant and say, 'Oops, I was wrong' in his bunker. We'll be long gone by then, so what does he care?

Very little, in all probability. Bush is a bit like an unhinged iconoclast who has arbitrarily decided he doesn't believe in cows, and loudly and repeatedly denies their existence until you get so annoyed you drive him to a farm and show him a cow, and he shakes his head and continues to insist there's no such thing. At which point it moos indignantly, but he claims not to hear it, so in exasperation you drag him into the field and force him to touch the cow, and milk the cow, and ride around on the cow's back. And, finally, he dismounts and says, 'That was fun'n'all, but dagnammit, I still don't believe in no cow.' And then he shoots it in the head regardless, just to be on the safe side. Just so it isn't a threat.

Come to think of it, Bush is so vehemently fact-phobic, he might as well expand the war on terror into an outright war on reality, in which anything palpably authentic is the enemy. There'll be an 'Axis of Real Stuff', encompassing everyone and everything from hairbands to dustmen, all of which Must Be Eliminated. 'If it's provable, we can kill it.' That's our new motto. God's on our side, because he can't be proved or disproved. He's one of our most valuable allies – the others being Santa Claus, the Tooth Fairy, ghosts, the bogeyman, and Bigfoot. Not to mention a vast fleet of UFOs, which the enemy won't have a chance of defeating because it never existed in the first place. Our armies won't be constrained by the laws of physics, and even if we lose, we'll simply say we won, even if we have to say it from an afterlife which doesn't exist either. That's the power of unwavering denial. It makes deities of us all.

Of course, by rejecting anything he doesn't want to hear, Bush is simply proving he's human. Humans hate the truth. Once someone's made up their mind, they rarely change it, no matter how much evidence to the contrary you show them. Changing your mind or admitting you were wrong is seen as weak, as though life itself were an almighty pub quiz where incorrect answers are penalised. The only option left is to interpret the facts in a new and interesting way that supports your overall position. This is what Bush has done. He says that since the report indicates that Iran halted its weapons programme in 2003, there's a clear possibility it could start it up again. The very fact that the Iranians don't have a nuclear bomb proves they might still develop one. Therefore, Iran is dangerous.

That's a clever thing to say, because (a) the future is unknowable, so it's impossible to tell him he's wrong, and (b) the more he says it, the more likely it is to come true. Since Bush has shown that he'll view Iran as a nuclear threat regardless of whether it's got the bomb or not, the Iranians might as well build one. What have they got to lose?

Also, the report doesn't say whether the Iranians are developing a giant laser beam capable of sawing the sun in two, but that's no reason to assume they won't be starting work on it next week. Picture a world in which Ahmadinejad holds us to ransom by threatening to plunge one sawn-off half of the sun into the Atlantic, sending 900-foot waves of boiling water rushing toward our shores. We can't let that happen. We've got to get in first: drive a space shuttle into the sun and blow the damn thing up before the enemy get their hands on it. It might solve global warming too. Let's hope the Pentagon is across this. Don't let us down, guys. Knock that baby out.

Another benefit of ignoring the report and piling in regardless is

that at least this time round we'll know for sure that the invasion
and subsequent war is based on a false premise in advance, which
beats finding out later and feeling a bit disgusted with ourselves.
Forewarned is forearmed. It's a narrative tweak which keeps things
fresh and interesting. The TV series *Columbo* used a similar device:
instead of being served a common-or-garden whodunnit, you'd see
the murderer committing the crime at the start, so the fun came
from watching his plan slowly unravel. There's no danger of that
happening to Bush though, because he doesn't believe in plans
either. So nothing unravels. It's a win-win situation. He should
unleash the hounds tomorrow. Go ahead, George. We'll be fine, out
here, outside the bunker. Don't you worry about us.

Lulu's Christmas Dream   [17 December 2007]

It's beginning to look a lot like Christmas. Well, on TV it is anyway.
At this time of year, every ad break turns into an extended brainwashing exercise as one campaign after another hammers its way
into your head by dint of sheer repetition alone.

'It's beginning to look a lot like Christmas' is, of course, the
theme song of this year's offering from Argos, which affects solidar-
ity with the average hard-shopping prole by depicting the high
street as a hellish dog-eat-dog war zone straight out of *Saving
Private Ryan*, the only thing missing being the occasional eye-
popping shot of a young soldier getting his leg blown off – which,
to be fair, wouldn't really be in keeping with the Yuletide spirit.

Stephen Fry's voiceover complains that Christmas should be
'more . . . well, Christmassy', at which point it cuts to a shot of an
Argos delivery van pulling up outside a suburban home, as though
that's the very essence of all things 'Christmassy', which it isn't. The
birth of Christ, a crowded train, a party-hatted boss drunkenly
molesting a co-worker – that's Christmassy, you idiots.

Apart from Boots, whose 'Here Come the Girls' celebration-of-
vapidity is at least entertaining, all the high street stores seem to
have got it a bit wrong this year. Iceland's ads are the most lurid, as
they continue to hawk an increasingly terrifying range of oven-

ready vol-au-vents (Loaded Prawns, Filo Parcels, Squirrel-and-Onion Swastikas and so on) using the dream-team combo of Kerry Katona and a Nolan sister. These ads precisely evoke the queasy sensation of drifting off in front of a bloated 90-minute festive edition of *Birds of a Feather* following an over-rich pudding and three Baileys too many. And maybe that's the point.

Celebrities feature heavily in supermarket ads. Asda continues its intensely patronising 'stars in the aisles' campaign, in which well-loved faces slum it among the downtrodden workforce. Sainsbury's dumps Jamie Oliver into a sort of Dickensian pop-up book filled with miniature slaves. Morrisons has really dropped the ball, with an excruciating advert called 'Lulu's Christmas Dream', in which Lulu wanders through a cosy, snow-caked market town peopled exclusively by a baffling combination of minor celebrities. There's Gabby Logan carving her turkey, Nick Hancock having a snowball fight, Denise van Outen giggling on a balcony, Diarmuid Gavin winking at Lulu as though recalling a particularly grubby one-night stand, and Alan Hansen filling his trolley with 500 tins of Miniature Heroes, all of it backed by Take That's 'Shine'. It's like a low-rent Ocean's Thirteen. If it had used Alan Partridge instead of Lulu, and ('I Believe in Miracles') 'You Sexy Thing' by Hot Chocolate instead of Take That, it could have been the best Christmas commercial ever. As it is, it's just embarrassing.

Speaking of embarrassments, the Spice Girls have managed to imbue their long-awaited comeback with all the glamour and class of a hurried crap in a service station toilet by whoring themselves out to Tesco. The first instalment, in which the Girl Power quartet try to hide from each other while shopping for presents, represents a important landmark for the performing arts: Posh Spice becomes the first human being in history to be out-acted by a shopping trolley.

Marks & Sparks win a nerd rosette from me for managing to authentically replicate the style and tone of late-50s/early-60s movie trailers, although the undertone of its commercial is a tad suspect: it took me three or four viewings to realise it, but Twiggy and co are desperately showing off in a bid to impress Antonio

Banderas, who looks a bit like a CEO in a brothel trying to decide which prostitute he fancies using. I keep expecting him to point out two of them at the end, and for the advert to cut suddenly to a grotesque scene where both of them pleasure him at once in a velvet boudoir, filmed in the same style as the slow-mo food porn it uses for its other commercials. All of which isn't very Christmassy either. But maybe that's just me.

Said ad is accompanied by yet another vintage song: 'It's the Most Wonderful Time of the Year'. Presumably the ad agencies hold some sort of summit each year in the run-up to Christmas, where they negotiate who has the right to use each track, just so there's no duplication. 'You can have Winter Wonderland provided we get to keep Wizzard.' That kind of thing. Old-fashioned crooning is in vogue this year. I'm expecting the Bing Crosby/David Bowie take on 'Little Drummer Boy' to make an appearance next time round – in a Currys ad, accompanying a shot of a wireless inkjet printer or something. You know. In keeping with the original sentiment of the song.

A Right New York State [7 January 2008]

As I type these words, I'm sitting in New York, failing to enjoy myself. Not because I'm a miserable curmudgeon (I'm not – I'm a sparkling sunbeam) but because I neglected to tell the Halifax that I was going abroad, and it has punished me by putting a security block on my card. It's like a parent-child relationship. I went out to play without asking permission and subsequently I've been grounded. Sorry mummy. Sorry daddy.

I was trying to buy a coat and some earmuffs – it's minus 10 million degrees out here and like an idiot I arrived woefully unprepared – when the block kicked in. It's pretty embarrassing when a shop assistant hands your card back, smiles weakly and says it's been rejected. If you're like me, you ask them to try again, and they reluctantly do so while a queue builds up behind you. And if you're really like me, the card's rejected again, this time in front of an impatient crowd, so to save face you apologetically huff something about 'calling your bank to bollock them' and demonstratively whip out your mobile, only to discover you can't get a signal until you walk all the way out of the shop, which makes you look precisely like you're trying to sneak away.

Standing on the pavement, with the phone almost fused to my ear with the cold, I'm told I won't be able to withdraw any money until tomorrow, because it's night-time in England and the Halifax security team have all gone home. Still, it's thoughtful of them to employ someone to sit at the end of the phone 24 hours a day just to empathise.

Since I have only $22 on me, my options for New York fun are suddenly extremely limited: specifically, they're limited to returning to the hotel to sit indoors ordering room service. I'm under house arrest.

Still, at least there's a TV. I sigh and switch it on, immediately plunging headlong into a high-octane showbiz news atrocity called *The Insider*. It's like being hit in the face with a pan. The hosts simultaneously smile and shout, and it's edited so quickly you feel like you're glimpsing events through the side window of a speeding car. The big news is that Lindsay Lohan was spotted swigging champagne from a bottle on New Year's Eve. They have a two-second clip of this which they loop and repeat about 600 times, sometimes zooming in, sometimes zooming out, sometimes accompanying it with spinning CGI lettering and sparkles and whoosh noises. Then a man with more teeth than sense whooshes in to replace her, loudly pledging to bring us 'all the latest Lohan updates on this developing story' throughout the remainder of the show. Then he's replaced by an advert for an anti-constipation pill.

I look out of the window. Outside, New York sparkles and bustles. But without a coat, I can barely even step out of the door. I grit my teeth and return to the box.

Time passes. The all-new celebrity edition of the US version of *The Apprentice* begins. It's fronted by Donald Trump and his optical-illusion hairstyle, who's rubbish compared with Alan Sugar. Among the cast is simpering human perineum Piers Morgan, furthering his showbiz career with another deliberately smug turn. Half the others are unrecognisable to me, partly because they're

American celebs, partly because they've had a bit too much plastic surgery, which always gives people a strangely generic, faintly cro-magnon look, as though they're part of a new species descended from, but not directly related to, us regular human beings. Morgan is sneering at one of them when my attention is drawn to a ticker-tape scrolling across the bottom of the screen announcing that Barack Obama has won the Iowa caucus. Then the whole thing's replaced by an advert for lasagna rollatini with sausage, something that looks so utterly ghastly that even Iceland wouldn't consider it.

At some point I fall asleep, only to wake up a few hours later midway through a speech by Mike Huckabee, the Republican candidate who's also won in Iowa. He's worrying for several reasons: (1) he's an ultra-religious Baptist minister who doesn't believe in evolution, (2) he looks a bit like Charles Logan, the corrupt president from season 5 of *24*, and (3) he's quoting G. K. Chesterton: 'A true soldier fights not because he hates those who are in front of him, but because he loves those who are behind him.' Standing directly behind him as he says this: Chuck Norris. Then there's a commercial for Advil. New York, meanwhile, continues to twinkle through the window, infuriatingly out-of-reach.

By now I'm out of my mind with despair, so I call the bank again simply to vent some frustration, and end up being horrible to the man on the other end, who's only doing his job. This makes me feel so low that I call back a few minutes later to try to apologise, but get put through to someone else, and they just think I'm weird. Now it's the next morning and I'm still waiting to discover if the bank's going to let me go outside. I've learned my lesson, OK? It's protecting my money by stopping me getting my hands on it, just in case I'm not me. And right now I'm not me. The real me would be out seeing the sights. Muggins me is locked indoors drinking Pepsi for entertainment. I clearly deserve everything I get.

Day of the Norovirus   [14 January 2008]

Fear stalks the land; stalks my land at any rate. I've landed a starring role in my own personal horror movie: Day of the Norovirus.

Gastric flu, the winter vomiting bug, spewmonia: whatever you want to call it, it's out there, somewhere, festering on every surface, waiting to infect me. Britain is diseased: a septic isle bobbing on an ocean of warm sick.

The media have had a field day, and to an emetophobe like me (someone with an uncontrollable, inbuilt fear of puking), this merely amplifies the terror. A headline such as 'Vomiting bug spreads across nation' sets my pulse racing twice as effectively as 'Mad axeman on loose'.

Even worse are the war stories: vivid blog postings from survivors, gleefully describing the full extent of their biological meltdown. They're trying to outdo each other.

'I had to lie naked on the bathroom floor for three days, blasting hot fluid from both ends, spinning around like a Catherine wheel.'

'Yeah? Well I vomited so hard, all the hair on my head got sucked inside my skull and flew out my mouth.'

'Pfff – think that's bad? At one point I spewed with such force, the jet fired me backwards through a stained-glass window, and I literally burst apart on the patio, sending a geyser of shit and vomit 600 feet into the sky.'

And if they're not online, they're crawling into the office to tell you all about them. While still infectious. If I was running things, it'd be dealt with like a zombie outbreak: shoot all victims in the head at the first sign of infection, then barricade the windows till the end credits roll.

Worse still, it apparently strikes without warning. Infection takes 12 to 28 hours to come to fruition, quietly making its way to your small intestine, and, at first, you're none the wiser. The physical symptoms come on so suddenly, you only truly know you've got it when you suddenly spot a jet of vomit flying away from your face. And then you're locked in. It's like knowing the sun could explode at any second and being powerless to prevent it.

Naturally I want to avoid it like the plague, because it is a plague. And I've become an expert. Here's how to avoid it yourself.

Forget those fancy anti-bacterial hand gels. They're pointless. Don't worry about breathing it in; unless you're unlucky enough to inhale a fresh droplet of sick or faeces (which can happen if some-one explodes right beside you), you can still get away unscathed even if someone in your immediate vicinity comes down with it. It's not carried in saliva either. The one thing you must do is wash your hands with hot water and soap for a minimum of 15 seconds before putting them in your mouth, nose or eyes.

Easier said than done. Once you're aware of it, it's incredible how often you touch a shared surface, then your mouth, without even thinking. Say you pop to the newsagents and buy a bag of crisps: that door handle could be caked in sick germs, and you've just slid them down your gullet along with the salt and vinegar. Or you're in an office: you use someone else's keyboard, then eat a sandwich. Why not lick a toilet bowl and have done with it?

But even washing your hands is tricky. Take the workplace toilet. The door handle, the taps and the button on the automated dryer may all be infected. You have to turn the tap with your elbow, wash for 15 seconds (time it: it's longer than you think), then turn the tap off with the other elbow. Then you'll need two paper towels: one to dry yourself, and the other to open the door with on your way out. Unless you do all of this, you're doomed.

I've become an obsessive compulsive disorder case study, repeatedly washing my hands like Lady Macbeth on fast-forward, acutely aware of where my hands are at all times, what I've just touched, and where they're heading next. It's exhausting, like con-sciously counting every blink.

Yesterday, in an attempt to prod some sanity back into my life, I went to a restaurant. Eating out is insane: even if your chef is hygienic in the first place, unless he's devoutly following the paper-towel hand-washing routine outlined above to the letter he may as well wipe his bum on your plate. Nonetheless, I decided to risk it. Giving in to emetophobia would be like giving in to the terrorists, yeah? End result: I lay awake for hours last night, convinced that I'd start hurling any second.

There's one chink of sunlight for us emetophobes: we hardly ever actually vomit. There are various theories as to why, and it's all a bit chicken-and-egg: either we're so naturally hardy that vomiting is a rarity (and therefore more traumatic when it does occur), or we're so psychologically averse to it, we can will ourselves to stop. In fact, if I was on *Heroes*, that would be my superpower. A few years ago I caught a noro-style gastric nasty that made all my friends spew like ruptured fire hydrants. I lay in bed with cramps and a fever, battling extreme nausea for four days, and somehow didn't snap. Although what was happening at the other end of my body was another story altogether. Magic powers only stretch so far. That's why Superman wears rubber knickers.

Anyway, it'll blow over soon. The media have already got new scare stories to torture us with. In the meantime, if you're reading this on a bus, in an office, or at a shared computer, and you're eating your lunch – God help you. Now wash your hands.

Not enough buttons   [21 January 2008]

According to a survey, two-thirds of people think gadgets are becoming too complicated. They're packed with features they don't understand, and subsequently never use. One newspaper illustrated the story with a photograph of 'a typical TV remote' featuring '43 baffling buttons', annotated with captions telling you what each of these buttons did, just to make it look even more complex and bewildering: 'cursor up', 'cursor down', 'A/V input connector 1', 'device mode', and so on.

Thing is, there weren't enough buttons for my liking. I love a complicated TV remote. They should have more stuff on them: dials and joysticks and flashing lights. I dream of a remote with its own mouse.

And I don't want a manual. I like to work out what each nubbin does through trial and error, poking it and staring at the screen. Best of all is the 'menu' button, which grants you access to a whole new array of onscreen options, replete with little icons and sliding scales. Sit me in front of a brand-new telly and it's the first thing I'll reach for, because new tellies often come with surprising and exotic new features provided by the gods of technology.

Coo! I can design my own font for the subtitles! Wow! I can flip the picture sideways so I don't have to lift my head if I'm lying perpendicular on the sofa! And look! There's a slider for adjusting the level of regional accents! Now I can make the Geordie guy who narrates *Big Brother* sound like a Cornish fisherman.

I'll happily spend hours fine-tuning everything to my liking. Woe betide anyone who hits the 'restore default settings' button. That's like smashing a piece of ornate pottery I've created. The other day, a Sky repairman turned up and breezily started playing with my settings, adjusting the contrast and colour balance as if he owned the place. I was outraged by the violation, as though he'd pulled my trousers down and nonchalantly examined my goolies.

I tend to assume other people share my obsessive need to examine the settings until everything is just so, and get genuinely enraged when I go to someone's house and discover, say, that they're watching programmes in the wrong aspect ratio. People over 50 are the worst offenders: they'll blithely sit through a *Dad's Army* repeat that is unnaturally stretched across the screen so that the entire cast look as if they had difficult births that left them with flattened skulls. Faced with this, I get acute back-seat-driver anxiety, and end up hectoring them like an exasperated pilot trying to teach a four-year-old how to fly a helicopter.

Recently, I was on a plane, sitting beside an 80-year-old woman who couldn't comprehend how the in-flight entertainment system worked. It had a touch-screen monitor and an additional set of controls in the armrest. Thing is, she didn't understand the difference between my armrest and hers. There I was, watching a movie in a bid to distract myself from the terror of being 30,000 feet up in the sky, when she patted cluelessly at my controls and switched it off. I started it again. Then she hit my fast-forward button.

At this point, I politely explained what was going on and attempted to help her operate her system. She nodded and went 'ooh' and 'ahh', but try as I might, she just didn't get it. Ten minutes later, she stopped my film again, and kept doing so intermittently throughout the flight, sometimes switching my overhead light on for good measure, just to annoy me. Her screen, meanwhile, displayed nothing but the synopsis for an episode of *Everybody Hates*

Chris, which she'd selected by accident but never played. She just sat there, staring at the synopsis for about three hours. I think she thought that was the entertainment.

Shamefully, I found myself starting to genuinely hate her – her doddering incompetence somehow rendered her less than human. Reverse the situation – put me in a 1940s household, say, and ask me to operate a mangle, and the chances are I'd earn her contempt with an equal display of ineptitude. But it isn't the 1940s. It's now. So snap out of it. Hit the right buttons or get left behind, you medieval dunce. Do you want the robots to take over? Because that's what'll happen if we don't all keep up. How dare you jeopardise the human race like that. How dare you.

And if people still refuse to learn, let's force them into it. Replace all supermarkets with complex remote-control vending machines that dispense food only if you can successfully navigate your way through a 25-tier menu system. And make it illegal to pass the food to anyone else. Before long, we'll starve the idiots out of existence; manufacturers will never have to simplify anything ever again, and we'll enjoy a golden age of buttons and options and adjustable sliders and A/V input connectors. Now that's progress.

– After writing this piece, I was reminded of something that happened to a friend of mine: he was sitting at work when his mum rang up out of the blue.

'It's your father,' she said. 'He's had an accident.'

My friend froze, steeled himself for the worst, and asked her what had happened.

'Well, he's deleted the printer icon from his desktop. How does he make it come back again?'

CHAPTER SIX

*In which young men are the enemy, Michael Portillo hosts
a warthog parade, and the Iraq war becomes a set of dizzying
numbers*

Coke 'n' cheese party   [26 January 2008]

When I was a kid, *Panorama* was a serious news programme consisting of grainy footage and a voiceover going 'blah blah OPEC blah President Carter blah' for six hundred days. To my young head, this was especially disappointing because it had such a thrilling theme tune – like an orchestra describing a hurricane – that I regularly forgot how boring I found the show itself. I'd hear the music and run for the TV, only to slink off in disgust five minutes later.

That was then. Now *Panorama*'s more like *Dancing on Ice* than *Newsnight*: a 'pop-news' show in the vein of *Tonight with Trevor McDonald*. People who complain about such shows 'dumbing down' with celebrity 'reporters' miss the point by an inch. There's nothing wrong with the news attempting to reach a wider audience – it's the choice of subject matter that's the problem. They shouldn't get Denise Van Outen to investigate the Maddy mystery. They should use stars properly. Send Girls Aloud to cover genocide in Darfur.

I'm not kidding. Years ago, Channel 4 were apparently planning a 'Celebrity Guantanamo' one-off in which famous people underwent borderline-torture methods used by the United States. It never made it to air. Panorama should've done it. *Tonight with Trevor McDonald* should've done it. Seriously. It'd raise awareness of a bona-fide global scandal, reaching millions of people who normally don't give a toss about 'the issues'.

Since I don't have a problem with celebrities acting as bait, gently luring the viewer toward a serious subject, I don't mind in the slightest that this week's *Panorama* stars former Blur bassist Alex James. But we'll get onto that in a moment. First: is it really necessary to start every edition of *Panorama* with an opening link in which Jeremy Vine stands shivering outside the BBC's Media Village in White City at night, with the wind and rain howling round his ears? He looks like a tramp on a pavement, mournfully gazing through the window of a fancy restaurant at the diners within, except instead of a window it's your TV screen, and instead of staring pleadingly at a dinner-jacketed posho tucking into a plate of foie gras, he's looking directly at you.

Anyway, Alex James: he's investigating cocaine. This is a subject he knows well, having famously blown £1m on booze and conk-dust during his Blur days. In fact, he did so much coke, the president of Colombia wrote him a personal letter. That's not a joke. He reads it out at the start of the show. I'm paraphrasing slightly, but basically it says: 'Dear Alex from Blur, I understand you're a clean-living farmer these days. And you make your own cheese. Woo hoo. Nice one. But once upon a time you were a notorious chalkhead. Why don't you come over here with a film crew and see how much misery cocaine is wreaking in my country? PS We've already approached Kate Moss but she's ignoring us.'

The resulting film is surprisingly good. James gets into several dicey situations (including an unnerving encounter with a contract killer with a loaded gun) and openly admits to feeling scared and out of his depth. He's also immensely saddened by the human cost of cocaine production, but realistic about the likelihood of the situation changing any time soon (and about the film's chances of dissuading existing cokehounds in Britain: 'They'll probably just hate themselves a bit more,' he says ruefully).

The only gauche moment comes when he meets the Colombian president and is so impressed by his uniform and general mannerisms, he develops a weird schoolboy crush on him and starts cooing to the camera crew about how lovely he is. And even that's sort of charming, in a gawky kind of way.

It's only half an hour long though. And then it's back to outdoorsman Jeremy for a final goodbye link. For God's sake, someone on the production team give the man an indoor desk. Never mind the cocaine wars – your host's turning blue, you maniacs.

The forgotten tortoises   [2 February 2008]

There's far too much stuff in the world. Check Wikipedia if you don't believe me. Hit the 'random article' widget on the left three times in a row, then guff your own legs off with amazement as it coughs up a trio of things you've never ever heard of before.

I've just tried this myself, and it introduced me to (1) an Australian Aboriginal tribe called the 'Gunwinggu', (2) *Something Wicked*, a 1993 album by Nuclear Assault, and (3) former computer games designer Demis Hassabis. Infuriatingly, I've actually met Demis Hassabis, so that's another theory left bleeding by the roadside.

Anyhow, the point I'm failing to make is that there's so much stuff out there, you can't possibly remember it all at once. Which isn't to say you delete it. Most of it you simply file away, somewhere at the back of your mind, by the bins. And there it stays for weeks, months, years, until something jolts you into retrieving it, at which point: bam! Instant recall.

I fear I'm not making sense, so let me explain. While watching the new David Attenborough series, *Life in Cold Blood*, I suddenly realised I'd completely forgotten about tortoises. I can't have thought about a tortoise in any shape or form for at least a year. They've been dead to me. Obviously, stuff like this happens all the time inside the human brain, usually zipping past unnoticed, but since I'm currently training myself to pay attention to every thought I experience, like a ninja, I caught myself being surprised by the realisation. I actually thought, 'oh yeah, tortoises, I remember them.'

But the beauty of a programme like *Life in Cold Blood* is that having reintroduced me to the concept of tortoises, it then astonishes me by depicting them doing something I've never seen them do before, namely fighting. Yes, tortoises fight. Did you know that? I bloody didn't. They've even got little jousting staves built into their shells, all the better for flipping one another on to their backs with.

Even the things you think you've seen before have a new and exciting twist. We see a python dislocating its own jaw in order to swallow a small deer. It starts with the head and slowly engulfs the whole body until it's coating the thing like a living condom. Familiar territory? Maybe so. But then Attenborough points out that the deer's head is so huge the snake can't breathe, so it sicks up its own windpipe and pokes it out the side of its mouth, like a floppy pink snorkel, puckering for air. Truly revolting. And new. And clever: it's the sort of thing Jack Bauer would do, if he had several million years to evolve his way out of a crisis.

Attenborough is routinely praised to the point where future historians might mistake him for a minor god, and quite right too. Few TV shows in any genre make you feel anything whatsoever, apart from a vague awareness that you're wasting your life, whereas his programmes, with their signature blend of understated commentary and magnificent footage, induce awe every five minutes. And not a sentimental, dewy-eyed kind of awe either, but a sobering one. In their own way, these are among the most nihilistic programmes on television. If your mind wanders at all during the tortoise fight, for example, it's likely to contemplate war, or terrorism, specifically dwelling on the extent to which conflict is an inbuilt human trait, just as it's an inbuilt trait in tortoises, which you'd previously thought of as a race of comically benign Cornish pasties, good for sleeping in boxes or appearing in the *One Foot in the Grave* title sequence, and not much else.

This is likely to be Attenborough's last major series: the final chapter in an extraordinary legacy. To change the way millions of people see the world is no mean feat, and he's done it with quiet assurance, humour, and respect.

TV can be many things. Nowt wrong with a bit of mindless entertainment now and then. But when someone with purpose seizes and commands it, it can also do this. Incredible.

Tony, don't be a hero [9 February 2008]

It's a basic psychological truth that the more someone appears not to want you, the more you'll go out of your way to win their attention. That's why nice girls fall for bastards, and nice boys end up following said nice girls around like lovelorn puppies, doomed to be a best friend, not a lover, until they cotton on and start acting like bastards themselves. It's the way of the world. You want what you can't have.

Teenagers don't seem to care about television, which is why television's all in a froth about them. As the internet, videogames and mobiles chew their way through the ratings, tempting back the young has become an obsession, giving rise to all manner of dumb theories about what 'they' – them, that 'youthy' lot – actually want, as though they're a different species.

Most TV types with authority are over 30, which isn't that old, but clearly old enough for them to forget that most people's teenage years consist of agonised introspection and enthused curiosity, not jumping up and down and going 'Wooo!'

Consequently, 'Wooo!' is the first port of call: gaudy colour schemes, strobe-paced edits, thumping beats, pretty faces, celebrity guests and sneery, aspirational horseshit. And it works, up to a point. But only for a narrow slice of the youth demographic. Only for the idiotic ones, or the smart ones slumming it because hey, there's nothing else on. TV's great at harnessing idiots. It's the rest of us it tends to ignore.

When I saw the initial trails for the first series of *Skins* last year, I harrumphed like a 400-year-old man. It looked like *Hollyoaks* getting off with *Trainspotting* on the set of Christina Aguilera's *Dirrty* video. The advert showed Tony, one of the main characters, romping in a shower with two girls at the same time, which looked about as far away from my teenage years as it was possible to get. And when episode one rolled by, my harrumphing appeared justified. The minute I saw Tony in action, I thought 'oh, so he's the hero, is he? Supposed to think he's cool, am I? Well I don't. I think he's an arsehole. Ha! Take THAT, *Skins*.'

But the series had wrong-footed me. It thought Tony was an arsehole too, and spent episode after episode showing his friends slowly coming to the same conclusion. He was shallow and cruel, and the final episode ended with him getting hit by a bus. If I was a teenager, that's precisely what I'd want to see.

In between now and then, Tony's been in a coma, emerging just in time for the start of the second series. The cocksure grin has been replaced by a hundred-yard stare. His brain's taken such a kick to the nuts, other people have to cut his food up for him. He can't write his own name or unbutton his flies. And the memories of most of his sexual conquests have been wiped, unlike his back-side, which he has to clean using an automated spout on a special toilet.

In short, Tony's eating humble pie by the fistload. So having spent series one setting him up as a hideous bell-end, the pro-gramme now invites you to pity him. It's a great start. A confident one, too: in fact, the show oozes confidence from the off, opening with a wordless dance routine in a church, just to confuse you.

And as it goes on, it becomes clear *Skins* isn't a youth show at all, but a proper drama, far closer to Jimmy McGovern's *The Street* than *Hollyoaks*.

Instead of attempting to pander to an imaginary audience of whooping teenage cretins, it merely seeks to entertain regular people. Yes, regular people. Remember them? They used to watch television in their millions, back in the days before it got obsessed with targeting niche groups.

In an age when the bulk of contemporary television is drearily defined by who it's aimed at, anyone of any age could tune in to *Skins* and draw something from it. Which makes it weird. And somewhat wonderful.

Imaginary young males   [16 February 2008]

Is there a single worse force in the universe than swaggering, cock-sure, stupid young men? Because I'm struggling to think of one.

You see them everywhere: lurching around in messy haircuts and idiot trousers, thinking about cars, or babes, or babes in cars, laughing too loudly and blaring things like 'classic!' or 'quality!' or 'genius!' or 'mental!' and every one of them, without exception, is a cee to the yoo to the enn to the tee of towering, awful proportions.

And the thing is, the real ones aren't even real, so to speak. The archetypal swaggering, cocksure young man is an insulting media construct, designed to star in beer commercials. Some 90% of their real-life equivalents are merely emulating these idealised buffoons in the tragic belief that this is what the world requires of them; that the first step on the path to acceptance consists of adopting a mockney accent and shouting 'get in!' when your team scores a goal. The remaining 10% are authentic wankers who'd do that anyway, of course – but there are probably some decent people lost among the ill-advised majority: trapped inside their shallow, posturing cocoons, yearning to break out but too scared to try. We should pity them. And when that fails, attack them with hammers.

Nuts TV is a station aimed at imaginary young males. It's not despicable or even particularly offensive to women (except, perhaps, the whiniest, most humourless ones). No. It's just shit. Utterly, astronomically shit. It might even be made out of shit: the sets, the cameras, the lighting rigs – all actual, genuine chunks of crap, carved into shape by the unseen hand of some insanely misguided God. And powered by piss instead of electricity. This is in no way an exaggeration.

It doesn't have tits, incidentally. Lingerie and hot pants, but not really tits. Although it does have presenters. Chief amongst them are the two men from *Big Cook, Little Cook*, who present a regular live strand from the studio, ironically chatting about boozers and sex and ninjas and so on. Stringing your programmes together with live in-studio links instead of pre-recorded continuity is a good idea for a digital channel: it gives it a sense of identity. But it's a drawback in this case. You'd be hard pressed to find anyone anywhere looking more pleased with themselves than the ginger one (formerly Little Cook) does here. He literally never stops smirking at his own casual brilliance. At one point I found myself smirking back – not because he'd said or done anything funny, but because of some cowardly inbuilt ape-like response. I actually felt pressure to join in, as though I was stuck in a train carriage with two overbearingly ironic lads and had decided to agree with everything they said or did, simply because the alternative – a crushing, awkward, echoing silence – would be too gruesome to bear.

It has programmes. It has *Fit and Fearless*, a sort of *Most Haunted* knock-off in which three 'babes' strip to their underwear and run around spooky old buildings, squealing with fright. It largely consists of night-vision camera footage, and looks like a bit like a *Carry On* film shot from the point of view of the *Predator*. Presumably you're meant to masturbate while watching, although actually doing so would make you a terrifying psychopath.

Here's what should be on Nuts TV: live footage of a swaggering, cocksure young man trapped within a revolving metal drum, the inner surface studded with nails. A different specimen each night. At the start of the evening, he falls in, screaming. He dies within five minutes, but the broadcast continues for another four hours, so we see nothing but his mute, punctured body tumbling around in the drum, accompanied by a soundtrack consisting of nothing but Oasis and Razorlight.

Yeah. That might cure things. If you want a vision of the perfect future, picture a boot stamping on a gurgling blokey face – forever.

A Toad of Toad Hall lookalike contest

[23 February 2008]

This week! Comin' atcha with all the passion and glitz of an over-sexed circus troupe freewheelin' its way down Las Vegas Boulevard, it's . . . The Conservative Party! Yeah! *Portillo on Thatcher: The Lady's Not for Spurning* is a 90-minute journey into the crazy world of the Tory party, and mark my words, it's the most arousing pro-gramme you'll see this decade. If you're the sort of person who screws frogs, that is.

And assuming you are, then prepare to spoo yourself inside-out, because everyone in this show looks like a frog. Nigel Lawson's in it. So's Norman Lamont. And David Mellor. It's like a Toad of Toad Hall lookalike contest. Or a *Spitting Image* reunion. But mainly the former.

Just about the only interviewee who doesn't look like a frog is David Cameron, and he looks like Brian the Snail. Cameron pops up from time to time to peep away in his peepy little voice, playing a tune on his Fauntleroy git-whistle: otherwise it's old school Tory warthogs all the way, with Michael Portillo leading the charge as chief inquisitor. More on him later.

The show itself is largely concerned with the legacy of Maggie

Thatcher (who appears in archive footage, haunting proceedings throughout). The trouble with Maggie, reckon Portillo and co, is that she was so hugely successful at redefining the Tories, they lost all sense of purpose the moment she left. I say 'left'. They hoofed her out, and the bitterness caused by her abrupt removal poisoned the party for years, causing them to pick one no-hoper leader after another: John Major (ineffective comedy nerd), William Hague (cheery dot-eyed cueball), Iain Duncan Smith (solemn dot-eyed cueball), Michael Howard (schoolmaster) . . .

Ah, Michael Howard: now there's a prick. Even here, interviewed by a former colleague, he can't answer the simplest of questions without pausing for two minutes first, with an anxious grin fritzing round his chops like an android going wrong. Either he's choosing his words carefully or there's a live anchovy stuck up his arse that keeps tickling his G-spot. Unlikely. He's choosing his words. Why? Because he's the sort of politician who's programmed to avoid straight answers by default. Each time his brain approaches a straight answer, it's instantly repelled, as if by an opposing magnetic field.

If Michael Howard was in a restaurant, and the waiter asked whether he wanted still or sparkling water, he'd sit there fritzing a grin for 10 minutes before replying 'neither'. No wonder we didn't vote for him.

Portillo, meanwhile, is pretty likable, if only because he's disarmingly frank about how vastly unpopular he became. When he lost his seat in the 1997 election, the entire nation cheered so hard the French got earache. Everyone hated him, myself included. In fact I even called him a cee-yoo-enn-tee to his face once, around 1999. I say 'called' – actually I shouted it. And it wasn't 'to his face', more the side of his head. I was sitting in a cab, quite drunk, and he was on the pavement, so I pulled down the window and bellowed it at him while zooming past. He looked a bit upset and I felt immediate remorse.

All things considered, he took his nationwide humiliation rather well; vowed to learn from it politically, and when that didn't pan out, jumped ship and went into broadcasting, where he's subsequently carved a niche as a pundit (*This Week*), occasional stunt journalist (getting CS-gassed for *Horizon*) and political historian.

Fair enough – although this particular show is rather meandering, unfocused and not nearly revelatory enough to justify the running time. Oddly – and here's a sentence I never thought I'd write – there's not enough Margaret Thatcher. Still, if you want to gawp at a parade of wobbling old Tory faces and remember how much you despised them, here's your chance. Throw spitballs. Knock yourself out.

The wheel of hate [1 March 2008]

Hello. Welcome to this week's Screen Burn. I'm afraid our writer is busy at present, so you've been placed in a queue and will be dealt with shortly. If you'd like to continue into the next paragraph, press one now.

Thank you. Please continue to use your imaginary keypad while using this service. To find out what programme is being discussed this week, press two now.

Thank you. This week's column relates to *Cutting Edge: Phone Rage*. To proceed straight to the article, press three now.

I'm sorry, five is not a valid request. To proceed to the article, press three now.

Thank you. The voice you hear in your head while reading may be recorded for training purposes.

Hello? It's me. Yes. I was going to talk about this week's *Cutting Edge*. A journey into the dark heart of the call centre that somehow manages to sum up everything that's wrong with our world. It starts by introducing us to three hideously ugly average schmoes, each of whom has been driven insane by call centres. They whinge to camera for a bit, then we see them in action: being held in a queue, arguing with the poor sod on the other end, sighing with despair, and so on. It's a joyless existence, made all the more depressing because it's so easy to relate to.

One of them sorrowfully describes how he sometimes finds himself venting his anger by shouting at the hapless lackey at the other end, even though he knows it's pointless, and that by doing so he's simply contributing to what he calls 'the cyclical wheel of hate'.

Then the cameras venture inside a call centre – for Powergen – and we discover the staff are so used to being shouted at, they scarcely even notice any more. Half their job seems to consist of simply letting the customer scream for a bit to blow off steam. You roar yourself purple; they sit and soak it up, like an anger sponge. The cyclical wheel of hate is revolving in a vacuum.

Then we visit a different kind of call centre: a smiley one belonging to First Direct. The thinking here is that the happier the staff, the happier the customer. So the staff are forced to be happy.

They hold sumo wrestling tournaments in paddling pools full of foam balls. They have to form teams with wacky names (like pub quiz teams) and attach kerrrazy photos of themselves to the 'team wall'. The boss says things like 'Hey, who wants to win a Creme Egg? First one to get the phrase "that's tremendous" into their next call . . .'

And they're coached in 'Above the Line Language', so they only ever say things like 'I'd love to' or 'I'd be happy to' instead of 'I must'.

It's the most terrifying, awful place I've ever seen, and it's the size of the National Exhibition Centre, for Christ's sake. It's madness. Any sane person working there would pray daily for a massacre. As the gunmen burst in, firing indiscriminately, the first genuine smile in six months would spread wide across your face, and you'd leap, giggling, into the line of fire.

And just when you think things can't get any more tear-jerking, we're introduced to Mandisa, a black single mum in South Africa, who hopes her new call centre job should make ends meet. Thing is, it's for a UK firm, so first she has to attend an 'Accent Reduction' course, which knocks all the fun out of her voice, so she won't frighten the horses.

Then she's given a crash course in British culture, which involves watching *The Full Monty* on DVD. Then she sits an exam. She passes! She's excited! She goes to work, smiling broadly! And the British phone up. Yeah, us. And we sigh and we whine and we hang up and shout at her. Her smile shrivels into oblivion. The cyclical wheel of hate turns again. And somehow you know it won't ever, ever stop.

Ireland's industry [8 March 2008]

Of all the music in all the world, easy-listening pop is the very best kind there is. That's why minicab drivers listen to nothing else. I've debated this with imbeciles who think the drivers are only listening to Heart or Magic or Smooth or whatever FM in the first place because they think that's what their customers want to hear. Rubbish. It's what the cabbies want. They've had hours on the road. They've tried all the other stations. This is the music that makes them happiest. Every single minicab driver in existence, regardless of age, background and position on the sex offenders' register, winds up tuned to easy listening. All roads lead to Rome. Like I said, it's the best music there is.

Now, a lot of this music is sneered at by rock aficionados, who'd rather we brushed our teeth to the uncompromising sound of British Sea Power and emptied our bums while listening to Devo on our iPod shuffles. We secretly want to hear Dolly Parton and Lionel Richie. But we can't. They're guilty pleasures.

That's the idea behind sing-along special *Guilty Pleasures*. It's a real curio. On the one hand, it features plenty of acts you don't often see on ITV1, like the Magic Numbers. On the other, it feels precisely like any number of bog-standard karaoke talent contests of the sort we've been bombarded with for the past five years. Except it isn't a talent contest: they're just doing it for fun (and exposure of course, but fun definitely comes into it).

Of course, this being mainstream ITV, they've also felt the need to rub an extra bit of shit all over it by interrupting proceedings with talking-head contributions in which a galaxy of ITV stars, such as GMTV presenter Andrew Castle, babble about how we all had big hair and shoulderpads back in the 80s ha ha ha ha ha ha yes we did didn't we ha ha HA HA HA. *Guilty Pleasures* deviser Sean Rowley also pops up in these segments, disguised as an Edwardian postman for some mad reason.

Just to underline its mainstream credentials, it's presented by Fearne Cotton – a genetic splicing of the twins from last year's *Big Brother* and Beaker from the *Muppet Show*. I always feel vaguely sorry for her without ever knowing why.

Still, if you can mentally edit those sections out as you go, the show itself represents a chance for several non-ITV acts to show-case themselves on ITV, and that's surely a Good Thing For ITV To Be Doing . . . like *Top of the Pops* with an old setlist. Except the moment it starts, confusion enters the building. The Feeling kick things off with a decent cover of 'Video Killed the Radio Star', a song approximately 200 times better than anything The Feeling have written themselves, and whose pleasure doesn't strike me as particularly guilty.

It soon transpires that for the purposes of this programme, 'guilty pleasure' sometimes simply means 'old song'. For instance, two-thirds of Supergrass close the show by covering Michael Jackson's 'Beat It' – again, there's nothing 'guilty' about that particular track, unless you're spectacularly uptight.

Worse, the acts themselves have roughly a 75% failure rate. KT Tunstall farts out an awful version of 'The Voice' by John Farnham. Craig David (looking a tad burly) has a feeble, watery take on Terence Trent D'Arby's 'If You Let Me Stay'. The aforementioned Magic Numbers utterly slaughter Dolly Parton and Kenny Rogers' 'Islands in the Stream' (a song I used to think was about 'Ireland's Industry', incidentally). And Amy Macdonald sings 'Sweet Caroline' in a weird, low register that doesn't suit her, the song, or anybody's ears or mind.

Sophie Ellis-Bextor pulls off a reasonable 'Yes Sir, I Can Boogie', and that Supergrass closer isn't bad, but overall, you're left wishing that instead of watching these guilty pleasures performed live on the telly, you were enjoying them in their natural habitat: sitting in the back seat of a minicab at 3 a.m., listening to 'Say You, Say Me' by Lionel Richie dribbling through the stereo, as the driver skims you home.

The war that isn't there   [15 March 2008]

Is it just me or is everything a sham? The real world doesn't feel real any more, as though we're separated from it by a thick layer of Perspex: we can see it, but can't sense it. Perhaps it isn't there.

Take the war. Not the Afghan war, not the 'war on terror', but the other one: Iraq. I call it a war, but really it's a TV show – a long-running and depressing one that squats somewhere in the background, humming away to itself; a dark smear in the Technicolor entertainment mural. We know it's happening – we catch glimpses of it happening – but we don't feel it any more. It's like a soap we don't watch, but keep vaguely up to speed with by osmosis.

Even as it unfolds, we have to strain to remember it's there. News stories about suicide bombers bringing death to Baghdad markets are as familiar as adverts for dog food. Our bored brains filter them out. Novelty and sensation – that's what our minds crave. Iraq just offers more of the same: death after death after death after death, until each death becomes nothing more than a dull pulse on a soundtrack; the throb of a neighbour's washing machine we learned to filter out months ago; the invisible ticking of a household clock. We'll notice if it stops, but not before. The average response to the rash of programmes marking five years since the start of the war is likely to be: 'Hey, is that still happening? Bummer.'

ITV1 are doing their bit with *Rageh Omaar: Iraq by Numbers*, which, should you even detect its existence, is a violently dispiriting ground-level look at the life of the average Iraqi civilian. Rageh Omaar, of course, is the 'Scud Stud' who became a minor celebrity back during the war's earlier, more exciting episodes. Because he's a celebrity, his name comes before that of the war in the programme's title: someone's decided you're more likely to tune in if you see the words 'Rageh Omaar' in the EPG. Certainly worked on me.

In some ways, this feels like a comeback special: he left the BBC in 2006 to join Al-Jazeera's English-language service, and the majority of viewers won't have seen him since. So when he walks onscreen it's all, Ooh, it's him – the bloke from that thing. Used to stand on the balcony with all the bombs going off behind him and all sorts. Shock and awe or whatever it was. I used to like him. Think I'll watch this.

Which isn't Omaar's fault, of course. If he's 'using' what celeb status he has, then he's doing so simply to encourage us to pay fresh attention to an ongoing tragedy that's grown too stale and too sad for us to even notice. To ease the viewer in gently, he pitches the show to us as a personal journey, not a stone-faced journalistic investigation. He meets one of the civilians who tore down Saddam's statue. He revisits a hotel where one of his cameramen was killed. He tours the Green Zone with some US troops. And he goes in search of his old friends.

Trouble is, seeking out old friends requires him to travel abroad, because so many of them have fled the country in fear of their lives. In Syria, he's reunited with one (his former driver), who was kidnapped and threatened. As his friend recounts his story, Omaar weeps on camera. Normally such a reaction would seem cynical and contrived: here, it feels justified and honest.

Interspersing each encounter are the numbers of the title: bald statistics served up as chilling graphics. Particularly striking is the figure regarding the total number of Iraqi dead – striking because it's so huge, and so vague. It lies somewhere between 150,000 and 1 million.

Between 150,000 and a million. That leaves 850,000 people who may be dead or alive. We simply don't know. They currently exist, or do not exist, within a cavernous margin of error. Our minds can't process this degree of horror. No wonder we change the channel. No wonder nothing feels real.

CHAPTER SEVEN

In which celebrities perish, Valentine's Day fails to raise hopes, and smokers are threatened with paperwork

The so-called 'Stock Market'   [28 January 2008]

Let's see if I've got this straight: an out-of-control French Cityboy has accidentally lost the Société Générale bank the grand sum of £3.7bn – a large amount by anyone's standards. And how did he do it? By betting the wrong way, then trying to dig himself out of the hole by continuing to bet the wrong way, covering up the mess he made along the way using some cunning ninja-style inside knowledge of how the system's 'warning lights' worked, which meant he was pissing money away undetected until the losses grew so huge they were visible from space.

Some analysts say the actions of this one poor panicking sod may have helped cause the stock market hoo-hah that kicked off last week: nice to know that even in today's world of faceless global corporations, the little guy can still make a difference.

If it's hard to imagine what £3.7bn looks like, it's even harder to picture an absence of £3.7bn. Presumably it resembles a dark, swirling vortex, like a portal to another dimension in a supernatural thriller. All the money got sucked into it, and emerged . . . um . . . where? Where's it gone? Is it lodged away somewhere to the side of the stock market, slightly to the left of the screen, where computers can't get to it?

As you may have gathered, I don't understand the stock market, because it's so boring my brain refuses to get to grips with it. Say the word 'economics' and I reach for my pillow. But even I know enough to realise it's largely an imaginary construct: abstract numbers given shape by wishful thinking. If the traders suddenly stop believing it's healthy, millions of people lose their jobs. Maybe one day they'll stop believing in it altogether; they'll collectively blink and rub their eyes, and the entire global economy will vanish, like a monster under the bed that turns out never to have existed in the first place, or an optical illusion you've suddenly seen through. And on *News at Ten* that night they'll say, 'Business news now . . . and, er, there is no business news. It's gone.' At which point we'd better come up with some kind of replacement barter system, pronto. Let's hope it's not based on

117

sexual favours, or a simple trip to the supermarket's going to be downright harrowing.

In order to maintain their mad conviction that the economy is real, City traders adopt all manner of belief-bolstering strategies, such as awarding themselves vast bonuses when they 'do well' in the 'stock market'. This reinforces the notion that it's possible to play the market with a modicum of skill, which it isn't, because (a) it isn't there in the first place and (b) it's random. They're like pub gamblers convincing themselves they've developed a 'system' for beating the fruit machine, except they get paid in Ferraris rather than tokens.

In his excellent book *Irrationality*, the late Stuart Sutherland cited several surveys in which the advice of financial experts has consistently been proven to be markedly less reliable than random guesswork. Professor of psychology Richard Wiseman went one further in his book *Quirkology*, conducting an experiment in which a professional investment analyst, a financial astrologist and a four-year-old girl all chose stocks to invest in. The four-year-old couldn't even read, so her choices were made by writing the names of 100 stocks on pieces of paper, throwing them in the air and grabbing a few off the floor. No prizes for guessing who consistently came out on top, by an impressive margin, even when the value of the stocks was tracked for a full year.

In other words, the French rogue trader is only really guilty of dreaming that little bit harder than everyone else. Rather than punish him, perhaps they should simply wish him out of existence.

After all, it's been done before: a Chinese metals trader called Liu Qibing racked up immense losses in 2005 by betting the wrong way on the price of copper at the London Metal Exchange. In the immediate aftermath, despite fellow traders claiming to know him as China's main copper trader, the Chinese State Reserve Bureau simply denied he'd ever existed in the first place.

A vintage year for celebrity deaths
[4 February 2008]

This is already shaping up to be a vintage year for celebrity deaths. First Heath Ledger, then Jeremy Beadle. In both cases I first heard of the sad demise through the miracle of text messaging. Friends clearly felt compelled to be the first to break the bad news: in Ledger's case this was probably because his death came as a shock (an especially tragic one, given his age), and in Beadle's . . . well, my theory is that everyone in the country secretly loved Jeremy Beadle, but kept it quiet because the general consensus seemed to be that he was 'hated'. And when he died, we all felt slightly guilty that we hadn't piped up sooner. There was a palpable sense of 'aww', because whatever your views on his TV shows, there was little doubt we'd lost a real character – and that somehow we'd failed him.

Anyway, having my mobile beep twice in a fortnight, like a coroner's pager, made me feel as though I'd unwittingly subscribed to some kind of instant deathwatch service. Which isn't a bad idea, actually. Let's brainstorm!

OK. It's called 'eVulture'. You sign up for free on a website, and choose the category of celebrity you're interested in. This being an age of dazzling consumer choice in which the customer is routinely indulged like a spoilt medieval prince, the whole thing is super-configurable. You can decide to ignore everyone but the biggest Hollywood star, for instance, or specialise in minor characters from half-remembered TV shows, the sort of person whose passing probably wouldn't be mentioned in a mainstream news bulletin. So if you want to be contacted the moment one of *Blake's 7* shuffles off this mortal coil, or the Milk Tray man winds up in a box of his own, this is the service for you.

Meanwhile, back at eVulture HQ, a team of dedicated researchers monitors the news feeds, scans the death notices in local papers and, if necessary, phones around to ask if anyone's seen that bloke who was in that thing lately. GPs are bribed to report any celebrity who dies on their watch (at the end of the year, they receive a hamper full of cakes and wine – the quality and quantity depending on the number of tips they passed on).

As soon as a death is confirmed, the relevant subscribers receive a text alert, which arrives with a discreet little advert attached (that's how the money rolls in). Anyone receiving a deathtext is likely to feel slightly depressed for a few minutes: an ideal condition for advertisers, because you're talking about people with their guard down here. Research suggests that messages for comfort products such as chocolate or alcohol should perform particularly well under these circumstances. There's also scope for some revenue-generating user interaction, too, such as an option to send flowers, sign a virtual book of condolence, or order a rush-released DVD box set containing the deceased's greatest performances.

Future plans include a scheme in which celebrities are voluntarily fitted with microchips that monitor their current health status, and automatically transmit a personalised farewell message to fans the moment their heart stops beating. At present, we can only offer raw text messaging, but soon hope to provide a full range of MMS-epitaph features such as animated icons, background music, and CGI video clips of the star in question waving goodbye and ascending to heaven.

That's the business plan in a nutshell. I've copyrighted the idea, but if someone else wants to set it up, I'm more than happy to let them. You work out all the complicated stuff; I'll take 25% of the profits. Actually, scratch that. Under that setup, I'd soon find myself looking forward to celebrity deaths – willing the cast of *Hollyoaks* to die so I could buy some new gold fittings for my yacht or something – which probably isn't good for the soul. Plus it'd make good business sense to go around actively bumping people off. No. I can't do it. Plough my share into wind farms or something. That should help eVulture subscribers assuage their guilt, while simultaneously providing a fitting tribute to the deceased. Perfect.

Incidentally, in case you're appalled by the idea (on the flimsy grounds that it's monstrous), it's worth noting that despite its name, eVulture only steps in once death has occurred. Not before. The tabloids already have the ghoulish-rubbernecker market sewn

up, as evidenced by the hand-rubbing coverage of Britney Spears'
increasingly tragic predicament, or the extended hounding of
Amy Winehouse, all of which strikes them as a tremendous paper-
shifting wheeze.

If Britney Spears appeared on a window ledge tomorrow, a fight
would break out below. Half of the assembled hacks and paps
would scream at her to jump, and the rest would urge her to go
back inside, but remain as tormented as possible. One or two
might offer professional help, provided that it resulted in an
exclusive.

And in the resultant coverage, the mob itself wouldn't even be
mentioned, none of their shouts or cackles recorded, as though
they had exerted no influence at all. At best, a few detached
smartarses might mutter something boneheaded about publicity-
courting celebs bringing it on themselves. And then the lot of them
would vanish into smoke, only to reappear at the scene of the next
'inexplicable meltdown'.

Under the circumstances, eVulture looks positively acceptable.

Unvalentine's Day [11 February 2008]

This week, millions of people across the country will celebrate the
crippling delusion known as 'love' by sending flowers, booking
restaurants and placing stomach-churning small ads in newspapers. Valentine's Day – the only national occasion dedicated to
mental illness – is a stressful ordeal at the best of times.

If you've just started seeing someone, the day is fraught with
peril. Say your current dalliance only began less than a month ago:
is sending a card a bit full-on? What if you ignore it, only to discover they've bought you a 5kg Cupid-shaped diamond in a presentation box made of compressed rose petals?

Few things are worse than receiving a heartfelt Valentine's gift
from someone you're still not sure about. It's a crystallising
moment: chances are you'll suddenly know, deep in your bones,
that they're not the one for you. And while your gut contemplates
that sad reality, your brain repeatedly screams at your face not to

give the game away, and you have to gaze at them with a fake smile and a fake dewy expression, until the pressure and shame involved in maintaining the facade makes you start to hate them for point-less reasons, like the stupid way they sit, or the stupid way they breathe, or the stupid way their pupils dilate when they look at you, planning your life together.

For those in established relationships, it's a perfunctory, grinding ceremony. On February 14 restaurants nationwide play host to joy-less couples begrudgingly sharing an overpriced meal in near-silence, each of them desperately trying to avoid a row because, well, it's Valentine's Day, and nothing says 'I sort of love you, I think, although I can't really tell any more' quite like the ability to sustain an awkward, argument-free detente for one 24-hour period a year.

And, of course, if you're single, it's a thudding reminder of your increasingly desperate isolation. You're stranded somewhere out on Thunderbird Five, picking up chuckles and kissy-sounds from the planet below, separated from the action by the cold gulf of space. It's especially sharp if you've just been dumped and are feeling pretty raw about it, thanks. Under those circumstances, it's a cruel joke: you're like a one-legged man on National Riverdance Day.

What's required is something to redress the balance: an Unvalen-tine's Day, if you will. A day that actively celebrates love's festering undercarriage. February 15 is ideal: there will be plenty of willing participants by then. Of course, if Unvalentine's Day is going to succeed, it will require commercial backing – which shouldn't be a problem, because there are loads of money-spinning opportunities here.

First off, how about a range of Unvalentine cards containing bit-ter messages for ex-lovers? Typical example: a mournful cartoon bunny with a harpoon lodged in its chest cavity, staggering blank-faced into oncoming traffic, with YOU RUINED MY LIFE printed across the top in massive, scab-red lettering. Or perhaps a Photo-shopped image of Hitler snoozing in bed, accompanied by the words HOW CAN YOU SLEEP AT NIGHT? Naturally, each card would have a little poem on the inside, something such as: Roses are red/ Violets are blue/ I'm a meaningless robot/ Molested by you.

There would also be a range aimed at disillusioned long-term couples: epithets include I CAN'T TAKE MUCH MORE OF THIS, IT ISN'T REALLY WORKING, and our bestseller, the starkly effective DYING INSIDE.

The aforementioned restaurants can get in on the act too, by hosting Unvalentine meals specially designed for couples on the verge of a break-up. There'd be no red wine, so you can chuck drinks over each other without ruining your clothes, and all the food would be incredibly spicy, so when you tell your partner of seven years that you're seeing someone else, and tears start pouring down both your faces, anyone nosey enough to look on will simply think you're reacting to the chillies. The toilets would be manned by male and female prostitutes, so you can indulge in some cathartic, self-hating rebound sex within five minutes of getting the old heave-ho.

Cheating on your partner, incidentally, is actively encouraged on Unvalentine's Day. Consider it a 24-hour carte blanche to shag whoever you please. Developing an obsession with someone in the office? Get it out of your system on February 15! Let's face it, it's probably good for both of you in the long run.

As well as celebrating the death of existing loves, Unvalentine's Day can also accommodate all the loves that never were: the thwarted crushes, unrequited yearnings, and hopeless unspoken dreams. So if there's a friend you're desperately holding a candle for, even though they've pointed out time and time again that it's never going to happen, this is your 'me-time': you're permitted to call them up and howl down the phone for half an hour, or stand pleading outside their window like a sap. And for one day only, it's illegal for anyone to pity you.

In summary, Unvalentine's Day promises to be the most coldly practical celebratory festival in history – a far healthier affair than Valentine's Day itself. True love is so uncontrollably delightful, there's no need to set aside a mere day in its honour. As for love's torments – well, it's probably best to compress and release them in a single, orderly burst, once a year. And that day is February 15. Mark it in your diary. Beside the tearstains.

No smoke without paperwork [18 February 2008]

Morning, citizen! The grandly titled Julian Le Grand, chairman of a ministerial advisory board called Health England, has a humdinger of an idea for you: smoking permits. He proposes a ban on the sale of tobacco to anyone who can't flash a licence at the cashier.

Good news for smokers: Le Grand reckons said licence should cost only £10. Bad news: he wants to make the application process as deliberately complex as possible. You'd have to fill out a lengthy form, attaching a photograph, proof of age and a fee, and send it all to a central Smoker's Permit processing centre and wait for your licence to come back, by which point, let's face it, you would have probably died. Oh, and the licence expires after a year, so you have to apply all over again each time it runs out.

Why leave it there? Why not make it expire every 24 hours, so you have to reapply each morning? Or include a Sudoku on the application form? Or force the tobacco companies to sell cigarettes inside complicated Japanese puzzle boxes? Or change the name of the brands each week, without publicising the change, while simultaneously making it illegal for a shop to sell you anything you haven't asked for by name, so you have to stand at the counter fishing for codewords for an hour?

Or here's a good one, Julian: make it a requirement for smokers to walk around with a broomhandle stuck through their sleeves, running behind the neck, so their arms are permanently splayed out, like a scarecrow's. To spark up under those conditions, they'd have to work together in pairs, flailing around in the outdoor smoking area like something out of *It's a Knockout*.

His paper, incidentally, also proposes 'incentives for large companies to provide a daily "exercise hour" for staff'. Welcome to your future life: having struggled into work suffering withdrawal pangs because today's smoking licence didn't arrive in the post, you're forced to spend 60 minutes doing squat-thrusts in the car park.

And each time you start crying, a man in a helmet comes round to gently remind you that it's all for your own good. Through a loudhailer.

If that sounds like a nightmare, don't worry: you can still wriggle out of the squat-thrusts, provided you're carrying a valid Laziness Licence, whose application process involves climbing a ladder to reach the forms (stored at the top of a 200-foot crane), ticking 900 boxes with a 7kg pencil, and finally posting it into a motorised mailbox that persistently runs away from you at speeds of up to 25mph. In other words, you still have freedom of choice. Provided you're carrying a valid Freedom of Choice Permit, that is.

Getting your hands on a Freedom of Choice Permit is pretty straightforward. The application form requires only your name and signature. Admittedly, you have to deliver it in person to the Freedom of Choice Licensing Agency, which is open only between 4.15 a.m. and 4.18 a.m., and is based in an unmarked office in the Falklands, but nevertheless, thousands have already applied, if the queues are anything to go by. The current waiting time is a mere nine weeks, although you'd be advised to get there early and guard your place in line because there have been reports of disturbances.

Anyway, once you've got your Freedom of Choice Permit, you're free to do as you please, within reason, provided you notify the Central Scrutiniser six days in advance of any unapproved activity, quoting your 96-digit Freedom of Choice Permit code in full, which isn't printed anywhere on the permit itself, but is given to you once and only once, whispered quickly into your ear at the desk in the Falklands, by a man standing beneath a loudspeaker barking out other numbers at random.

The permit itself, incidentally, is shaped like a broomhandle, and is designed to be threaded through your sleeves at all times.

If you couldn't be bothered with all that, you will just have to do as you're told, which isn't that bad, to be honest. There's a compulsory exercise hour or five, and an approved list of foodstuffs, but that's about it. You will still have at least 10 minutes a day to do as you please, although we've just banned violent videogames, which are bad for your head, and there are one or two ideologies we'd rather you didn't discuss with friends or on the internet, which is why we're not issuing any Freedom of Speech Permits for the time being – although if you'd like to be notified when they're available, simply book yourself into one of our underground holding pens and remain there until your name is called, or not called, or time itself comes to an end. Whichever takes the longest.

Once upon a time, in between scrawling allegorical fables about lions and wardrobes, C. S. Lewis said something prescient. 'Of all tyrannies,' he wrote, 'a tyranny sincerely exercised for the good of its victims may be the most oppressive. It would be better to live under robber barons than under omnipotent moral busybodies.

'The robber baron's cruelty may sometimes sleep, his cupidity may at some point be satiated; but those who torment us for our own good will torment us without end, for they do so with the approval of their own conscience.'

You can nod your head in agreement if you like. Once you've got your Nodding Permit. Don't want you straining your neck, now, do we, citizen?

The Punchbag Hotline   [25 February 2008]

Shortly before writing this sentence, I literally punched myself in the head, because I'm unbelievably angry for no good reason. OK, for one good reason – I'm 24 hours into what must be my 20th attempt at quitting cigarettes for good (that 'smoking permit' horror story was the final straw – I'd rather quit now, on my own terms, thank you, not six months down the line when I've got to apply for a licence to keep on puffing, courtesy of some titwit advisory board).

I was what you might call a 'furious smoker' in that the very act of smoking annoyed me, and I tended to smoke when annoyed. Now that I've (hopefully) stubbed out my last one, the nicotine's been temporarily replaced by a steady, swelling rage, which I can feel surging just behind my eyes even as I type, as though I'm preparing to transform into the Hulk at the slightest provocation. This is not a healthy state to be in. It's a shame I'm currently single, because I'd like nothing better than a massive, pointless argument right now – the sort that suddenly and unexpectedly blows up over something trivial, such as 'Where did you put the towels?', before rapidly degenerating into a self-righteous festival of bellowing that only comes to an end when one or both of you breaks down in tears out of sheer confusion, and winds up crawling around on the kitchen floor like a dog, wailing and howling, with a glassy pendulum of snot swinging off the end of your nose. I get misty-eyed just thinking about it.

Some people feel this angry all the time. I encountered more than my fair share of them back when I was a shop assistant – an alarming number of our fellow citizens who apparently walk around simply aching for a fight. Once a man strolled in, pointed to something behind the counter, and gruffly asked if he could have it for five pounds off. He was wearing tracksuit bottoms, and had one hand absent-mindedly stuffed down the front, playing with his balls, as he studied my face for a response. I politely explained that the price was the price, haggling wasn't an option, and so on. He asked if I wanted to step outside. When I said I didn't, he swore at me, kicked the counter, and stormed out. The entire exchange lasted less than 30 seconds.

A man that angry probably picks a fight with himself in the mirror each morning. God knows how he gets through life. He was about 27, with no visible scars. Miracle. By now he must be dead or in jail. Or possibly both: in a jail for dead people. Rotting in his cell. Turning to Porridge.

There ought to be a telephone service for people perpetually as furious as him – or temporarily as angry as me; a cathartic, anger-management equivalent of the Samaritans, which you can call 24/7 to vent your frustrations at a live human punchbag. The average conversation would start like this:

THEM: Hello, Punchbag Hotline.

YOU: What sort of way to answer the phone is that?

THEM: Sorry?

YOU: (*sarcastic lisping voice*) 'Hello, Punchbag Hotline.' Prick.

THEM: There's no need to . . .

YOU: SHUT YOUR HOLE!

It would continue in much the same vein until you'd shouted your way back to normality. Sounds pointless, but I guarantee it would save lives.

Three short and unreasonable paragraphs on skiing [25 February 2008]

It's almost the time of year when the nation's braying upper-middle-class idiot quotient collectively decides to stand up and go skiing. Good for them. Speaking as a control freak, I'm opposed to skis, snowboards, and skates on principle. I like to know where I'm going, how soon I'll arrive there, and how quickly I'll stop. I can't imagine doing that on skis. They're slidey. I don't like slidey.

But that's not the main reason I've never been tempted to go skiing: it's the people. The moment anyone tells me they're going skiing, I start to dislike them. This is because I've constructed my own imaginary version of a skiing holiday in my head: it involves a fistful of self-satisfied bastards called Dan and Izzy and Sam and Lucy sharing a chalet together, drinking wine while listening to Mark Ronson on Izzy's iPod speakers, taking 15,000 photos of each other guffawing and pulling silly faces, and occasionally venturing outside to slide down a hill on a pair of glorified planks, at which point with any luck they hurtle headlong into a tree, snapping at least three limbs in the process, and the holiday ends with them lying on their back, twitching like a half-crushed spider, exposed shards of shinbone gleaming in the winter sun as they scream for an air ambulance at the top of their idiot lungs.

That's my imaginary skiing holiday, and since it's populated exclusively by bastards, I assume anyone who goes skiing in real life must be a bastard too. And at the time of writing, I'm yet to be proven wrong.

All the fun of an MRI scan [3 March 2008]

Today is my birthday. Let joy be unconfined. There won't be a party. Too stressful. The trouble with birthday parties, in my experience, is that you tend to group different friends into different pockets – you have work friends, and college friends, and various groups of random friends you've picked up along the way . . . and since they're all quite different, you behave differently with them. I might be a swearing lout with one friend and an urbane sophisticate with another. Mix them all together in the same room and it gives me an identity crisis: suddenly I don't know who I am any more, and I panic and smash chairs against the wall until everyone goes home.

So instead of holding a birthday party, I plan to mark the occasion by screaming and crying. That's what I was doing the day I was born, so it's fitting. And besides, I've got cause for tears: apparently, I'm middle-aged. I'd always assumed middle age began somewhere in your 40s – the *Oxford English Dictionary* defines it as 'the period between youth and old age, about 45 to 60' – but today's ruthlessly youth-oriented Reich has shifted the entry point ever closer, while I've grown steadily older to meet it. As I turn 37, I have to accept that I'm yesterday's news.

And just to underline how despicably aged I am, life has dealt me a small yet significant blow. For a while now, I've found that it hurts to type. Within moments of sitting at my keyboard, a headache-like sensation grows in my arm. The muscles creak. The elbow feels hollow. I'd always assumed that people with RSI were just making it up, the crybabies. Now I'm one of them.

So I've been seeing a physiotherapist. And, troubled by an apparent lack of progress on my part, she sent me for an MRI scan to see if there was anything going on in my neck.

Having an MRI scan is a barrel of laughs. First you sit in a waiting room, wondering why everyone else has (a) come in pairs and (b) looks so stressed. Then you realise they're probably waiting to find out about life-threatening tumours, while you're only there for an achy arm. This makes you feel a bit ashamed and unworthy, like someone simply having a go on the machine for a laugh. It also prompts you to contemplate your own mortality, or at least pull a face as though that's what you're doing.

Then you get changed, which simply means emptying your pockets and removing your belt, because while you don't have to be naked for an MRI scan, taking anything metal in with you will make the machine spark, fizz and explode, leaving behind a black hole into which all the matter in the galaxy will be slurped. 'Destroyer of Universes' doesn't look good on a CV.

Next you're led into a room occupied by a gigantic white machine with TOSHIBA printed on it. This is undeniably exciting, because you're going to lie down and go inside the big white tube and everything, like people who are ill on the telly do.

You lie down on a motorised tray. A chirpy assistant places rubberised ear-mufflers next to your head ('You'll hear a loud knocking sound in there'), then passes you a tube with a squeezy bulb thing on the end of it. If you start freaking out, squish it in your fist and they'll pull you out of the machine. 'Ha!' you think. 'Why would I freak out in the first place?'

And then you go inside the machine.

You glide inside surprisingly quickly, to find yourself staring upwards into a universe of featureless white. And then the noise starts. It didn't sound like knocking to me: more like an Aphex Twin gig. A series of stop-start electronic tones, buzzes, rumbles and alarms resonated through my head and neck.

'This is what being a modem must be like,' I thought, gazing into the bleached nothingness.

It lasted about 20 minutes: more than enough time for anyone to start feeling seriously weird. Soon I began to suspect I was in a sci-fi thriller, having my mind wiped. Two minutes longer and I'd have been squeezing the freak-out teat and babbling about seeing through the Matrix.

On the way out, they give you a CD with your images on it – like a souvenir snapshot from a ride at Alton Towers, except instead of being depicted grinning on a log flume, you're dissected into slices. This is a bracing sight, and pretty good for kick-starting far deeper thoughts about your own mortality than the ones you were pretending to have earlier for the benefit of the people in the waiting room. As such, it makes perfect desktop wallpaper. Now, every time I minimise a window, I catch sight of my innards and contemplate death. This keeps me vibrant and alive and characteristically cheerful.

Anyway, the upshot of it all was, the scan revealed my neck is older than I am. That is, a combination of bad posture, bad habits, and bad everything means part of my cervical spine appears prematurely clapped out. If I'm middle-aged, my neck's a pensioner. This is non-reversible, which means the resultant arm pain won't go away any time soon. Instead, I'll have to work round it, doing neck exercises like a codger. Age comes to us all, but I've managed to invite some of it to the party early, simply by not sitting correctly for 37 years. It's a humiliating birthday present, not to mention infuriating. I'd punch the wall in despair, but that'd make things worse.

Perhaps I should hold a birthday party. After all, at my current rate of decay, next year's will be a wake, so I'd best make the most of each remaining moment. Just don't expect handwritten invites, okay?

The Dead Parrot defence [10 March 2008]

I got caught cheating once. Actually, not strictly cheating – I'd split from my girlfriend at the time, but it was pretty soon after the break and there was still some doubt as to whether we were going to get back together or not, and then I met this girl, and . . . long story short, my ex was in the flat we'd shared together, picking up some of her things, when she spotted a pair of alien knickers on the radiator.

'Whose are these?' she asked.

'They're yours,' I said, shrugging nonchalantly, like it was obvious.

'I'd recognise my own knickers, for Christ's sake. Just tell me whose they are.'

'Ohhhh,' I said, like it was all coming back to me, 'remember I told you about that work trip I went on? Where we all went to Paris? Well, on the way back, a couple of people gave me their laundry, and I washed it, and it must've all got jumbled up with mine.'

The trip to Paris was real. The laundry story clearly wasn't. I'd hoped the fact of the former would somehow obscure the lie of the latter. It didn't work.

'Why did they give you their laundry?'

'Huh? Oh. They don't have washing machines of their own, that's all,' I shrugged again, chucking in a quick, 'God, you're so suspicious!' for good measure.

At which point she started crying. In desperation, I'd adopted a 'Dead Parrot Defence' – named after Michael Palin's lying shopkeeper in the famous Monty Python sketch. The Dead Parrot Defender is hoping that if they lie long and hard enough, reality itself will bend to accommodate them. Well, duh. It doesn't pan out that way, genius.

A classic Dead Parrot Defence consists of an overtly preposterous central premise cooked up in the heat of the moment (bonus points if it ignores a few well-known laws of nature), coupled with an obstinate, huffy denial of the facts. A few years ago, while trying to hide a smoking habit from a (different) girlfriend, I accidentally dropped a lighter on the bedroom floor. It rolled past her. She stared at it. And I indignantly claimed it had fallen through the ceiling, from the flat upstairs.

Until recently, Dead Parrot Defences have been the farcical preserve of adulterers hiding in cupboards and schoolkids whose dog ate their homework. But now things are getting serious. Recently, a spate of ridiculous alibis put forward by desperate murderers in high-profile cases has raised the art of the Dead Parrot Defence to awful, heartbreaking heights.

First, 37-year-old Mark Dixie confessed to having sex with teenage model Sally Anne Bowman's corpse, but denied being her killer. 'All I saw was a pair of legs,' he explained, 'and I took advantage of her . . . I thought she'd passed out drunk or fallen.' In fact, she'd been stabbed seven times – although he claimed not to have noticed that. He only realised she was dead, he said, when she failed to react to him biting her repeatedly on the face and neck.

And last week, 27-year-old Karl Taylor denied murdering 31-year-old businesswoman Kate Beagley during a first date. His version of events ran as follows. Earlier that day, while in a 'suicidal and despondent' mood, he'd borrowed a carving knife from a friend, hidden it up his sleeve and forgotten about it. That evening, he and

Beagley were sitting on a bench drinking wine. The knife fell from his sleeve; he picked it up and put it on the seat. Moments later, while he was distracted by a phone call, she picked up the knife and stabbed herself 31 times in the face, neck and throat.

When the prosecutor handed Taylor a 'knife' made of rolled-up paper and asked him to demonstrate precisely how Beagley took her own life, Taylor initially refused, saying he wasn't 'in an emotionally fit state to do that', until the judge ordered him to do as he was told. When asked how long the incident had lasted, he replied 'minutes'.

'That's a very long time,' noted the prosecutor, before asking why Taylor – a fitness instructor – hadn't attempted to stop her. The exchange that followed read like excerpts from a tasteless comic sketch.

'What am I going to do, use my martial arts to get the knife out of her hand?' complained Taylor.

'Why not?' asked the prosecutor.

'But it was an unanticipated situation,' Taylor protested. 'How was I going to take the knife out of her hand? What am I going to do, kick her unconscious? Your ideas are so outlandish.'

'What's outlandish about suggesting you try to save her life?'

'I've already told you what I did. I stepped forward and stuck my hand out. It was an awkward situation to be in.'

'It was an awkward situation to be in' would be a great final line if this was a sketch, not a real-life murder. By inadvertently turning their trials into jet-black farces, Dixie and Taylor added insult to injury. That's the trouble with the Dead Parrot Defence: it makes things worse. It hurts more.

In which case, perhaps the punishment should fit the crime. Squeeze them into a grotesquely undersized cell and when they complain, shrug and say, 'Sorry, the building's shrinking.' Feed them nothing but gravel on toast, while claiming it's the latest gourmet trend. Offer them no-strings lifelong parole, only to withdraw it at the last minute because a dog ate the concept of liberty. Let them end their days as a comic victim, trapped within a prison of absurdist lazy lies. That'll do it.

Because you're not worth it [31 March 2008]

So *The Apprentice* has started again, bringing with it a fresh batch of free strangers to hate. The men in particular are an especially gruesome crew this year – half have got stupid sticky-uppy design-er haircuts and faintly resemble lapsed Gillette models; the other half look like face-transplant recipients queueing for a ghost train. What's up with Raef, for instance? He's the absolute spit of Uri Geller staring at a pin. Horrible.

And that's before they've opened their mouths. The minute they do, the usual torrent of hideous yah-boo moneyspeak comes tum-bling out, reaffirming your gut objection to their every waddling molecule. Their arrogance is breathtaking. Or at least it appears to be in the eight-second soundbite I'm judging them by, and sod it, that's enough. I'm a busy man. I don't have time to develop long, festering grudges. Give me knee-jerk hate figures and I'm happy.

As they stand on screen burbling away about their personal mis-sion statements and saying things like, 'I'm a red-shelf player; I give 120%; I'll kick, scream and gouge my way to the top of the board-room and no force in the universe can stop me', it occurs to me that what these people really need is a dose of humility. Clearly, no one's ever taken them aside and said, 'Er, you sound like a bit of a bell-end here. Perhaps you ought to sit down and be quiet.' What they need is a good slagging.

Being slagged off is good for you. It thickens the skin and strengthens the backbone. And I'm no stranger to it, in part because each week this column – written originally for the lo-fi steam-powered paperware edition of the newspaper – is replicated on the *Guardian*'s dazzlingly futuristic Comment Is Free site, held aloft in cyberspace by pixels and sheer willpower. As the name suggests, each article on Comment Is Free is accompanied by a dangling thread in which passers-by can leave comments, obser-vations, witticisms and – yes – capsule slaggings.

And every week, without fail, various world-weary travellers will stop by to tell me I'm not as good as I used to be, or wasn't any good to start with, or have bored them into the afterlife, or can't write, or can't think, or should stop typing immediately and drown myself in the bath, assuming I can manage that, which I probably can't, what with being so rubbish and all.

Now, when you read stuff like that, your brain does two things at once: on the one hand, it marvels at the haughty self-importance of the failing human sneer who bothered writing it. And on the other, it agrees with every word they say. Lurking deep within everyone's brain are two interdependent creatures. One's an insecure, quivering homunculus; the other a needy egomaniac. So long as they both take turns pulling the levers, everything works out OK. But the balance is a fine one. The homunculus thrives on negative feedback. Deprive it of a regular slagging, and it eventually withers and dies, leaving the egomaniac to take over. At which point you're swaggering around thinking you're it, describing yourself as a 'red-shelf player' and so on. Cruising for a bruising. Swerving your speedboat into the rocks with an insouciant grin on your chops.

And there's a surplus of arrogant titheads around because we don't, as individuals, receive anything like enough negative feedback these days. Instead we're all led to believe we're somehow unique and important, that we have a destiny, that we matter in some way. But this doesn't add up. There are billions of us. An infinite swarm of haircuts and anuses, that's humankind for you. We can't all be 'special'. The vast majority of us are meaningless energy blips, and we'd do well to remember the fact. Maybe if we saw ourselves as merely part of the herd (which is, after all, what we are), we'd be more inclined to work together to solve the planet's problems.

But that's not going to happen until regular, repeated personal slaggings become an important part of everyday life. Technology can help. It's far too obsequious at present. Switch on your computer and it's all 'Hello' this and 'My Documents' that, and 'Would you like me to help you with that?' Enough bumlicking already. Each time you boot it up, it should growl, 'What do you want?' and start tossing you stuff with a shrug. iPods could get in on the act by automatically inserting subliminal messages into your favourite album tracks – invisible voices that whisper, 'You are despicable' directly into your subconscious.

135

TV can do its bit, too. If I were in charge, every episode of every soap would be legally obliged to include a five-minute sequence in which one of the main characters turns directly to camera and tells the viewer they're nothing but a random assembly of atoms, of less consequence and meaning than the average fencepost, which at least has a definable purpose. The national suicide rate may rise slightly, I grant you. But overall it'd be character-building.

Finally, I'm ready and willing to be called on as a personal 'anti-life coach' for anyone who's currently too pleased with themselves. I can offer energy-sapping depressitudes and personally targeted invective round the clock, for just £3,000 a month. Unless you're an *Apprentice* candidate. Then it's free.

CHAPTER EIGHT

In which The Apprentice *provokes confusion, the Gladiators change their names by deed poll, and a TV show baits real-life paedophiles for chuckles*

Kiddywink Kastle [5 April 2008]

Babies give me the jitters. The way they stare at you – I'd say 'drunkenly' but actually it's like someone far, far removed from our dimension. If a stranger sat opposite you on a train and stared at you the way babies do, you'd pull the emergency cord within six seconds. I think the horror stems from the fact that since I don't know what babies are thinking – because they have no language to think with – it feels a bit like being stared at by a pet. A dog, say. Except it's a small, hairless dog with a quasi-human face. Brrr. It's just not right, is it? So babies give me the jitters. They can't possibly be natural.

And how the hell are you meant to look after them anyway? I had to mind one for a whole afternoon once. Nightmare. It just lay in the corner of the room, gurgling and bawling and pooing like the world's thickest employee. I sat in a chair, reading a book and trying to ignore it, like you might try to ignore rain leaking through a tent. It just wouldn't go away.

If babies had control panels studded with large, clearly-labelled buttons, I might be able to handle them. Just tap the button marked 'sleep' with a stick and walk away. But they don't have control panels, because they're selfish.

In summary: I'd make an awful single mother. Which makes it somewhat hard to judge the inhabitants of *Pramface Mansion*. Sorry, did I say *Pramface Mansion*? I meant to say *Young Mums' Mansion*, because that's what they've changed the name to. When the title Pramface Mansion was first announced, it was immediately held up as a quintessential example of the sensation-seeking yukkiness of contemporary TV; although since you had to be a snickering, in-on-the-gag media arsehole to know what the term 'pramface' meant anyway, probably because you'd been using it yourself for the past six months on self-consciously sassy trash culture messageboards, it's hard to know (or care) precisely whose sensibilities were being offended in the first place.

Incidentally, I'm so dismal and out-of-it I had to look the word 'pramface' up and I still don't think I really 'get' it. I mean, as terms

139

of abuse go, isn't it a bit weak? If you're going to sneer at the under-class, grow some balls. Come right out with it. Call them 'paupers' and 'scum', and sit on your balcony hurling buttered rolls at them while guffawing. Buy a top hat and a monocle, and preface every 'chav'-bashing comment with the words, 'I say, Godfrey. . .' I mean, you ARE being a snob, right? In which case, do it properly – out here, on the other side of your tissue-thin veil of irony; out here where we can see you.

Still, two wrongs don't make a right. *Pramface Mansion* was an objectionable title all round: the last-minute name-swap is a small victory for our collective human dignity. But the show itself? Whassat?

For starters, the new title automatically makes it feel 200 times less exploitative and more like, well, like a not-entirely-unreason-able premise for a TV show, really, although I'm prepared to take that back if they start nailing the kids to the ceiling on day 28. Basi-cally, a bunch of single mums – not all 'young'; they range in age from 19 to 35 – and their offspring share a mansion for four weeks, taking turns to set the 'house rules' to see if they can learn anything new about parenting from each other. And to see if it's entertaining. Along the way there's a bit of moaning, some trauma, and an un-believable amount of weeping – on the part of the mums.

In fact, the main lesson seems to be this: put a bunch of single mums together and within six seconds they'll be sobbing down each other's shoulders for some kind of cathartic release. And why not? Owning a kiddywink looks like a study in stress. Let them keep the mansion, for God's sake.

The déjà-vu dimension   [12 April 2008]

It's good. It's bad. It's gad. What is? *Battlestar Galactica*, that's what – one of those shows that annoys and delights in equal measure, playfully rubbing your thigh with one hand as it jabs you in the eye with the other. The pluses outweigh the minuses overall and it's curiously addictive . . . but, my God, it rubs me up the wrong way sometimes.

If you haven't seen it, it's an accomplished 're-imagining' of the original *Battlestar Galactica* – television's answer to *Star Wars*, which hit bulbous old-school screens worldwide way back in 1978, when all other TV shows were made of wood. The initial excitement of the show's deep-space dogfighting soon palled, though, when viewers realised they were effectively watching the same sequences again and again and again. Special effects were so laborious and expensive back then the makers could only afford a limited number of money shots, which were remixed each week ad nauseam until the whole thing seemed to be taking place in the Déjà-vu Dimension.

By contrast, the new *Galactica* nonchalantly pisses out one state-of-the-art FX sequence after another, making it look easy. Its space battles are immense, densely populated affairs that often veer into psychedelic complexity. Yet the show offers them up with a shrug because the dogfights are little more than pleasant distractions; it's far more concerned with pursuing its complex allegorical storyline.

And said storyline is so complex and so allegorical, there's hardly any point in trying to sketch an explanation for newcomers, mainly because I don't really understand it myself. There are humans and Cylons, see. The Cylons are these sort of robot things that look like people, and they're the bad guys, except sometimes they're not.

The two sides are at war, with the Cylons being a bit like the terrorists and the humans being a bit like the Americans, except sometimes it's the other way round. Oh, and it's essentially a religious war because the humans believe in lots of old-school multiple gods, like the ancient Egyptians (who they may or may not be closely related to), while the Cylons believe in 'the one true God', who presumably has a microchip for a face and sits on a big throne of pixels in the sky.

In other words: if you haven't watched the show before but fancy tuning in this week, don't bother. It'll make less sense than a wool piano. Go back to the start on DVD first. It's well worth it, although you'll have to adjust your filter in order to overlook some glaring drawbacks: half the cast look like underwear models, there's a lot of gung-ho *Top Gun* bullshit, and it often takes itself so insanely seriously you start wishing someone would bend over and blow off in a Cylon's face or something just to lighten the mood.

Regular viewers, meanwhile, will be pleased to know that as season four opens, it's business as usual, i.e. moody and complicated. All your favourite characters are present and correct. The deeply conflicted Colonel Tigh stands on the deck hammily swivelling his one good eye around like a tortoise impersonating a pirate, while pineapple-faced Admiral Adama stands alongside emanating one gruff, depressive sigh after another. And my favourite character – sweaty, panicking, Withnail-look-and-sound-alike Dr Gaius Baltar – is still getting space-pussy thrown at him by the bucketload for no apparent reason: now a reluctant guru, he's been whisked off and hidden away in a sort of Temple of Quim, full of lithe young women worshipping his every pube.

Overall, it seems just as preposterous, glum and strangely compelling as ever, so hooray. This being the last season, they're presumably going to reach Earth in the final episode and live unhappily ever after, squinting suspiciously at each other until the end of time.

Possessed by the spirit of nothing at all
[19 April 2008]

No, I don't get it either. Why fire Simon? Why? Why? Why, Sir Alan, why? You could carve the reasons directly on to my mind's eye and I still wouldn't understand. Why? Why? Why?

By some measure the most likable, competent candidate in *The Apprentice*, Simon was inexplicably hoofed out this week, in perhaps the most dispiriting miscarriage of justice since the trial of the Birmingham Six. I'm writing this on Tuesday, the morning before the broadcast, and can only imagine the nationwide outpouring of indignant fury that accompanied his sacking. The rest of Europe probably stopped what it was doing and looked round to see where all the yelling was coming from. Bet you could hear the shouts on the moon.

It was the final proof that the show is a SHOW first and foremost, not a test of business acumen. Even so, it may prove too audacious a narrative twist for the audience to bear. Killing the hero in week three? Jesus.

The Apprentice traditionally engages in a little sleight of hand during its opening weeks, hiding the eventual winner somewhere at the back, letting them slip past unnoticed until somewhere around the final three episodes where they suddenly transform into a serious contender. That's what's happened with the previous three winners, all of whom were 'the quiet one' in their respective packs. Since the victors are essentially boring, the show instead concentrates on villains and clowns – yer Katie Hopkinses and Syed Ahmeds.

But this year, there seems to be a surfeit of shitbags – not one central baddie, but three: Jenny, Claire and Alex. All three employ the same basic tactic: blame and belittle your opponent at every turn.

Jenny was the first to emerge from the undergrowth, pummelling the hapless Lucinda into a blubbering heap with her monotone cosh of a voice. There's a terrifying lack of emotion to Jenny at the best of times, but it really comes to the fore when she's dishing out a bollocking. She becomes possessed by the spirit of nothing at all. The light in her eyes goes out. Her elocution flatlines. It's like being nagged by a Sat Nav. If you ever wondered what it'll be like when the machines rise up and take over, look no further. Forget images of robot warriors thrashing us with electric whips; it'll be an army of Jennys slowly talking us to death.

Claire, for her part, is essentially Ruth Badger gone wrong. Apparently convinced she's a bastion of straight-talking common sense, she instead comes across as a huffing, eye-rolling bully. It's easy to picture her standing up to give her two cents' worth in the audience of *The Jeremy Kyle Show*, which is surely reason enough not to employ her.

And rounding out the bastard pack, my least favourite of all: Alex, who I've disliked intensely since week one. If the final edits are anything to go by, Alex is an objectionable, buck-passing, jumped-up, passive-aggressive, know-it-all streak of piss with a short fuse, a sour mouth, and a petty, needling, finger-pointing demeanour. Unless you're a woman, of course, in which case he's a blameless dreamboat. Every girl I know swoons like all the oxygen's vanished the moment he dribbles onscreen, which only serves to make him even more irritating. I want to run in front of them clapping my hands and clicking my fingers, like a man trying to prevent the invasion of the bodysnatchers. Can't you see, girls? Can't you see? He's tricking you with his beauty! Wake up! See through the matrix! He's a bastard! Stop batting your eyelashes like that! That's how he feeds! Stop feeding him! Stop it!

Anyway, the sheer amount of bad feeling from these three threatens to unbalance the show as a whole. Who are we supposed to like, exactly? My current favourites are posho Raef and weepo Lucinda; the former because he's an affable arse, and the latter because the girls keep kicking her around like a rag doll and I'm a sucker for underdogs.

They'll do. But Simon was my first choice. Why? Why Sir Alan? Why?

Smashed in the face with a mobile disco
[26 April 2008]

I haven't been stabbed in the eyes recently, but I've got a fair idea how it might feel thanks to some of the weekend's early evening entertainment. There's been a spate of programmes of late which seek to disguise their inherent ordinariness by distracting you with set designs apparently based on the climactic scenes of *Close Encounters of the Third Kind*. Neon strips, sweeping floodlights, brightly coloured bulbs – it's like being smashed in the face with a mobile disco.

Take *The Kids Are All Right*, a gameshow which has absolutely nothing in common with Sky's *Are You Smarter than a 10-Year-Old?* aside from a near-identical premise. At heart it's a cutesy-poo bit of fluff, in which fully grown adults pit their wits against a team of cleverclogs kiddywinks. Twenty years ago it would've been a daytime show hosted by Michael Aspel, with a beige set and a title sequence backed by simpering acoustic guitar music. This being the cold, hard 21st century however, it looks and feels like a night-time SWAT raid on a robot factory.

The host is *Torchwood* and *I'd Do Anything* star John Barrowman, a man so insanely ubiquitous he's rapidly becoming the TV equivalent of desktop wallpaper. To ensure you notice him, Barrowman spends most of *The Kids Are All Right* bellowing at the top of his voice. And he's the quietest thing on the show. Thumping great sound effects punctuate every onscreen decision. The camera swings in and out. Gaudy graphics whizz past at dizzying speed. You can only broadcast this sort of thing on a Saturday evening. Put it out in the morning and you'd kill people.

There's even a round where John Barrowman shouts, 'It's time for INFORMAAAATION OVERLOOOOAAAAAADDDD!!!!!' and we're treated to a nonsensical three-minute montage of archive footage, unrelated bursts of dialogue, flashing words, and cut-out photographs of ice-cream cones spinning around the screen. Ostensibly it's part of a memory test, but that's clearly a cover story. I've seen *The Ipcress File*. I know a psychedelic brainwashing technique when I see one.

Apart from the visuals, the funniest thing about *Kids . . .* is that the format requires Barrowman to make repeated reference to adults beating children. At one point he said something like, 'OK, remember: beat all six kids and you win pounds 20,000.' Blind viewers who aren't paying attention must think civilised society has collapsed completely.

Speaking of beatings, the following night ITV treats us to the clunkily titled *Beat the Star*, which dares to couple an even noisier set with an even more mundane set of activities. The premise: each week a member of the public has to conquer a famous sportsperson in a series of games. Woo hoo. Last week, it was a policeman versus Amir Khan. Round one: who can hammer nails into a plank the quickest? Remember: if they bend, it doesn't count! This proved so exhilarating, the audience screamed and shouted throughout, just like the terrified passengers from *Snakes on a*

Plane. Later on, Khan and the copper went head-to-head in a cow-milking contest. There was also a round where they had to look at a scrambled photo and guess which famous person it represented. Photo number two was Alistair Darling. This was exciting. And in between each round, the set exploded in a cornea-skewering frenzy of searchlights, neon, and Vernon Kay's nuclear-white teeth.

Beat the Star is about 75 minutes long, incidentally.

Just to reiterate: 75 minutes.

Are you clear about that? Good. Tomorrow night it's a fireman versus Darren Gough. With any luck there'll be a round where they have to see who can hang a dessert spoon off the end of their nose the longest. Or just a quick game of pass the parcel. Either way, it's sure to be an unforgettable thrill ride, or at least resemble one thanks to the near-death-experience whirlwind of flashing lights that's bound to accompany it. Buy a glow stick, neck a few pills, and you can join in at home – provided you're not brainwashed into vegetative oblivion first.

Bring back twerping   [3 May 2008]

Is it just me, or should the current series of *The Apprentice* come packaged with its own laughter track? Last week's edition in which we bade farewell to Kevin, the bizarrely self-assured Frank Spencer/Daffyd hybrid, was the funniest, most sustained work of comedy I've seen in months. I'm still not quite convinced it was real. The whole thing felt like pure mockumentary.

Poor Kevin. Poor boy-faced Kevin and his daft bloody gob. I watched the episode with a friend of mine and each time he appeared onscreen she guffawed and said 'he really is a twerp'. And sadly she was right. A twerp. Judging by the heavily edited, skilfully packaged evidence, there's no better word to describe him. And it's a term of abuse that deserves a revival. It's fun to say. Try it. Twerp. Twerp twerp twerp. Bring back twerping, say I.

Anyway. Charged with the task of inventing a new 'special occasion' designed to shift their own range of greetings cards, Kevin's team plumped for National Send A Sanctimonious, Hectoring And

Ultimately Wasteful Card To Show How Concerned You're Pretending To Be About The Environment Day – a notion as dumb as it was oxymoronic, as it was dumb again as it was rubbish. Why not launch a range of diet books encased in a three-inch chocolate shell, you dum-dums? Every single member of his team deserves firing for not pointing out the obvious contradiction at its heart (with the exception of Sara, who was picked on throughout the task, partly for being much smarter than the others but mainly because the regular whipping boy, Lucinda, happened to be on the other team this week).

The environmental greetings card 'concept' sprang from the addled mind of the increasingly nightmarish Jenny, a woman so pig-headed she's probably got a curly tail at the back of her skull. Jenny has managed to achieve the impossible by making Katie Hopkins (last year's villain) seem warm-hearted and gregarious, albeit only in retrospect. You could imagine having a drunken laugh on a boating holiday with Katie Hopkins, chuckling as you negotiate a lock in the dark. Whereas, after 28 minutes on a barge with Jenny, you'd leap ashore and dash your own brains out against the nearest tree, just to be rid of that droning self-assured station announcer's voice, offering nothing but relentless criticism disguised as mission statements. There just doesn't seem to be any humanity there, goddammit. Did you see her attempt at a welcoming smile? It was like watching a horse climb a ladder. It wasn't natural. It didn't go.

My pet hate, the dreamboat tosspot Alex, was disappointingly quiet for the duration of the episode. His input largely consisted of repeatedly practising his nervous lip-pursing tic, which he's developing into quite a piece of performance art. Whenever he spots something bad looming, he anxiously sucks and clenches his lips until his mouth starts to resemble a cat's arse.

Before long, project leader Kevin was in the boardroom, swallowing and gulping like Churchill the nodding dog trying to bluff his way through a police interview as Sir Alan dished out the kind of obligatory monstering he can probably now do in his sleep, while Nick Hewer sat beside him, peering so hard you could almost hear his scalp straining under the pressure. Sir Alan, incidentally, is looking pretty dapper this year. I'm not making it up: go and find a repeat of one of the earlier series and see the change for yourself. He used to look like a water buffalo straining to shit in a lake. Now he's Russell Crowe. He's clearly lost weight and may well be working out (perhaps by lugging box after box of unsold Em@iler phones into an almighty skip). Perhaps he's been on *Ten Years Younger*. However he's done it, for the first time in *Apprentice* history, he's now better-looking than most of the contestants.

OK, perhaps 'better-looking' is a stretch. 'Less weird-looking' is closer. But admit it. You fancy him. You fancy Sir Alan Sugar. Just a bit. Don't deny it. Yeah you do.

Now I'm livin' in Exeter   [10 May 2008]

Sometimes I think the whole of humankind can be separated into two types: those who pay attention to song lyrics, and those who don't. And those who don't should be rounded up and throttled to death. By robots. With merciless strangling hands.

I'm exaggerating, but only slightly. I love lyrics. If you don't listen to the words, you're no friend of mine. The words are where 50 per cent of a song's meaning resides, and it's shocking how many people just don't seem to hear them, even when they're startlingly clear. I once had to explain to someone what 'Common People' by Pulp was about, even though they'd listened to it a billion times. How wilfully dumb can you get?

Perhaps I find it frustrating because I've been cursed with an almost autistic ability to memorise song lyrics after one or two listens. But rather than recall them accurately, I tinker about and replace them with new words for my own amusement; and it's these re-written versions which ultimately remain lodged in my mind.

I can't hear 'Thinking of You' by Sister Sledge, for instance, without assuming the chorus goes: 'I'm thinking of you/ And the things you do to me/ That make me love you/ Now I'm livin' in Exeter'.

My current favourite internalised mental replacement lyric is a disarmingly basic one in which I simply substitute the name Eleanor Rigby with 'Robert Mugabe', because it scans. Every time I watch the news and something about Zimbabwe comes on, I hear Paul McCartney lament that Robert Mugabe died in the church and was buried along with his name. Nobody came. This is why I'd be hopeless on *Don't Forget The Lyrics!*, a new Shane Richie gameshow whose primary game mechanic is explained in its title.

And it's quite bossy, that title. It sounds like the sort of thing an insane Nazi commandant forcing a yard full of PoWs to perform a musical at gunpoint might bark at the top of his voice just before shooting someone for fumbling the chorus of 'Frosty the Snowman'. They should've called it 'Nicht Forgetten Das Lyrics!', or 'Schtumbleword Verboten!'.

Or 'Don't Forget the Lyrics, Mofo!', which isn't very German, but accurately conveys the urgency of the situation.

Anyway, the show is just like *Who Wants to Be a Millionaire* only with karaoke instead of questions. Each week, an annoying member of the public comes on and jumps up and down and says how excited they are until you want to punch them all the way to Barbados and back.

Then Shane asks them to pick a category of song: pop, say, or glam rock, or TV theme tunes; we're talking crowd-pleasers, OK, so there's no Joy Division or anything. Then the in-house band starts playing, the lyrics come up on a big screen, and the contestant wails the song as cacophonously as possible while maintaining the beatific grin of the thuddingly stupid.

And then! Suddenly! The on-screen lyrics are whisked away! And the singer has to finish the next line FROM MEMORY! If they get every single word right, the pot increases and they proceed to the next round, eventually hitting a jackpot of £250,000.

If a contstant gets it wrong, Shane leads them to a desolate, snowblown corner of the stage, commands them to get down on their knees and unloads a single bullet into the back of their head. The body is left in plain sight for the remainder of the programme as a warning to others of its kind: DON'T FORGET THE LYRICS!

Yet another superb episode of *The Apprentice* last Wednesday, although for some reason no matter how many people Sir Alan ejects, it feels as though their overall number fails to dwindle. Two got the chop last week, and there's still eight of the bastards in there. Still, at least this means you can pick more than one favourite: for me, it's got to be Raef, Sara or Lucinda.

Them to win. Go them. Go them.

Return of the Gladiators   [17 May 2008]

An end to war? Environmentally friendly alternatives to oil? The second coming? No. What the world has been crying out for, apparently, is the return of *Gladiators*, which vanished from our screens eight years ago.

I don't recall much protest at the time. No one established an emergency helpline or threw themselves under the controller of ITV's car. Not a single leading newspaper ran a wounded editorial lamenting its demise and pleading with God for a revival. There were no dazed crowds of jonesing *Gladiators* fans wandering the street in a sorrowful funk, dumbly bumping into shop windows without even noticing, quivering in a puddle of tears in the cold and distant grief dimension. Its passing went largely unnoticed. A gentle nationwide shrug rolled across the country like an underfed Mexican wave. *Gladiators* had passed away, and we, as a nation, moved on.

But, like the song says, you don't know what you've got till it's gone. A year after *Gladiators* disappeared, 9/11 shook Planet Earth's axis to its core, creating a new landmark paradigm in watershed epochs. The world was left stunned, reeling. 'Where are our *Gladiators* now?' it wailed with its mouth, 'Because we need something to take our minds off this shit.' And in the years following, with the invasions of Afghanistan and Iraq, widespread economic meltdown, and the growing awareness of impending environmental disaster, the clamour for the return of the soothing balm of *Gladiators* grew ever more cacophonous.

Now the dark ages are at an end: *Gladiators* is back, and it's better than ever. And by 'better', I mean 'the same': an hour of people in leotards running, tumbling, wrestling, jumping, and hitting each other over the head with padded sticks, inside a cavernous crash-mat-and-searchlight repository.

Gladiators has never felt very British. The audience shriek and hoot throughout, and they're all waving outsized foam hands with pointy fingers, which must make it nigh-on impossible to see. Perhaps they're not baying for blood at all, but just shouting at the person in front to get that stupid foam hand out of the way.

Everything in the arena is either red or blue or a 20,000-watt lightbulb – apart from the *Gladiators*, whose costumes are monochrome and more individually 'pimped' than before. Spartan, for instance, has some vaguely Ancient Roman-style strappy bits hanging down round his balls, leaving him looking like a cross between a promotional poster for the film *300* and a collector's edition of *Boyz* magazine.

Incredibly, he's not the gayest-looking male *Gladiator*. That honour goes to Atlas, who has a body made of raw, bulging muscle, but the head and face of a woman. In his introductory ident, he appears to shake his flowing locks and wink coquettishly at the viewer. They should've called him Dorothy and had done with it.

Keeping with the homoerotic theme, you may have noticed that all the male Gladiators have names that sound like gay nightclubs. Oblivion, for instance, sounds like a steaming 4 a.m. sinbox filled with strobe lights and shaved heads. But it isn't. It's a 6ft 3in bell-end in black trunks. The producers have given Oblivion a complex personality: he's angry and he complains a lot. This makes him different to Predator, who brags and looks hard. The level of characterisation pisses all over *The Wire*.

The lady Gladiators are slightly less absurd, apart from Inferno, who looks like a pornographic Manga sketch of Geri Halliwell circa 1998, and Battleaxe – a champion hammer-thrower, and the least ladylike of the bunch. She may look beefy and stern, but calling her Battleaxe seems a tad harsh. Perhaps next year they'll bring in one called Dog. Or Moose. Or Boiler.

Actually, in this interactive age, they should throw the naming of the Gladiators open to the public. How about one called Bastard?

Or Perineum? Any other suggestions? Send them to charlie.brooker @guardian.co.uk and we'll make it a contest.

The names pour in [24 May 2008]

Good on you, reader. Last week, while musing on the preposterous monikers chosen for the *Gladiators*, I invited you to send in suggestions of your own. I expected nine or 10 entries. I got hundreds – many of which I'm reproducing here.

Just to recap: the following are all proposed names for new Gladiators, should Sky One's pointless revival of the long-unmissed ITV series bother returning for a second series. To draw full value from each name, you have to imagine an excitable commentator bandying it about during an intense Gladiator-vs-pleb battle. In your mind's ear, hear him saying something like 'Roy's running for the finish . . . but oh! [GLADIATOR NAME] is determined to shut him down! A nasty blow from [GLADIATOR NAME] there! And so on.

Without further ado, here are your suggestions. Contestant ready? Gladiator ready? Good. Here we go.

First, the men. You suggest: Paxman, Pigeon, Badger, Schlong, Asbo, Baghead (who 'carries a syringe'), Pornographer, Blunderbuss, Columbine, Blister, Hessian, Menthol, Tractor, Fist, Embryo (a 'lad with the brain of an amoeba and the reflexes of a pot of Colman's mustard'), Burden ('obese bloke that can't move too fast'), Kraken, Pollution, Opprobrium, Battlebus, Boswelox, Guff, Sodom, Wetwipe, Surcharge, Meatpole, Thrutch, Breezeblock, Pasquale, Kemp, Climax, Radion, Thermostat, Dalek, Infidel, Prolapse, Vas Deferens, Void, Spasm, Jaw, Enema, Pussyole, Prepuce, Alan, Mongol, Travesty, Hibernator, Mustang, Fellatio, Bickle, Bareback, Pummel, Hurtyman, Sheath, Bananaman, Dunce, BluRay, Guantánamo, Pedalo, Caramac, The Hesitator, Astroglide ('it's a sexual lubricant'), Pamphlet, Bukkake, Loner, Simpleton, Shitclown, Santorum, ZX-H8-U, Narcissus, Nibbles (an 'Uncle Monty-shaped gastronaut who rolls after people'), Girth, Spork, Mondeo, Thrombosis, Tepid, Fighty, Shipman, Kilimanjaro, Stryker ('a nod to Jeff'), Skytrot, Phrenum (who 'could have a creepy helmet bowlcut like Javier Bardem'), Fuhrer, or – my favourite – Fritzl.

In between the male and female categories, we have Mirrorball ('the first transgender Gladiator').

Now the ladies. Fewer entries here, but a spirited showing nonetheless (if somewhat anatomically-obsessed). You propose: Gash, Cameltoe, Butch, Labia, Frown, Growler, Rub-n-Tug, Dworkin, Estrogen, Thyroid, Ringtone, Meringue, Windolene, Aneurysm, Angina, Chlamydia, Mrs Hitler, Mudguard, Testosterod, Plankton, Femsil, Slattern, Armourdildo, Grindstone, Turpentine, Pumice, Killwhore, Binlids, Chemical Sally, Botox, Spinster, Tampon, Fallopian, Lactator, Seapig, Yeastro, Tearjerker, Gomorrah, Dingleberry, Glans, Harridan, Crevice, Menstrualator, Jizzelle, Widdecombe, Handshank ('blue-collar everywoman who belts herself in the face with a spanner to show how good she is'), Schadenfreude, Hernia, Clitorisk or – my lady favourite – Mauve.

Special mention to 'Mark C' who came up with some of the more elaborate entries above. The winner, though, is 'Sophocles' – suggested by Alex Maple – because it's a timely reference to Michael Sophocles from *The Apprentice*, the most furious man on TV (although not, perhaps, quite as angry as the average viewer following Sir Alan's current record of unfair dismissals). Despite the boyish face and drippy wet eyes, ol' pressure-cooker Sophocles appears driven by barely suppressed rage. He resembles a small boy, tired out during a shopping trip, simmering on the verge of a tantrum. Each time I see him in the boardroom I think he's about to seethe 's'not fair, s'not fair' in a peevish mantra, then wig out and start huffing and kicking the table. Or one of his fellow contestants. Preferably Alex. Or Claire. Or Helene. I can't stand any of them. Lee's okay – albeit dumb as a cupboard – but really, with Raef gone, Lucinda's the only deserving victor. Even though she's a bit too 'aromatherapy' for my liking.

Pity the kidfuckers [31 May 2008]

When a TV show makes you feel sorry for potential child rapists, you know it's doing something wrong. *To Catch a Predator* is that show. It hails from America, where it's not some wacky bit of far-out cable madness but a mainstream network broadcast; a staple feature of Dateline NBC (a sort of *Tonight with Sir Trevor McDonald* minus Sir Trevor).

Here's the set-up for this week's episode: fearless, crusading adult volunteers for an anti-paedo watchdog group called Perverted Justice go on the internet and pretend to be 13-year-old girls. They wait until contacted by grown men, play along with the conversation when the subject turns to sex, then invite them over for an illegal fumble. When the men turn up, they're greeted by an attractive young actress (who could just about pass for 13) who leads them into the garden and asks them to wait by the hot tub while she changes into something sexier.

The men pace excitedly, awaiting Lolita's return. But oh! Out pops Dateline's Chris Hansen instead! He's male, pushing 50, and doesn't look like he wants to play. Their faces fall like the Twin Towers. They mistake him for a cop. 'Did you come to have sex with a 13-year-old?' he asks. 'Oh no, sir,' they splutter, 'nothing could be further from my mind.'

Then he brings out a transcript of their original web chat and asks them a bunch of questions about it – not to titillate, no God no – but in order that we viewers might forge a better understanding of the twisted mindset of the child sex predator. And because it'll make us guffaw like cartoon donkeys when they desperately try to explain away all the references to blowjobs and penis size in their chatroom chinwag. It's the back-pedalling Olympics.

After making them sweat for several minutes, Chris reveals his camera crew and tells them they're on national television. Ta da! You're on Paedle's About! At this point their faces tend to fall still further. They start crying and begging. Some of them probably poo themselves, although they don't show that. But the worst is yet to come: at this point, Chris unexpectedly waves them goodbye, and they walk out, sighing with relief . . . only to walk face-first into a bunch of armed police who hurl them to the ground and arrest them. Then we get to see them being interviewed AGAIN, this time by the police, who aren't quite as debonair and charming as Chris (and are markedly less keen on poring over all the online sex talk than him).

And then it's over. Justice prevails – provided you overlook the several billion troubling aspects to the show. The overpowering whiff of entrapment, for one thing. The collusion between reporters, vigilante groups and police for another. And that 'attractive young actress' who greets them by the door: make no mistake, she's hot. And at 18, she's US legal. Presumably someone at *To Catch a Predator* HQ sat down with a bunch of audition tapes and spooled through it, trying to find a sexy 18-year-old who could pass for 13. They'll have stared at girl after girl, umming and ahhing over their chest sizes, until they found just the right one. And like I say, she's hot. But if you fancy her, you're a paedophile.

It's a pity robot technology isn't more advanced than it is, because the ultimate *To Catch a Predator* show could do away with the actress altogether. Instead, the men would be greeted by a convincing 17-year-old android, who'd instantly start having sex with them. But oh! Just before they reached climax, a hatch would open in the top of her head, and a robotic version of Chris Hansen's face would emerge on a big bendy metal neck, barking accusations at them, and then the android's vagina would snap shut, trapping the pervert in position, and the robot body would transform into a steel cage from which they couldn't escape, and start delivering near-fatal electric shocks every five minutes to the delight of a self-righteous, audience, chanting Justice Prevails, Justice Prevails. Justice Prevails. Forever.

The job interview from heck   [7 June 2008]

Just before *The Apprentice* shimmies to a conclusion, let's go back – way back – all the way to last Wednesday, and the penultimate 'job interview' special. By now an *Apprentice* tradition, this is the episode that routinely sorts the wheat from the chaff. It's also the point at which the show's narrative gears start audibly crunching. Squint closely, and the notion that the series represents a genuine test of business skill is exposed as the preposterous gobbet of cockflob it is.

We know the drill for this episode by now. The candidates are grilled by some of Sir Alan's business buddies, including Bordon Staryface and a stubbly Johnny Vegas type who looks like he's just chucked a chip wrapper in the bottom drawer seconds before calling you into the room. Their job is to sit opposite the contestants pulling unimpressed faces. Having spent the previous 10 episodes making each candidate look like a twat tied to an arsehole, the programme suddenly performs an about-face. No one wants a bastard to win, so it must persuade the viewer that – hey! – there ain't no bastards here. All sorts of previously hidden positive qualities are brought to the fore.

Take human cat puppet Helene. Since week one she's been shown rolling her whopping great fist-sized eyes and lazily bullying Lucinda. But within minutes of the job interview starting, she's asked about her hitherto-unmentioned troubled background and is instantly transformed into the plucky outsider who triumphs over adversity. She's been in the background throughout each task; now it's impossible not to root for her on some level. This is the Michelle Dewberry manoeuvre and – just to be clear – it's the programme being devious, not Helene herself appealing for sympathy at the last minute. Each candidate will have been thoroughly vetted beforehand. The producers knew her heart-rending back story. They just hid it until now, because it makes for a good twist.

Ditto the white lies on Lee's CV. His fibs about attending university for two years instead of four months could have been (and almost certainly were) detected at some point during the audition stage. If Sir Alan was genuinely solely interested in selecting the best candidate, it'd make sense to comb through each candidate's CV in the first 10 minutes of the very first episode, quizzing them over any inconsistencies. But that'd make boring television. Far better to introduce a note of jeopardy for Lee at the 11th hour.

While we're on the subject of Lee, there was a glaring example of the show unfairly setting him up to look like a prick the moment his interview kicked off, when Johnny Vegas asked him to impersonate a pterodactyl, then sneered at him for not taking the interview seriously as soon as he did so. What is this, Guantánamo Bay?

Why not really dick with his mind by asking him to take a seat, then kicking it out from under him and calling him a subservient seat-taking imbecile? Still, making Lee look a bit dumb is easy. Making the sour, defensive, prickly Alex seem likable is a trickier prospect, one even the magic of the edit suite couldn't quite pull it off. Instead it banged on about how young and handsome he is, like it's an audition for a daytime soap.

They have to accentuate the positive in Alex's case because, like Helene, he's a weaker candidate. Presumably they go positive on the weak ones and negative on the strong ones to make the final feel like less of a foregone conclusion. Claire, for instance, has been an obviously strong contender for weeks, and appeared to sail through her interviews. But that's dull, so Sir Alan had to loudly voice doubts about whether she's too gobby for him.

Anyway. The mechanism may be visible, but the machine itself works. It's entertainment. I won't be missing the climax, although I'm worried about the way the teams are split, because it raises the hideous prospect of either Alex or Helene winning – in which case they might as well have picked the winner at random by flipping a coin.

– *Lee won, in the end. You know. Lee. LEE.*

CHAPTER NINE

In which the idiots start winning, Boris runs for mayor, and the sexual habits of various animals are contemplated

The idiots are winning   [7 April 2008]

Man the lifeboats. The idiots are winning. Last week I watched, open-mouthed, a *Newsnight* piece on the spread of 'Brain Gym' in British schools. I'd read about Brain Gym before – a few years back, in Ben Goldacre's excellent Bad Science column for this newspaper – but seeing it in action really twisted my rage dial.

Brain Gym, y'see, is an 'educational kinesiology' programme designed to improve kiddywink performance. It's essentially a series of simple exercises lumbered with names that make you want to steer a barbed-wire bus into its creator's face. One manoeuvre, in which you massage the muscles round the jaw, is called the 'energy yawn'. Another involves activating your 'brain buttons' by forming a 'C' shape with one hand and pressing it either side of the collarbone while simultaneously touching your stomach with the other hand.

Throughout the report I was grinding my teeth and shaking my head – a movement I call a 'dismay churn'. Not because of the sickening cutesy-poo language, nor because I'm opposed to the nation's kids being forced to exercise (make them box at gunpoint if you want) but because I care about the difference between fantasy and reality, both of which are great in isolation, but, like chalk and cheese or church and state, are best kept separate.

Confuse fantasy with reality and you might find yourself doing crazy things, like trying to wave hello to Ian Beale each time you see him on the telly, or buying homeopathic remedies – both of which are equally boneheaded pursuits. (Incidentally, if anyone disagrees with this assessment and wants to write in defending homeopathy, please address your letters to myself c/o the Kingdom of Narnia.)

Perhaps the Department for Children, Schools and Families confused fantasy with reality the day it endorsed Brain Gym. Because while Brain Gym's coochy-coo exercises may well be fun or relaxing, what they're definitely good at is increasing the flow of bullshit into children's heads.

For instance, according to the Brain Gym teacher's manual,

performing the 'brain button' exercise increases the flow of 'electromagnetic energy' and helps the brain send messages from the right hemisphere to the left. Brain Gym can also 'connect the circuits of the brain', 'clear blockages' and activate 'emotional centering'. Other Brain Gym material contains the startling claim that 'all liquids [other than water] are processed in the body as food, and do not serve the body's water needs . . . processed foods do not contain water.'

All of which sounds like hooey to me. And also to the British Neuroscience Association, the Physiological Society and the charity Sense about Science, who have written to every local education authority in the land to complain about Brain Gym's misrepresentation of, um, reality.

Wander round Brain Gym's UK website for a few minutes. It's a festival of pseudoscientific chuckles where impressive phrases such as 'educational kinesiology' and 'sensorimotor program' rub shoulders with bald admissions that 'we are not yet at the stage where we have any scientific evidence for what happens in the brain through the use of Brain Gym'.

Look at the accredited practitioners of the art: top of their list of qualified Brain Gym 'instructor/consultants' is a woman who is apparently also a 'chiropractor for humans and animals'. That's nothing: I read tarot cards for fish.

And check out the linked bookshop, Body Balance Books. Alongside Brain Gym guides and wallcharts, it stocks titles such as *Awakening the Child Heart* and *Resonance Kinesiology*, which, apparently, 'holds information on how to move forward with truth, without the overlays of people's beliefs and ideas about what is best for themselves and others'. Huh?

If we mistrust the real world so much that we're prepared to fill the next generation's heads with a load of gibbering crap about 'brain buttons', why stop there? Why not spice up maths by telling kids the number five was born in Greece and invented biscuits? Replace history lessons with screenings of the *Star Wars* trilogy? Teach them how to whistle in French? Let's just issue the kids with blinkers.

Because we, the adults, don't just gleefully pull the wool over our own eyes – we knit permanent blindfolds. We've decided we hate facts. Hate, hate, hate them. Everywhere you look, we're down on our knees, gleefully lapping up neckful after neckful of steaming, cloddish bullshit in all its forms. From crackpot conspiracy theories to fairytale nutritional advice, from alternative medicine to energy yawns – we just can't get enough of that musky, mudlike taste. Brain Gym is just one small tile in an immense and frightening mosaic of fantasy.

Still, that's just my opinion. Lots of people clearly think Brain Gym is worthwhile, or they wouldn't be prepared to pay through the nose for it. If you're one of them, here's an exciting new kinesiological exercise that should dramatically increase your self-awareness – and I'm giving it away free of charge. Ready? OK. Curl the fingers of your right hand inward, meeting the thumb to form a circle. Jerk it rhythmically up and down in front of your face. Repeat for six hours. Then piss off.

Please God not Boris   [14 April 2008]

A few years back, during the run-up to the Nathan Barley TV series, my co-author Chris Morris and I briefly kicked around a storyline about an animated MP running for election. When I say 'animated', I mean literally animated. He was a cartoon – the political equivalent of Gorillaz – fashioned from state-of-the-art computer-generated imagery so that he could move and talk in real time, like Max Headroom. His speech would be provided on-the-fly by a professional cartoon voice artist working in conjunction with a team of political advisers and comedy writers, so he'd have an impish personality not dissimilar to the genie in Disney's *Aladdin*. Debating against him would be impossible because he'd make outrageously goonish statements one minute and trot out cunning political platitudes the next. Because he wasn't real, he'd never age, die, or be bogged down in scandal – and huge swathes of the population would vote for him just because they found him cool or fun or different.

Fast-forward to now. On 1 May London chooses its mayor, and

I've got a horrible feeling it might pick Boris Johnson for similar reasons. Johnson – or to give him his full name, Boris LOL!!!! what a legernd!! Johnson!!! – is a TV character loved by millions for his cheeky, bumbling persona. Unlike the cartoon MP, he's magnetically prone to scandal, but this somehow only makes him more adorable each time. Tee hee! Boris has had an affair! Arf! Now he's offended the whole of Liverpool! Crumbs! He used the word 'picaninnies'! Yuk yuk! He's been caught on tape agreeing to give the address of a reporter to a friend who wants him beaten up! Ho ho! Look at his funny blond hair! HA HA BORIS LOL!!!! WHAT A LEGERND!!!!!!

If butterfingers Johnson gets in, it'll clearly be a laugh riot from beginning to end, like a series of *Some Mothers Do 'Ave 'Em* in which Frank Spencer becomes mayor by mistake. Just picture him on live TV, appealing for calm after a terrorist bombing – the scope for chuckles is almost limitless.

Assisting Boris in his run, the London *Evening Standard* is running an openly hostile anti-Livingstone campaign, which means every other page carries a muckraking down-with-Ken piece from crusading journalist Andrew Gilligan, played by Blinky, the three-eyed fish from *The Simpsons*, in his byline photo. All the articles blend into one after a while, but their central implication is that Ken's a boozy egomaniac surrounded by a corrupt circus of cronies, so you might as well vote for a rightwing comedy pillock instead. You know, him off the telly. With the blond hair. LOL!!!! WHAT A LEGERND!!!!!

Now, even if the *Standard* photographs Ken carving a swastika into a dormouse's back, I'll vote for him for the following reasons:

1. I'm genetically predisposed to hate the Tories. It's my default, hard-wired position. If Boris wins, their simpering pudge-faced smuggery is going to be unbearable. Picture the expression Piers Morgan makes when he's especially pleased with himself, then multiply it by 10 million, and imagine it looming overhead like a Death Star. That's what it's going be like. Therefore I don't care who wins provided Johnson loses, and loses hard, preferably in close-up, on the telly.

2. Ken's other main rival is solid-but-dull Lib Dem candidate Brian Paddick. He probably deserves a shot, but as he's not going to win, voting for him would be a waste of a perfectly good X, which might otherwise be used to pinpoint buried treasure, indicate affection, or mark a plague victim's door.

3. I wouldn't trust Boris to operate a mop, let alone a £10 billion Crossrail project.

4. On a related note, I don't believe in my gut that Boris gives even the faintest hint of a wisp of a glimpse of a toss about London, or indeed humanity in general. Both of which are fairly important in a job like this.

5. But on the other hand OMFG LOOK AT HIS FUNNEEE HAIR LOL!!!! BORRIS IS A LEGERND!!!!

Anyway, if the worst happens and Boris gets in, then provided he doesn't obliterate the capital in some hilarious slapstick disaster, or provoke war with Portsmouth with a chance remark – provided, in short, that London still exists in some recognisable form – the rival parties should fight fire with fire by running equally popular TV characters against him in the next election.

It doesn't even matter if they're real or not. Basil Brush would be a shoo-in. Churchill, the nodding dog from the car insurance ads – he'll do. Or if we're after the ironic vote, how about Gene Hunt from *Life on Mars*? Or Phil Mitchell? At least he's a Londoner.

They might as well. Desperate times call for desperate measures, and there's no more desperate sign of the times than the current wave of LOL OMFG!!!! BORIS DONE A GUFF!!!! ROFL!!!!!!! THE MAN IS A LEGERND I TELL YOU LOL!!!!! I CARNT WAIT 2 SEE HIM RUNNING THE INTIRE CITTY!!! BORRIS 4 KING!!! LOL!!! LOL!!! LOLLL!!!!!!!!!!!!!

– In case you need reminding, Boris Johnson won.

Morning versus night [21 April 2008]

If the morning and the night had a fight, who'd win? My money's on mornings. Nights may be sleeker and, on the face of it, more dangerous, but mornings are definitely harder. It's strange that staying up late at night is somehow regarded as 'cooler' than getting up at the crack of dawn, when it's the latter that truly separates the men from the boys. Any wuss can stay up until 4 a.m. swilling cocktails and jabbering, whereas queuing silently for a bus at 5.30 a.m. in the middle of winter requires a level of genuine grit normally reserved for the likes of the Ancient Mariner.

At what point, incidentally, does the night officially turn into morning? I'd say, regardless of whether the sun has bothered rising yet or not, the morning only truly starts at the point where you wouldn't have to apologise to your neighbours if you accidentally set off a bullhorn in your living room. Somewhere around 8 a.m., in other words. Anything earlier than that is just inhumane.

The night/morning divide has been on my mind of late because my current circumstances have required me to become an early riser. I'm not a natural morning person. Left to my own devices, with no work commitments or sense of purpose, my sleeping pattern tends to drift into student mode, ambling further and further past the horizon until it gets to the point where I'm waking up at 1 p.m. and hitting the sack around six in the morning. I eventually become fully nocturnal – like a vampire, but more of a loser, and with markedly less capacity for transforming into a bat and flapping around a castle scaring virgins.

Traditionally, anyone unfortunate enough to find themselves working with me discovers very quickly that there's little point scheduling meetings first thing in the morning, because I'll either miss the start by 45 minutes (then waste another half hour defensively explaining that my alarm didn't go off and so on), or turn up bleary-eyed and useless, having stayed awake all night because I was so spooked by the thought of oversleeping.

But all that's had to change of late. I've somehow got into the habit of rising early and, boy, oh boy, it's an exciting journey into a whole new world. For one thing, I've discovered an entire species of human being that I rarely come into contact with: London's commuters.

Their existence never fails to surprise me. I'd always thought of the mornings as essentially uninhabitable, like the planet Mercury.

But no. I head out the door at 7 a.m. and there they are – actual live people! – making me jerk with astonishment each time. It's like lifting a rock and seeing life unexpectedly teeming below. Although it's not actually teeming most of the time. A lot of it is simply standing around, lined up silently at the bus stop like a sorrowful row of Antony Gormley figurines, suffering one indignity after another. Cramped conditions, busted LED signs, bursts of syncopated marching interspersed with the occasional frenzied dash, freezing skies, freezing breath, freezing, pissing rain . . . their lives are a hilarious cycle of misery. Or rather, it would be hilarious if I didn't have to join them each morning.

Still, apparently that's all on the way out. According to *The Economist*, thanks to the ongoing technological revolution, the commuter of yesteryear is gradually being replaced by the 'urban nomad' of tomorrow. A combination of burgeoning Wi-Fi access and increasingly smart-arsed gadgetry is making location increasingly irrelevant for many workers: wherever they are, they can still communicate with colleagues, access documents, and type up blisteringly dull reports.

There's no need to physically head into work, unless you work in a chip shop, and even then scientists are close to cracking a method for frying potatoes via broadband and emailing them direct to your customers' stomachs.

The upshot of all this being that the early morning commute is set to slowly dissipate from a concentrated frenzy of furrow-browed scampering into a sort of fuzzy, laid-back cloud in which worker bees drift hither and thither, sometimes staying at home, sometimes buzzing round town, touching down in a Starbucks every five minutes to stare at a BlackBerry or something modern like that. The very notion of geography has been shattered as surely as if someone had written the word 'geography' on a plate and hurled it to the floor in a touristy Greek restaurant. And it'll be a bit less cramped at the bus stop as a result.

Having conquered space, technology should now set about conquering time. It's all very well being able to hold a video conference without leaving your own toilet, but there's still that pesky need to communicate with people in real time, which means being awake at the same moment they are. And in my experience other people have an irritating tendency to get up early and stand around tapping their watch. What I want is a Sky+ system for all human interactions, so I can store conversations up and then play them back at a time that suits me, preferably the middle of the night, which is my natural habitat.

But then there are all sorts of things I want that the world of science has yet to deliver. The real-world Sky+ system is just one of them. There's still no sign of the hovercar, the robot butler, or the pill that tastes like an entire Sunday roast, and I distinctly remember ordering all three way back in 1978 when I was seven years old and capable of soaring optimism. Now I'm older, I'd settle for a lie-in. Still, that's the way the aspiration crumbles.

Bowl, Barack, bowl [28 April 2008]

Is Barack Obama elitist? Will his middle name harm his campaign? Are voters turned off by his lack of bowling prowess? Did he give Hillary the finger during a speech in Raleigh, North Carolina? When he picks his nose, which digit does he use? And what does that say about him?

The first four questions were genuinely posed by US TV news over the past few weeks. The nose-picking question wasn't. But it's no more puerile and pointless than the ones that were. The answers to the real questions, incidentally, run roughly as follows:

1. Is Obama elitist? Of course he is. He's running for president. It doesn't get much more elitist than that. Still, in terms of privilege, he'd have to go a long way to beat the ding-dong incumbent. Bush hails from a family of oil barons, billionaires, CEOs, former presidents, Scrooge McDuck and Daddy Warbucks. He's slept in a gigantic rustling money nest every night since the day he was born. And he's got an uncle made of gold. But since he also looks like Alfred E. Neuman and talks like he's ordering ribs, he's viewed as a straight-talkin', down-home regular Joe, albeit one with so much blood on his hands it's surely in danger of caking and congealing and turn-

ing his fists into heavy balls of scab, each one the size of a cabbage, good for thumping against desks and doors but not much else. Although even if that did happen, even if Bush called a press conference on the White House lawn and stood there demonically beating out a funeral march with his scabby orbs on a nightmarish drum fashioned from human bones and skin – even under those circumstances, you sense he'd somehow get away with it. Because that aw-shucks grin looks good on camera.

2. Will Obama's middle name – Hussein – harm his campaign? Depends how often and how insidiously you pose the question, really.

3. Are voters turned off by Obama's lack of bowling prowess? Hard to say. While campaigning in Pennsylvania, he took part in a photo opportunity at a bowling alley. It didn't go so well. He bowled a miserable 37; half his balls sailed into the gutter. In summary, he looked like a dick. The clip immediately entered heavy rotation on the TV news channels, becoming one of those modern snatches of footage that instantly take on iconic status by sheer dint of repetition; looping hypnotically, repeating ad nauseam against a soothing background of dull pundit birdsong, permanently stitching themselves into the fabric of your mind's eye. And the hosts ask whether this makes him look elitist, and the pundits umm and ahh over whether it does, and the word 'elitist' is bandied about again and again over the image of Obama looking like a dick, an elitist dick, an elitist can't-bowl dick, and it all starts to feel like brainwashing, albeit inadvertently, albeit only because they've got a simple, juicy clip and 10 billion hours of airtime to fill. So yes, voters might be turned off by Obama's lack of bowling prowess, because it's been shoved in their faces and smushed around like an oily rag.

4. Did Obama give Hillary the finger during a speech in Raleigh, North Carolina? This one's easy. The answer is no. Of course he didn't. While discussing his opponent during a campaign speech, Obama momentarily scratched his face using his middle finger. That's all. But hang on: we've still got a lot of airtime to fill, so let's loop it again and again while we try to work out if it might've been

a deliberate gesture, or a subconscious giveaway, or nothing at all. Was it nothing at all? This. Look at this. Was this nothing at all? Here it is again. What about this time? And this time? And this?

When you stand at a distance and survey this level of nitpicking idiocy, taking in the full landscape of stupidity and meaningless analysis, it's hard not to conclude that 24-hour rolling news is the worst thing to befall humankind since the Manhattan Project. The focus on conjecture and analysis has reached such an insane degree that pundits are chasing some kind of meaning in the way a presidential candidate scratches his face. This is what lunatics do when they think people on television are sending them person-alised messages. Where the rest of us see Vernon Kay hosting a gameshow, they see evidence of a conspiracy, and they scan every wink, nod, and eyebrow twitch for veiled threats or coded instructions.

Except the lunatics have an excuse: they're lunatics. Lunacy is what they do. It's in their job description. News networks are sup-posed to offer news. Instead they serve up loops and chatter. They might as well show footage of passing clouds and invite their pun-dits to speculate on which one looks most like a kettle and which one looks most like a pony. And let the race for the presidency be settled by a bowling match.

You are here [5 May 2008]

There's a characteristically brilliant Peanuts strip which opens with Linus sitting on the living-room floor, anxiously clutching his mouth. Lucy enters and asks what's wrong. 'I'm aware of my tongue,' he explains. 'It's an awful feeling! Every now and then I become aware that I have a tongue inside my mouth, and then it starts to feel lumped up . . . I can't help it . . . I can't put it out of my mind . . . I keep thinking about where my tongue would be if I weren't thinking about it, and then I can feel it sort of pressing against my teeth.'

Loudly declaring this the dumbest thing she's ever heard, Lucy scowls away. But a few steps down the corridor, she stops dead in

170

her tracks. She clutches her own mouth. Suddenly she's aware of her tongue too. She runs back and chases him round the room, shouting, 'You blockhead!' with her gigantic booming gob.

Occasionally, late at night, while trying to sleep and failing, I experience something similar – except instead of being aware of my tongue, I'm aware of my entire body, the entire world, and the whole of reality itself. It's like waking from a dream, or a light going on, or a giant 'YOU ARE HERE' sign appearing in the sky. The mere fact that I'm actually real and actually breathing suddenly hits me in the head with a thwack. It leaves me giddy. It causes a brief surge of clammy, bubbling anxiety, like the opening stages of a panic attack. The moment soon passes, but while it lasts it's strangely terrifying.

I asked around and discovered to my that relief I'm not the only one. Many of my friends have experienced something similar and have been equally spooked. One of them, a smartarse, pointed out that Jean-Paul Sartre was so rattled by the sensation that he was inspired to write an entire book about existential dread called *Nausea*, which became a student classic. I prefer Charles M. Schulz's take. It's far more succinct and comes with funny pictures.

Anyway, what troubles me about such moments of heightened awareness isn't the dizzying headrush that accompanies them, but the implication that the rest of the time I must be essentially asleep, cruising around on autopilot, scarcely even aware that I'm alive. Here, but not here. Like I'm watching a TV show. That's the bulk of my life. I might as well set the video and nod off completely, catching up later while eating a takeaway dinner.

I didn't mention this to my smartarse friend – but if I had, they'd doubtless point out that Kurt Vonnegut was so rattled by this sensation that he was inspired to write an entire book about it. In his 1997 novel *Timequake*, a bizarre rift in time sends everyone on Earth back 10 years – but only in spirit. Trapped inside their own heads, mere spectators, they're forced to watch themselves living their day-to-day lives for an entire decade, making the same mistakes, experiencing the same joys and heartaches – and they're powerless to intervene. Naturally, they get bored and drift off, leaving themselves on autopilot. At the moment the timequake eventually ends, and they're back in the present day, most of them simply drop to the floor, confused – it's been so long since they were at the controls, they've forgotten how to walk and talk for themselves.

That's the stuff of science fiction, but it increasingly applies to our everyday lives. The gap between your stupid face and cold hard reality is increasing all the time. We plod down the street holding remote conversations with voices in little plastic boxes. We slump in front of hi-def panels watching processed, graded, synchronised imagery. We wander through made-up online worlds, pausing occasionally to chew the fat with some blue-skinned tit in a jester's hat. We watch time and space collapse on a daily basis. Our world is now running an enhanced, expanded version of reality's vanilla operating system.

As a result, it's all too easy to feel like a viewer of – rather than a participant in – your own life. And living at one remove can be crippling. You spend more time internally criticising your own actions, like a snarky stoner ripping the piss out of a bad movie, than actually knuckling down and doing stuff.

All of which means that those late-night moments of lurching fear, of existential nausea, of basic 'I'm alive!' horror, now feel more extreme than ever. The gap has widened. Our sleep is deeper. We're like mesmerised rabbits. That explains why we fail to do anything in the face of mounting dangers. We've done piss-all about global warming, the Bush administration, and Piers Morgan's rising media profile – each of which has the potential to destroy us all – because we hardly know we're born.

That's my theory anyway. Clearly, the only solution is for us to set about smashing up every single machine in the world, before we nod off completely. Yeah. That's the best conclusion I can draw at present. Because I didn't set out to write a weird existential column this morning, but hey: I'm fast asleep myself. Sue me when you wake up.

The return of selfishism   [26 May 2008]

You're a passenger in a car that someone else is driving, and your
hands are tied, and up ahead is a container lorry full of hot liquid
manure that you're definitely going to run into the back of, but
your driver's deaf and blind and not slowing down, so there's nothing you can do except writhe in your seat and brace yourself for the
impact.

That's roughly how I feel following the Crewe and Nantwich by-
election. Thanks to a 900% swing to the right (or thereabouts),
a Cameron-fronted Tory government now looks like not just an
alarming possibility, but an awful, grinding, inescapable certainty –
yet another preordained slice of doomsday, like climate change or
the *War Against the Machines*. The countdown has already begun.

Clearly some kind of self-defence is in order, which is why I've
already started mentally withdrawing from the real world. It's easy:
all you have to do is imagine that the whole of life itself is just a
low-budget daytime TV show, one you're watching uninterestedly
from the sofa with one eye while reading a magazine with the
other. You know: *Cash in the Attic*, something like that. To help
sustain the illusion, imagine a cheapo theme tune playing each
morning when you wake up, and again each night before you go
to bed. Before long, the day in between will feel like zero-conse-
quence schedule-filling fluff, thereby lifting an almighty weight
from your shoulders.

With practice it's possible to become so psychologically distanced from issues that affect you, you could comfortably watch
your own leg being sawn off by an unhinged bearded intruder,
without doing more than raising an eyebrow and muttering, 'That
looks painful,' before returning to an article you were reading on
the history of mashed potato. That's the state of mind I intend to be
in the day Prime Minister Cameron gives his victory speech from
the front steps of No. 10.

Perhaps I needn't bother. Perhaps there's no need to insulate
myself against the Tories at all. What am I scared of, precisely?
During the London mayoral election, I had two main fears. The

first, obviously, was that Boris was going to win. For weeks I repeat-edly voiced that fear to everyone I met – to no avail as it turned out. But the second fear, the one I kept tucked away somewhere near the back of my head, was far more sinister. It was this: what if Boris won – and then turned out to be really good at his job? That might force me to question my cherished anti-Tory prejudice, which is so ingrained and instinctive it feels like something hand-stamped on my DNA.

That flouncy genetic analogy may not be far from the truth, incidentally: in recent years, scientists have begun exploring the notion that your political leaning may be hardwired into your biology, invisibly imprinted on your cells. This would explain a lot. For instance, I know in my bones that rightwing policies are wrong. Obviously wrong. They just are. It's Selfishism, pure and simple. Nasty stuff. Consequently I don't 'get' Tories, never have and never will. We don't gel. There's something missing in their eyes and voices; they're the same yet different; bodysnatchers run-ning on alien software. Yet that's precisely how I must seem to them: an inherently misguided and ultimately unknowable idiot. (I'm right and they're wrong, of course – but they can be forgiven for not working that out. They can't help it. They were blighted at birth.)

According to tradition, you're supposed to get more rightwing as you grow older, as wide-eyed youthful idealism is gradually replaced with growling, frightened, fat-arsed self-interest. I say 'gradually', but what worries me is the thought that such a transfor-mation could occur with terrifying speed, a real Damascene con-version. I came close once after glimpsing David Miliband on TV: I couldn't hear what he was saying, but something about his face – just his sodding face – revolted me on a deep and primal level. It was chilling, unsettling – like watching a haunted ventriloquist's dummy slowly turn its head through 360 degrees. 'Who is this grinning homunculus,' I thought, 'and what does he want from me?'

This either means my genes are shifting, or Miliband is a rightwing imposter. Or maybe he's simply not of this world. Perhaps I merely behaved like a farm animal reacting to an extra-terrestrial intruder – howling in distress without knowing why.

Ghastly and nightmarish though Miliband may be, he's got nothing on gloomy Gordon Brown, who increasingly resembles a humourless, imposing old butler slowly creaking the mansion door open in a Frankenstein movie. Prime Minister Igor, the shuffling fun-free zone. No wonder the nation's fallen out of love with him. Imagine playing a carefree game of frisbee with Brown at a summer barbeque. You can't. That's why the poor bastard's doomed.

And why we're doomed along with him. Because here comes Cameron and the Bullingdon massive, swept to power by default on a wave of resentment, surliness and festering boredom. Selfishness returns. I'm weaving my cocoon early. Wake me in 2018 when the New Tory revival is over.

Hardcore animal sex   [2 June 2008]

Not that it's a slow news day or anything, but Bill Oddie is in trouble with viewers for providing unnecessarily racy commentary on *Springwatch*. According to reports, the former Goodie backed footage of two sparrows mating with the words: 'The female is asking for it – and getting it, basically . . . She's doing that wing-fluttering thing as if to say: "I am a baby, feed me now" . . . and is getting quite the opposite . . . That's a wing-trembler she's just had there.'

Later, while watching two beetles having sex, he proclaimed: 'One thing's for sure – this boy is horny,' before going on to role-play the part of the female: 'Come on, big boy, come and get it . . . Oh, be gentle with me!'

Now this is bloody sexy stuff. No one could hear that without getting dangerously turned on. In fact, according to the state-of-the-art Raunch Gauge based at Wookey Hole in Somerset (founded in 1978 to monitor fluctuating levels of steaminess in network broadcasts), that particular edition of *Springwatch* was the second most arousing broadcast since records began – eclipsed only by the notorious 1984 edition of *News at Ten* in which a trouserless Sandy Gall vaulted the desk and violently rubbed his crotch against the lens for 10 whole minutes in a desperate bid to perk up a report on Sealink ferries.*

Gall's shenanigans took place 24 years ago – a long time in broadcasting, where memories are so short that even top TV executives regularly forget where their own mouths are while eating, which is why The Ivy is full of grown men and women smearing food all over their faces like babies and slapping the table in a panic. The horror had long since faded. Consequently Oddie's XXX-rated outburst caught the population unawares. Within minutes, millions of viewers nationwide found themselves driven into an uncontrollable frenzy of slavering lust, grinding themselves against the nearest person or object in a desperate bid to satiate their desires. The carnage was indescribable, hence the glaring lack of newspaper reports about it.

Once they'd finished mopping up, viewers picked up the phone to complain. Stop making animals sexy, they screamed. It's freaking us right out.

And they're right. Animals aren't sexy, especially when they're having sex. Let's list the reasons why.

Reason One: the lack of experimentation. It's all rut, rut, rut as far as the animal kingdom's concerned. You never see goats giving blowjobs or a pair of foxes trying out the reverse cowgirl position. Two dogs banging away in a shop doorway won't even look round to check out their own reflections. They'll sniff each other's bums, but that's about as warped as they get. There's a crushing lack of imagination in animals' sex lives . . . which might go some way to explaining reason two . . .

Reason Two: the lack of facial expressions. Human beings perform all manner of crazy facial distortions during intercourse – Peter Sissons one minute, Marty Feldman the next. It's all part of the fun. Sometimes it's tempting to break off in the middle just to point and laugh, especially when your partner pulls a face like someone who's recently dropped a piano on their foot but is trying to conceal their agony.

* This is absolutely not true.

Animals, on the other hand, don't pull any expression at all – or at least nothing we humans can interpret. They look the same as always, i.e. glazed and bored and impossibly dumb. Concentrate on their faces and it's like watching furry handymen changing a plug. There's no passion there. Not even any kissing.

Reason Three: their genitals are all over the shop. Animal penises, in particular, are the stuff of nightmares. Kangaroos have a bifurcated penis – and 'bifurcated', for those of you watching in plain English, means 'forked'. The echidna pushes the envelope even further: its penis has four distinct heads. Dolphins have retractable prehensile cocks which snake about like monkey's tails, grabbing passing objects and throwing them into the air. Fun at parties? Yes. But sexy? No.

Anyway, while it's legal for humans to watch animals having sex, it's illegal if we decide to join in. God knows why, since the act of bestiality itself is surely punishment enough. It certainly doesn't look like a barrel of laughs. Years ago, while I was working in a second-hand record shop on a quiet day, a fellow staff member surreptitiously passed me a gaudy A5 magazine called something like *Zoo Fun* or *Farmyard Hunger*, filled with depressing photographs of humans and animals locked in congress. One image, in particular, burned itself into my mind: a man standing on a tree stump having sex with a cow. Both he and the cow appeared bored out of their minds; two colleagues begrudgingly completing a chore on a cold, cloudy day in Denmark. That's not sexy. That's a bad day at work.

In summary then: animals are rubbish in bed, and you shouldn't have wayward thoughts about them. No matter what Bill Oddie says.

CHAPTER TEN

In which ethnicity is admired for the sake of it, Christianity is misrepresented, and Dale Winton threatens to bring on the wall

They're, like, totally ethnic [14 June 2008]

Hands up everyone who thinks they're the most important person in the world. Come on. Stop lying. You all do, you pampered, ego-centric worms. And you're wrong. In the grand scheme of things, none of us mean jack squat. No matter what you think, say, or achieve during your lifetime, however you strive to make some kind of impact, you'll have absolutely zero influence on the overall course of the universe. You're a drop in a bathtub. A tile in a mosaic. A solitary pixel on an immense and frightening LCD monitor.

If reading these words sent you temporarily crazy, and you ran outside and stripped naked and pressed your bum cheeks against the nearest Starbucks window – really pushed them apart so everyone inside got a gruesome view up your rear aperture – and then started defecating against the glass to a backdrop of tumbling lattes and horrified screams . . . if you did THAT, it might irrevocably alter your life, what with the ensuing court case and all, but it would make absolutely no difference to the trajectory of history. In summary: you're pointless.

This is a terrifying thought, of course, which is why we in the West tend to overcompensate by convincing ourselves that we're actually all massively interesting and special and unique. At its simplest, you can see this trait reflected in advertising slogans like 'Because You're Worth It' – and at its most insidiously offensive in shows like *Tribal Wives*.

Here's the premise: in each episode, a different British woman is flown across the world to spend some time living among a charmingly authentic tribe of some description in order to see what life-affirming message she can glean from their humble hut-dwelling existence. This week, our volunteer is Sass Willis, an unmarried 34-year-old from Oxford. Sass feels like she's missing out on something but isn't quite sure what it is. Perhaps a week with the Kuna Indians of Panama will help?

Guess what? It does. Within about 10 minutes they're painting her face with henna and grinning at her with endearing, gappy mouths in which half the teeth are missing. They have wooden bowls and hammocks and brightly coloured robes. They carve statuettes and hold ceremonies and travel around in canoes. They're, like, totally ethnic.

Naturally this means that (a) we get a load of panpipe music farted down our earholes for an hour while (b) the narration implies the Kuna possess a simple spiritual wisdom which Sass can both learn from and heal herself with. It helps that they appear to speak in simply worded, easily translatable platitudes, and spend much of their time telling her to settle down and get married when she returns to the UK. Cue plenty of video diary entries in which Sass tearfully discusses how the Kuna have changed her life forever and made her see what's really important and how from now on she'll have a new perspective on things and blah blah blah . . . because she's worth it.

Well pardon me. Not to single out Sass or the Kuna or anything, but why does every other programme about exotic tribes have to spend the entire duration of its running time making out that every single one of them is massively, inherently wise? Statistically, half of them are going to be idiots, for Christ's sake. Those simple chuckles and gap-toothed smiles you're so enamoured with? That unvarnished, basically worded advice? What if they are just signs of stupidity? What if you've travelled halfway round the world and sought spiritual insight from a bunch of cretins? After all, a berk is still a berk, whether they're eating chips in Rhyl or dancing round a fire in the rainforest.

Once, just once, can't we have a travel show in which the presenter lives with a remote tribe for a week and comes away shrugging and calling them a bunch of boring, backward arseholes? Even if it isn't true. In fact, especially if it isn't. Can't we? Please?

'I feel so terribly sad after watching it'   [21 June 2008]

Ping! An email arrives. From a reader. Called simply Matthew. And he writes: 'Please, please, please write something publicly in your Screen Burn column about *Class of 2008*. I feel so terribly sad after watching it. I feel your evaluation of it would somehow help me live with myself for a bit longer. Sorry if you think I am asking for a request or anything. It's just that they are all such complete cunts.'

Plaintive. But I don't do requests. Although luckily for Matthew, I'd resolved to write about *Class of 2008* anyway. In case you haven't seen it, it's an aspirational youth-oriented docu-soap that follows a group of sickeningly privileged, jumped-up little piss-drips as they embark on various glittering careers in music, modelling, and clubland. It's like watching a roomful of monocled adolescent toffs loudly applauding their own farts. Only worse. Because farts can sometimes be funny.

It's introduced by a look-at-me turdhole who calls himself 'Flash Louis'. Louis lives with his parents in Hampstead. Louis lives with his parents in Hampstead. I said that twice because it's worth repeating.

He's also a DJ and aspiring promoter and possibly the most emptily self-satisfied person ever to grace a television screen. Across the series he's shown attempting to arrange a glittering club night, and for some mad reason we're expected to give a toss without ever being told why.

Anyway, Louis is merely our narrator, our anchor, our foothold in a dizzying whirlpool of bottomless shittery starring his privileged chums. Chief among his pals are a gangly ginger posho called Will, who plays in a band (the bass player's called Rory, which is all you need to know), and apparently famous international supermodel Daisy Lowe. Last week much of the action centred on Will and Daisy flying off to swank around at Milan Fashion Week as guests of Dolce & Gabbana. Cue footage of them receiving free clothes and slap-up meals, swaggering round their luxurious hotel suite, blithely wiping their bums on the world's face. At no point are we given any indication of what they've done to deserve all of this, other than being in the right place at the right time, surrounded by the right constellation of absolute twats.

Throughout the programme, my body reacted in unusual ways. First, the lyrics to 'Common People' by Pulp began swirling in my mind. Then I became dimly aware of a low grinding noise on the soundtrack, which turned out to be my teeth. This was followed by a strange blurring effect in the visuals, which turned out to be me gouging one of my own eyes out with my thumb just so I'd see 50 per cent less of their awful grinning gobs.

And the worst thing about it? Like I said, it's a youth show. That really isn't on. Listen here, BBC, if you MUST broadcast an almighty, air-kissing celebration of upper middle-class dilettantes, for God's sake don't do it in front of the children. Faced with this level of posing, pretension and self-congratulation – effortlessly funded by God knows who – 99 per cent of the (young, impressionable) audience are going to come away feeling inadequate or disadvantaged or angry or miserable. What was it Matthew said? 'I feel so terribly sad after watching it.'

Is that what you want, BBC? To make us feel terribly sad? Well, is it? And if so, why? Do you hate us? Is that it?

Still, there is one up side. Sometimes I get depressed about the way the world's heading. I'm scared by the prospect of widespread food or oil or water riots. Late at night I lie awake and I wonder: what if civilisation collapses completely? If the seas rise and the oil runs dry and we all end up fighting each other with spiked cudgels on a tiny circle of gore-sodden wasteland? I visualise it happening, and I despair.

But now I have an escape hatch. I think about *Class of 2008* and cheer up again. Because if we're all going to suffer come the apocalypse, they will too. Only their faces'll be an absolute picture.

– After this article appeared, one of the Class of 2008 *– the one going out with Daisy Lowe, I think — emailed me to say that while he could understand why him and his friends probably came across as over-privileged twats on TV, they (a) weren't actually very rich and (b) were all nice people really. His email was reasonable and pleasant and modest, and rather left me feeling like I'd been a bit of a bastard I'm afraid.*

Minds wide shut   [2 August 2008]

Must be frustrating being a scientist. There you are, incrementally discovering how the universe works via a series of complex tests and experiments, for the benefit of all mankind – and what thanks do you get? People call you 'egghead' or 'boffin' or 'heretic', and they cave your face in with a rock and bury you out in the wilderness.

Not literally – not in this day and age – but you get the idea. Scientists are mistrusted by huge swathes of the general public, who see them as emotionless lab-coated meddlers-with-nature rather than, say, fellow human beings who've actually bothered getting off their arses to work this shit out. The wariness stems from three popular misconceptions:

(1) Scientists want to fill our world with chemicals and killer robots; (2) They don't appreciate the raw beauty of nature, maaan; and (3) They're always spoiling our fun, pointing out homeopathy doesn't work or ghosts don't exist EVEN THOUGH they KNOW we REALLY, REALLY want to believe in them.

That last delusion is the most insidious. Science is like a good friend: sometimes it tells you things you don't want to hear. It tells you the truth. And we all know how much that can hurt, don't we, fatso?

Many people find bald, unvarnished truths so disturbing, they prefer to ram their heads in the sand and start dreaming at the first sign of scientific reality. The more contrary evidence mounts up, the harder they'll ignore it. And even the greatest, most widely-admired scientists can provoke this reaction. Take Darwin. Or rather, take *The Genius of Darwin*, the latest documentary from professional God-hatin' Professor Yaffle impersonator Richard Dawkins, which sets out to calmly and lucidly explain (a) why Darwin was so ace, and (b) just how much evidence there is to support his findings.

Darwin's theory of evolution was simple, beautiful, majestic and awe-inspiring. But because it contradicts the allegorical babblings of a bunch of made-up old books, it's been under attack since day one. That's just tough luck for Darwin. If the Bible had contained a passage that claimed gravity is caused by God pulling objects toward the ground with magic invisible threads, we'd still be debating Newton with idiots too.

Since Darwin's death, Dawkins points out, the evidence confirming his discovery has piled up and up and up, many thousand feet above the point of dispute. And yet heroically, many still dispute it. They're like couch potatoes watching *Finding Nemo* on DVD who've suffered some kind of brain haemorrhage which has led them to believe the story they're watching is real, that their screen is filled with water and talking fish, and that that's all there is to reality – just them and that screen and Nemo – and when you run into the room and point out the DVD player and the cables connecting it to the screen, and you open the windows and point outside and describe how overwhelming the real world is – when you do all that, it only spooks them. So they go on believing in Nemo, with gritted teeth if necessary.

What was it that spooked them so? Probably natural selection's lack of reassuring narrative. It lays the ruthless, godless world pretty bloody bare. As Dawkins says: 'The total amount of suffering in the natural world is beyond all decent contemplation. During the minute it takes me to say these words, thousands of animals are running for their lives, whimpering with fear, feeling teeth sink into their throats. Thousands are dying from starvation or disease or feeling a parasite rasping away from within. There is no central authority; no safety net. For most animals the reality of life is struggling, suffering and death.'

Woo-hoo! Compare and contrast with the plot of *Finding Nemo* and it's easy to understand why people would rather believe in the purdy singing clown fish. But this is our reality, people. Like the man says, there's no safety net – so since we're all in this together, we'll have to make our own. And we can't do that with our eyes and minds wide shut.

It's a sin [9 August 2008]

You know what organised religion needs? More power and influence. Thank God, then, that Channel 4 are on hand to give it the helping hand it so desperately requires in the form of *Make Me a Christian*, a spiritual makeover show in which four hardcore Goddites attempt to convert a rag-tag band of sinners into full-blown Jesus freaks in just three weeks.

In true oversimplified TV-conflict tradition, it's a clash of absurd extremities. The Christians, for instance, consist of an evangelical preacher, a lady vicar, a Catholic priest and – very much heading up the pack – the Reverend George Hargreaves, founder of Operation Christian Vote, and the Christian Party, and the Scottish Christian Party, and the Welsh Christian Party. If it's Christian and a Party, chances are George is its figurehead. He scatters Christian joy like a muckspreader flings shit: indiscriminately and everywhere.

Said Christians are pitted against a group of volunteers containing the following widely representative social types: a lesbian schoolteacher, a tattooed militant atheist biker, a white Muslim convert, a boozing fannyhound who claims to have slept with over 150 women, and a lapdancing witch. Nice work, C4. I'm sure we can all learn from this. Let battle commence.

Following a trip to York Minster, George hands each of the volunteers a Bible. The word 'Bible', he tells them, stands for 'Basic Instruction Before Leaving Earth'. He instructs them to read it every day. This makes the atheist biker kick off, so George graciously talks over him until he walks out.

The group seems pleased to see biker boy go. After all, what's the point of participating if you're not prepared to learn? As William (the Muslim convert) says, 'Step one to learning is silence, and step two is listening.' Step three, presumably, is absolute cocksucking obedience – or it would be if cocksucking wasn't a sin.

Almost any form of sex is a sin. Take Fay, the occult lapdancer. George takes one look at her lifestyle (spangly bras and tarot cards) and announces she's 'on a trajectory to hell'. Sobbing, Fay slinks away to her boyfriend's house for a few days of comforting. When she emerges later, George bollocks her for having sex outside marriage. 'While the world might call it "making love",' he says, 'the Bible calls it fornication.'

Fay's clearly unhappy and wracked with issues about her appearance, but you can't help wondering if introducing her to Gok Wan might've been a tad kinder.

Not that George and co would approve of Gok. After all, we get to see what they make of exuberant gayness when Pastor Wally (the evangelical preacher) commands Laura (the lesbian teacher) to remove all evidence of same-sex activity from her home. Her saucy party snaps, her books of Sapphic erotica – they have to go.

George agrees. His Christian Party takes a notably dim view on homosexuality. He says things like, 'The ancient city of Sodom could have been saved, if only righteous people could be found,' in its election broadcasts. And in 2006 he personally pledged £50,000 to assist the nine Scottish firefighters disciplined for refusing to hand out fire-safety leaflets at a gay parade.

Given that George also wrote and co-produced Sinitta's 1986 gay disco anthem 'So Macho' (sample lyric: 'I'm after a hunk of a guy, an experienced man of the world . . . He's got to be so macho/ He's got to be big and strong, enough to turn me on'), this is surprising. Still, he's a surprising guy. In 2007 he campaigned to have the iconic red dragon removed from the Welsh flag as it was 'nothing less than the sign of Satan'.

With his polarising views and divisive political campaigning, George is just the man to be fronting a makeover show, and the broadcast will doubtless be accompanied by the percussive sound of thousands of Christians enthusiastically smashing their foreheads against the wall with delight at the way they're represented. Still, let's not blame Channel 4. Let's forgive them. Just like Jesus n' shit, yeah?

Fun with brains [16 August 2008]

The human brain is a wonderful thing, but you wouldn't want to kiss it. It's an ugly, quivering, corrugated blancmange. If it wasn't permanently shrouded from view by that opaque bone helmet you call a skull, you'd never get laid.

Just as well, because if the top of your skull was missing, and you accidentally banged your naked brain against the headboard during a one-night-stand, you'd probably start jerking around and going 'buhhhhh' and pulling a face like Robert Mitchum having a stroke. And that's completely different to what you normally do during sex, right?

Anyway, if you don't fancy gazing into a bucketful of peeled minds, avoid *Blood and Guts: A History of Surgery*, which explores the evolution of brain surgery in unflinching detail. I say 'unflinching': the show didn't flinch once. I, however, flinched like a man with his glans in a sandwich toaster.

Make no mistake, this is graphic stuff. Shot after shot of heads being sawn or jimmied open, and exposed, pulsating brains being prodded with sticks. But if you manage to stay conscious (by pinching the back of your hand and breathing slowly through your nose), it offers some incredible sights.

For instance, early on we see a woman undergoing surgery to remove an errant bit of cranial yuck that's been causing epileptic fits. They whizz the top of her skull off and peel away a gossamer-thin coating to reveal her bloody, gelatinous brain, which they repeatedly squirt with a spray bottle, to wash away the claret and expose the pale pink jelly beneath. We see blood vessels throbbing in her mind, and then – cue the incredible bit – we spin round to the other side only to discover she's STILL AWAKE and enjoying a chinwag with one of the nurses.

She has to remain conscious, see, because the surgeon needs to know if he's about to cut out anything important, and the best way of ascertaining that is to zap individual sections of her brain with an electrode, then ask her how it feels. One bit makes her hand twitch about. Another makes her eyes roll back. Gradually he builds a rough 'map' of her brain, and adjusts his scalpel swipes accordingly. It helps to avoid unpleasant surgical side-effects, such as spending the rest of your life bumping into furniture and mooing.

Truth be told, watching this woman calmly lie back and natter while the surgeon probed her brain sent me a bit giddy. I'd be useless on either side of the equation. If I were the patient, I'd suddenly freak out, leap to my feet and run screaming down the corridors, sloshing brain goo up the walls as I went, getting stupider with each spillage, and eventually collapsing, drooling, by the lifts. And as the surgeon, I wouldn't be able to resist going mad with the electrode, making her jump like a puppet, or seeing if I could fritz her mind in such a way that she'd start seeing noises, or hearing colours, or thinking the air in the room had the texture of biscuits or something.

Speaking of mad surgeons, there's a fair few of them on display here, such as Walter Freeman, inventor of the transorbital lobotomy, which involved hammering an icepick through the eye socket and into the brain, then wiggling it around until the nerve fibres connecting the frontal lobes to the thalamus were severed. Freeman thought that it cured mental illness, which is a bit like thinking you can fix your computer by jamming a knitting needle through the hard drive.

There's also an interview with a Spanish surgeon who planted electrodes in a bull's brain, then jumped in the ring with it, and stopped it goring him to death by pushing a button on a remote which made it spin around in confusion. The footage of that is pretty funny, if you despise animals.

Anyway, great show. Make a note of it now. On your brain. With a sharp stick. And try not to poke the bit that switches your bum on and off while you're up there.

So macho [23 August 2008]

No apologies, you absolute bastards, for this column returning once again to the horror of crass religious makeover show *Make Me a Christian*, which draws to a close this week having prompted much wailing and gnashing of teeth – 98% of it in my living room, where each episode has been accompanied by a storm of cries, squawks, and outraged splutters. The bellows came so regularly and automatically (as an instinctive physiological response to what I was seeing and hearing) that after a while I actually forgot it was me making them. They'd become part of my flat's natural ambient soundtrack, like the ticking of the clock or the sound of mould growing in the fridge. Yell, yell, yell. It was like living on top of a yell mine.

If you were to measure the volume of my shouts and plot them on a graph, you'd discover that the number of sonic peaks corresponded precisely to the number of close-ups of head Christian mentor Reverend George Hargreaves' simpering tortoisey face. A few weeks ago, after watching episode one, I was so incensed by his self-satisfied air of stubborn intolerance I Googled him as soon as the credits ran. Before long I'd uncovered his astonishing back story: that in the distant past he'd been a DJ and songwriter (responsible for Sinitta's 'So Macho' and 'Cruising') before becoming the head of the insanely right-wing Christian Party, which wants to denounce homosexuality, teach creationism in schools, reintroduce the death penalty, ban abortions, remove the 'satanic' red dragon from the Welsh flag, and basically make a bollocks of everything. (Fortunately, they're not very successful, what with the general populace being aware it isn't AD1500 any more. In the recent Haltemprice and Howden by-election, George received 76 votes. But, hey, perhaps this TV exposure will build his profile.)

Anyway, George's background is so juicy and mad, I fully expected the show to make the most of it. You know: wait till he's admonishing Laura (one of the show's volunteers; a lesbian) for her sinful gayness, then have the voiceover say, 'But George hasn't always been so opposed to homosexuality . . .' and BAM! – cut to Sinitta performing 'So Macho' on *Top of the Pops* in 1983 with a caption explaining who wrote it. And move from there into a cute VT package detailing his loopy political ambitions. Didn't happen in show one. Or show two. Aha, I figured. They're saving it for the finale: a classic 'reveal'. Look! He's been a vaguely sinister weirdo all along! Gotcha!

But no. His past and his party never warrant a mention. Instead we get the standard makeover show ending: a few participants scratching around for reasons why they feel a bit better about themselves having gone through the sausage machine. Ignore the faintly upbeat veneer and it's all pretty feeble: none of them appear to have undergone any spiritual transformation whatsoever. They may have enjoyed several of the 'tasks', such as helping the elderly or throwing a barbecue for the neighbours, but that's because doing good deeds is fun. You don't need Christ whispering in your ear to appreciate the value of loving thy neighbour.

In fact, the biggest hurdle each of them has had to overcome throughout the series is George himself: his robotic intolerance; his haughty judgements; his stomach-churning opinions stated as fact. Choosing him as its 'star' has created a bizarre tension at the heart of the programme: the volunteers have been repeatedly told that Christianity is all about love and acceptance by a man who insists the world must adhere to his dementedly fundamentalist interpretation of the Bible. And by giving George a mainstream televisual platform without once pointing out what a marginal and extremist figure he is, the show is hugely unfair on yer average non-lunatic churchgoer, the majority of whom are far more likely to offer you a pot of homemade elderberry jam than hysterically denounce you as a fornicating sinner.

Yeah, that's right. I'm an atheist defending moderate Christians. Wanna make something of it?

White people rapping   [6 September 2008]

Empathy lives! If you've ever doubted your ability to feel compassion for your fellow man, try sitting through the recent DFS commercial in which various out-of-work actors have to mime along to the shit Nickelback song 'Rockstar' without squirming yourself half to death with embarrassment-by-proxy. The sorrow and humiliation is overpowering. I can barely stand to watch. Which bit's the worst? The bit where the porky thirty-something bloke does air guitar, or the bit where the old woman in sunglasses mouths the chorus? Bet they had to repeatedly halt the shoot because people were completely breaking down on camera – collapsing into helpless shuddering fits. Having sex with a dying goose in exchange for basic rations on some apocalyptic porn site would be less demeaning.

The only thing in the universe more shameful than old people miming rock songs is the sight of white people rapping. Not all white people, you understand – about 15% are good at it. The rest come across like Leslie Nielsen in an unseen and unfilmed *Naked*

Gun sequence in which Lieutenant Frank Drebin has to black up and infiltrate a hip-hop video shoot. (In the 1980s, it was the law that every family movie or sitcom had to include a bit where the 'Dad' character performed a rap, replete with lots of hand gestures and the word 'yo', although the practice was eventually abandoned when audiences began committing suicide en masse.)

Consider that a protracted warning about *Scene Stealers*, a new teenage 'life swap' show which as of this nanosecond forms part of the BBC's yoof strand Switch. Essentially an amiable take on the *Faking It* format (or a shameless rip-off, depending on whether you own the rights to it or not), *Scene Stealers* is all about tribes. Teenage tribes.

Of course being part of a tribe is easier when you're young, although some types age quicker than others. Stay slim and you can convincingly pull off the Camden indie kid look into your early 30s. Goths spoil sooner. They start to look a bit tatty around the age of 25. Still, no matter which tribe you've chosen, there comes a point where you've just got to admit defeat. I dimly recall seeing men in their 50s still walking around dressed as teddy boys in the late-70s and early-80s. Even as a child I knew it was heartbreaking.

So if you must experiment with tribery, the full bloom of youth is the only sensible time to do it. This week's *Scene Stealers* takes two slightly posh kids and tries to transform them into south London rappers. Just to make things that bit more difficult, both kids are firm tribe members already. The first, Nikita, is a 'plastic'. I'm pretty certain they've made this 'tribe' up especially for the programme: basically 'plastics' dress and act like they're in Girls Aloud. The other is Josh, who looks like Howard Jones and describes himself as 'an alternative 80s punk'. He's got a synth in his bedroom and knows the chords to Gary Numan's cars.

Josh and Nikita are whisked to London to meet their mentors – two aspiring rappers called Fret-Deezy and Rampz, who have 48 hours to turn them into convincing Channel U types who spit rhymes and rep their endz and all dat. It'd be more interesting to see Fret-Deezy and co become punks, but that's doubtless in store for week two.

193

In the meantime, this episode inevitably builds to a climax where Josh and Nikita have to rap in front of a panel of hip-hop 'experts'. Nikita's not bad. Josh grew up on a farm. How good do you think he's going to be?

No successful rapper has ever hailed from a farm. It's one of the immutable laws of creation. During his gruesome rap, you'll pray for the DFS ad to appear, just for some light relief. But it won't, because this is the BBC. You're stuck watching him flounder.

Overall: harmless fun, provided you're 19 or under. Any older and it'll make you feel like a wheezing cadaver. And that's not a tribe, that's your future, that is.

Vice President MILF [13 September 2008]

Pssst. You know the American election, yeah? That unfolding spectacle across the Atlantic; the one you've been a bit worried about of late? Well, the good news is you can stop fretting. It doesn't matter. It isn't real.

But don't take my word for it. I'm a cretin. Ask an egghead channel. As part of this week's US election mini-season, *President Hollywood* takes a squint at the curious co-dependent relationship between fictional and real US presidents. Each has informed and influenced the other, it seems: Hollywood and the entertainment industry swap positions as regularly as enthusiastic rutters in an even-handed one-night-stand. One minute Kennedy's giving the world of fiction a blowjob by providing a role model for noble decency that survives to this day, and the next, TV's slurping straight back, preparing the ground for Obama courtesy of *The West Wing*'s Matt Santos.

As a result, the lines between fiction and reality are almost hopelessly blurred. And probably a bit sticky. Voters would dearly love to elect some kind of mythic 'innocent outsider', the archetype for which was defined way back in 1939 by Jimmy Stewart in *Mr Smith Goes to Washington*. That's why both Obama and McCain attempt to portray themselves as warm-hearted agents of change.

Bush pulled the same trick, of course, although his down-home aw-shucks act rings fairly hollow these days, what with the war and the waterboarding and all that. Nixon's ignoble spell in the White House inspired a string of conspiracy thrillers and slippery, sinister commanders-in-chief. But Nixon impersonations are growing stale. If nothing else, Bush's legacy should at least provide an exciting new template for movie presidents: the war-mongering pseudo-rube.

Anyway, *President Hollywood* itself is a pretty interesting programme with one glaring flaw: it was made before anyone knew Sarah Palin existed. If, as the show suggests, every election campaign somehow resembles a movie plot, this was the moment a rough'n'ready Dolly Parton/Erin Brockovich character stepped in to dispense a little butt-kickin' straight talk on behalf of everywoman. Or at least that's how Team McCain is spinning it. As a way of distracting everyone from the perceived weaknesses of friendly-but-doddery McCain himself, it appears to have worked, and worked well.

But their inspiration seems to have been drawn not from Hollywood at all, but the world of reality TV. The structure is markedly similar. Palin arrived as a complete unknown, which meant the news media had to spend hours explaining who she was in little VT packages; bung some gaudy pop and a few lens flare effects on top and you could've been watching a contestant biog on *The X Factor*. It helps that she's hot. Hot for a politician, that is. In the street she's a standard Milf. Stand her next to 500-year-old John McCain and she's a Barely Legal covergirl. While half the electorate argue about her hardline stance on abortion, the other half is debating which hole they'd do her in first. Not out loud, you understand, but in their heads. Or online.

Furthermore, as a moose-hunting former beauty queen, Palin is a kooky character – precisely the sort of person a producer would home in on at the auditions like a dog sniffing meat. Obama's a stock character too, of course – the 'likable try-hard' – but although he ticks precisely the same reality boxes as Palin (unknown, good looking, etc), he's not as obviously kooky. Given a choice between 'kooky' and 'able' in a talent contest, reality viewers reward 'kooky' every time. And why shouldn't they? They're watching a TV show, not picking the next government.

Except they are in this case, obviously. It just doesn't feel that way. The unreal whiff of reality TV has overwhelmed the senses, and now, if some booming voice-of-God suddenly announced the whole thing would be decided in a live election day sing-off, none could raise an eyebrow in wholly honest surprise.

Another prick in the wall [20 September 2008]

I've seen some dumb things in my time. Take *Die Hard 4.0*. That's astronomically dumb; like being smacked in the face with a mallet made of super-compressed dumb.

Merely watching it made me feel like a simpleton reading a Ladybird book on a dodgem. Then there's *Bad Boys 2*, which I didn't so much 'watch' as 'catch glimpses of' – it was showing on a plane while I kept intermittently nodding off: literally every time I opened my eyes a car was corkscrewing through the air in slow motion, surrounded by explosions, and I'd go back to sleep. It was dumb enough to sedate me.

But these are Hollywood epics. It took millions of dollars and hundreds of hours of gruelling labour to create such monuments of transcendent stupidity, such overwhelming pyramids of thick. The BBC, brilliantly, has managed to bring us something equally (and shamelessly) dumb at a fraction of the cost. You'd glow with national pride, if only they hadn't done it by merely adapting a Japanese format.

I speak, dear reader, of *Hole in the Wall*, which is by far the stupidest gameshow I have ever seen. Just to be clear: in this context, 'stupid' isn't necessarily an insult. It's so openly, obviously and knowingly stupid, the whole thing is virtually immune to criticism. It's the television equivalent of a gurgling jester repeatedly honking a horn.

It's been described as 'human Tetris', which it is. Each week, two teams of celebrity contestants go head to head. One by one, the players stand on a pad in front of a pool while a wall moves slowly toward them, ready to shovel them into the water. The wall has a hole in it. A person-shaped hole. The sort of hole Wile E. Coyote would leave in the side of a cliff when blasted through it by a cannon. The contestant has to contort themselves into the right position, like a key going through a lock, so the wall can pass them by without knocking them into the drink.

Just to make things stupider, the contestants are required to wear figure-hugging silver Lycra jumpsuits designed to be as humiliating as possible. One of the Hairy Bikers takes part this week; scarcely a moment goes by without someone cracking a joke about how big and wobbly he looks. All of them sport visibly crushed goolies or spectacular cameltoes.

If you've ever wanted to see former Blue Peter presenter Zoe Salmon lying on her back and hoisting her hips in the air, here's your chance – although be warned: in a bid to ward off potential masturbators, Anton Du Beke's standing in the background wearing a costume so tight his nuts are spread halfway across his pelvis, as though they've been buttered into position with an enormous pallet knife.

Anyway, that's it. The first time you see the wall appearing and get a sense of how it works, I guarantee you'll laugh out loud. Then it happens again. And again. And again. And then you realise there's little or no variation: that's all that happens, for the full half-hour. You're watching celebrities being knocked into a pool, over and over, while the audience shrieks and applauds, and it all starts to resemble not just a dumb gameshow, but an almost nightmarishly dumb gameshow, the sort of gameshow you'd find in a dystopian science fiction film about an insane futuristic society. And you have to hold your head to quell the giddiness.

That's how dumb it is.

But really, so what? We've been here before. It's basically a Nintendo version of *It's a Knockout*. And, what's more, once you factor in the knowledge that the contestants are competing for charity, it looks less like the death of civilisation and more like a daft game at a village fete, writ large.

This is TV blowing off and giggling for 30 unrelenting minutes.

My only complaint is the variety of contestants: before the end of the series here's hoping that we'll get to see Simon Schama, Brian Sewell and Prince Philip adopting the position. And the Lycra.

The lost boy   [15 November 2008]

How many more series, do you reckon, before *The X Factor* ditches this whole 'singing' thing completely and just concentrates on the storylines? I ask in the wake of the shock decision last week to punt Laura White off the stage, which – according to a bunch of squeaking voices in the tabloids – was the most unexpected thing to happen on live television since 9/11, and only marginally less upsetting. Knockerbrains. They protest too much. It wasn't that big a surprise. It wasn't like a hatch suddenly opened in the middle of her forehead and a mouse rode out on a motorbike. The public merely exercised its right to vote for performers it felt sorry for and, unfortunately for Laura White, the same tabloids had sealed her fate by claiming she was seeing an '*X Factor* executive' and banging on and on about the age difference between them.

Incidentally, I've only just noticed I'm saying 'Laura White' instead of simply 'Laura'. They've started using the contestants' surnames this year, presumably because they're in danger of running out of unique forenames. They must've had 28 Lauras by now, surely?

Actually, I've just looked it up and they haven't. So why they've done it remains a mystery. Still, at least it means we get to enjoy Eoghan's preposterous moniker in full. It's Eoghan Quigg. Eoghan Quigg. That's not a name, that's a Countdown Conundrum. It looks like what happens when you hastily type a URL with your fingers over the wrong keys. If they still allowed text voting, he'd have been out weeks ago.

Or maybe not. Because the moment Eoghan bounds on stage, he triggers a dormant maternal instinct in millions of grandmas up and down the nation, enough to overcome any spelling barrier. Last week an elderly neighbour aahhed herself to death halfway through his performance of 'Anytime You Need a Friend'. Because Eoghan's got a baby face. And I mean that literally, as in someone's grafted a baby's face on to the front of his head. Tiny little eyes and a ruby-red mouth. He's like a cross between the Test Card clown and a crayon portrait of Jamie Oliver. Weird. Eerie. Like the spectral figure of an infant chimney sweep that suddenly appears in an upstairs window, gazing sadly at your back as you walk the grounds of a remote country mansion on a silent Christmas afternoon; alerted by an indefinable chill, you turn and, for the briefest moment, his wet, sorry eyes meet yours . . . and then he's gone.

That's Eoghan, the ghost of *X Factor* present. Even if he gets voted out, I'm frightened I'll still spot him intermittently in the dead of night, popping up on screen during old black-and-white films, pleading through the glass like a kitten in a microwave. Swear to God, if he's not gone by New Year's Eve I'm having my television exorcised by a priest.

Daniel Evans is this year's comedy entry, because he looks like Ricky Gervais and injects 400 tonnes of cheese into every word he sings. Simon and Louis are rude to his face every week, which is a bit rich since what he's doing sums up *The X Factor* as a whole better than 200 hours of the histrionic wibbly-wobbly showboating most of the other contestants offer. He's tacky and he sounds insincere. So what? The only difference between him and the average *X Factor* boot-camp joinee is volume. He can't belt it out like the others can. Surely that's a bonus in this case? At least he's not a fucking ghost.

Anyway, either Alexandra or Diana (assuming she recovers) should win. The former because she's got the best voice, the latter because she's got the most interesting voice: sometimes she lets out curious little peeps and whistles when she sings, as though she's accompanied by a baby bird randomly blowing air across the top of an empty milk bottle. Either that or there's something seriously wrong with my television. We'll know for sure when the priest gets here.

OK, Robert . . . [22 November 2008]

Must be nearly Christmas: *I'm A Celebrity . . . Get Me Out Of Here!* is back. How many times have we heard that wah-wah calypso atrocity of a theme tune now, looping as a music bed while Ant and Dec read out the voting details? They've added an extra little saxophone bit to it this year, which, as it turned out, provided just enough novelty to distract me from the noose I'd started tying. A rare humanitarian gesture from ITV there.

I'm writing this on Tuesday morning. So far, Brian Paddick's got his bum out and that's about it. I don't recall previous series being this light on incident, even at this early stage. They need more drink.

We want the Page Three girl to flip out and start knocking pots over. We want Esther in a fist fight. We want Kilroy-Silk to drop his guard and say something so offensively terrible he has to live in the jungle for ever rather than risk the flight home.

Still, what with reality show twists being what they are, let's assume at least four of the celebrities will have killed and eaten each other by the time you read this, and another four will have been helicoptered in to take their place. I'm guessing Georgina Baillie, Ian Brown, Martin Daniels, and the plastinated body of Princess Margaret, on wheels.

I get £10 per correct answer, payable by YOU. There'll be a knock at the door in the next few minutes. That's me. Collecting. Get your wallet.

Aside from Kilroy, the rest of the camp is pretty nondescript. Carly Zucker freaks me out because her name sounds like a baby trying to say my name. Either Martina Navratilova or Joe Swash will win; the former because she's strong-willed and funny, and the latter because he's dopey and chuckly and looks like a half grown-up version of the sort of grinning freckled ginger boy you'd see painted on the front of a packet of cake mix circa 1978. He's upholding what's become a grand tradition for ex-Albert Square residents: *I'm a Celebrity* is now the official decompression chamber for anyone leaving *EastEnders*. There's probably a door somewhere round the back of the Queen Vic that magically deposits them in the jungle.

Being an emetophobe, I found the first of the signature 'eating' tasks difficult to watch, thanks to Swash's wussy habit of violently retching each time he popped another insect in his mouth. It sounded like his stomach was repeatedly yanking his throat in the belief it was some kind of escape rope, and frankly it was uncalled for.

The dishes served up were nowhere near as disgusting as the kangaroo anus chewed on by Matt Willis a few years ago. They still haven't topped that, and on current form they're unlikely to either. The tasks badly need an overhaul. They're getting too complex and samey. Testicle-eating, ravine-crossing, swamp-dunking . . . we've seen it all before.

What's required is a fresh blast of brutal simplicity. Here are some cheap and effective Bushtucker Trials they could do tomorrow, offered free of charge in the hope that Robert Kilroy-Silk has to tackle them on live television:

1. OK Robert, you have four minutes to jerk off five of our unit drivers. As you can see, they're wearing blindfolds and earplugs; they think you're Esther Rantzen. Try to imagine the sort of technique she'd apply, and mimic that.

2. OK Robert, you have 30 seconds to blind this kangaroo with a tent peg.

3. OK Robert, here's a tab of breakdown-strength LSD. Put it on your tongue, and step into this cave full of glow-in-the-dark dolls' heads. You've got six hours to find the one that looks like it's crying.

4. OK Robert, here's a loaf of bread. You've got 10 minutes to stick the whole thing up your backside. Tear it, moisten it, roll it – whatever helps. But the entire loaf has to go or it's no stars for the camp.

Any of those would be a TV moment to cherish. Write them down, ITV. WRITE THEM DOWN.

CHAPTER ELEVEN

In which deadly marketing strategies are brainstormed, conspiracy theorists grow upset for the 85th time, and Britney Spears is depicted naked

Killvertising [16 June 2008]

Pity ITV. No really – drop to your knees and pity it. Last week the culture secretary Andy Burnham refused to accept a European Union directive that would have paved the way for product placement on British television. On hearing the news, ITV's face fell. Its shares soon followed suit.

As advertising revenue continues to dwindle, money is leaking from ITV's business model like blood from a harpooned steak. Cutbacks will be inevitable, and chances are we'll see the results on screen. Forget dumbing-down; fear cheapening-up. Instead of a star-studded *Doctor Who* knock-off stuffed with pricey CGI dinosaurs, the next series of *Primeval* will be a reality show in which Patrick Kielty and Lembit Opik drive around Staines in an ice-cream van trying to catch dogs in a net. *Loose Women* will become *Loose Woman*, a daytime talk show in which a menopausal fishwife stands alone in a cupboard-sized studio, staring into a mirror and gossiping about herself. And in a bid to cut down on location fees, from now on the detectives in *Lewis* will be solving murders that have taken place in their imaginations; each episode will consist of nothing but footage of Lawrence Fox and Kevin Whately sitting in chairs screwing their eyes up and frowning a bit.

Boo hoo hoo. Bad news for telly.

On the face of it, Burnham's reasons for rejecting product placement couldn't be more sound. Trust in television is already at an all-time low following last year's string of call-in scandals, when viewers were effectively pickpocketed by the box in the corner of their living room. Many people now stare at their TV set for hours not because they like the programmes it shows, but because they're worried it might start nicking stuff while their back's turned. And Burnham recognises that blurring the line between shows and ads won't exactly help matters. 'Product placement exacerbates this decline in trust and contaminates our programmes,' he said. 'As a viewer I don't want to feel the script has been written by the commercial marketing director.'

He's got a point there, although it might be worth giving the commercial marketing director a go – just once, in the spirit of fair-ness – to see what he comes up with. Love in the Time of the Arrow Information Paradox? The New Adventures of Spreadsheet, PI? Brand Awareness Way? OK, so the dialogue might be impenetrable, but it couldn't possibly be as boring as the latest Poliakoff exercise in mastur-guff.

Anyway, Burnham's right. But the world is wrong. ITV's got to pay for its programmes somehow and, in the current environment, prohibiting product placement altogether seems a bit like telling a bunch of starving plane crash survivors shivering in a lifeboat that they're not allowed to start eating corpses for sustenance. No one wants to switch on the box and see Fireman Sam banging on about the great taste of Disprin, but desperate times call for desperate measures.

One solution is to allow product placement after all, provided it's subtle, and provided the advertisers have no say in the editorial content. Lingering pack shots, or dialogue such as, 'Taggart, according to an animated multimedia text I've just received on my new Sony Ericcson t85X, there's been a murder' are out, obviously. But I for one couldn't give a toss if Doc Martin is shown spreading Marmite – proper, branded Marmite – on his toast. Actually, I don't care if he spreads it on his balls, because I don't watch *Doc Martin*, but you get the point – if Marmite wants to pay to stock his on-screen kitchen, and that makes the show cheaper, which in turn means fewer ad breaks in the middle of it, therefore allowing me to spend more time wallowing in a world of uninterrupted fiction, then I'm happy. Well, OK, not happy – never happy – but not much closer to suicide either. That's a plus.

Another option is to advertise in new and exciting ways. A few weeks ago Honda ran a live skydiving commercial. Why stop there? Why not stage your own advertorial Olympics consisting solely of 30-second sponsored events broadcast live across the globe? (Nanoseconds after typing this I've realised it's a brilliant idea, so any ad agencies reading this should consider it copyrighted by me as of now. Use it if you like, but it'll cost you – give my slice of the royalties to Amnesty International, just to annoy the Chinese.)

Or turn hardcore. Let's say you're trying to launch a new soft drink. Traditionally you'd have to spend millions on a commercial, and millions more booking airtime for it. Screw that. Here's what you do: put up one billboard. Just one. Somewhere on a route near Buckingham Palace or Downing Street. Point a camera at it 24/7. Then simply pay a sniper to assassinate someone of global importance when they pass in front of it. Bingo! The clip will run on an endless loop on every news channel in the world, for eternity. Even as viewers gasp in horror watching the victim's head explode like a watermelon, they'll simultaneously be thinking 'What's that? New Plum-Flavoured Pepsi? Cool!' each time a chunk of skull flies past your logo.

Talk about brand awareness. That's the future, right there. All it needs is its own twatty marketing-speak buzzterm – something like 'Killvertising' or 'Atroci-publicity' – and within about six months it'll even seem halfway acceptable. Go creatives. Go you.

Love and hat   [23 June 2008]

Know what I've decided to hate this week? Hats. Yes, hats. Who do hats think they are? They contribute nothing to society, and don't even display basic manners. Has a hat ever held a door open for you? No. It hasn't.

While the rest of us work our fingers to the bone, sweating litres, trying to keep this crazy world going, hats just lounge around on top of our heads like they own the place. If you're currently wearing a hat, take it off and stamp on it. Down with hats. All hats are wankers.

And never was there a more sickening display of archetypal hat arrogance than ladies' day at Royal Ascot, which took place last week. The British press seems to view it as a harmless, tittersome annual tradition-cum-photo opportunity; a playful contest in which an assortment of leathery upper-class crones and willowy swan-necked debutantes compete to see who can wear the silliest piece of headgear.

Every year it's the same thing: a 200-year-old countess you've never heard of, who closely resembles a Cruella De Vil mannequin assembled entirely from heavily wrinkled scrotal tissue that's been soaked in tea for the past eight decades, attempts to draw attention away from her sagging neck – a droopy curtain of skin that hangs so low she has to repeatedly kick it out of her path as she crosses the royal compound – by balancing the millinery equivalent of Bilbao's Guggenheim museum on her head, and winds up forming the centrepiece of a light-hearted photomontage in the centre of whatever newspaper you happen to be reading that day, accompanied by a picture of Princess Eugenie in a headdress, and some milky underfed heiress with the physique of a violin-playing mantis, wearing nothing but a diamante cornflake on each nipple and a hat made out of second-hand dentures or something equally avant-garde.

That's how ladies' day at Ascot comes across in the papers. Pro-Hattist propaganda, plain and simple. Tee hee hee, look at us hats – aren't we just marvellous? Isn't hat-wearing just peachy? Make more hats, make more hats. Come on, humans – make more hats. And we lap it up.

Honestly. It's stomach-churning.

Still, such hatstravagance pales into minnow-like insignificance compared to some of the hats on display in the Tower of London. I went there somewhat randomly last week, accompanying a friend from out of town. And at first it was fun, playing tourist in my own city. I chortled at a beefeater. Gawped at a bit of old stone. Sniffed a few ravens. As you do.

And then we headed for the jewel house to see all the crowns and shit. We ambled in and immediately found ourselves part of a slow-moving caterpillar of sightseers, which shuffled through the vaults with hushed, painstaking reverence, past immense glass boxes displaying gaudy old tat of mind-mangling financial value.

There were gigantic golden spoons. Gigantic golden soup tureens. Royal gowns apparently woven from angel hair and diamond string. Countless sceptres and orbs. God knows why you'd need one sceptre, let alone a four-metre cabinet full of them, but here they were regardless, each more gilded and unnecessary than the last. P Diddy would look round the room and laugh at the absurdity. It took the concept of 'bling' and pushed it beyond comprehension.

But it was the crowns that did it for me. What are crowns? They're hats with ideas above their station. Impractical hats at that. They're cumbersome, fragile, and disappointingly uniform. Most have got bloody great holes in the middle. King Frederick the Great once said, 'A crown is merely a hat that lets the rain in', and whoever the hell he was, he sounds like someone who'd know.

The sole purpose of a crown is to make anyone not wearing one feel like an insignificant pauper. They're obscene to the point of satire. If Donald Trump walked through Manhattan wearing a top hat made of banknotes, we'd call him a crass, tasteless idiot. Yet each year, at the state opening of parliament, the Queen rocks up wearing the Imperial State Crown – a hideous ornamental nest containing almost 3,000 diamonds, 277 pearls, 17 sapphires, 11 emeralds and four rare rubies. Or five rare rubies, depending on which bit of the internet you ask, because it's encrusted with so many wildly expensive jewels, no one seems entirely sure quite how many there actually are.

One thing's for certain – the Queen could, if she so chose, open parliament by whipping off the crown and saying: 'You know what? This is absolutely taking the piss, isn't it? This hat's got to be worth at least nine hospitals. And I don't even need it: there's loads more of these things back at the Tower. Tell you what, let's flog this one to a Russian oligarch and use the money for saving lives or research-ing sustainable energy sources or something.'

She could do that. She's the Queen. But no. She'd rather sit there balancing a pile of unimaginable riches on her head while we scrabble for beans in the dirt.

This tells you all you need to know about the sort of person who voluntarily elects to wear a hat. And I'm not simply bitter because I've got a weird, boxlike head that no hat or cap or woollen beanie can sit comfortably on. No. That's not the root of it at all.

The graveyard of privacy   [7 July 2008]

I've got the opening scene of a dystopian thriller all worked out. It's a hot summer night in a typical suburban flat. A young woman (let's call her Alison) stands over the body of her boyfriend, who she's just killed in a fit of madness. A crime of passion. She didn't mean to do it, but gah – now look at the mess she's made.

She's quivering, gazing down at the body like someone staring into a hitherto undiscovered dimension filled with swirling nightmarish tapestries, still clutching the murder weapon in her dismal little fist, breathing through her nose like a cornered church mouse, and somewhere in the background the phone is ringing. Ringing, ringing, ringing. It takes her an age to notice. In a daze she answers it, her eyes still harpooned to the corpse. She presses the receiver to her ear and someone in a call centre greets her by name.

'Hello Alison,' says the voice, which – while friendly – sounds as though it's reading from a card, for the 50,000th time. 'I'm calling from OmniCorps Ltd, and according to our predictive software there's a 97.8% chance you've just murdered your boyfriend. Now, we're obligated to pass this information on to the authorities, which means the police are already on their way, but before they arrive we'd like to offer you the opportunity to take advantage of an exciting offer. So if you'd like to go to your window and look outside, our escape van should be arriving any moment . . .'

Alison parts the curtains: it's already there, impatiently tooting. 'Just get in the van,' says the voice. 'Get in, and we'll take care of the rest.'

Still in a trance, she goes downstairs. She gets in. In the back are three other people. All have committed similar crimes within the past hour. Speckled with blood, they stare at each other in crazy silence as the van pulls away.

It turns out that the marketing arm of OmniCorps Ltd has been automatically tracking the entire nation's internet activity, viewing habits, credit card transactions, use of public transport etc for years, in order to build an exhaustive database of consumer profiles. They've become so good at profiling, they're able to accurately predict whether a given individual will commit a crime, and if so, what time of day they'll do it. They're like the 'Pre-Cog' department in *Minority Report*, except that, instead of arresting murderers, they offer them an escape route. But once Alison gets in the van, she's driven off to a gigantic underground sweatshop, where she and thousands of other murderers are doomed to spend the rest of their lives slaving on a production line, creating bargain-basement products for – you guessed it – OmniCorps Ltd.

That's the basic idea. It needs work. OmniCorps Ltd needs a better name, obviously. Also the story doesn't have a second or third act (some sort of prison breakout is in order, I guess). Worst of all, our main protagonist is a murderer, so the average non-murdering audience member might find it hard to empathise with her. Originally, Alison was a man; I made her a woman to sweeten the pill a tad, but maybe her boyfriend needs to have been a serial cheat, or a violent drunk, or at the very least have a taste for plodding indie stadium-rock or something, so we can comfortably forgive her for bashing his skull in with a steak tenderiser or whatever she used.

Anyway, it'd be worth watching, if only because the premise is 23% more plausible now than it was five years ago when I thought of it. Back then, my biggest fear was the mild intrusion of Nectar points. Now I simply assume everything I do is comprehensively probed by the invisible fingers of the central scrutiniser as a matter of course.

In my flat, there's a full-length balcony window, with no curtains, situated right outside my bedroom. I sleep naked, so if I go for a piss in the middle of the night, I end up flashing the neighbours twice – once on the way to the bathroom, and once on the way back. First time it happened, I vowed to put up an opaque blind. But I haven't. Partly because after a while I figured, hey, they've seen it all before – why deprive them now? But mainly because I live in London, European Graveyard of Privacy.

This place is a joke. Each day I move around carrying a mobile phone (traceable) and an Oyster card (trackable), monitored, on average, by 10 times as many CCTV cameras as there are in the Big

Brother house. Wherever I go, a gigantic compound eye peers at the back of my neck. I'm another bustling dot in the ant farm.

Hide indoors? Ha. I've got Sky TV. I can't even draw the curtains and watch *Bargain Hunt* without some whirring electronic prick making a note of what I'm doing. And forget the internet. Today I blew 20 minutes pointlessly looking up an old kids' TV show called *Animal Kwackers* on YouTube. A record of this decision will soon be automatically winging its way to Viacom. I haven't just wasted my own time; I've wasted theirs too. The way things are going, I half-expect to hear a quiet electric 'peep' noise each time I flush the toilet; another bowel movement logged by Bumland Security.

But I don't get angry. I shrug. They won. They won years ago. Like a bear in a zoo, I can rub my head against the wall in despair, or ignore the onlookers and forlornly shuffle around as normal. Past that balcony window. Where each time they get an eyeful, an electric peep sounds somewhere in the dark.

Yeah. Never mind a boot stamping on a human face forever. A smug electric peep each time they catch sight of your bumhole. That's your future, right there.

Naked emperors of Pluto [14 July 2008]

I've got a theory – an untested, unprovable theory – that the more interesting your life is at any given point, the less lurid and spectacular your dreams will be. Think of it as a balancing procedure carried out by the brain to stop you getting bored to death.

If your waking life is mundane, it'll inject some thrills into your night-time imaginings to maintain a healthy overall fun quotient. So if you work in a cardboard box factory, and your job is to stare at the side of each box as it passes along a conveyor belt, to ensure they're all uniform and boxy enough – and you do this all day, every day, until your mind grows so dissociated and numb you can scarcely tell where the cardboard ends and your body begins – when your daily routine is THAT dull, chances are you'll spend each night dreaming you're the Emperor of Pluto, wrestling a 6-foot green jaguar during a meteor storm in the desert just outside Vegas.

All well and good in the world of dreams. But if you continue to believe you're the Emperor of Pluto after you've woken up, and you go into work and start knocking the boxes around with a home-made sceptre while screaming about your birthright, you're in trouble.

I mention this because recently I've found myself bumping into people – intelligent, level-headed people – who are sincerely prepared to entertain the notion that there might be something in some of the less lurid 9/11 conspiracy theories doing the rounds. They mumble about the 'controlled demolition' of WTC 7 (oft referred to as 'the third tower'), or posit the notion that the Bush administration knew 9/11 was coming and let it happen anyway. I mean, you never know, right? Right? And did I tell you I'm the Emperor of Pluto?

The glaring problem – and it's glaring in 6,000 watt neon, so vivid and intense you can see it from space with your eyes glued shut – with any 9/11 conspiracy theory you care to babble can be summed up in one word: paperwork.

Imagine the paperwork. Imagine the level of planning, recruitment, coordination, control, and unbelievable nerve required to pull off a conspiracy of that magnitude. Really picture it in detail. At the very least you're talking about hiring hundreds of civil servants cold-hearted enough to turn a blind eye to the murder of thousands of their fellow countrymen. If you were dealing with faultless, emotionless robots – maybe. But this almighty conspiracy was presumably hatched and executed by fallible humans. And if there's one thing we know about humans, it's that our inherent unreliability will always derail the simplest of schemes.

It's hard enough to successfully operate a video shop with a staff of three, for Christ's sake, let alone slaughter thousands and convince the world someone else was to blame.

That's just one broad objection to all the bullshit theories. But try suggesting it to someone in the midst of a 9/11 fairytale reverie, and they'll pull a face and say, 'Yeah, but . . .' and start banging on about some easily misinterpreted detail that 'makes you think' (when it doesn't) or 'contradicts the official story' (when you misinterpret it). Like nutbag creationists, they fixate on thinly spread, cherry-picked nuggets of 'evidence' and ignore the thundering mass of data pointing the other way.

And when repeatedly pressed on that one, basic, overall point – that a conspiracy this huge would be impossible to pull off – they huff and whine and claim that unless you've sat through every nanosecond of *Loose Change* (the conspiracy flick *du jour*) and personally refuted every one of its carefully spun 'findings' before their very eyes, using a spirit level and calculator, you have no right to an opinion on the subject.

Oh yeah? So if my four-year-old nephew tells me there's a magic leprechaun in the garden I have to spend a week meticulously peering underneath each individual blade of grass before I can tell him he's wrong, do I?

Look hard enough, and dementedly enough, and you can find 'proof' that Kevin Bacon was responsible for 9/11 – or the 1987 Zeebrugge ferry disaster, come to that. It'd certainly make for a more interesting story, which is precisely why several thousand well-meaning people would go out of their way to believe it. Throughout my twenties I earnestly believed Oliver Stone's account of the JFK assassination. Partly because of the compelling (albeit wildly selective) way the 'evidence' was blended with fiction in his 1991 movie – but mainly because I WANTED to believe it. Believing it made me feel important.

Embrace a conspiracy theory and suddenly you're part of a gang sharing privileged information; your sense of power and dignity rises a smidgen and this troublesome world makes more sense, for a time. You've seen through the matrix! At last you're alive! You ARE the Emperor of Pluto after all!

Except – ahem – you're only deluding yourself, your majesty. Because to believe the 'system' is trying to control you is to believe it considers you worth controlling in the first place. The reality – that 'the man' is scarcely competent enough to control his own bowels, and doesn't give a toss about you anyway – is depressing and emasculating; just another day in the cardboard box factory. And that's no place for an imaginary emperor, now, is it?

Britney nude [NSFW]

Miley Cyrus, Angelina, Israel vs Palestine, iPhone, 9/11 conspiracy, Facebook, MySpace, and Britney Spears nude. And not forgetting Second Life, Paris Hilton, YouTube, Lindsay Lohan, World of Warcraft, *The Dark Knight*, Radiohead and Barack Obama. Oh, and great big naked tits. In 3D.

Let me explain. Last week, I wrote a piece on 9/11 conspiracy theories which virtually broke the *Guardian* website as thousands of 'truthers' (painfully earnest online types who sincerely believe 9/11 was an inside job) poured through the walls to unfurl their two pence worth. Some outlined alternative 'theories'. Some mistakenly equated dismissing the conspiracy theories with endorsing the Bush administration. Some simply wailed, occasionally in CAPITALS. Others, correctly, identified me as a paid-off establishment shill acting under instructions from the CIA.

Now to sit here and painstakingly rebut everything the truthers said would take three months and several hundred pages, and would be a massive waste of the world's time, because ultimately I'm right and they're wrong – well-meaning, but wrong. What's more, I've woken up with an alarming fever and am sweating like a miner as I type these words. On the cusp of hallucinating. Consequently my brain isn't working properly; it feels like it's been marinaded in petrol, then wrapped in a warm towel. So I'm hardly at my sharpest. Actually, sod it: you win, truthers. I give up. You're 100% correct. Inside job, clearly.

Whatever. Now pass the paracetamol.

Anyway, because it contained the words '9/11 conspiracy', the article generated loads of traffic for the *Guardian* site, which in turn means loads of advertising revenue. And in this day and age, what with the credit crunch and the death of print journalism and everything, the use of attention-grabbing keywords is becoming standard practice. 'Search engine optimisation', it's known as, and it's the journalistic equivalent of a classified ad that starts with the word 'SEX!' in large lettering, and 'Now that we've got your attention . . .' printed below it in smaller type.

For instance, according to the latest *Private Eye*, journalists writing articles for the *Telegraph* website are being actively encouraged to include oft-searched-for phrases in their copy. So an article about shoe sales among young women would open: 'Young women – such as Britney Spears – are buying more shoes than ever.'

On the one hand, you could argue this is nothing new; after all, for years newspapers have routinely jazzed up dull print articles with photographs of attractive female stars (you know the sort of thing: a giant snap of Keira Knightley doing her *Atonement* wet-T-shirt routine to illustrate a report about the state of Britain's fountain manufacturers). But at least in those instances the actual text of the article itself survived unscathed. There's something uniquely demented about slotting specific words and phrases into a piece simply to con people into reading it. Why bother writing a news article at all? Why not just scan in a few naked photos and have done with it?

And if you do persevere with search-engine-optimised news reports, where do you draw the line? Next time a bomb goes off, are we going to read 'Terror outrage: BRITNEY, ANGELINA and OBAMA all unaffected as hundreds die in SEXY agony'?

And wait, it gets worse. These phrases don't just get lobbed in willy-nilly. No. A lot of care and attention goes into their placement. Apparently the average reader quickly scans each page in an 'F-pattern': reading along the top first, then glancing halfway along the line below, before skimming their eye downward along the left-hand side. If there's nothing of interest within that golden 'F' zone, he or she will quickly clear off elsewhere.

Which means your modern journalist is expected not only to shoehorn all manner of hot phraseology into their copy, but to try and position it all in precisely the right place. That's an alarming quantity of unnecessary shit to hold in your head while trying to write a piece about the unions. Sorry, SEXUAL unions. Mainly, though, it's just plain undignified: turning the journalist into the equivalent of a reality TV wannabe who turns up to the auditions in a gaudy fluorescent thong in a desperate bid to be noticed.

And for the consumer, it's just one more layer of distracting crud

– the bane of the 21st century. Distracting crud comes in countless forms – from the onscreen clutter of 24-hour news stations to the winking, blinking ads on every other web page. These days, each separate square inch of everything is simultaneously vying for your attention, and the overall effect is to leave you feeling bewildered, distanced, feverish and slightly insane. Or maybe that's just me, today.

Actually, it's definitely just me. Like I say, I'm ill, my brain's not working. Which is why opening this piece with a slew of hot search terms probably wasn't a brilliant wheeze.

Perhaps if I close with a selection of the LEAST searched-for terms ever, I can redress the balance. Worth a shot. Um . . .

JOHN SELWYN GUMMER . . . PATRICK KIELTY NUDE . . . UNDERWHELMING KNITTING PATTERNS . . . FULLY CLOTHED BABES.

There. That should do it.

On tonsillitis [28 July 2008]

Regular followers of my dismal 'existence' may recall last week that I broke off in the middle of a thrilling piece about internet search terms to complain I had some sort of fever and boo-hoo-hoo poor me. Turns out I had tonsillitis. Now, if you're anything like I was a fortnight ago, the mention of tonsillitis right there won't do anything for you. I mean, what is it anyway? A kiddywink illness? Bit of a sore throat? Pah. That's how people who've never had tonsillitis tend to think about it. I certainly did. Whereas now, I can confidently report that it's worse – far worse – than international terrorism and child abuse combined.

Why didn't I know this before? Either there's some sort of weird conspiracy going on that involves the general public collectively underplaying its horrors, or I just didn't listen whenever someone recounted what happened when they had it. I suspect the latter. I suspect each time they opened their mouth I thought: 'Boo-hoo, bit of a sore throat, yeah?' in a loop, trying to disguise my contempt as I stared at their stupid babbling face, waiting for my turn to speak. And I think everyone's done this. No one's listened to the sufferers, ever. Not even their own doctors. And that's why we all, as a nation, have failed to acknowledge how nasty tonsillitis actually is. Yup. I blame society. Now, it's possible we never 'got' tonsillitis because the survivors' descriptions weren't lurid enough. Let's redress the balance.

It starts with an achy throat. One day I went 'ahh' in the mirror, and glimpsed some kind of mouth ulcer at the back of my throat. Urgh, I thought, reaching for the antiseptic mouthwash. That should take care of it.

A week later, a heavy flu-like sensation suddenly descended; a sultry cloud locking itself into position over the sun. I've got a cold, guessed my idiot brain. I lay on my sofa, sweating and listlessly channel-surfing, until I realised I couldn't even follow the plot of *Celebrity MasterChef*. I crawled into bed at 9 p.m. Next morning I had to write last Monday's column, but the sweats and shivers were so bad I couldn't type properly. Did I go to the doctor? No. Because I live in London, where to get a doctor's appointment you have to consult Old Moore's Almanack six months in advance to work out when you're going to be ill and book an appointment accordingly. And also because that afternoon we were filming for a TV show I've written. We were shooting outdoors in the rain.

During the shoot, I spent most of my time staring anxiously at a helicopter overhead, convinced it was planning to crash into us as part of some terrorist attack. I'd become feverish and paranoid, like Ray Liotta in *Goodfellas* minus the coke jitters. Meanwhile, my throat throbbed like a beaten stepchild.

That night I thrashed in bed, sweating like a punctured dinghy, unsure if I was still outside watching the helicopter or not. This went on for six hours until I passed out, only to lurch awake 45 minutes later and discover I could scarcely swallow or speak. My voice had mutated beyond recognition. When I spoke, I sounded like Janet Street-Porter slowly listing vowels through a hose.

I went to the mirror, opened wide and peered in. The back of my throat now resembled a sandblasted foetus, or an endoscopic close-up of a diseased bowel. My tonsils had been dragged down a gravel path and slammed in a car door. An emergency appointment was in order.

Two hours later an appalled doctor was gazing into my raging, pustulated throat and bollocking me for not seeking help sooner. Prescribing antibiotics, she warned things would get worse before they got better. She was right. The fever is the easy bit. The throat itself: that's the thing.

It isn't even your throat any more. It's torment in a pipe. Swallowing feels like someone forcing a spiked kneecap down your neck, and for some reason, your mouth decides this represents a golden opportunity to generate gallons more saliva than usual, so you get to experience the joy of agonised swallowing again and again, around the clock. You can't sleep through or ignore it. It's a constant jabbing that slowly drives you mad. Within 48 hours I'd gone feral: staggering around my flat like a confused and angry animal, slapping the walls and howling inside my head.

Not that there's much energy for slapping walls. Not when you can't eat food. Forget solids. Even a glass of water becomes a cup of shattered twigs. Ice cream or scrambled egg: that's your lot. Gargling with warm salt water is the sole thing that buys five minutes of relief. Before you know it, the kettle and sink hold the same significance as a crack pipe. You're constantly Winehousin' for saline.

And it goes on and on, until somewhere round day three, when you're seriously contemplating suicide (anything but hanging, what with these tonsils) the drugs kick in and the cloud starts lifting. And you run out into the street (because you can run again!) and collar passers-by (because you can talk again!) and you try to tell them just how bad tonsillitis is. But they're staring at your stupid wobbling face, waiting for their turn to speak.

If this strikes you as a trivial subject to write about, you're wrong. Really. Bollocks to the rest of you. I could've sat through live 3D news footage of some gruesome bloody war, watching starving women and children being machine gunned in the face by Terminator rebels, and I'd have just shrugged. So what. Stop crying. They're only bullets. Try having my throat. Try some genuine suffering, you pussies.

The worst that could happen   [4 August 2008]

Here's a real-life nightmare for you. Late last Wednesday night, passengers on a Canadian Greyhound bus had their enjoyment of the on-board movie, *Zorro*, soured when one of their fellow travellers suddenly launched into an appallingly violent and apparently unprovoked attack on the stranger sitting beside him. Following a frenzied assault, the attacker decapitated his victim with a hunting knife, then held up the head for the horrified passengers (who by now were standing outside the bus, holding the doors shut) to look at.

Every aspect of this story is terrifying. I don't know what frightens me most. There's the fear of suddenly falling victim to a violent killer, obviously. Then there's the behaviour of the killer himself: according to witnesses, he'd been sitting on the bus behaving entirely normally for at least an hour before the attack. What if he'd been behaving entirely normally his entire life, then suddenly went crazy without any warning whatsoever? What if that could happen to anyone? One minute you're sitting at home watching *Cash in the Attic*, the next you're nodding in slavish agreement as a six-foot crocodile with fruit-machine reels for eyes commands you to torch the house next door. How long does it take to go irretrievably mad anyway? Is there a speed cracking-up record? It's not a comforting thought.

Then there's fear number three: the thought of witnessing a life-changing atrocity first-hand. Being hopelessly morbid, I contemplate this sort of thing all the time. For instance, when sitting in a cinema, I often get slightly distracted by the thought that a bomb might be about to go off. Once a thought like that has entered my head, I can't shift it; I imagine the flash and the blast and the screaming. Bits of kidney landing in my popcorn, that kind of thing. You try concentrating on *Mamma Mia!* with a brain full of ominous foreboding. It's impossible.

Someone cleverer than me once described this condition as having an 'Alfred Hitchcock mind', in reference to the way many of Hitchcock's movies contain a sequence in which a scene of everyday mundanity is given a macabre spin by the viewer's certain knowledge that something terrible is about to happen (*The Birds*, in particular, is full of moments like this). I prefer to think of it as being perpetually stuck in the opening moments of an episode of *Casualty*, where every stepladder, plug socket, and loose-lidded food processor is a grinning, lurking deathtrap.

Perhaps you normalities pity us sufferers. Wrong. You're hardly awake. We live on the edge. Wouldn't you prefer each of your daily activities to come imbued with this kind of nervous frisson? I can scarcely cross the street without imagining, in punishing detail, how it would feel to be run over by an oil tanker – to feel my own sense of awareness becoming distorted in new and grotesque ways as my brain is squished between the treads of its tyres. Would I hear my own skull pop open beneath the wheel? Or would I be unconscious by then? That's the level of grisly contemplation I like to wallow in. Consequently, each time I successfully make it to the opposite pavement, I feel genuinely glad to be alive. Who needs extreme sports? Why jump from a plane for kicks? Jesus, don't you have an imagination? Sod that trip to the airfield. Stay in the kitchen, where you could potentially slip on a floor tile and skewer your eye on a potato peeler. That's all the excitement you need.

A weird side-effect of this frankly dubious mindset is that, while I love gruesome fictional horror (which tickles those same morbid synapses for entertainment), I can't bear to witness real-life nastiness. Recently someone tried to show me a YouTube clip of some unfortunate yobbo having his leg crushed beneath a collapsing brick wall. But I couldn't even listen to the damn thing, let alone look at it. Genuine violence and gore tends to leave me feeling dizzy, cold, and somewhat changed. Not everyone is the same. Apparently, said YouTube video is accompanied by all manner of 'LOL his knee iz shattered!!!' user comments, left by warm-hearted viewers who found the spectacle as gently amusing as a *Vicar of Dibley* Christmas special.

Perhaps I should toughen up. I recently spent some time on the set of a forthcoming apocalyptic TV show involving lots of fake blood and gore. For several days on the trot, there were smashed cars, flames, smoke, corpses and exposed innards everywhere I looked. At first it's genuinely depressing. Then you grow warmly accustomed to it. Before long I was kicking dead women and children around for a laugh. It's probably desensitised me just enough to cope well in the immediate aftermath of a small nuclear explosion. While everyone else is screaming just because a few charred limbs are dangling from lamp posts, I'll be calmly scouring the rubble for weapons. All the better to fight gangs of marauding bikers with.

In fact, I'm wondering if it's worth setting up some kind of holiday theme park specifically aimed at desensitising visitors to real-life atrocities they may encounter in the future. Basically, it would be exactly the same as Center Parcs, but with burnt trees and ultra-realistic latex corpses strewn around the place, some of them featuring state-of-the-art in-built animatronics, so they can slowly claw their way across the ground toward your kids, screaming and twitching with their eyes popping out. Hey, it's character-building. A holiday with real purpose. Beat that.

The great taste of risk   [11 August 2008]

Here's a news story guaranteed to provoke a fusillade of indignant spluttering, courtesy of your inner Clarkson: German politicians are reportedly planning to ban Kinder Surprise eggs on the grounds that they're a safety hazard.

In case you're not familiar with the concept, the 'surprise' inside each Kinder egg is a cheapo little toy housed within a plastic shell. Anyway, the Germans are worried that hungry, gurgling kiddy-winks might mistake the gifts for food and wind up choking to death. 'Children can't differentiate between toys and nutritional items,' said Miriam Gruss, a member of the German parliamentary children's committee.

What, really? Don't get me wrong – I think children are idiots. But even I find that statement a tad unfair and sweeping. I used to have a spud gun when I was a kid. In case you're not familiar with that concept either, it was a small metal pistol that fired chunks of potato. Not once did I aim the potato at anyone. Or try to deep-fry the gun. And I was thick as shit. I guess it was luck.

In fact my run of luck was pretty impressive. Other toys I failed to ingest include a Scalextric, several boxes of space Lego, the board games Operation and Mousetrap, and a complete collection of Paul Daniels' TV Magic Tricks – even though the latter included an egg-shaped gizmo called The Magic Egg. Somehow, miraculously, my conker-sized kiddywink brain managed to differentiate it from a real egg. Thus my life was saved by a whisker.

Gruss won't countenance such a slapdash approach to child safety. Not on her watch. 'It's a sad fact,' she said. 'Kinder Surprise eggs have to go.'

As you can imagine, the committee's proclamation has already caused a fair bit of outraged huffing, not least from the manufacturer, Ferrero, which until now has perhaps been best known for providing the catering at badly dubbed ambassadors' receptions in the late 1980s.

'There is absolutely no evidence that the Kinder Surprise eggs, as a combination of toy and foodstuff, are dangerous,' said Ferrero's spokeswoman. Then she snatched a golden-foil-wrapped nobbly chocolate bollock from a nearby silver platter and added, 'Monsieur, with these Rocher, you are really spoiling us.'

Now I'm no fan of Ferrero chocolate, which vaguely tastes like regurgitated icing sugar to me, but I can't help thinking that it would be hugely unfair on the company if an unsubstantiated link between Kinder eggs and danger began to form in parents' minds and sales suffered accordingly. Let's face it, even though Kinder eggs are generally bought for the gift rather than the sickly chocolate shell, and even though many of the toys are so ingeniously designed they could easily be sold on their own, munching through the outside to get at the inedible inside is half the fun.

What's more, jittery, neurotic parents don't need any more false scares to piss their pants over. They're already raising their twatty little offspring like mollycoddled prisoners: banned from playing outdoors in case a paedophile ring burrows through the pavement and eats them, locked indoors with nothing but anti-bacterial plasma screens for company, ferried to and from school in spluttering rollcaged tanks. . . . Christ, half these kids would view choking to death as a release.

No wonder they grow up to become tiresome whooping advocates for extreme sports. If I'd spent the first 18 years of my life doing time in a joyless cotton-wool cell, listening to some angsty bloody parent banging on about how precious and special I was every pissing day, I'd snowboard off a 300-foot cliff at the first opportunity too. Under those circumstances, tumbling down a rockface and cracking your skull open must feel like a declaration of independence crossed with an orgasm.

How did we get to this point? Our sense of self grew too strong. We gazed up our own bums for so long, we each became the centre of the universe. We're not mere specks of flesh, jostled by the forces of chance. We're flawless deities, and goddammit we deny – deny! – the very existence of simple bad luck. If we trip on the pavement, someone else is to blame. Of course they are. And we'll sue them to prove it if necessary.

In a bid to pre-empt our self-important litigiousness, armies of risk assessors scan the horizon, dreaming of every conceivable threat. You could bang your head on that branch. Crack a rib on that teaspoon. Choke to death on that chocolate egg.

Well, it stops here. And it stops now. Next week, I'm launching my own range of Kinder eggs. They're called Unkinder Eggs. And they don't contain sweets. They contain specially designed hazards. Spiked ball bearings.

Spring-loaded razor-blade traps. Flimsy balloons filled with acid. Miniature land mines powerful enough to punch holes in your cheeks and embed your teeth in the wall. The idea is to carefully nibble away all the chocolate without incurring a serious injury. Thrills! Tension! Chocolate! It's the confectionery equivalent of extreme sports. You'll love it.

And hey – that's not just cocoa butter and milk solids you're savouring. It's better than that. It's the great taste of risk.

The imaginary Olympics   [18 August 2008]

Thank God for dishonesty. I can't have been the only Briton to shift awkwardly in their seat throughout the opening ceremony of the Beijing Olympic games the other week. The Chinese mounted an unprecedented spectacle. Thousands of synchronised drummers, acrobats, fireworks, impossible floating rings made of electric dust (surely alien technology, that), dancers, prancers, singers and flingers. Maybe not flingers. I just threw that in to complete the rhyme. But you get the picture. It was amazing. It cost around £50 million and was probably rehearsed at the shooty end of a machine gun. Dance, beloved populace! Miss three steps and we take out your kneecaps. Miss five and we go for the head. Dance till your homeland is the envy of the world! Stop weeping and dance!

Yet even as my eyes took delight in the colour and magic, my spirits sank. I'm no patriot, but I feared for our national pride come the 2012 London Olympics. How the hell are we going to top a display like that? Our plans currently consist of six roman candles, Bernie Clifton riding his ostrich, and some *Britain's Got Talent* prick-a-ma-boob beatboxing on a trampoline. It would be less shameful if we all marched into the arena one by one, dropped our trousers, yanked our bumcheeks apart and let the entire globe gaze right up our apertures for an hour, while the Kaiser Chiefs perform their latest single in the background. If nothing else, it would give the rest of the planet something to think about. They'd never mess with us again, that's for damn sure.

But my defeatism, for once, was misplaced. The ceremony wasn't as spectacular as it seemed. An impressive swooping aerial shot of fireworks bursting in footprint-shaped constellations turned out to be a computer-generated lie. And the cute little girl singing the Chinese anthem was only miming to the voice of another girl, whom the authorities considered too hideous to warrant airtime.

Actually, they were right. The original girl was an absolute pig, with teeth so higgledy-piggledy you could be mistaken for thinking her skull was trying to chew its way out of her face. You could possibly use her head as the basis for the lead puppet in a children's programme set in Ugly Wood, provided you didn't mind your kids vomiting in fear and disgust each time she wobbled on screen.

Oh shut up. I'm joking.

Anyway, the deception didn't end with the opening carnival, but bled into the events themselves. Hordes of volunteers, known as 'cheer squads', have been been planted in the stands during under-attended events, to disguise empty seats and goad the rest of the crowd into whooping on cue.

What's remarkable about all this trickery isn't the trickery itself – but how ineptly it's been maintained. Even a six-year-old knows that once you tell a lie, you stick to it. You never admit the truth. Never. And when confronted with irrefutable evidence of your guilt, you dig your heels in further still – loudly denying reality until your accusers die of exasperation. It's a brilliant strategy that's kept the Bush administration going for years.

But the Chinese? A few timid queries and they admitted it all with a shrug. Yeah, they were computer-generated image (CGI) fireworks. Yeah, the kid was miming. Yeah, we're using cheer squads. So what? We're not arsed. Stop wetting your pants. What are you going to do about it anyway? Did you know that if we all stood up and sat down at the same time, the resulting tidal wave would destroy your capital cities? Ask us again if we're arsed. Go on. Fire away.

They didn't even try to cover it up properly before they were rumbled. The 'cheer squads', for instance, were hardly subtle – they were decked out in bright yellow shirts and huddled together in conspicuous clumps. They couldn't have been more noticeable if they'd had searchlights for faces and foghorns for hands. All of which provides an effective blueprint for us to follow circa 2012. First up, the opening ceremony, in which a volcano rises from the Thames, spewing flaming Olympic rings into the night sky while Big Ben – or rather, a genetically enhanced version of Big Ben, one with straighter teeth and bigger tits – pirouettes in the background, miming to the Kaiser Chiefs' latest single. This goes on for 15 hours or until the nearest superpower threatens to bomb us. Then the events themselves begin. None of them takes place in the Olympic stadium because there is no Olympic stadium. We've not bothered building one. Instead, we've got a host of exciting made-up CGI sports. Moon Snooker! Unicorn Wrestling! Quantum Deathball! Dissenter Beheading! Pac-Man with Guns! Naturally, none of the other countries has been allowed to practise any of these games, whereas we've had four solid years to develop and perfect them. So we're guaranteed, ooh, at least three bronze medals. We'll thrash Paraguay, that's for damn sure.

And as our virtual athletes (who aren't really there) take their place on the podium (which isn't really there either), thousands of specially trained spectators will loudly voice their appreciation at gunpoint. Then we'll kick the shit out of one or two overseas journalists and claim the whole thing's been a roaring success. Again and again, till we're blue in the face. Bish bash bosh. Job done. As a twat might say at the end of a column.

The black hole [1 September 2008]

There's a little-known and decidedly average George Romero movie called *Bruiser* which, despite turning rubbish and hysterical at the end, has a creepy and intriguing premise. In it, Jason Flemyng plays a successful young marketing exec who wakes up one day to discover his face has inexplicably transformed into a smooth, white, featureless mask. He stands horrified in front of the mirror, trying to remove it but failing because it's fused to his head. He has literally become a blank.

That's the best bit of the film. After that it all goes a bit daft, as Flemyng's newfound anonymity sends him doolally and he runs around Los Angeles killing people left right and centre (mainly centre) until you just don't care any more. I'd have preferred him to stand weeping in front of the mirror for the remaining 90 minutes because I found that bit exceptionally creepy. And you know why? Because I can relate to it, that's why. Thanks for asking.

I could relate to it not because I've got a smooth, featureless face – sadly, it's more like a lumpy relief map charting myriad disappointments – but because in the past few months I've grown increasingly concerned that deep inside, underneath, in my heart, at my core, in my bones, within the very centre of my soul, lurks a terrifying, all-consuming, awful, echoing blankness.

Just to be clear, this is not the same thing as depression, which would manifest itself as an actively negative mindset. Rather it's an absence of any definable mood whatsoever. It's not like glancing at the glass of water and seeing it as half-empty; more like glancing at the glass of water and seeing it as half-full, but shrugging indifferently and staring at the wall instead of running around giggling and setting off party poppers. And to be fair, vacant indifference is the only sane reaction to a mere glass of water in the first place. It's hard to muster much enthusiasm or despair either way. Which leaping great cretin at the Department of Psychological Metaphor decided your opinion vis-à-vis a glass of water should be the barometer of character anyhow? If you want to find out who's a pessimist and who's an optimist, don't faff around filling tumblers – water's a precious resource, for Christ's sake. Just ask them. Or issue them a form with OPTIMIST and PESSIMIST printed on it, and see which box they tick. It's not rocket science.

Anyway, back to my thudding personal blankness. It's probably a bonus. On the one hand, I take absolutely no pride whatsoever in whatever meagre professional achievements I can muster, take little interest in anything outside work and am essentially just a blinking, shuffling mannequin watching events in his life merely drift past like underwhelming prizes on the *Generation Game* conveyor belt. And on the other, I just don't give a shit. It's a win-win situation. Or it would be, if I had any concept of 'winning' in the first place.

Apparently this condition is known as 'anhedonia' – the inability to derive any pleasure from things that would normally be considered pleasurable. Hand someone truly anhedonic a slice of chocolate cake, and at best they'll think, 'Hmm, my tastebuds indicate this cake is delicious,' rather than simply enjoying it. They subject it to Spock-like analysis, swallow it, shrug, and then crap it out a few hours later, wearing a neutral, unchanging expression throughout. Well, that's me, that is.

And it's hard to see what the cure might be. If you've fallen out of love with life – not to the point of actually disliking it, you understand, but to such a degree that you merely tolerate rather than welcome each passing day – it's surely impossible to get the spark back. Any suggestions? Religious epiphanies and extreme sports are out. And I could do without raising a family, thanks: that looks like an almighty pain in the arse and to be honest I couldn't be bothered. I'd immerse myself in a hobby but they all look so pointless. You might as well sit alone in a shed counting numbers. I've tried cultivating a passion for the arts but that didn't work either. I mean, I quite like plays, live music, exhibitions, museums and paintings, but not enough to spend more than 25 minutes journeying to see them. Reading's all right, but be honest – turning the pages isn't ultimately worth the effort. Perhaps serial killing would help. Yeah. That'd give everything a welcome bit of edge. Although I'm prepared to believe even that gets boring surprisingly quickly: within two weeks I'd be yawning my way through yet another humdrum strangling.

Still, it could be worse. Having listlessly Googled anhedonia, I see it's related to a hilarious spin-off condition called 'ejaculatory anhedonia'. Apparently it mainly affects men, and as the name suggests, the unfortunate few who suffer from it are incapable of deriving any pleasure whatsoever from orgasms. They squirt a nutful of mess while staring impassively into the middle distance, like the human equivalent of a pushdown soap-dispenser, and that's it. Now that would be depressing.

Hello, boys [8 September 2008]

According to a pointless piece of eye-rolling anti-EU extrapolation that appeared in a number of newspapers, a smattering of MEPs are calling for the introduction of strict new advertising guidelines that could eventually lead to Eva Herzigova's breasts being taken out and shot.

At least that's the gist of it. As far as I can ascertain, the story largely represented a brilliant excuse to print the supermodel's infamous Wonderbra ad for the 80 millionth time, on this occasion under the headline 'Goodbye, Boys'. Even though the Hello, Boys campaign ran 14 years ago, editors just can't let it lie. Rather than fading into obscurity it has, if anything, grown to represent some kind of sexual Year Zero which still haunts their collective mind's eye to this day. Just as Philip E. Marlow from Dennis Potter's *Singing Detective* was obsessed by visual memories of his mum enjoying a bit of off-piste afternoon dick in a forest, so the image of a semi-naked Eva gawping with awestruck joy at her own overflowing cups is forever frozen in their consciousnesses, and they're doomed to reproduce it again and again in a bid to help themselves and their readers come to terms with its sheer psychological impact. It wasn't just an advert. It was the 9/11 of tits.

And now some killjoy EU busybodies want to travel back in time and ban it! Or something like that! Boo! Typical! Let's bomb Brussels! Or maybe just France! Etc!

But wait, it doesn't end there. As the *Daily Mail* goes on to explain, 'This being the EU, it is not simply raunchy advertising that is in danger . . . It wants anything which promotes women as sex objects or reinforces gender stereotypes to be banned . . . Any campaigns which are deemed sexist might have to go . . . [such as] the bare-chested builder with a can of Diet Coke in 1996 . . . Even famous adverts such as those featuring the Oxo family, with Lynda Bellingham as the housewife, might be deemed sexist.'

Inevitably, the minuscule conker of reality at the heart of this shitcloud is markedly less interesting than all this talk of a wild banning outbreak might suggest. Once you remove all the 'mights' and 'coulds' and other weasel words from the article, you're left with nothing but a report from the EU women's rights committee (doubtless a barrel of laughs at parties), which merely suggests governments should use their existing equality, sexism and discrimination laws to regulate advertising.

Nonetheless, 'The EU vote on the report is not legally binding but it could be used by governments to justify the biggest shake-up in the industry for years.' Or it could not. Who knows? Uh-oh, we've accidentally printed that photo of Eva again. Argh! Only one thing for it: we're all going to have masturbate our way back to sanity together. Right, readers? Three . . . two . . . one . . . go!

It's safe to predict this 'shake-up' will have as much impact as all the other quasi-fictional EU bans and regulations the press enjoys harping on about in pieces headlined 'OXYGEN TO BE OUT-LAWED' or 'NOW EU BUSYBODIES SAY MILK MUST BE SERVED IN CLOGS', and so on. Partly because all such stories ultimately turn out to be knitted from wisps of translucent flim-flam, but mainly because the only way to ban advertising that 'reinforces gender stereotypes' is to ban all advertising whatsoever.

What's the alternative? Only allow commercials that actively challenge gender stereotypes? I can scarcely picture what kind of patronising hell we'd be creating for ourselves there. And what if it worked? What if all our ads were suddenly filled with ladylike men eating chocolates and butch ladettes swigging beer, and these images proved so influential that everyone started behaving that way in real life, until these brave new anti-stereotypes had become stale old actual stereotypes, so we had to start all over again by subverting our old subversions? And so on and so on. Don't know about you, but I'd shoot myself some point around 2011. Probably while wearing a dress.

And besides, anyone with more than four atoms of cranial glop in their skull already knows that adverts don't provide a realistic field guide to the genders. In adverts, women are carefree sex kittens. In reality, they're just annoying. Especially the ones who whine on and on about gender stereotypes through the strange flapping hole they use for expressing simple-minded notions which is apparently located somewhere above their chests. (The *Guardian* has asked me to point out that this is a joke. Which indeed it is. Although, cleverly, it's also an optical illusion, because to uptight enemies of fun, it doesn't look like a joke at all, but a heinous slur. Still, at least complaining about it will give them something to do before they all die early of joylessness, leaving the rest of us to swap off-colour gags at their spartan little gravesides.)

When it comes to being objectified in ads, men lag way behind women, although they're gradually inching closer thanks to the aforementioned Diet Coke hunk and the Aero Bubbles guy and so on. Mainly, though, they're portrayed as gurgling dimwits whose sole reward in life is to be occasionally granted the opportunity to stare at a football through a pint of piss-coloured beer.

In other words, both genders are routinely insulted in adverts, but that's because adverts are inherently insulting to anything more sentient than a footstool. Of course they're demeaning, dum-dum. They're adverts. That's what they do. And attempting to regulate them further would be as big a waste of adult time and resources as telling a four-year-old not to make giggly jokes about poo.

Just as well that isn't going to happen, then. Cue Eva Herzigova photograph. Article ends. Goodbye.

The pubic consensus [15 September 2008]

The other day I was enduring *The Sex Education Show* on Channel 4, in which a self-consciously 'liberated' presenter called Anna ran screeching around the place like a one-woman hen night, banging on about boobs and willies in a bid to 'get Britain talking' about sex. And the script essentially ran as follows:

'Hey, Britain! Let's all be honest and open, yeah? Penises! There! I said it! Some are big, some are small! Here's a photo of one! Are you shocked? You mustn't be shocked! Although it's OK to be amused! Tee hee! Aren't we pushing back the boundaries? Isn't this healthy? Come on, we're all adults. This is good for us! Celebrate it! Vulva! Wow! Can you believe I just said that? Condom! Orgasm! Clitoris! Etc!'

Don't get me wrong: I'm all for snickering nob gags and frank images of nudity, but I'd rather not have them accompanied by some tissue-thin justification about 'healing the nation' or 'getting people talking'. Just tell us a joke, show us your bum and piss off.

Anyway, as luck would have it, Anna did show us her bum. Sort of. In a mirror. While she was trying on lingerie, because this was a modern documentary, see? Just as in London you're famously never more than 4 feet from a rat, so in 21st-century factual enter-tainment shows the presenter is never more than four minutes from a pointless TV stunt. Like trying on some frilly pants. Or getting a bikini wax.

The bikini wax section caused me some anguish. After braving a 'full Hollywood' (where they suddenly rip the whole lot clean away, like DLT having his face pulled off), Anna held a little chat with a studio audience, encouraging them to help heal broken Britain by loudly discussing their pubes. Things were ticking along predictably – ie a 50/50 mix of words and chortling – when something upsetting happened. They asked the men in the studio whether they trimmed their pubic hair, and almost every single one of them put their hands up.

Then they read out the results of a survey they'd done, which claimed that, yes, 60% of men trim their pubes. What, really? 60%? Huh? And then they asked the women in the studio if they preferred the male trimmed-pube look – and they all nodded like Churchill the car-insurance dog. First I felt woefully out of touch. Then I simply hated the world a little more. And then an uneasy thought came over me. If the majority of other men genuinely spend hours hoisting their scrotum over the bathroom sink with one hand, nail scissors in the other, meticulously snipping and pruning their man-bush into a tiny ornamental hedge, until their entire pubic region resembles a tranquil arboretum in miniature, albeit one with a cheerful bit of dick poking out of it, then maybe all my ex-girlfriends have been secretly revolted by my comparatively slovenly lower appearance. Did they think I was some sort of wild hobo? I phoned one up and asked her.

'What the hell are you talking about?' she asked.

I told her that according to something I'd seen on telly, most men trim their pubes.

'Well, duh. It was obviously bullshit,' she barked.

'Really?'

'Really.'

Phew. This was a relief. Aside from the icky pubic-hair aspect of the whole thing, no one wants to feel like the odd one out. I didn't want to be the sole dishevelled caveman in a world full of smooth, sculpted statues. I thought I'd missed a memo.

I've missed memos before. For instance I never bothered with scarves for years, because I couldn't work out how you were meant to wrap them round your neck without the dangling ends getting in the way. And then about two years ago someone showed me the method whereby you fold the scarf in half and poke the end through the loop and – hey presto – it all stays neatly in place. Wow, I thought. Everyone else has known this for years, and I've just found out now! I bought a couple of scarves to celebrate, and smugly paraded around in them like a child who'd just learned to tie his own laces.

And then a few weeks later I was sitting (uncharacteristically scarfless) with a friend having a drink, when she suddenly pointed at someone walking past the window in a scarf, and scowled, 'God! Why is everybody suddenly wearing their scarves that way, as if they're at university? They look like such tossers.'

I shrank in my seat, wondering how I'd missed not one, but three memos: the one that'd taught everyone else this particular method of scarf-tying, the second one that decreed it fashionable, and the third that decided it was passé.

Fortunately, it seems no pubic-hair memo has been issued at all: on closer inspection, the 'survey' that threw up the 60%-trim rating had only asked 50 men, with no indication of how representative these 50 men were. They could've been male strippers. Or indie Camden eyeliner types whose black jeans are so tight, they have to shave their minges off just to do up their flies. I wouldn't put anything past those twats. They probably don't have human-size testicles anyway. But that's an argument for another week, because we're out of space and time. Goodbye.

How to disappear incompletely [29 September 2008]

Take a holiday, said literally everyone I know. You're not being yourself. The smallest thing stresses you out. Last week you realised you'd accidentally bought some AAA batteries instead of the AA size, and instead of simply taking them back to the shop or buying a new set you ran outside and spent an hour screaming and slamming a dustbin lid against your garden wall. Try explaining that to the neighbours. Or to us. We're literally everyone you know, remember? Rarely do we speak in unison like this. Ooh, doesn't our collective voice sound funny? It's like a throat organ. Or a choir, but flatter. And more judgemental and needling. Anyway, pay attention to what it's saying. Obey. Take a holiday.

They had a point. I'd been working flat out on two different things at the same time, both complex, both demanding of time. One was a non-broadcast pilot that required me to watch news coverage of the Russian/Georgian conflict ad nauseam – disc after disc of it, again and again, in search of funny things to say about actual footage of war and bombs and people lying around looking thoroughly killed. And there are funny things to be said – no, really there are – but finding them definitely isn't good for your head.

In the middle of this, I wrote a column that struck me as a bit of light-hearted schtick about the comical pointlessness of existence, but which struck almost everyone who read it as a desperate and embarrassing cry for help. Readers emailed advice. Well-meaning zealots sent religious pamphlets. A few warm-hearted humanitarians explicitly urged me to commit suicide, on the basis that I was a prick and my writing was dismal, and that they were therefore owed blood. Hey, it's nice to know they're out there.

But friends told me to take a holiday. So I did, and I'm on that holiday right now. Yet somehow I'm also writing this, in a 'business centre' and internet hole, in a hotel, at midnight. Turns out I'm not very good at being on holiday, although I can't work out whether that's my fault, or the fault of human progress. The internet makes it easier to communicate with the folks back home, but it also brings the folks back home on holiday with you.

Britain doesn't simply go away when you leave it behind any more. It used to be the case that you'd fly home after a fortnight abroad and suddenly be astonished by a newspaper headline at the airport – BROWN: WHY I RESIGNED, or the suchlike. And you'd feel like you'd really missed out: What do you mean, the world carried on without me? It felt a bit like coming back from the grave, except instead of returning to deliver a haunting message from the afterlife, you had a few boring anecdotes about that nice restaurant where you had that thing, and a sunburned neck.

Today you can never really leave. For one thing, most of the world looks alike now anyhow. For another, if anything big happens back home, friends will text you. And not just big things either. They'll tell you who's been fired on *The Apprentice*. They'll phone you from the toilet for help in their local pub quiz.

Just to make things worse, shortly before leaving I bought a swanky new 'smart phone' aimed squarely at absolute cast-iron wankers. Go on, treat yourself, I thought. Be an unashamed cock and buy it. Turns out it does everything. Email, internet, GPS system, Google maps . . . there's probably a can opener on it somewhere. If you're standing in the middle of nowhere you can push one button to be told precisely where you are and another to find out where the nearest synagogue is. Or sauna. Or both. Punch in a query and it'll recommend eight local restaurants, cough up their phone numbers and invite you to ring them. Then it'll give you directions. Since I'm on a road trip, it's proved incredibly useful, partly for finding last-minute motels and the like, but mainly because gawping and poking at a tiny electronic screen feels a lot like work. In fact it's not a phone at all, but a pocket-sized job simulator, and this helps with the cold turkey immensely.

Because without an uninterrupted supply of bite-size chunks of work to occupy your head, how the hell are you supposed to stay sane in this world? Even on holiday, there's no escaping this planet or its people. BlackBerrys, iPhones and their imitators are very much tossers' playthings, but they're also providing a vital sociological service: they make their owners feel temporarily useful and important for just long enough to prevent mass suicides in the street. Hey! You replied to my email! For a few fleeting seconds, you really made a difference, buddy.

Now get back to your holiday. You are actually on holiday, aren't you? These days, it's hard to be sure.

INTERLUDE

An American road trip [25 October 2008]

The following piece originally appeared in the Guardian'*s travel section.*

I have a short attention span, so short I even got bored just then, halfway through typing the word 'span'. This means when planning a holiday, I tend to balk at the prospect of a week or two flopping on a beach. What if I get restless and walk into the sea? More to the point, and going on past experience, what if I get so sunburned on day one I spend the rest of the holiday staggering around like someone who's just crawled their way clear of a nuclear blast? There's only so many times you can say 'ouch' before you get tired of hearing yourself wince.

That's why my ideal holiday is a road trip. All that variety! And sitting down! It's like watching television, but better, because every so often you get to step out into the landscape you're watching and interact with it. And it's in 3D! Perfect.

Apart from one tiny problem. I can't drive. I've done road trips before – in the US, obviously, because that's the Kingdom of Road Trips – and each time, I've had to recruit/con (delete where applicable) licence-holding friends or girlfriends into coming. Since the ideal trip lasts around three weeks, and has a cast of more than two, arranging the details isn't always easy, particularly when you try to do it at short notice. I don't know many people prepared to drop everything to spend the best part of a month driving from state to state. Although it turns out I do know one: my improbable friend Aisleyne, tabloid staple and former *Big Brother* contestant. She, preposterous as it sounds, would be my rock, my 'core driver', for the duration of the trip. Others would accompany us for different sections: for the first leg, through California, my friend Urmee and an ex, Cat. For the second half, two other friends: Kelly and Ben, who'd fly out to meet us when we got to Las Vegas.

The whole thing was organised in a blur. It was only when I got to the airport that it struck me: none of these people knew each other. Most of them had never met. And they were a fairly diverse bunch. This was like throwing a bizarre mobile birthday party.

But I wasn't worried about that. I was worried about the flight. I'm not a good flier. I don't flip out on board and start hammering at the exits; I just sit there nervily envisaging a death plunge for the duration of the journey. And in the days leading up to take-off, I feel doomy and bleak, like I'm on a self-imposed death row. But this time around I had some valium. I'd never taken it before, and I'm glad I did. Neck the pill and 20 minutes later: bingo. Suddenly nothing really mattered. Instead of gripping the armrest during take-off, I lay back in my seat exhibiting the sort of blissful insouciance you'd normally associate with a man who's just been tossed off in a massage parlour.

We arrived in San Francisco and picked up our car: an unsexy people carrier the size and shape of an industrial refrigerator. A sports convertible may sound fun, but just try driving through the desert in one: within the hour you'd be hallucinating with sunstroke so badly, you'd swerve off the road, thinking you were traversing the rings of Saturn or driving inside Joan Collins's face.

Still, there was no driving at all for the first two days. There's scarcely any point taking a car into San Francisco: it's a collection of steep hills with no parking spaces. We explored on foot. The first day was spent aimlessly wandering around in a kind of daze as we tried to acclimatise. San Francisco is the US equivalent of Brighton. It's quaint, it's a gay mecca, it's by the sea, and it's foggy and cold.

I'd taken the precaution of pre-booking tickets for a night tour of Alcatraz (piece of piss: you buy them online and print the tickets yourself). It's essential to book in advance, and well worth the effort, if only for the bit on the tour where you stand in a solitary confinement cell listening to a former inmate explain how he kept himself sane in the dark by ripping a button off his shirt, throwing it in the air and spending the rest of the night searching for it on his hands and knees. If you enjoy harrowing glimpses into the dark heart of man's inhumanity to man, you'll have a whale of a time. I certainly did.

The next day we wandered around Haight-Ashbury. Once the birthplace of the hippy movement, it's now a sort of cross between Shoreditch and Camden: all trendy shops and organic cafés. Since I was accompanied by girls, I spent most of my time standing impatiently in clothes stores, listening to them coo over assorted pieces of fabric.

Still, at least I got to eat a gigantic burrito, which, as it turned out, would be my biggest meal of the entire trip. Women don't eat really, do they? At least, this lot didn't. All they wanted, every night, was sushi. Sushi, sushi, sushi. Before you accuse them and me of insufferable wankery, bear in mind that sushi in the States is far cheaper and better than in Britain. By the end of the trip I'd inhaled more fish than a sperm whale, but at least I hadn't clogged my colon with 10,000 burgers and steaks.

Then we got in the car and headed out. First stop: Santa Cruz. Satnav has transformed road trips, skimming hours from your journey time – not so much on the open road, but on the fiddly bits when you're looking for a motel. Get an address in advance and you arrive effortlessly, auto-piloted all the way to their front door.

I've been to Santa Cruz before. That time it was great: a sun-drenched, laid-back surfer's town with an old-fashioned beach-front fairground complete with wooden rollercoaster. This time it was overcast and all the girls had PMS, so we didn't hang around. The next morning we stopped in Monterey, checked out its superb aquarium (which features a mind-mangling display of artificially lit jellyfish, hovering in space like tiny galaxies), and decided to tackle the drive down Big Sur at sunset.

Big Sur is, as any guidebook will tell you, spectacular: all winding roads, cliffs, sheer drops, and the ocean. Being a media-saturated ponce, however, I couldn't quite shake the feeling that I was in an upscale car commercial, albeit a gloriously beautiful one. Television spoils everything.

Then it got dark. Big Sur takes longer than you think, and driving around the side of cliffs in the dark is Not Fun. There was, it's fair to say, a certain amount of screaming, especially when a spooky guy in a knackered van insisted on tailing us for a full hour. He was definitely a murderer. Definitely.

Eventually we made it to San Luis Obispo, to stay in the apparently notorious Madonna Inn: part-motel, part design nightmare. No corner of the Earth could be more gaudy. We sat at the bar. It resembled archive footage of 60s Vegas playing on a TV with the colour cranked up to hallucinogenic levels. Every surface was Pepto-Bismol pink or electric blue. A terrifying giant doll hung overhead, lolling back and forth on a mechanical swing. This is what serial killers see in their heads when they come. I recommend it wholeheartedly.

The next day, still rubbing our eyes, we made for Santa Barbara, a relaxing boutique of a town, clean to the point of artificial, with miles of beach. It's what you imagine California is like in your head when you're 12. Accommodation isn't cheap, but it's the perfect place to unwind – particularly if you enjoy sunbathing, which I don't. Disturbing sight of the day: a bikini-clad Paris Hilton-style beach bunny sitting on a towel with the words 'WHITE PRIDE' tattooed in gothic script across her lower back. Aisleyne had to be talked out of walking over and lamping her.

Next stop: Los Angeles. Sadly, the hotel we'd booked turned out to be (a) next to the airport, (b) a 40-minute drive from anywhere interesting, and (c) a self-consciously trendy hangout apparently designed to personally annoy me. The lifts played canned laughter when you arrived at your floor. That's not a metaphor: that's what they actually did. And the mini-bar didn't include cold drinks, but did have a packet of radish seeds and one of those little table-tennis bats with a rubber ball hanging off a bit of elastic. Q: What's the difference between quirky irony and infuriating 'You Don't Have to Be Mad to Work Here But it Helps!' wackiness? A: None.

Sadly, I had work to do in LA. Not high-powered meetings with movie execs. No. Just my usual *Guardian* writing duties. So I had to sit in the hotel room, tapping at a laptop, while the girls went off and swanned around. At one point I had a break and took a cab to an outdoor mall. Sinatra was being piped in from invisible speakers somewhere in the trees, and everyone was far slimmer than the last time I was here. Suddenly I felt like scum. It made me want to smoke. I quit smoking in February, and now the sheer Tupperware mock-pleasantness of everything surrounding me was threatening to undo my resolve. I bought a pack, lit one, and immediately extinguished it. No. No.

I was happy to leave LA. I was less happy with Cat's driving. We were heading for Vegas, and she appeared to be in a hurry. Perhaps she'd robbed a bank while I wasn't looking. Either way, she was hell-bent on squeezing a four-hour drive into 10 minutes. But when you can't drive, you're robbed of the ability to complain. Instead I distracted myself by selecting our driving soundtrack from an MP3 player. At least that way I'd be able to listen to the Beatles while the fire crew cut us from the wreckage.

Fortunately it didn't come to that and we arrived in one piece. Then things instantly turned strange. Knowing I was going to be staying in Vegas, the *Guardian* had sent out feelers to see if anyone was prepared to offer free, interesting accommodation to one of its writers. I'd get a nice place to stay, they'd get some publicity (good or bad, it's all publicity). That's how it works.

The Planet Hollywood Resort and Casino said yes. And because I would be covering it for this piece, they pulled out all the stops. I wasn't quite prepared for what happened. First, we were introduced to our own personal butler, the instantly charming Bisrat. He took us to our suite, which turned out to comprise four huge individual rooms branching off a massive lounge the size of a fashionable London bar. It had a pool table, a bar, a table football machine, a plasma screen on every available surface, some wacky sculptures, a breathtaking view of the strip, and – right there in the lounge – a free-standing shower with a lap-dancing pole in the middle of it.

Bisrat immediately uncorked a bottle of wine and poured us each a glass. I needed it. Drop me in the middle of opulence like this and I automatically feel like a burglar.

No matter how often I looked round the place, I couldn't get used to it. It looked like a set. You could film an entire aspirational drama series about hard-partying city hotshots in there, if you were an arsehole. Suddenly I wondered: what appalling scenes has this place witnessed in the past? How many hookers have twirled round that pole? Did housekeeping routinely wipe it clean each morning? Brrr.

Urmee and Cat flew home. Kelly flew in, followed shortly by Ben. I was talked, somehow, into going to a club. It was called Tryst, and was situated in the middle of the Wynn casino, a horrible slab of money and pretension designed to appeal squarely to absolute wankers. The club was rammed with beautiful women and hideous men. It had a waterfall, expensive drinks, and a dancefloor full of whooping twats throwing banknotes in the air. Good, I thought. The economy is tanking. This looks like the last days of Rome. Then another thought struck me: here I was, with two improbably glamorous women, in Vegas. Everyone thought I'd paid for them. Because that makes sense in Vegas.

Furthermore, going round Vegas with these two was like escorting two female models through a prison. The foul, hollow, forced party vibe I found bleakly amusing on previous trips now felt sickly and threatening. It's like a permanent New Year's Eve, my worst night of the year. Everyone pretending to let go and enjoy themselves. All of it fake, as fake as the replica Eiffel tower dominating Paris, the fake French casino. It's an atmosphere in which idiots thrive. The next day, by the pool, I saw a trio of muscled-up body-fascist lunkheads loudly haranguing an out-of-shape middle-aged man with lots of body hair. 'Hey dude, you're totally rocking that mohair sweater,' they yelled, again and again. They stood right over him. 'Seriously, it's awesome.' They said it over and over, until he left. Shamefully, I did nothing. They'd have killed me.

A few hours later, a drunk buffoon swiped Aisleyne's camera and took photos of his own spectacularly ugly testicles in a doomed bid to impress the ladies. The perfect metaphor for Vegas.

Back in the suite, while the Bellagio casino's multi-million dollar fountain display erupted across the road, every plasma screen was filled with Obama and McCain and red flashing numbers and

ECONOMY IN CRISIS. Las Vegas is mad at the best of times. In this context, it seemed downright insane. The trend in recent years has been for swankier and swankier casinos: the Bellagio and the Wynn are essentially *Dynasty* box sets made flesh. Now the credit crunch has left them looking like big, dumb relics. Towering, empty hangovers. They felt underpopulated compared to the down-market tack-pits which, comparatively, were overflowing. If gloomy economic predictions are correct, Vegas is going to turn very ugly very quickly.

Not that I spent the whole time scowling. After all, I was in the lap of luxury. The food, the service, the furnishings – it was all one unending blowjob. But it felt like a blowjob taking place seconds before a mushroom cloud appears on the horizon. Stupidly – incredibly stupidly – I started smoking, seduced by the novelty of being able to light up indoors, which felt as exotic as smoking underwater. Argh. By the time you read this, I'll be in the process of my umpteenth 72-hour quitting process. Thanks, Vegas. Once again, I was glad to leave.

By now we were behind on our itinerary. The next few days consisted of near non-stop driving. Another rule of road trips: allow far more time than you think you'll need. We sprinted through Monument Valley. Amazing landscape, yes: but when you're in a hurry it's essentially just another load of rocks. Then a mammoth drive all the way to Albuquerque.

If you find yourself anywhere near Albuquerque, go on the Sandia Peak aerial tramway. Just do it. It's the longest mountain cable car in the world, and it's terrifying and beautiful at once. Half your brain is lulled by the scenery, while the other half screams about death. There's a bar at the top. I drank a pint with shaking hands.

After Albuquerque, we stopped in a charming town called Truth or Consequences, named after a 1950s radio show that offered to broadcast an episode from the first town prepared to change its name to that of the show. Before that it was called Hot Springs, and with good reason. Because it's full of hot springs. Most of the motels double as spas. Go there. It's bloody lovely.

Between Truth or Consequences and the hill country of Texas, there wasn't much to do but drive, drive, drive, with the occasional overnight stop in a shithole. Thank God we were getting on, because it's a bit like being stuck in a small air-conditioned cell, albeit one with an interesting view out the window. The sheer amount of space in America can become overwhelming: the road is straight, and it stretches all the way to the horizon, forever.

Finally we made it to Bandera, Texas, for a two-day stay at the Running-R Guest Ranch. This was possibly the best part of the entire trip, and certainly the most relaxing. Stay in a cabin! Fall asleep in a rocking chair! Ride a horse! I've never ridden a horse before: fortunately, they're prepared for greenhorns. You just climb on its back and it follows the other horses, like a software-driven electronic car. I kept forgetting it was a real animal, except every so often it'd stop for a piss or stumble a bit on a rock. That wakes you up. All the staff were impossibly friendly: Kelly and Aisleyne were particularly taken with one of our cowgirl hosts, whose life they envied so hard it almost hurt them.

Our final destination was Houston, of which I saw little more than a soulless shopping mall, some skyscrapers and a thunder-storm. Oh, and a pair of swans, improbably bobbing around in a pool in the hotel lobby. Houston doubtless has far more to offer, but I didn't have time to see it. I had to fly home.

In summary: not a relaxing holiday, but an insanely eventful one. We tried to cram too much in to the time we had, which is why both the trip itself and this article were full of fleeting snapshots. For the distance we travelled (SF to LA to Vegas to Houston) I'd allow at least an extra week. Otherwise you spend a bit too much time rubbernecking and fiddling with iPods in the passenger seat. Nonetheless, the US is undoubtedly a great place to visit. Friendly people, stunning scenery, and if you pick your motels wisely, it's cheap, too. Go while it's still there.

CHAPTER TWELVE

In which the world as we know it comes to an end, Kerry Katona is defended, and the Daily Mail *pretends to be outraged by Russell Brand and a butterfly*

The end [13 October 2008]

Great. I go on holiday, turn my back for a few weeks, come back and what's happened? The banks are on fire and we're at war with Iceland. As I type these words (on a Friday morning, fact fans), Sky News is zooming in on a screen full of red flashing numbers, apparently willing them to fall yet lower. The problem is a lack of confidence, they keep saying, cutting away every so often to show a big plunging downward arrow or a shot of a City trader holding his head in despair.

I'm a bit sick of that whole holding-his-head-in-despair schtick, to be honest. It's about time they tried something more spectacular. Surely it's time for a revival of that great cliché of the 1930s, the ruined City whizzkid hurling himself out of the window? The credit crunch high dive. Extra points if you manage to pull a backflip on the way down, or crack your jaw on a window cleaner's cradle somewhere around floor 35. The ultimate high score goes to the first one who manages to successfully update his Facebook status using an iPhone seconds before slamming into the pavement. 'Danny is plummeting to his doom.' Click here to tag him in a photo. Look, there he is. That sort of gritty pink puddle with a few teeth and bits of hair sticking out of it? Next to the bin? Beside the horrified, vomiting pedestrians? That's Danny, your mate who got a career in the city. That's what the FTSE did to him. And you thought your job was bad. Who's laughing now? Not him. He can't. His windpipe's in the gutter.

Is this the end of the world? If so, it's a bit more boring than I'd imagined. So far, it's been an invisible apocalypse. Poke your head out the window and there's little evidence of charred debris. Perhaps that's yet to come. Like I say, I'm writing this on Friday morning. By the time you read it, it'll be Monday. Maybe we're already bartering with coloured pebbles or fighting over water or something.

Still, there's no point in worrying. If we're going to be plunged into some kind of barbaric medieval dark age, I might as well be philosophical about it, because there's no way I'll survive more than a month. I'd be hopeless at fighting over basic resources and don't have any essential manual skills, such as the ability to hunt and skin rats. Perhaps I can learn the lute and become a minstrel, or perform bawdy jigs in exchange for pennies. Assuming there are any pennies. Hey, maybe just before all currency is finally declared worthless we'll get to experience the whole wheelbarrows-full-of-worthless-banknotes thing, like they did in Germany just before the war. That'd be a blast.

It all seems particularly bizarre, because just over a week ago I was in Las Vegas, as part of a US road trip I'm writing up for the Travel section. The casino put me up in an outrageous suite the size of a millionaire's bachelor pad. It had a pool table, a butler, and a shower in the lounge with a lapdancing pole in the middle of it. The windows looked out over the Las Vegas strip; specifically over the multimillion-dollar fountain show at the front of Bellagio. I visited a nightclub full of pricks who danced around tossing bank-notes in the air, then returned to the suite, which alongside a pool table and a butler, also came equipped with about six gigantic, wall-mounted HD plasma TVs, every single one of which was screaming bad news about the economy. I felt like I was trapped inside a terrifying satirical sci-fi flick.

And it had to happen, obviously. For years, money was just appearing from nowhere, or so we were told. People bought houses and bragged about how the value kept zooming up, and up, and up. In fact they didn't seem to be houses at all, but magic coin-shit-ting machines. It was all a dream, a dream in which you bought a box and lived in it, and all the time it generated money like a cow generates farts. Great big stinking clouds of money. And none of it was real. And now it's gone. Your house is worth less than your shoes, and your shoes are now, in turn, worth less than your mouth and your arse. Yes, your most valuable possessions are now your mouth and your arse, and you're going to have to use both of them in all manner of previously unthinkable ways to make ends meet, to pay for that box, the box you live in, the one you mistook for an enchanted, unstoppable cash engine. I hope you've got a nice kitchen. Maybe that'll take your mind off things. And sell that

Alessi smoothie maker while you're about it. You can't afford fruit any more. It's tap water at best from now on. It's good for you! Really, it is.

All of it was a dream. All that crap we bought, all the bottled water and Blu-Ray players and designer shoes and iPod Shuffles and patio heaters; all the jobs we had; all the catchphrases we memorised and the stupid things we thought. Everything we did for the past 10 years – none of it really felt real, did it? Time to snap out of it. Time to grow our own vegetables and learn hand-to-hand combat with staves. And time, perhaps, to really start living.

An election in Narnia [20 October 2008]

Like virtually no one else in the country, I stayed up to watch the final US presidential debate the other night, which started at the user-friendly time of 2 a.m. and lasted 350 hours, if you count all the post-match analysis. All the rolling news channels were covering it live, of course, so my choice of network was largely based on aesthetics. Sky News had the colour turned up to cartoon levels, so that was out. The BBC had a more sober palette, and was showing it in widescreen, but there weren't enough distracting tickers and graphics to maintain my attention – I know they're bad, but I just can't help myself – so before long I started channel-surfing. The moment I alighted on CNN, I knew I was going to stay there. Why? Because they had an animated graph.

It looked like a heart monitor. For a moment, I thought it was displaying the opponents' pulses. Or maybe it was hooked up to a pad in their seats, and was scrupulously monitoring the amount of arse sweat they'd generate if a tricky question reared its head. But no. Instead it was supposed to be a visual representation of the ever-shifting mind-set of a group of uncommitted Ohio voters.

Rather than shoving electrodes into said voters' brains, so they looked like miserable cats in an anti-vivisection poster, CNN had taken the humane route and given them some sort of approval-rating widget. So if you were holding one, and Obama said something you didn't like, you turned the dial down, and if McCain said something you did like, you turned it up. And vice versa. There was one line for women and another for men, so you could see how the different sexes had different reactions. Sadly, that was the full extent of demographic separation. They could've broken it down a little further. It would've been fascinating to see how, say, over-weight ginger-haired postmen felt about the possibility of a new free trade agreement with Colombia, but the lazy bastards at CNN couldn't be arsed to tell us.

This shocking oversight aside, watching the wobbly line snake up and down as the candidates spoke was mesmerising. So mes-merising you couldn't really hear what they were saying. In fact, it turned the debate into a video game – like SingStar, the PlayStation karaoke thing where you get drunk and try to belt your way through 'Girls Just Wanna Have Fun' without hitting too many bum notes.

When the delicate subject of abortion came up, the line became yet more fiddly, and turned into one of those infuriating puzzles where you have to move a metal loop along a twisty-turny electri-fied wire without touching the sides.

Since it's impossible not to root for one candidate or another, this meant that you found yourself egging your favourite on in craven and bizarre ways. 'Shit, the line's dropping – quick, make a rash promise to the American people! Say you'll eliminate taxes! Claim to be Christ! Offer free hand-jobs! Anything!'

At one point I found myself thinking it'd be useful if people had those approval-monitor graphs on their faces in real life, so when you were talking to them at parties you could tell, at a glance, just how interested or bored they were. Then I remembered that's what basic facial expressions are for. Nature always gets there first.

Speaking of facial expressions, during the eight or nine nano-seconds I wasn't focused intently on the animated line, the linger-ing reaction shots provided much entertainment. The screen was split in two so you could see their faces while the other was talking. Obama smiled a lot, so much in fact that he started resembling a reality show contestant watching a compilation of his 'best bits'. McCain's face didn't know quite what to do with itself. It kept trying to look furious. Then you'd see him remember that looking furious doesn't play well, so he'd arrange his face into a tight, eerie grin, while appearing to grow increasingly furious with himself for failing to hide his earlier fury, thereby creating an unfortunate anger-based feedback loop. He should've worn a mask. Is the world ready for a masked president? Hell, yeah. How about one in a Sarah Palin mask? Or Chico Marx? Or Jason Voorhees from *Friday the 13th*? That'd really have thrown Obama off his stride, and given the networks something else to debate ad nauseam, thereby putting McCain back at the top of the news agenda. Is this a new maverick strategy, or a mental breakdown? The pundits would be at it for hours.

Despite the visual distractions, a few words and noises did register in my brain. Obama's voice is so soothing, I kept thinking he was about to start advertising coffee. 'I want to say to the American people: this is the finest, mellowest blend your money can buy.' McCain, meanwhile, was narrating a children's story about Joe the Plumber. Maybe it's a back-up plan: if he doesn't win the presidency, he's going to launch a stop-motion animation series on Nickelodeon. There's probably a warehouse full of Joe the Plumber action figures out there somewhere in the Arizona desert just waiting for the say-so.

I kept waiting for Obama to counter McCain's talk of Joe the Plumber by bringing up Boris the Spider or Dennis the Menace or something, but no. He started addressing Joe too. Before long they were both at it, appealing to Joe straight down the lens, which meant I had to keep looking behind me in case he was standing there, fixing a pipe.

Then it was over and I went to bed. At least I think I did. Perhaps it was all a dream. Certainly felt that way. An election in Narnia. And they all lived happily ever after. The end.

Picnicking in the despair of others [27 October 2008]

There's a lot of bleak and distressing news around at the moment. In fact, I've become so conditioned to expect bad news that if I

251

turned on CNN tomorrow morning and saw a report saying every kitten in the world had died of leukaemia during the night, accompanied by footage of sobbing workmen bulldozing their bodies into a mass grave, I'd probably just shrug and think: 'Yeah, that figures.' But grim though the news is, nothing of late has haunted me quite as much as a story I read some time ago – this time last year as it happens – about a man who was jailed for urinating on a woman who'd collapsed in the street, shouting 'This is YouTube material!' as she lay dying.

A reader reminded me of this last week. But only indirectly. I get a lot of emails from people asking me to read through stuff they've written to see if I think it's funny, or can give them advice and so on. And I rarely do, because (a) some of the stuff they send is even worse than my own (in which case they must be really straining), and (b) my inbox is perpetually over its size limit thanks to an endless swarm of whopping great PR emails containing 10MB JPEG invites to things I'm never, ever going to go to – so half the time I can't reply anyway.

But during a bored moment last Thursday I bucked a trend and decided to read one such submission: a comic mock-news article a reader sent in, concerning Kerry Katona's already-notorious appearance on *This Morning*. Said reader called Katona a 'mentally hilarious ex-girl band jizz puppet' and a 'pram-faced shit-muncher'.

LOL.

I couldn't quite work out which was worse – the fact that they'd written this in the first place, or the assumption that I, specifically, would find it funny. Having poured countless buckets of deliberately puerile abuse over people for several years, to the point where I've developed RSI, I figured I only had myself to blame. Then again, maybe not. Perhaps I'm mellowing in my old age, or perhaps I've grown 15% more human, but kicking real people when they're down doesn't really activate my chuckle cells.

Sure enough, Katona's apparent meltdown – assuming her slurring performance was a meltdown and not, as she claimed, a reaction to antidepressants – became 'YouTube material' within minutes of the broadcast. And although many of the comments underneath expressed concern or pity, there were plenty of cackles too. 'Haaaaaa haaaaaa haaaaaa,' wrote one warm-hearted chum of humanity, because a simple 'Ha ha ha' just wouldn't suffice.

Why leave it there, chuckles? Why not head down to your nearest addiction clinic and laugh yourself up a storm? Or better still, swing by the local hospice: it's a goldmine of comic misery. Except it isn't, because those are 'innocent' victims, none of whom have previously annoyed you by being famous, or courting attention with lad-mag photo shoots, which is, apparently, all it takes to convert basic human sympathy into side-splitting belly laughs.

Of course, if you want to be on the receiving end of this kind of point-and-giggle shittery it helps if you're a woman, and you've had your crotch flashed across the internet courtesy of some clammy paparazzo who held his camera at ankle-height and shoved it up your skirt as you clambered out of your car. Look! When we lie down on the pavement, utterly prostrating ourselves among the dog piss and fag butts, when we lie down here and gaze upwards . . . we can actually see your vagina, you repugnant! And from here on in, anything negative that happens to you has been instantly rendered hilarious. Lost your mind? Haaaaaa haaaaaa haaaaaa. Lost your children? Haaaaa haaaaa haaaaa. Here's hoping you get drunk and stumble into a threshing machine so we can print out the pictures and stick them on the office noticeboard and laugh till our noses run. And why? Because we're better than you.

Asserting an unearned, wisp-thin air of superiority: that's what it's really about.

The equation runs as follows: vacuous celebrities are trashy and annoying + I consider myself above them = HAAAA HAAAA HAAAA CHECK OUT THE SUFFERING LOL!!!!

It doesn't add up. If you look down on the genuine misery of those you consider beneath you, you're not just being an arsehole, but a snooty one to boot. The very fact that you're willing to get so annoyed by an irritating celebrity that you'll gleefully jettison any notion of sympathy is surely a bright scarlet warning light indicating just how empty your spiritual gas tank has become. We're talking about Kerry Katona here, not Jörg Haider. Do you want to end up like Carole Malone? No? Then for Christ's sake take up a hobby or something. Fly a kite. Phone a friend. Visit a museum. Play some Guitar Hero. Anything. Just gain a little cheerful perspective.

Because we're all just jerks in the playpen, when it comes right down to it. And tossing insults and brickbats is all part of the fun, especially when it's done with panache. But when anyone – no matter how annoying – stumbles and shatters their skull, you'd better be prepared to either shut up or help them. Why? Because you're also a grown up, stupid. And that's what they do.

Sexual acts on a butterfly [3 November 2008]

So it's here at last. The dawn of the dumb has broken in earnest. Two mistakes occur – first Russell Brand and Jonathan Ross overstep the mark with an ill-advised bit of juvenilia, then someone decides to broadcast it. Two listeners complained, but that's by the by: it shouldn't have gone out. But then the *Daily Mail* – not so much a newspaper as an idiot's guidebook issued in bite-size daily instalments – uses the incident as the starting point for a full-blown moral crusade. Suddenly everyone's complaining, whether they heard the broadcast or not, largely on the basis of hysterical, boggle-eyed descriptions of what the pair said. Poor Andrew Sachs, who, having been wronged, graciously accepted their apologies and called for everybody to move on, looked bewildered by the sheer number of cameras stuck in his face. Because, by then, apologies weren't enough.

The *Mail* was so incensed, it printed a full transcript of the answerphone prankery under the heading 'Lest We Forget' – and helpfully included outtakes that weren't even broadcast, so its readers could be enraged by things no one had heard in the first place. This was like making a point about the cruelty of fox-hunting by ripping a live fox apart with your bare hands, then poking a rabbit's eye out with a pen for good measure.

And now, like a lion developing a taste for human flesh after munching on a bit of discarded leg, the paper is on the hunt for fresh victims. First up: Brand's Channel 4 comedy show *Ponderland*. Readers were treated to a blow-by-blow account of what kind of depravity they could expect to see if they tuned in that evening.

'As his closing joke, he performs a graphic mime of sexual acts on a butterfly.'

Funniest. *Daily Mail* sentence. Ever.

Friday's paper included a rundown of other 'obscenities' broadcast by the Beeb, which the paper fearlessly 'uncovered' by recording some TV shows and writing down some of the jokes. To protect readers' sensibilities, all the rude words were sprinkled with asterisks, although since the *Mail*'s definition of 'rude' extends to biological terms such as 'penis', it was a bit like gazing at an ASCII representation of a snowstorm on a ZX Spectrum circa 1983. Perhaps next week it will produce a free sheet of asterisk stickers for readers to plaster over their own genitals, lest they catch sight of them in a mirror and indignantly vomit themselves into a coma.

One of the shows singled out was an episode of the romcom *Love Soup* transmitted in April that, the *Mail* insisted, depicted a woman being raped by a dog. I didn't see the show myself, but I doubt you saw it going in or anything, because I don't recall seeing Mark Thompson hanging from a lamp post while an angry mob kicked Television Centre to pieces. Maybe we can 'devolve' to that point in time for Christmas.

Still, if it's OK to be retrospectively enraged, why stop at April? Be ambitious! Keep going! There's an endless list of comedy shows that would qualify for the *Mail*'s hall of shame. How about *Monty Python*, which in 1970 included a gloriously tasteless sketch about a man eating his mother's corpse, then puking the remains into a grave? If *Python* had been banned, we'd never have seen *Fawlty Towers* or heard of Andrew Sachs in the first place – problem solved. *Steptoe and Son, Till Death Us Do Part, Porridge, Not the Nine O'Clock News, The Young Ones, Have I Got News For You, Blackadder, The Day Today, Little Britain, The Thick of It* . . . by the *Mail*'s reckoning, each of those shows surely deserves a place on the list too. Hundreds of hours of laughter you'd never have had.

The sad, likely outcome of this pitiful gitstorm is an increase in

BBC jumpiness. I have a vested interest in this, of course, because I've just started work on the next series of my BBC4 show *Screen Wipe*, on which we sometimes sail close to the wind. In the past, the BBC has occasionally stepped in to nix the odd line that over-steps the mark – as it should do, when parameters aren't out of whack.

But when the Beeb's under fire, those parameters can change. Last year, following the 'fakery' scandals, we recorded a trailer for the series in which I mocked a BBC4 ident featuring footage of seagulls, by fooling around with a plastic seagull on a stick and muttering about how you couldn't trust anything on TV any more. Pure *Crackerjack*. But suddenly it couldn't be transmitted, due to 'the current climate'. So God knows how restrictive things might get over the coming months.

And that's just my basic, low-level gittery. If something as sub-lime and revolutionary as *Python* came along today, the *Mail* would try to kill it stone dead, and it'd rope in thousands of angry old idiots to help, all of them bravely marching to the Ofcom web-site to register their disgust. What a rush. Feel that pipsqueak throb of empowerment coursing through your starched and joyless veins! You've crushed some fun, and it feels good to be alive!

Perhaps it's time to put a 'Complain to Ofcom' button right there on the remote control: if enough viewers press it, the show gets yanked immediately, like a bad variety act being pulled off stage by a shepherd's crook.

Or maybe, just maybe, it's time to establish 'Counter-Complaints': a method of registering your complaint about the number of knee-jerk complaints. And one should cancel out the other – so if 25,000 people complain, and a further 25,000 counter-complain, the total number of complaints is zero. It might lead to a lot of fruitless but-ton-mashing, but at least we can keep our shared national culture relatively sane. Because judging by the rest of the news, if the ship's going down, a few unrestricted taste-free laughs now and then might make things more bearable for all of us.

CHAPTER THIRTEEN

In which Sachsgate rumbles on, Bagpuss goes to sleep, and MTV introduce the most vapid TV show in history

Ofcom follies [29 November 2008]

So there I am, preparing to spew another column abusing some unfortunate *I'm A Celebrity* inmate – not Timmy Mallett, because I've started to love him, partly because he appears to have turned into a *Spitting Image* puppet of Jonathan King, but mainly because he spends the whole time cackling and chanting inane songs like a four-year-old singing about doing a poo, and it's driving the more uptight camp members out of their minds, to the point where I'm already fantasising about a follow-up show in which the producers permanently glue him to Nicola McLean's back and make them run Drayton Manor Park and Zoo for an entire year . . . So anyway, there I am, preparing to pen that sack of jollies when PING! Another email arrives. From a disgruntled member of the public, still annoyed about the Brand/Ross phonecalls. Still annoyed!

Actually, they're not just annoyed about Sachsgate. They're annoyed with me. What I'd done, see, both in print and on telly, was claim the resulting overreaction to the woeful calls, fuelled by an increasingly desperate press, might lead to an overall toning down of any and all potentially 'offensive' TV material, which in turn could deprive us of authentic gems in the future. I supported my case by citing all sorts of fantastic old bits of comedy we'd never have seen if broadcasters back yonder had been subject to the sort of kneejerk Ofcom-clocking that's become the norm: *Monty Python*, *Not The Nine O'Clock News*, *The Young Ones*, and so on.

Terrifically clear to you, me and the average cabbage. But not to the furiously hard-of-understanding, who decided I was comparing the Sachs phonecalls to such rare works of genius (which I wasn't) and thereby defending them (which I also wasn't). Enraged by their own misreading, they've been emailing me directly to point out how wrong the argument they haven't followed is. Thanks. Your voice has been heard. Each time you click 'Send' it's a fresh triumph for democracy.

Still, this latest email also took umbrage with one other point I actually DID make. I implied that people who retrospectively complain to Ofcom about material they've only read about second-hand are, in essence, a bunch of sanctimonious crybabies indulging in a wretched form of masturbation. In my defence, I only implied this because it's true.

Anyway, to expose my crashing wrongness on this issue, the sender points to an old column I wrote recounting my shock upon reading of a real-life incident in which a drunk pissed on a dying woman. 'Hang on,' counters the self-appointed barrister, 'You didn't see it first-hand – so do you have the right to be shocked or offended? Of course.'

He's right. I didn't have to witness it first-hand to be shocked. But then I didn't feel the need to report my shock to the police either. Unless I've got some useful information to offer, I'd rather not hassle them. Only a cunt would do that.

Nearly 40,000 people complained about the Sachs calls. Impressive. But a few weeks later Ofcom received a petition from 50,000 people equally pissed off about Laura White being voted off *The X Factor*, doubtless trying to outdo the Sachsgate mob. Perhaps I've misunderstood its purpose, but I don't think Ofcom was intended to be an all-purpose repository for bandwagon protest votes. In terms of raw numbers, the Laura White incident looks like the more serious crime. So these numbers are meaningless. Why add to them? Are things that bad at home?

And besides, if TV broadcast the kind of material you see in the press – if it paid women in lingerie to recount graphic celebrity fuck'n'tell stories, or shoved its cameras up the skirts of girls exiting taxis so viewers could wank to the sight of their knickers, or routinely broadcast grossly misleading and openly one-sided news reports designed to perpetuate fear and bigotry – if the box in the corner smeared that shit on its screen for 10 seconds a night, it'd generate a pile of complaints high enough to scrape the crust from the underside of Mars.

In summary: this correspondence is now closed.

Homosexualiteeheehee   [6 December 2008]

In 1975, ITV broadcast *The Naked Civil Servant*, a TV movie about the life of the flamboyant gay icon Quentin Crisp. I say 'flamboyant gay icon', although he didn't actually become one until the programme itself was broadcast and made him famous. It made John Hurt famous too, which pretty much sums up the difference between TV drama then and TV drama now. A 90-minute prime-time ITV movie about an unknown homosexual played by a relatively unknown actor? With no Martin Clunes or Robson Green or David Jason? It's a true story, you say? And he isn't a serial killer? Uh, leave it on the desk and we'll get back to you some time around, ooh, never o'clock?

Except maybe it would happen. For one thing, they're shooting a sequel (*An Englishman in New York*, starring Hurt again). And for another, ITV is something of a clandestine queer issues champion. *Coronation Street* has been a camp powerhouse for decades; then there's *Bob & Rose* and, most recently, *I'm A Celebrity . . . Get Me Out Of Here!*, which this year featured a scene in which three gay people, all of them over 50, were seen crying with joy after receiving letters from their partners (and in the case of George Takei, his husband).

OK, so it also showed them rolling around in rat shit and bickering over hammocks too, but – hey! – it's social progress of a sort and precisely the kind of thing the *Guardian* normally embraces. It's certainly hard to imagine the BBC broadcasting something similar in primetime without trying to turn it into a self-consciously noble 'issues drama'.

Actually, until recently, the life of Brian Paddick would've looked like a good basis for a self-consciously noble 'issues drama' about a high-profile gay policeman who runs for mayor of London. Now, hilariously, any scriptwriter currently adapting his biography with one eye on a Bafta is going to have to include a scene in which he beats Timmy Mallett in a competition to see who can down a pint of liquidised crocodile penis the fastest. Whichever way you cut it, Paddick's had a weird 2008: appearing on *Newsnight* opposite Boris

Johnson and Ken Livingstone in April; listening to Joe Swash blow off in the jungle in November.

Speaking of Swash, I'm assuming he's won by the time you read this. Certainly at the time of writing it looks inevitable, what with him being the only one left who's wholeheartedly nice. George Takei doesn't count because he's been almost completely invisible. I think he's using the Predator's shimmery see-through stealth armour; quite fitting in the jungle. He popped up now and then like an unseen narrator, reading out a fresh chapter heading in his synthesised baritone voice, but that's about all he did.

In fact most of the campmates turned out to be underachievers. Paddick got his bum out and wandered around like a passive-aggressive cross between C3PO and John Major. Nicola McThing spent hours grumbling on her back in a bikini, which made her fake tits resemble two giant wax testicles resting on her ribcage like immovable paperweights. David Van Day was predictably deranged and ridiculous. Simon from Blue said five words, six of them dull, and Martina Navratilova spent the whole time pulling a face like she was working in an Eastern European shoe factory and was neither upset nor uplifted by the experience.

Joe Swash, on the other hand, was unrelentingly funny. Partly because he looks almost exactly like Alfred E. Neuman, the eerie *Mad* magazine mascot, but mainly because he quickly revealed himself as an exasperated human rights campaigner, becoming outraged by the smallest injustice. Every three minutes the show cut to a shot of him leaping off a log to scream about the unfair treatment of Timmy Mallett in the style of an eight-year-old throwing a tantrum. If it fancies a few ticks for its public service record, ITV should get him to front a six-week series on human rights abuses around the world, called That's Bang Out Of Order, That Is. With Shami Chakrabarti as co-host, please.

When Bagpuss goes to sleep [13 December 2008]

Another week, another column diverted from its planned trajectory at the last minute.

I was supposed to write about *Horizon: Where's My Robot?*, an affable lightweight documentary about the world of science's ongoing attempts to create proper walking, talking mechanical men. The most unusual and affecting sequence in the programme involves a Japanese professor's efforts to create a lifelike android, and the difficulties that involves. He's built several eerie likenesses, of himself, his daughter, and an attractive young woman – only to discover that they freak people out. The trouble is they look almost human, but also markedly lifeless, with cold eyes and uncreased skin. Visitors react with revulsion at the very sight of the things because there's no soul.

Anyway, I sit down to write about that, check the internet for a bit of last-minute procrastination and . . . oh no. Oliver Postgate's just died. There it is on the BBC News website. I can't write about anything else now. I have to type this off the top of my head. And the first thought that strikes me is that, in stark contrast to the creepy Japanese android guy, here was a man capable of effortlessly breathing gallons of soul into even the most basic of artificial lifeforms. A saggy old cloth cat. A steam engine made of paper, puffing cotton wool balls for steam. A tribe of miniature pink aliens on the moon.

Together, the team of Postgate and Peter Firmin were apparently incapable of creating anything less than timelessly wonderful whenever they sat down to work. *Pogles' Wood*, *Noggin the Nog*, *Ivor the Engine*, *Bagpuss*, *The Clangers* . . . each of them would instantly hypnotise and charm the viewer. And each was infused with a uniquely British sense of genteel eccentricity; they became a key element in countless individual childhoods, informing the dreams and imaginations of millions of people. All of it forged in a former cowshed in Kent, sewn into being like an enchanted tapestry made of 16mm film.

The stories were simple, the animation basic, the puppets and drawings polite yet charismatic, but together they were far more than the sum of their parts. Close your eyes and picture them and you can't help but feel genuine warmth; these films were made with love. It glowed from the screen.

Postgate himself was a committed pacifist, and forgive me if I sound like a wuss, but I swear you could hear it in his voice, which never shrieked or gurgled or patronised, but maintained a steady, dreamlike pace on each soundtrack. It was recorded quite basically, so it often sounded like he was speaking from a cupboard in the corner of the room, but that merely added to the charm. Stuff your bird or whale song, forget about breezes in cornfields or lapping waves and waterfalls: there is no more calming sound in the world than the voice of Oliver Postgate. With him narrating your life, you'd feel cosy and safe even during a gas explosion. It floated above all these stories, that voice; wound its way through them. It was the kindest, wisest voice you ever heard, and now it's gone.

As have all the other sounds, which you'll now hear in your mind's ear as I mention them in turn: Ivor's pshht-a-coo engine mechanics; the Clangers' whistles; Bagpuss yawning; Gabriel the toad swallowing; professor Yaffle climbing down from his bookend to inspect some new artefact; the squealing mice. All gone now, too.

The character design, the writing, the narration, the sound effects, the music: each individual element of every Smallfilms creation was absolutely pitch-perfect. That's not just rare, it's almost unprecedented. That it all appeared effortless is a testament to their genius: it's a level of craft that's impossible to achieve by anyone aiming for it on a conscious level. It's either in you or it isn't. It was in Oliver Postgate, and that's why he was – for my money, and without the slightest whiff of hyperbole – the greatest children's storyteller of the last 100 years.

Rest in peace, sir. You earned it.

My close friend Coolio [10 January 2009]

Having failed to destroy the world in 2007, *Celebrity Big Brother* returns with a surprisingly high-profile line-up: considering the nuclear fallout generated last time, you could be forgiven for expecting a cast list comprising the bloke from the Admiral Insurance ads, John Noakes's PA, three random Guatemalans and a photograph of Cheryl Baker glued to a broom. Instead, there are at least three or four people you've at least heard of, even if the last time you heard about them was six or seven years ago. I've even met one of them, albeit briefly. I'm talking, of course, about Coolio.

OK, so I didn't so much 'meet' Coolio as serve him in a shop, but it still counts. It was some time in the early 90s when I was working in a video game emporium just off Oxford Street. We prided ourselves on being a countercultural sort of place. Staff chain-smoked behind the desk while the stereo blasted Aphex Twin into customers' faces. We stocked obscure Japanese grey imports on holier-than-thou formats, Jamma boards and secondhand British titles. Kids hung around playing beat-'em-ups and swearing. One day Coolio bounded in, bellowing at the top of his voice without even trying. I think he bought a copy of Samurai Shodown II on the Neo-Geo. He knew his games, did Coolio.

Anyway, apart from MY VERY CLOSE FRIEND COOLIO, there are a few other recognisable faces – and Ulrika Jonsson, whose face isn't as recognisable as it used to be. It's changed, yet stayed roughly the same, as though it's made from different material. Material from space. It makes her look like someone else wearing special effects makeup to make them look like Ulrika Jonsson. Maybe that's the twist. Maybe it's actually Bob Mortimer underneath all that. The truth will out.

Then there's Verne Troyer, aka Mini-Me. He's simply too small; the size of a baby. Watching him walk up the red carpet on launch night made me feel giddy and feverish, like I was teetering on the verge of an uncontrollable psychotic episode, one where the dam in my head finally bursts and vision itself ceases to make sense and the walls start shouting and demons and witches and melting Nazi elephants crawl from the carpet to drag me away to Mad Land. He takes up four pixels on the average LCD television. For the first time in Screen Burn history, the photo accompanying this column will be (a) a full-body shot, and (b) actual size.

LaToya Jackson: there's another recognisable one, although it's Michael and Janet you're recognising when you look at her. She's essentially Betty from *Some Mothers Do 'Ave 'Em* with a US accent.

Terry Christian, for his part, is transmogrifying into Jack Palance and coming across quite well in the process.

Of the rest, Mutya, Michelle and Ben are flavourless sandwich filling, so until Tommy Sheridan reveals himself to be a massive preening bighead – a moment I keep anticipating but which, irritatingly, hasn't yet arrived – the ones annoying me most are Tina Malone and Lucy Pinder.

Malone because she's got a habit of dragging the conversation round to herself: even when LaToya Jackson was describing some harrowing domestic abuse, Malone managed to deftly convert it into an appraisal of her own uncompromising no-nonsense scouse attitude. Pinder, meanwhile, went from 'sexy' to 'plain' in a nanosecond: as soon as she mentioned her Tory outlook in her introductory VT, you could hear intelligent penises shrivelling across the nation.

I've got nothing against curvy, booby glamour girls, but the moment they start banging on about the Conservative party they turn into ugly, soulless dolls. As a result, she could don lingerie and spend the rest of the week doing rude aerobics, and it still wouldn't help. Now you know what's in her head, the exterior's been rendered so unattractive she might as well be excreting dog food through her (presumably) shaved and talcum-powdered orifices. Seriously, only a psychopath could find that attractive. And when you're supposed to be sexy for a living, that's a major problem.

Question everything   [24 January 2009]

Ask anyone with a Sky box: the problem with the multi-channel universe is how samey it all is. Hundreds of stations pumping out the same palliative mulch. But every so often a new start-up channel emerges with a left-field agenda. It's always worth tuning in once, just for the surprise value. There was Isle of Wight TV, which seems to have vanished now. And SoundTV, which consisted of old-school variety and interviews with Richard Digance. That's gone too. These rogue stations don't tend to last long.

Well here's a new one: Edge Media TV, 'a platform for alternative and suppressed viewpoints'. In other words, it's chock-full of conspiracy theories. Conspiracy theorists need to believe their viewpoints are being suppressed, rather than, say, assessed and dismissed as ropey and ludicrous. Which makes a channel devoted to spreading these viewpoints a bit of a paradox. If 'the system' was even 1% as efficient and sinister as they believe, their station wouldn't exist.

But it does, broadcasting programmes with titles like *Question Everything* and *Hidden Agenda*, and a talkshow called *Esoteria*, which according to the host is 'a SHOW, not a PROGRAMME – we aim to SHOW you alternative viewpoints rather than PROGRAM you to accept a particular point of view'. He must be proud of that bit of mind-expanding wordplay because he repeats it quite a lot. A bit like he's programming you, actually.

And herein lies the tragedy. The other day I tuned in to *Eerie Investigations*, in which the host, a strangely simpering woman with *Eerie Investigations* printed on her T-shirt, conducted vox-pop interviews with people at an anti-ID card rally. There are a thousand valid reasons for opposing ID cards and questioning everything the government does, but instead both the host and her interviewees spent most of their time talking about how we're all going to have microchips planted in our heads as part of the New World Order (which, naturally, orchestrated the 9/11 attacks), intermittently breaking from this theme to dismiss the general public as idiotic, docile sheep with such towering self-assurance it made you actively wonder whether labouring under a fascist police state in which government computers monitored your dreams and doled out electric shocks each time you had a subversive thought would be preferable to living in freedom alongside these massive wankers.

Maybe 'wankers' is a bit harsh. These are essentially clever people gone wrong. Having learned to mistrust the powers that be, they take a giant leap, mistaking bossiness and incompetence for ultra-organised and sinister plotting – and then compound the error by mistaking themselves for journalists or scientists. The result is a depressing descent into fairytales backed with risible 'evidence';

fairytales told with the defensive assertion that anyone who doesn't believe them is a shill or a sheep.

Consider *Ludicrous Diversion*, an Edge Media documentary which implies the 7/7 bombers weren't really bombers at all, but patsies framed by 'the system'. Rather than offering any hard evidence for this startling claim, it highlights minor anomalies in the official version of events, the police's reluctance to release CCTV footage, and references to past miscarriages of justice such as the Guildford Four, then expects the viewer to add two and two to make 25. It's like a lazy and badly made *Power of Nightmares*, convincing only to the eagerly paranoid.

In between the programmes, there are adverts for Cillit Bang (whose exact role in the New World Order has yet to be established) and a seven-hour – yes, SEVEN-HOUR – 'DVD presentation' from David Icke, in which he tells the viewer how the world really works. And presumably apologises for not employing an editor.

In summary: it's bunkum. But then I would say that, wouldn't I? I'm a mainstream media shill. They've got to me already. And now they're coming for YOU.

Here goes nothing [31 January 2009]

The landmark sitcom *Seinfeld* was famously described by its own makers as 'a show about nothing'. But it wasn't really. It was a show about minutiae and neurosis and social transgression. And jokes. In fact it was a show about everything, brilliantly disguised as a show about nothing with a breezy, relaxed, sardonic style. That's why it's still such a great show, once you adjust your filter to disregard the infuriating slapped bass peppering each episode like a squelching fart cannon.

Seinfeld appeared in 1989, which means we've been waiting 20 years for an authentic 'show about nothing'. Now we've got one. And in a neat reversal, it's a show about nothing disguised as a show about something. On the surface, *The Celebrity Agency* is a modern docusoap. But that surface is tissue-thin. Beneath it: nothing.

Once you strip away the adverts and titles, the premiere episode is a mere 20 minutes long – edging on nothing, although it feels longer because there's so much nothing crammed into it. It details the day-to-day workings of Jonathan Lipman Ltd, a talent agency without the talent. It's a company which 'represents celebrities': arranging PAs with WAGs, photoshoots with *Big Brother* contestants, and promotional events in which Kenzie from *Blazin' Squad* eats a Pot Noodle on an open-top bus . . . that kind of thing. Incredibly, they manage to facilitate this without ever once staring into the middle distance while hacking at their wrists with a penknife in a desperate bid to leave this meaningless universe behind. Instead they seem to enjoy it.

The first episode features two photoshoots. One involves Bianca Gascoigne looking sultry at a Manchester carwash for a lads' mag. The other is an *OK Magazine* 'look at my lovely home' puff-piece starring Imogen from *Big Brother* in a house that isn't even hers. Absolutely nothing occurs at either location, but even these nilch-vacuums are overshadowed by a staggering detonation of nothing taking place in London.

The agency's biggest signing, Paris Hilton, is in town for a personal appearance at the Mahiki nightclub. And here's what happens: Paris Hilton has a spray tan (off-screen); Paris Hilton receives suitcases full of promotional freebies (on-screen); Paris Hilton eats a meal (off-screen); Paris Hilton stands in a nightclub for about an hour (on-screen); Paris Hilton gets paid an estimated 30,000 for her trouble (off-screen).

As you may have noticed, half of what Paris Hilton does takes place off-screen, which means – yes! – LESS THAN NOTHING is happening. It's the first successful transmission of televisual anti-matter. That's because the show isn't actually about her, but the staff of the agency, starting with Jonathan Lipman himself, who seems to be the kind of super-self-confident cock-of-the-walk that makes you actively pray for Armageddon the nanosecond he swaggers into view. He sports one of those half-spiky, half-swipey haircuts that only exist courtesy of about 28 pots of a futuristic micro-fibre styling clay with a name like 'Punk Mud' or something.

He is, to put it mildly, an aching great dick of the highest order.

Which isn't to say he spends his time beating his chest and loudly proclaiming his own brilliance. Far from it. He's actually rather low-key and casual and is probably quite a nice guy. Somehow, that only makes it worse. He's cheerfully promoting the adulation and elevation of nothing, like a man selling vague sections of air for a living, and he hasn't even got the decency to seem bitter and frightened about it. Instead he stands at the very centre of this whirling vortex of shitstink with his hands in his pockets, tapping his toe to 'Umbrella' by Rihanna, waiting for the paparazzi to arrive. And photograph nothing.

You'll choke on it but only momentarily. The nightmare tide of nothing quickly overwhelms you. It kills all thought and meaning and replaces them with nothing. Submit, human. Submit. There's nothing you can do to stop the nothing. Nothing. Nothing.

CHAPTER FOURTEEN

In which Barack Obama is elected, Santa dies, and Tatler *prints an exhaustive list of the biggest cunts in Britain*

A quick bit of good news   [10 November 2008]

President Barack Obama. President Barack Obama. Nope, still can't get used to it. It's literally too good to be true. I must've died in my sleep and am now having an insane fantasy pumped into my head by the Matrix. Any minute now Salma Hayek is going to float through the door with a tray of biscuits and I'll know the game's up. Or perhaps I've just come round from a coma. The election took place 10 years ago, and what I've just sat through was actually a Hollywood movie loosely based on real events. And in a bid to appeal to the multiplex crowd, they decided to jettison all semblance of subtlety.

On the one hand, you had Obama (Will Smith in admittedly impressive makeup, although the ears never really convinced). He was practically walking on water. No one's that nice. And pitched against him, the Republican campaign, which was so nakedly horrible it could only have been orchestrated by Skeletor. Nudge-wink comments about 'the real America', underhand attempts to link Obama with terrorism, automated robo-calls whispering desperate fibs into the ears of voters . . . if Obama's grandmother had died while he was at her bedside in Hawaii, they'd have erected billboards claiming he couldn't be trusted around white women. Jesus, guys, why not just change your name to the Bastard Party and march around in long black capes? Vote for us, we're openly despicable.

The scriptwriters clearly decided to balance the nastiness by introducing some satirical comic relief in the form of Sarah Palin, but she was scarcely plausible either. And they never really nailed her story arc, instead being content to have her wandering through every scene she was in, screeching inept banalities like a rightwing version of Phoebe from *Friends*. And what was with the whole Joe the Plumber sub-plot? I mean, c'mon, they invited him on tour and everything. As if. In the real world, no one would've bought that for a second. That's precisely the sort of thing that breaks the all-important suspension of disbelief. It didn't help that the guy they cast to play him, Michael Chiklis, is instantly recognisable from his leading role as the corrupt, brutal cop Vic Mackey in the hit TV series *The Shield*.

And the ending was far too saccharine. Dancing in the streets? Tears of joy around the globe? Oh please. I give it four out of 10. A rental at best.

On *Tatler* [17 November 2008]

One drawback – or possibly advantage – of being known as an easily riled automated curmudgeon is that people tend to hurl recommendations my way. 'Here, look at this,' they chortle, holding something irritating under my nose. 'You'll hate it.'

Usually the item in question is merely a bit disappointing. But the other day someone urged me to buy the latest copy of *Tatler* and read the Little Black Book section. 'It's absolutely unbelievable,' they said. I was intrigued enough to pop to the newsagents and cough up my £3.80. Even though I don't think I've ever read an edition of *Tatler* in my life, I had a general sense that being seen with it in public was a bad idea, so I turned the magazine around, hiding the cover against my chest as I left so no one could see what I was carrying. Better to let the passersby assume I'm carrying a porn mag, I figured – although the whopping great advert for Cartier diamond jewellery on the back probably gave the game away. I don't think they advertise in *Barely Legal*.

Once I was safely out of sight, I gingerly opened the magazine and started reading. Three seconds later, I was furious. Before getting to the Little Black Book section, I'd alighted on an article about a 'sexy Holland Park billionairess and her fabulous life'. She was called Goga Ashkenazi, and she was pictured swathed in fur, diamonds dripping pendulously from her ears like shimmering globules of semen in a bukkake movie. She was clutching a miniature dog that looked like it'd been peeled; one of those scrawny upholstered canine skeleton-creatures with the facial tics of a tiny frightened bird. Given the alarming way these micro-dogs pant 5,000 times a second, I always think they're about to die, that their pea-sized heart might suddenly burst like a popcorn kernel inside that rodenty little ribcage. That worries me.

But Goga wasn't worried. She was smiling. As well she might. If she wanted, she could buy a million dogs and spend a month hurling them into a threshing machine for chuckles. According to the article, she's so rich she 'summons private jets like most people hail cabs', and once lost a '£500,000 piece of wrist candy', shrugged, and simply put on another one. It describes her as 'a sort of 21st-century Holly Golightly', which seems a bit harsh. Holly Golightly was a call girl. Ashkenazi is an oligarch with her own goldmine. And maybe she's lovely, but the article was so fawningly, nauseatingly dazzled by how much money she's got, it'd be impossible for any sane human being reading it not to thoroughly despise her by the end.

Shaken, I turned to the Little Black Book section, which turned out to be an authoritative A–Z of overprivileged arseholes (most of them still in their early 20s), plus the occasional celeb, rated and compiled by the single biggest group of wankers in the universe.

You're supposed to want to sleep with these people, and the text attempts to explain why. It's the ultimate in self-celebratory nothingness, 2,000 times worse than the worst ever article in *Heat* magazine. It includes five lords, six ladies, four princes, five princesses, two viscounts, three earls, a marquess, and 16 tittering poshos whose names are prefixed with the phrase 'The Hon' (which, I've just discovered, means they're the son or daughter of a viscount or baron). Names like Cressida, Archie, Guy, Blaise and Freddie feature heavily. How annoying is it? Put it this way: James Blunt is also on the list, and he's the least objectionable person there.

Each entry takes the form of a chortling mini-biog guaranteed to make you want to punch the person it describes flat in the face. Thus, we learn that 'Jakie Warren' is 'the heart-throb who lives in the coolest house in Edinburgh and has the initials of all his best friends tattooed on his thigh. You can touch them but he'll make you buy shares in the racing syndicate he co-owns with Ed Sackville . . . Good in bed, we hear.'

Or consider 'The Hon Wenty Beaumont': 'The growl, the growl – girls go weak for the growl . . . Utterly divine Christie's kid who enjoys nothing more than playing Pass the Pig during weekends at the family estate in Northumberland or in Saint-Tropez.'

In other words, the only thing these waddling skinbags have going for them is unrestricted access to a vast and unwarranted fortune. Ignore the bank balances and it reads like a list of the most boring, horrible cunts in Britain.

As an additional poke in the ribs, each entry is accompanied by a tiny photograph, so you can squint into the eyes of the cosseted stranger you've suddenly decided to hate. The girls are technically pretty in a uniform, Sloaney kind of way, while the men are more varied, falling into three main categories: dull preening James Blunt types, dull preening indie types, and simpering ruddy-cheeked oafs who look like they're about to pull a pair of under-pants over their head and run around snorting like a hog in a bid to impress a drunk debutante.

In summary, it's an entire alternate dimension of shit, a galaxy of eye-stinging fart gas, compressed into a few glossy pages. It will have you alternating between rage, jealousy, bewilderment and distress, before dumping you in a bottomless slough of despond. Buy a copy. No, don't. Stand in a shop flipping through the pages, deliberately fraying each corner as you go. Drink it in. Feel your impotent anger levels peaking. The headrush is good for you. Try it. You'll hate it. Thanks for the recommendation. I'm off for a cry.

Hope it's chips, it's chips   [24 November 2008]

It's great being a shambles. Just peachy. Rather than gliding through a staid, predictable life full of contentment and friendship, you lurch from one crisis point to the next, constantly challenged by your own ineptitude. One day I'm going to write a 24-style thriller in which the main character is under constant threat, not from terrorism, but himself. A typical episode would open with him being woken from oversleeping by having his house repos-sessed because he's forgotten to fill out some forms. It might sound dull at the moment but trust me – once we've layered a pulsing soundtrack over the top you'll need to sprout fingernails at an unnatural rate to keep up with the amount you're chewing off.

I practise incompetence at an Olympian level. It recently took me 21 days to get round to replacing the lightbulbs in my kitchen, which for several weeks had been blowing one-by-one until finally the room was plunged into darkness. For 21 days I had to feel my way into the room like a blind man, then prop open the fridge door in order to have enough light to be able to see. Your eyes get used to it after a while. So does your brain. It became a routine. Soon opening the fridge felt as natural as flipping the light switch. Standing there, chopping onions in the artificial gloaming, all felt well with the world. It took an incident with a broken glass on the floor and a shoeless foot to nudge me in the direction of the nearest lightbulb stockist, and even then I instinctively used the fridge as an impromptu lamp for another two days before re-acclimatising myself to the concept of ceiling-based light sources.

Adding to the confusion, I'm tired. Strike that – exhausted. Working on a TV show might look like a parade of easy-going giggles from the outside, but on the inside it's an endless treadmill that eats time like a sperm whale eats plankton: in immense, cavernous gulps. Yesterday I rose at 9 a.m. after three hours' sleep, then stayed in the edit until 6 a.m. this morning. At 7 a.m. I arrived home and tried to sleep, in the knowledge that I was supposed to be up in about two hours' time. Knowing the builders next door would start clanging scaffolding poles around like an open-air tribute to the musical *Stomp* at about 8 a.m., I found some wax earplugs and wedged one in each lughole. But there was another problem. Light was streaming through the windows. I searched for an eye mask and failed. But while scavenging through the bottom of an old drawer, I found a pair of black knickers belonging to an ex-girlfriend. That would have to do. I pulled them over my head like a Mexican wrestler until they covered my eyes, and lay down. I probably looked quite dashing.

I tried to sleep. But exhaustion is a funny thing. It sends the brain haywire. Deaf and blind, I lay there with the old Birds Eye Steakhouse Grill song looping endlessly in my head. Hope it's chips, it's chips. We hope it's chips, it's chips.

In between verses I worried that my boiler might malfunction and kill me with carbon monoxide fumes if I fell asleep. I'm not one for keeping up appearances, but even I blanched at the thought of my neighbours seeing my blue, icy cadaver being hauled out on a stretcher with a pair of knickers on its head. That's what they'd remember me for. The fear of this kept me awake until some time around 8.30 a.m., when my bladder complained that it needed to go to the toilet. I got up, but in my confusion – hope it's chips, it's chips – I attempted to make my way downstairs to the loo without taking the pants off my head. I walked into a door. Now I was performing slapstick for the benefit of no one.

I pulled them up just above my eyes, headed downstairs and drained myself. On the way out of the bathroom I caught sight of myself in the mirror, wearing the knickers like a skullcap. The other thing about exhaustion is that it encourages hysteria. I laughed, then saw myself laughing, and laughed some more. I returned to bed, still giggling, and lay there in the dark with the singing Birds Eye workmen driving their van around in my mind. Hope it's chips, it's chips. We hope it's chips, it's chips. I think I even said that aloud at one point. For a moment, I was genuinely insane. At some point I lost consciousness.

I overslept of course, and awoke at 1.30 p.m. in a state of some confusion, stumbled downstairs and opened the fridge door so I could see the kettle – unnecessary, what with the daylight and all. I drank a coffee, phoned the *Guardian*, and said I was going to start writing. Then I typed the first sentence of this column. Then I wrote the rest. And then you read it. This proves I can, at least, maintain a veneer of efficiency amid the self-inflicted mundane chaos of my life, even if in doing so I end up slightly wasting your time. Other columnists write of glamorous parties and faraway lands, of politics, or romance, despair and elation and the unending mysteries of the human condition. On this page you find nothing but the fevered hope that it's chips, it's chips, and for that I apologise.

It's not so great being a shambles. But it's the only life I know.

Chain Gang Betties   [1 December 2008]

Petty criminals of Britain! Stop breaking into that shop for a moment and bloody well pay attention. As of today, those of you doing community service are required to wear a new uniform. It's a high-visibility orange bib with the words COMMUNITY PAYBACK printed across the back in bold black type. How'd you like them apples? Not so carefree now, are we? Consider yourselves well and truly shamed.

That's right. Community Payback bibs. It might sound stupid, but this is Jack Straw's idea and he wants it taken very seriously indeed, which is why he's been pictured in the *Daily Mirror* holding one of the new bibs aloft while maintaining a preposterously solemn expression on his fizzog, staring straight through the lens like either (a) a sinister stage magician trying to stop the cameraman's heart or (b) Droopy preparing to knock on the door of a close friend and inform them of the death of a beloved relative. Pick your favourite of those two similes and apply it to his face. That's what he's done. He's thought, 'Jesus, this is ludicrous; better look like I mean business and see if I can front it out,' and as usual he's pulled it off with quite brilliant aplomb. No one does a face-of-death quite like Straw. Despite possessing an inherently comic, kindly and rubbery face, which in any sane world would make him a shoo-in for the role of a goonish neighbourhood postman doing pratfalls in a broad sitcom, he's learned to overcome this affliction and can now resemble utterly authentic doom incarnate whenever the situation demands it. Look at this latest snap and the temperature drops in the room. You'd think he'd been born without laugh muscles and raised in a civilisation that never invented the smile. Bravo.

Pity about the bib, though. For one thing, even though it's clearly designed to demean the rapscallion wearing it, the government's 'respect tsar', whose real name is Louise Casey, says it isn't. 'The point of the orange jackets is not to humiliate people but to make the punishment visible,' she claims.

You've got to respect her opinion, mainly because she's the

respect tsar so she'll definitely notice if you don't – but really, that line of argument isn't fooling anyone. It's a bib, for Christ's sake. And besides, if 'visibility' is key, she's missed a few tricks. In fact the whole project is far too timid. Just be honest, announce you're going all-out to humiliate, demean and belittle, and we, the nation, will embrace it. Ignore the carpers. They'll never like it anyway. So don't wuss out. Go for broke.

Start by changing the wording. 'Community payback' is rubbish. 'Community' is pure British wonk-speak – the simpering language of milquetoasts – while the embarrassing yee-haw showboating of 'payback' must have been included in a half-arsed attempt to impress the tabloids. Put the two words together to make 'community payback' and the result just sounds lame, like the mistranslated overseas title of a below-par Schwarzenegger action movie in which he launches an all-out assault on a hardened gang of litter louts holed up in Chertsey.

And how are we, the snickering public, supposed to refer to these recidivist saps when we spot them emptying the poop bins anyway? Do we call them 'paybackers' or 'CPs', or what? If you're going to label them, at least come up with something populist. Something we can use. How about 'SCUM SLAVE'? Or 'CHAIN GANG BETTY'? That last one would definitely catch on. I might start shouting it at them in the street tomorrow. So put that on the back of the jacket. And, bearing your stated aim of 'visibility' in mind, don't just stop at bold capital letters: the typeface should physically light up, like a Vegas casino hoarding. Actually, the whole jacket should light up. And it shouldn't be a jacket. It should a fluorescent green leotard with a transparent panel located over the testicles, so you can see them squashed up against the window like depressed balding commuters and, above it, a small flashing sign with the words 'HA HA LOOK AT MY HILARIOUS BALLS' accompanied by an arrow pointing at them, picked out in multicoloured LEDs visible from half a mile away. Blind pedestrians who wouldn't otherwise get to enjoy the spectacle should be catered for too, thanks to a looped iPod soundtrack consisting of assorted celebrities describing precisely how ridiculous the miscreant's balls look, backed with comedy tuba music blasting from a heavy iron tannoy mounted on the offender's head.

That's a more effective deterrent than a little orange bib. And perhaps Jack Straw could model one at the press launch, doing one of his trademark sober expressions. He could probably even pull a serious face with his balls, so they looked suitably noble and statesmanlike even while flattened against the transparent pane, thereby underlining the scheme's commitment to visibility and aversion to humiliation. If anyone can do it, he can.

The day Santa died   [8 December 2008]

'Santa's gone home. Santa's fucking dead.'

As theme park slogans go, it's a winner. Sadly, it wasn't the official tagline for Lapland New Forest, the temporary Christmas attraction that was forced to close last week after furious visitors demanded their money back. Instead, the 'Santa' line was shouted at a *Sun* reporter and a 'handful of queuing families' by a member of staff disconsolately closing the gates for the last time.

Lapland New Forest sounds like a barrel of laughs. The publicity material promised a glorious winter wonderland replete with animal attractions, an ice rink, log cabins, a nativity scene, a snowy 'tunnel of light', and, of course, Santa's grotto. But according to incensed visitors, it turned out to be 'little more than a mud-covered car park'. They complained that the generator for the ice rink had malfunctioned, turning it into a pool of water, the 'tunnel of light' was actually a few fairy lights dangling from trees covered in artificial snow, the nativity was an amateurish billboard, the log cabins were green sheds, and the animal attraction was a handful of reindeer and several 'thin-looking huskies chained up in a pen'. To keep the kids happy, there was apparently a four-hour queue for Santa's grotto, at the end of which families were charged £10 for a photo with the man himself. Oh, and refreshments weren't cheap either. Five drinks and a baguette would set you back £17.

Many visitors, who'd paid around £25 per ticket, weren't especially impressed, and the mood quickly turned ugly. One of the security guards told the BBC he'd quit, partly because he was 'really, really ashamed' to work there, and also because of the level of violence he and the rest of the staff had been subjected to by irate customers. 'Santa got attacked,' he explained. 'One of the elves got smacked in the face and pushed in a pram.'

So now it's closed, which is a shame, because it sounds great to me. I love underwhelming theme parks. Slick, showy ones with hi-tech rollercoasters may be entertaining on the day, but really they're all the same. I've been to Euro Disney, Alton Towers and several others in that snazzy corporate vein, but they all blend into one in my memory. Mostly, I remember the queues. Give me a ramshackle DIY attraction any day. Those are the ones that stay with you.

I'll never forget the Concrete Menagerie, for example. Picture Madame Tussauds, but with the celebrity waxworks made out of concrete. And instead of stunning likenesses of the rich and famous, imagine a group of misshapen figurines that were scarcely recognisable as human beings, painted by an especially hamfisted group of GCSE art students in a hurry. That was the Concrete Menagerie. It was housed in the back garden of a house in Northumberland. A full-scale model of Jaws (the shark, not the Bond villain) which resembled a giant grey phlegm glob with eyes was one highlight. Another was a figurine of Lawrence of Arabia sitting astride a camel. Lawrence had a set of real false teeth stuck in his mouth, leaving him with an unsettling rictus grin.

Recently, a friend excitedly recounted a family trip to Collector's World, 'a highly popular tourist attraction in Norfolk', according to its website. He, his wife and their offspring got lost on a driving trip and found themselves drawn mysteriously towards it. It consisted of room upon room of bizarre, apparently unrelated artefacts. There was a 'Pink Room' dedicated to Barbara Cartland, a telephone museum, a collection of antique cars, some sort of hideous-sounding 'gynaecological chair', and best of all, a hall filled solely with memorabilia relating to the actor Liza Goddard, which apparently included pullovers and a mug she'd once drunk out of. Exhilarating and frightening in equal measure, I'd imagine, especially if you're Liza Goddard yourself.

So popular are skew-whiff theme parks, in fact, that there are two whole books devoted to collecting the best of them: *Bollocks to Alton Towers* and *Far From the Sodding Crowd*, which contain opening times and travel information for a veritable goldmine of enchanting and/or eccentric attractions, including the British Lawnmower Museum, Gnome Magic, the Margate Shell Grotto, and Cuckooland (a collection of 550 vintage cuckoo clocks). That Lapland New Forest has closed its gates before the team had a chance to include it in a third volume is almost – almost – a national tragedy.

Besides, if they'd somehow managed to keep it going, the weight of publicity its sheer thudding, sprawling crapness has generated over the past week could surely have turned things around, at least in terms of ticket sales. Thousands of people would doubtless have made the ironic pilgrimage, and the worse they'd found it, the better. A disappointing trudge through a car park to be ripped off by a man in an ill-fitting Santa costume.

It's hard to think of a more appropriate Yuletide experience.

Bathing with neighbours [5 January 2009]

Only one thing's going to get us through 2009, and that's romance. And possibly cannibalism. But mainly romance.

In case you missed the bulletin in your post-festive daze, let me bring you up to speed. According to the latest predictions, here's what we're in for this year: MISERY. Yes, not just misery, but MISERY. In capitals. Just like that.

Dim your lights. Here's the highlights reel. The worst recession in 60 years. Broken windows and artless graffiti. Howling winds blowing empty cans past boarded-up shopfronts. Feral children eating sloppy handfuls of decomposed-pigeon-and-baked-bean mulch scraped from the bottom of dustbins in a desperate bid to survive. The pound worth less than the acorn. The City worth less than the pound. Your house worth so little it'll collapse out of shame, crushing you in your bed. Not that you'll die peacefully in your sleep – no, you'll be wide awake with fear, worrying about the situation in the Middle East at the precise moment a chunk of ceiling plaster the size of a flagstone tumbles from on high to flatten your skull like a biscuit under a shoe, sending your brain twizzling out of your earholes like pink-grey toothpaste squeezed from a tube. All those language skills and precious memories splattered over your pillows. It'll ruin the bedclothes. And instead of buying expensive new ones, your grieving, impoverished relatives will have to handwash those bedclothes in cold water for six hours to shift the most upsetting stains before passing them down to your orphaned offspring, who are fated to sleep on them in a disused underground station for the rest of their lives, shivering in the dark as they hear bombs dipped in bird flu dropping on the shattered remains of the desiccated city above.

Welcome to 2009.

So what do we do? Well, as with any scary situation, we could try scrunching up our eyes and wishing it all away, but that rarely works, unless you're driving a bus across a busy junction and couldn't give a fig for convention. Instead, we're going to have to co-operate with one another if we're going to get through this. I know, I know: ugh. The concept of sharing has been knocked out of us. For years it's been all about you, your nice things, your signature dish and your plasma screen, and everyone else can go swing. Now we'll have to knock on doors and swap cups of sugar. But maybe it won't be so bad. Picture yourself sharing a meal with a neighbour. Or maybe a bath. A bubble bath. Look, there are little tealight candles round the edge of the tub. And you're having a glass of red wine together! It's lovely! Assuming you have attractive neighbours. If not, sorry. Just close your eyes and wish it away, especially when they stand up, turn round and bend over to search for the soap.

Actually that whole bath scenario might represent the way forward. It sounds quite romantic, and authentic romance has been in short supply of late. Authentic romance makes life more enjoyable, but more importantly it costs nothing. Buying flowers and baubles and Parisian city breaks – that's not authentic romance. That's lazy showboating. Authentic romance could flourish in a skip. Prove this to yourself. Invite someone on a date and spend the evening sitting in a skip making each other laugh with limericks or something. Get through that and you've bonded for life. Or maybe a week. It's hard to tell when you embark on a new relationship. Still, if you split up: time for more romance with someone else. Everybody wins.

Mark my words, you'd be wise to practise your romancing skills now, because when, circa October, we're huddled together in shelters sharing body heat to survive, the ability to whisper sweet nothings could prove useful. Come the dawn, you'll need to pair up with someone to go hunting for supplies with, and it'll help if you've been cuddling all night. The world outside will be dangerous, so there'll have to be two of you. One to root through the abandoned Woolworth's stockrooms and another to stand outside warding off fellow scavengers with a flaming rag on a stick.

Obviously if two is better than one, it follows that three is better than two, especially in the thick of a food riot. Rather than forming boring old duos as per tradition, polygamous unions involving up to 30 or 40 participants will emerge victorious, roving the landscape in packs by day, writhing around in obscene configurations in their papier-mache huts by night – strictly for the purposes of generating heat, of course. We can all do our bit. I, for one, am fully prepared to take on 50 wives if it'll help make the world more manageable, provided I don't have to talk to them and I get to wear a crown and issue decrees and everything. We'll create a kingdom in a cave somewhere and kill and eat unfortunate passers-by, like Sawney Bean and his family. Now they had vision. First potential wife to contact me with full Ordnance Survey reference numbers for a suitable location (warm cave, close to major thoroughfare) gets to be Minister of Skinning Trespassers Alive and Sticking Their Heads On Poles as a Warning to Others of Their Kind.

All things considered, this may be a bleak year but at least it'll be more interesting than, say, 2006, during which nothing happened. So grit your teeth and meet 2009 head-on, because it's not going anywhere until 2010 at the very earliest.

In summary: happy new year.

Life partners and joy thieves

Sigh. Yeah, that's right: sigh. Two years ago, almost to the day, I wrote a piece about the world's bizarre insistence on marrying me off, prompted by three separate incidents in which strangers chuckled at my shambling incompetence and suggested that what I needed was a proper sorting out, which could only arrive in the form of a wife. Cue much indignant spluttering on my part. For one thing, how did these strangers instinctively know I wasn't already married? Even gargoyles get hitched, sometimes. And for another, I didn't actually want a wife, thanks for asking.

Nothing beats living alone. Why shackle yourself to a fellow human being for the rest of your days? Because you're in love? Don't be a wuss. That'll fade after a few years and all you'll be left with is a walking catalogue of tiny, grating quirks gleefully pointing out your shortcomings. To avoid murdering each other, you'll have to keep yourselves anaesthetised with DVD box sets and the occasional holiday. Life partner? Joy thief, more like.

But maybe that's a lie, the kind of lie you live by in the face of mounting evidence to the contrary. There are a billion valid reasons to avoid settling down, but the root cause of most commitment-phobia is something else entirely. Namely terror. Raw terror. The terrifying prospect of falling in love in the first place.

Love can be genuinely awful. Worse than the norovirus on a coach trip. When it goes wrong – and it usually does – it kicks a hole in your ribcage and voids its bowels in your soul. Get burned badly and from that point on, falling in love is like inviting a werewolf into your home: you sit there fascinated, watching it eat at the table and admiring your curtains. You make conversation and share private jokes. But try as you might, you're not quite relaxed and you're not quite yourself; you're on tenterhooks, aware that any moment now it's going to turn round and bite your throat out.

In the face of love's potential destructive fury, you're left with three options. (1) Pull down the emotional shutters and try to avoid it. (2) Find someone you admire or like, rather than love, and try to make do, rendering both of you miserable in the process. Or (3)

Throw caution to the wind and gingerly place your fragile, beating heart in the hands of another human being and hope they don't crush it in their fist for giggles. On paper, the first option seems like the only sensible choice.

But gah and damn and blast and argh: it isn't. Not really. To carry it off with any degree of success involves suppressing all vestige of romance, which ultimately atrophies your insides and turns you into either a loner or a bastard, or some maddening, alternating combination of the two. And you can't entirely kill off the romantic impulse. When you're queuing in the supermarket on your lonesome, clutching a basket full of meat and veg, all of which has been carefully weighed and packaged into portions big enough for two apparently just to underline the folly of your isolationist policy, it's hard not to gaze enviously at the couples in front of you, even if they're bickering over a cheap jar of pasta sauce. They might be unhappy, but at least they're united by misery. The rest of us have to pick holes in ourselves. They get to share.

So maybe a wife isn't such a bad idea, I figured, as 2009 started to dawn. The problem is finding one. I've fantasised before about a society in which single people are assigned partners arbitrarily by the government.

But that's not going to work, because my checklist of desired attributes is impossibly lofty: I refuse to be satisfied with anything less than a clever, funny, misanthropic supermodel who spends 98% of her time ignoring my existence (because basic psychology dictates that nothing's going to maintain your interest quite like being dangled on a string for eternity), and the remaining 2% offering sickening reassurance. Thus far the universe has stubbornly refused to offer this up, and since no one on earth can possibly match up to this deluded ideal, which I don't deserve anyway, perhaps it's time to widen the net by aiming low. By which I mean below the realms of the human. Animals are out: they don't live long enough to make the social revulsion your union would provoke worth bearing. Unless you count tortoises, but they're too hard and aloof and ultimately unknowable to seriously consider settling down with.

No. A robot wife will do just fine. It wouldn't have to be terribly advanced: a crudely animated face on a stick offering relentless criticism and the occasional rude limerick would probably keep me sufficiently entertained to the grave. I'm aware even that might be aiming a bit too high. I'm not getting any younger, so give it a few years and I'll be content with a bag of gravel in a hat. Although just to keep things spicy, it'd be an open relationship: I'd let other men have sex with my gravel-bag wife, provided I could point and laugh as they did so.

Pour all your romance into a bagful of gravel? Yeah, I can see that. And it is, I suspect, the only conceivable future in which true and lasting happiness lies.

Chocolate Guernica [14 January 2009]

Here's another few millimetres shaved from the national joy quotient: the Food Standards Agency is launching a scheme to get restaurants to print calorie information on their menus alongside the name of each dish.

What used to happen was this: at the end of the meal, the waiter arrived clutching a dessert menu to ask if you wanted pudding, and you and your companion shared a quick jokey conversation along the lines of 'I'll have one if you have one' or 'if you order the Chocolate Guernica, I'll have one mouthful . . . just the one, mind', until the waiter smiled and said, 'I'll get two spoons,' and a few minutes later you enjoyed guiltily tucking into a velvety mass of warm brown mush together, then went home and had sex to underline what a decadent pair of naughty revolutionaries you'd been.

Now that same dessert menu will become a dossier of sobering statistics. It'll still be accompanied by descriptions of moist sponge enrobed in an oozing burqa of dark chocolate sauce, but no amount of unctuous wordplay can distract from those cold, hard numbers. Five hundred calories? The waiter might as well tip a jug of freezing water directly into your laps. Perhaps if it was also accompanied by a list of physical activities you'd have to undertake in order to burn off all that fat and sugar, the balance would be redressed. A scoop of vanilla ice cream? Ten minutes of kissing in a shop doorway. Caramel cookie surprise? That'll be accompanied by a pornographic instructional line-drawing complete with arrows pointing out precisely what you'll have to put where, and how firmly and repeatedly you'll have to repeat the action. And so on.

The one drawback: business lunches with the boss would be rendered awkward and excruciating. But that's a small price to pay. Another upside: parents wouldn't bring their children to restaurants.

Unless they do that, all the scheme will achieve is a rise in the national level of food-related neuroticism, which is surely peaking in conjunction with obesity statistics. A similar system in New York restaurants apparently reduced the average diner's intake by around 100 calories. A success, on the face of it, although the figures don't show how many of them went home and tucked into a bowl of Ben & Jerry's because they wanted dessert but also didn't want to be judged an indolent slob by the waiting staff.

The whole calorie-counting business is far too anal anyway. It encourages fat people to waddle around with a headful of damning numbers, perpetually totting up their score like a failing bookmaker carrying out an internal audit. It's the same with alcohol and units. Literally no one understands the units system.

Around Christmas the NHS ran a campaign called Know Your Units which looked a bit like the periodic table: rows of different-shaped glasses full of different drinks, each with the relevant unit number finger-painted in condensation on the side. Not only did it underline how baffling the units system is, but because the forbidden beverages were all lovingly shot, cool and inviting under studio lights, it actually made you want to try drinks you wouldn't normally contemplate. Hey, that vodka and tonic I saw this morning looked refreshing. How many units was it again? I can't remember. God, I'm useless. I hate me. Think I'll have 10. That should blot out the failure.

Rather than bashing us over the head with numbers, the healthy-living Reich needs to employ more creative means to make the indolent, slobbering populace bend to their will. For starters, how about hooking every chair in every restaurant up to a weighing machine? Having instantly gauged how disgusting you are, a computer prints out a menu with the most gluttonous items removed. Or you could do away with the waiters entirely, and replace them with a food pipe. You sit down on the weighing chair and shove the pipe down your gullet, and a nutritionally balanced river of mulch is pumped directly into your stomach from a giant processing unit in the kitchen which hums ominously and has lights that blink on and off and a giant rotating swastika on top just to spook the underlings gingerly filling it with low-fat chicken stock.

That might prove expensive. Wing mirrors on the cutlery, however, would be cheap: distorting funhouse mirrors specifically angled to reflect your own wobbling, bloated face from the most unflattering angle as you shovel hunks of lamb casserole into your despicable gaping mouth. To make the experience more unpleasant, they could train a dog fed exclusively on onions and beer to run in from a back room and quietly blow off under the table each time you raise the fork to your mouth.

Actually, why not just ban food? Step one: make owning a kitchen illegal. Step two: replace all supermarkets and cafes with trucks that rove the streets three times a day dispensing bite-sized meal-pellets. Make sure the trucks are controlled by a computer, so they adjust their pace each time a crowd approaches, forcing them to break into a run and gain essential exercise.

Alternatively, they could carry on patronising and nagging and prodding and hectoring until everyone in the country gets so utterly sick of it all they take up arms and start a violent revolution. Beating your way through a flank of riot police to smash down a government building with a sledgehammer burns off thousands of calories. And afterwards you can sit down in the rubble and skeletons eating mouthfuls of pie, secure in the knowledge that you've earned yourself a treat.

President Superman   [26 January 2009]

Last week I watched the most frightening horror movie I've ever seen. It was about three hours long, and, incredibly, it all unfolded live. I'm talking, of course, about the inauguration of Barack Obama. Yes it was inspiring, yes it was uplifting . . . but it was also genuinely terrifying on a very human level, because just like you I was watching it with the terrible nagging suspicion that he might get shot at any moment.

At this point it's worth stating unequivocally that I've never wanted to see anyone being shot, thank you very much, whether they're a president or the world's biggest arsehole or both. And fortunately, such things rarely happen. But I've seen too many films, and far too much 24. I've been conditioned to almost expect it. So now, whenever the news cuts live to a politician – any politician – making a speech, I'm gripped by an eerie sense of dread and have to change the channel.

Obama's inauguration, however, was too big to miss. All that hope and expectation distilled into one man whose election has, at a stroke, reminded the world of all that is good and remarkable and inspiring and simply downright wonderful about the most exciting nation on earth: America. For the last eight years, watching America at work was like watching the scenes in *Superman III* where Superman, under the influence of red kryptonite, goes 'bad' and grows stubble and gets drunk and starts vandalising the city and shouting at kids. He's only stopped when his geeky alter ego Clark Kent magically fights his way out from within, and stands blinking before him, in his nerdy suit and thick glasses. Evil Superman scowls, and the pair have a cathartic bust-up in a junkyard – at the end of which Evil Superman is finally vanquished. As a battered but unbowed Clark Kent gazes up at the heavens, the theme music swells, and he pulls his shirt open to reveal – ta da! – a fresh, clean Superman costume he'd been wearing underneath the whole time. Then he flies off and beats up Robert Vaughn or something, which is a shame because until then it had all been a pretty good metaphor for the redemptive spectacle of last November's election.

And now it's just a silly action movie I probably shouldn't have mentioned in the first place.

Still, Obama really has been elevated to the position of Superman in many minds, to the point where it's hard to keep a check on expectations; we're all yearning for him to single-handedly save the world. Hearing him referred to as 'President Obama' on the news still seems too good to be true, like waking up the morning after falling in love and wondering whether you're dreaming.

But we're also aware he isn't a Man of Steel; painfully aware too that the world contains its fair share of racists and paranoid gun nuts, which is why many of those tuning into the inauguration did so with a mixture of joy and trepidation.

Everyone I know had voiced the same dark fears, even in the face of constant updates from the news networks regarding the mammoth security operation surrounding the day. We were told Obama would be travelling in a mortar-proof vehicle thronged by secret service vans, each filled with about 200 tiny Jack Bauers, packed in like sardines; there were radio jammers to prevent the detonation of bombs and a magic experimental gas enveloping the Mall capable of transforming bullets into harmless glitter. Nonetheless, the entire thing unfolded like one of those scenes in a slasher flick when the heroine heads into a spooky old house on her own, and it all goes quiet, and you tense uncontrollably in your seat, knowing that at any moment someone in a hockey mask is going to burst from a cupboard wielding a threshing machine or something.

The rolling news networks, which rarely shy from exploitative gimmicks, clearly missed a trick by not offering an alternative commentary option in which a jittery, paranoid viewer accompanied proceedings with jittery, paranoid narration. 'Here's the presidential motorcade now . . . oh Jesus, he's stepping out! He's in the open! Where's security, goddammit? Look at the size of that crowd . . . let's hope they frisked everyone on their way in. He's approaching the podium . . . That bulletproof glass is a bit low for my liking. Oh Christ I can't watch.' And so on.

When the ceremonial cannons went off following the swearing-in itself, you could actually hear buttocks clenching around the world. Did they really have to do that? It just felt downright mean. Because, quite frankly, the vast majority of people on this planet would be far happier if, for the remainder of his presidency, Obama only makes public appearances encased within a gigantic iron-and-concrete ball, addressing crowds via a Wi-Fi link to a nearby tannoy. And even then, it'd be more comforting to assume that this was, in fact, a bluff: that the concrete ball was empty, and the man himself was actually speaking to us from a deep underground bunker, ideally one situated on a different planet, made of cotton wool, in another universe altogether, unmarked on any map, somewhere round the back of our most peaceful and powerful collective dreamings.

CHAPTER FIFTEEN

In which Noel Edmonds rants down a lens, Knight Rider *makes an ill-advised comeback, and* Greece Has Talent

Noel's Wide-a-Waco Club [14 February 2009]

I've mentioned Sidney Lumet's 1976 satire *Network* before, but really: it looks more like a documentary with each passing second. The film revolves around Howard Beale, a newscaster who goes crazy and threatens to commit suicide on-air. Rather than sack him, the network notes the ratings spike generated by his outburst and promotes him as a 'mad prophet of the airwaves'. Soon, record audiences are tuning in to watch him deliver increasingly deranged rants to camera. I won't spoil the rest; rent it tonight if you haven't seen it. No, actually: don't. Just tune into *Noel's HQ* instead.

Noel's HQ – Noel's Party Headquarters, if you like – is the strangest programme on TV. A live Saturday night 'shiny floor' show with conspicuous altruism at its core, it's essentially a cross between *That's Life*, *Surprise Surprise*, and some unmade episode of *I'm Alan Partridge* in which Alan snaps and runs into traffic with his shirt off, smashing windscreens with a cricket bat.

About 90% of it consists of Noel Edmonds introducing members of the public who've suffered tragedies, or set up charitable trusts, or both – and then doing nice things for them. Last week, two charming old ladies who'd established a children's charity were whisked away to the *Strictly Come Dancing* live tour and left with huge grins on their faces. Nice people being rewarded for niceness: only a shit could find fault with that.

It's the remaining 10% that's troublesome: specifically the bits where Noel shouts about petty-minded local councils, and the studio audience cheers or boos and waves union flags and the whole thing starts to resemble a disturbing political rally.

Last week the show featured an item about a badly injured marine who, having lost both legs in Afghanistan, was denied planning permission for a specially adapted bungalow by his local council. It was a tale that would irritate more or less anyone – the guy's lost his legs, so cut him some slack, for Christ's sake. Following an emotive VT on the subject, Cheggers (Noel's eternal sidekick; someday they'll be buried together) read a statement from the council saying they were prepared to negotiate with the marine and his family.

297

Good. But not good enough for Noel, who wanted them there in the studio. Worse still, the council's press officer, Jim Van den Bos, told a researcher that Wealden District Council wouldn't talk to 'an entertainment show'.

This was the cue for an astonishing three-minute down-the-lens rant during which Noel yelled that Jim Van den Bos, and people like him, were 'at the heart of everything that's wrong with this country', while the audience cheered and yelled. He went on to suggest, via the medium of bellowing, that the people of Wealden should 'have their say' at the next local election – and that hopefully they'd be 'advertising for a new press officer soon'. All of which slightly overshadowed the bit where he read a statement from Gordon Brown supporting the construction of the bungalow. Council policy aside, what really irked Noel, it seemed, was being dismissed as an 'entertainment show', even though: (a) it's listed on the Sky EPG under 'entertainment', (b) The studio audience wear big foam gloves with 'Noel's HQ' printed on them, and (c) It opens with a theme tune that sounds like a pinball machine malfunctioning on a bouncy castle.

Highlighting the story would've been enough: instead, Noel stood before a baying TV mob calling for the instant dismissal of a press officer who doesn't make planning decisions, had already issued a statement, was presumably simply doing what he was told, and possibly has a family to feed.

Next time, maybe Noel should concentrate on the nice surprises for charity workers. Otherwise, before we know it, he'll be carrying out live public executions – death by gunging for bureaucrats – while the audience fires pistols and Cheggers sticks heads on poles. Either that or he'll be running for office. Presumably on behalf of the House Party. Noel's HQ? Number 10. FEAR THIS.

The colour of horrid   [21 February 2009]

Taglines are generally a lie. 'A journey beyond your imagination' usually transpires to be a phutting clown car ride down Guffington Crescent, while 'the movie event of the year' happens six times a month and refers to anything from Abbott and Costello Meet the Ombudsman to Attack of the 100-foot Bum Monsters.

Here's one that bucks the trend. *The Colour of Money* is billed as 'the most stressful game on television' and – by golly! – it turns out it genuinely is the most stressful game on television, at least until they bring out a gameshow in which the recently homeless have to solve dot-to-dot puzzles at gunpoint to win a new house before a swinging sharpened pendulum cuts their foot off.

It's hosted by Chris Tarrant, whose neck is growing increasingly alien and fascinating by the day, so much so you spend more time staring at his neck than his face, which means they might as well draw a pair of cartoon eyes on it and zoom the camera in until the top of his head is cut off and you can just get on with the job of staring at his neck without feeling guilty about not looking at his actual face. If you follow me.

Anyway, never mind that. *The Colour of Money* is effectively a blend of *Deal or No Deal* and bomb defusal. Chris welcomes a contestant into the studio, which looks a bit like the inside of a Cylon baseship from *Battlestar Galactica* crossed with a neon graveyard filled with onyx, outsized iPods. The giant iPod things turn out to be 'cash machines', each containing a different sum of money. The players pick a machine (each differentiated by a different 'colour', hence the title) and stand staring at the screen while a cash figure steadily rises. The trick is to shout 'stop!' before the machine hits its total and 'locks you out'. Since you don't know how much cash it contains, this means balancing greed against nerve.

To increase the tension, each contestant has to do this 10 times, and is given a set target at the start. Say it's £64,000: this means they have to get an average of £6,400 from each machine, and if they don't manage that, they get piss all.

Look, I know you're baffled: trust me, it makes sense when you see it, just like all gameshows (except *Goldenballs*, which has more rules and clauses than the European Convention on Human Rights). What it boils down to is this: endless gnawing anxiety as the players attempt to defuse one potential bomb after another. Somehow the makers have hit on a game that provokes one of those indefinable yet intrinsic human sensations: just as Tetris is inherently satisfying, so *The Colour of Money* is inherently nerve-racking. At times I found the preview DVD so unbearable I had to hit the Mute button and look away until the next round. It's like watching a blindfolded man running back and forth across a level crossing. Totally horrible.

In case the game itself wasn't stressful enough, ITV has decided to play up the human angle with a chilling remorselessness that borders on the psychotic. Each player is introduced via an emotive *X Factor*-style VT in which they explain, in quavering vulnerable voices, just how precious and important the money would be to them. There are lots of references to the credit crunch and 'these difficult times'. The first contestant is a mum-of-two whose husband is about to be sent to fight in Afghanistan. This becomes a break-bumper sting. 'With her husband recalled to the army, can Diane secure her family's future?' asks the voiceover, over footage of Diane hyperventilating and blinking back tears.

All of which is tasteless, and not very British. Completely unnec-essary too, since the game itself is so compelling, tense and yet ultimately random, it's likely to be a huge worldwide hit. Unless someone in Argentina has come up with something even more tense, like a game in which new parents have to watch their gur-gling offspring crawl obliviously through a cave of whirring chain-saws towards a pot of shining gold. Give it a week.

Perspex soup   [28 February 2009]

Perspex Soup. Wind and Pineapple Biscuits. Absinthe and Dildos. One of these is genuinely on the menu in *Heston Blumenthal's Feast*, which is without doubt the most mental cookery programme you'll ever see, unless you're in the habit of necking six LSD tabs on a weekend morning and staring at *Saturday Kitchen* until James Martin's face turns into a singing horseshoe in space.

I've decided I very much like Heston Blumenthal, who recently seems to have become the most omnipresent of all the TV chefs.

Unlike the others, he doesn't scream at failing restaurant managers or tut at overweight schoolkids. He doesn't even pretend to teach the viewer to cook. He just does demented things with food, clearly enjoying himself as he does so. He's the culinary equivalent of Wilf Lunn, the mustachioed 'mad inventor' who used to show up on kids' TV in the 80s, demonstrating various self-built Heath Robinson devices which performed some abstract function for a few minutes before exploding in his face. There's something scary about both of them: a true lunatic's glint.

This new series is the best showcase for Blumenthal's talents so far. *In Search of Perfection*, the BBC2 show in which he set about anally creating 'perfect' burgers and so forth, was too prissy, while *Big Chef Takes On Little Chef* came across as awkward. In *Feast*, however, he's merely required to create the most preposterous dishes possible.

That's the full extent of the format: Heston researches and cooks something absolutely psychotic, then serves it to a table full of celebrity guests (fittingly, a weird selection, encompassing Richard Bacon and Rageh Omaar). It's like a special edition of *Come Dine With Me* hosted by the unhinged artisan murderer from the movie *Se7en*.

Each week there's a vague overall historical theme (this week, the Victorian era), but that's really only a springboard to inspire Heston to do something daft and usually quite frightening. And he really does go above and beyond in his quest to create mad food; at times it borders on insane ritualistic behaviour. At one point this week, he cheerfully boils a cow's head in a pan, reduces it to a con- centrated stock, then freezes the resulting fluid into the shape of a fob watch before serving it to his guests in a tea cup. He also deep- fries a mealworm and injects it with mayonnaise.

And then there's the dildos. For dessert, Heston decides to serve an outsized jelly with terrifying sexual overtones, which means spending an afternoon experimenting with gelatine and vibrators in a Hoxton sex shop. The jelly itself contains absinthe. Rather than just pouring a load in, he first travels to France to have a drinking contest with an absinthe expert, to discover whether the drink will, as rumoured, induce visions. Some way into the boozing session he looks confused and turns to camera.

'I've got no hallucinations yet,' he says unsurely, 'but I always think bananas taste better with three-legged cows in a vegetable shop.' I had to rewind and check three times: that's what he says, word for word, with no further explanation offered. Shortly afterwards he announces he can't drink any more and goes to bed.

This really is one of the most creative shows I've seen in quite a while; not in the construction of the programme itself (which takes the familiar 'mission' format to provide a fairly spurious narrative), but in Blumenthal's inventive craziness. It's basically a bloke deliberately dicking around to extreme effect for an hour, dabbling in a weird form of art, seeing how far he can go. Halfway through, I realised why this was so refreshing: you very rarely see such genuinely ingenious and imaginative processes being followed this clearly on TV. Each course Blumenthal serves is like an edible *Python* sketch: meticulously constructed and very, very silly.

There's absolutely no need for this show to exist, or for old Mad Specs the Chef and his helpers to put so much effort into it. But it does, and they do. It's daft and great. Hooray for this.

All ears [7 March 2009]

The digital station FX punches above its weight in terms of top-notch TV series. *The Wire. Generation Kill. Dexter. Breaking Bad.* All of them received their first showing over here on Sky channel 164. Well now it's got *The Listener* to add to that list. Just to bring down the average.

The Listener isn't a very good example of a high-quality American import. Mainly because it's Canadian, but more importantly because it's rubbish. In fact even the title is rubbish. You know why it's called *The Listener*? Because the main character listens to things.

OK, so they're not common-or-garden things. He listens to people's thoughts. He's telepathic, just like the chubby Keanu Reeves-lookalike policeman in *Heroes*. That's actually a fairly interesting premise, so why pick the most boring title imaginable? It's like creating a Superman series and calling it *The Flyer*.

Anyway, the Listener himself is a paramedic called Toby. And this is the next disappointment; he's a massive puss. He looks like a cross between Frodo Baggins and the mono-browed teenage pie-full-of-twat who used to star in the 1989 Yellow Pages commercial about the kid who needed a French polisher to fix a scratch on a coffee table following an early example of a *Skins* party in his parents' house. Apparently Toby's been a telepath since birth, which is odd, because each time he hears a thought dribbling out of someone's skull he pulls a confused face, as though it's never happened before. I call it a 'confused face': actually he just looks gormless, as if he's about to start going 'buhhhhh' and bumping into the scenery. It's like he's trying to impersonate a stupid dog being amazed by its own bowel movements.

His powers aren't even particularly impressive. For one thing, he can't hear everything, only just enough stuff for the writers to be able to move the plot along a few notches. In the first episode, he's trying to find out where a bad guy has hidden a kidnapped woman and her kiddywink, yet despite standing RIGHT NEXT TO HIM several times, he doesn't pick up anything, thereby forcing him to break into said bad guy's house later to look for clues. For all the good his powers do him, he might as well be pulling fortune cookie predictions from his arse and following their instructions to the letter. That would pull in 20 times more viewers, even if they stuck to their literal-titling policy and called it The Adventures of Magic Bum Man.

Anyway, 99% of the stuff he does manage to hear (when the screenwriters let him) consists of useless trivia. At one point he hears his boss thinking, 'Man, I'm grumpy when I don't get to watch the wrestling', so he decides to cheer him up by offering to lend him a WWF video. It really is that exciting.

And wait! It gets even worse than that. The writers can't even decide exactly how his powers work, because sometimes he sees thoughts as well as hearing them. For instance, he 'sees' the bad kidnappy guy in a vision at one point, which is why he recognises him when they cross paths later. That's not listening! That's look-ing! Why didn't they call it The Looker-and-Listener? These people are idiots.

I could go on, because the questions keep mounting up. Why, in the dull romantic subplot, doesn't the Listener just immediately know whether his girlfriend wants to continue their relationship or not? Why is the version of Toronto the Listener lives in so incredibly underpopulated that a whopping great 4x4 vehicle can crash in the middle of a central city street, and end up on its roof, on fire, with-out a single bystander looking on? Why does the whole thing feel like a bad cut-scene from a late-90s 'interactive movie' CD-ROM game? Why? Why? Why?

I doubt the Listener himself knows. The thought processes involved in creating this series must've been so horrendously unfo-cused that no matter how hard he strained, they'd just sound like a low fuzzy hum. Or, more accurately, an uninterrupted 55-minute raspberry.

A pillock of Apprentii   [28 March 2009]

The Apprentice throws up many questions. Such as: what's the plural of apprentice? Apprentii? Apprenticeese? Let's go with the former. And now we've established that, what's the correct collec-tive noun for a group of Apprentii? A pillock of Apprentii? A wankel? A swagger?

Swagger it is. Right. Now we can proceed.

As this year's swagger of Apprentii marched into view over the Millennium Bridge, I was struck by two things. Firstly by the way that during the initial stages when there are far too many of them to really focus on, they all fall into one of two categories: inter-changeables and aliens. The interchangeables are nondescript, hovering around in the background as though auditioning for Nick and Margaret's job, a bit like visual filler. Sometimes you'll spot one in the boardroom and scratch your head trying to remember their name. But don't be fooled: the series is always, always won by an interchangeable. They start developing names and personalities somewhere around week five. Think of them as hatchlings.

The aliens, meanwhile, draw the eye. I was once told that the mark of a well-designed cartoon character is that they remain recognisable even in silhouette – think of Bart Simpson or Mickey Mouse. Some of this year's Apprentii already fall into that category: there's one physical characteristic or affected visual quirk that makes them stand out. Mona, for instance, has fascinating eyes: beautiful, but exactly the same as Nookie Bear's (Google it if you don't believe me). Howard is a genetic cross between previous winners Simon and Lee, albeit one with the downward gaping mouth of a depressed coelacanth moaning about all the damp weather they've been having underwater. Ben looks exactly like hitherto-undiscovered footage of Aidan Gillen (AKA Tommy Carcetti in *The Wire*) playing a local businessman in an imaginary episode of *Emmerdale* from 1999. Even so, as I mention their names, chances are you won't quite be able to recall who I'm talking about yet. There are just too many of them. It's still just a swagger of Apprentii.

A youthful swagger at that. The cliché that you know you're getting old when policemen start looking young applies even more strongly to Apprentii. Half of them dribble. One is seven years old. I keep expecting them to pull out a set of toy cars during the boardroom scenes and start making brrmm brrmm noises while Sir Alan's trying to bollock them.

Speaking of Sir Alan, it's heartening to see that these stormy financial times haven't beaten an ounce of humility into him. Despite an ongoing makeover which sees him becoming physically leaner and slicker each year, his character remains constant: the level of unwarranted, snarling belligerence hasn't dropped a single share point. Even though last week's inaugural task was a fairly pedestrian car-washing challenge, he conducted the final showdown like a murder trial – not any old murder trial, but a gangland, kangaroo court, *Long Good Friday* sort of trial, the sort that takes place in an abandoned warehouse and ends with one of the defendants being hung upside down and having their knees sliced off with an angle grinder.

If he's this angry during week one, with any luck by week six he'll be throwing furniture around in a rage and grabbing candidates by their ties. And instead of sending the fired loser out of the room to meekly collect their suitcase, he'll nod a small gesture in Nick's direction and leave the room.

At this point Nick quietly taps a button under the desk (locking the doors), silently pulls on some tight leather gloves and advances slowly towards the victim, brandishing a syringe filled with a sinister clear liquid. The victim beats their fists against the exit to no avail, as Nick moves in, smirking coldly, moving ever closer, relentless as a Terminator. Close up on the glistening tip of the needle as it draws near. Cut to black. Tortured scream. Roll credits in silence.

This, my friends, is precisely the kind of entertainment we need during a recession.

Against Philip [25 April 2009]

Sorry for being away for weeks. I've had a pain in the neck, literally. Not just the neck, but the shoulder, elbow, fingers . . . you name it, it's screwed. I'm told it's probably a herniated C7 disc, and it's a constant source of joy. Numbness, tingling, a ceaseless sharpening ache . . . it's not agonising, more accumulatively infuriating; like sitting in a cinema with someone continually kicking the back of your seat. And you can't get out of your chair.

Each day brings a revolving carousel of dispiriting symptoms, all of them apparently set on 'shuffle'. On Monday the tingly numbness in my fingers might be a main concern. Tuesday may feature unrelenting shoulder pain. Enfeebling tricep weakness on Wednesday. And so on.

I bring this up not because I want your pity (well, maybe slightly), but because it's the perfect metaphor for the current series of *The Apprentice*, in which the primary source of discomfort shifts with each episode.

A fortnight ago, for example, I decided Ben was the villain of the piece. Everything about him irritated me as much as someone tossing a handful of staples in my face. For starters, he displayed an almost satirical level of self-confidence, claiming to the best at this and the champ at that and the King of the Galaxy and so on. He seemed to earnestly believe he had the ability to cleave entire universes in two using his mind alone, like Doctor Manhattan from *Watchmen* but markedly less blue and without a big pubeless dick swinging around like a loose sleeve, threatening to slap the entire front row in the face.

And if Ben's manner alone wasn't enough to earn him a poke in the mind's eye, his silly head was there to take up the slack. What's with the surprised eyebrows and the trim cartoon eyelashes? He looks like Top Cat with stubble. Or a He-Man figurine with the head of a six-year-old girl. Where's his neck? Has he got a neck? His head seems to be growing straight out of his chest cavity, like an emergent conjoined twin suddenly gasping for your attention. Perhaps he's got a second head sprouting from his arse, dribbling business-speak between each greasy fart and turd.

Anyway, that's what I'd have said if you'd asked me about Ben a fortnight ago. But it seems a bit cruel and unnecessary now. He's calmed down a tad, and besides, he's only 22. Who isn't a prick at 22? I certainly was.

No. The real enemy is clearly Philip, the 29-year-old former estate agent with the Durham accent. He was actually my favourite for a while. Not any more. He's flared up. He's gone horrible.

Philip seems to spend 98% of his screen time shouting his own opinions over anything anyone says. And if they're a woman, he'll shout twice as loud, for twice as long, like some previously unseen character from *Life on Mars*, only less amusing because he's wearing a smart suit and some hair gel instead of a zany kipper tie. And boy does he love himself.

He looks like he throws himself roughly on to the bed each night, hungrily moving his hands all over his own body, trying to kiss himself deep in the mouth. If it were legal or even possible to do so, he'd probably marry himself, then conduct a long-term affair with himself behind himself's back, eventually fathering nine children with himself, all of whom would walk and talk like him. And then he'd lock those mini-hims in a secret underground dungeon to have his sick way with his selves, undetected, for decades.

If you asked Philip if he thought the world revolved around him, he'd blink and ask you what exactly a 'world' was, then go back to staring in the mirror, drooling and smiling and pointing and saying 'Philllllippp, Philllllipppp' over and over again like a mantra.

Next week, I'll probably dislike another candidate more. But right now? It's Philip, Philip, Philip all the way to the Shit Shop and back.

Male physical splendour   [2 May 2009]

Extreme Male Beauty is the title it says here on the preview DVD, so naturally I assumed it was a documentary about me. I am terrifyingly beautiful. People often scream and hurl themselves under passing trucks the moment they spot my physical splendour gliding towards them. Embittered naysayers may claim my face resembles a damp curtain billowing in the squall of a bison fart, but these people have neither eyes nor souls. Let's be honest. I make David Beckham look like a sockful of piss.

But some men, it seems, don't share my obvious psychological confidence. Men like radio DJ Tim Shaw, who presents this show. He spends half the intro detailing what an average schmoe he is – indolent, a bit flabby, probably flatulent – and generally projects such a familiar everyday air you'll probably think you've met him at some point or another, as though he's thingummy's boyfriend you met a few years back at that barbecue thing for Sarah's birthday. Any sense of mutual acquaintance is dashed, however, when it gets to the bit of the show where he shows you his pale, gingery penis. Especially because his penis isn't just hanging there like a crippled finger, but being stretched by some kind of metallic device, like it's had a fight with an articulated corkscrew and lost. And you never saw that at the barbecue, did you?

The point of the programme, apparently, is to 'explore' the increasingly demented body-image issues afflicting British men. Men have completely lost their minds in recent years, buying hair straighteners and eyeliner and stupid bloody clothes in their millions in a concerted bid to craft themselves into a cross between a Manga character and a *Big Brother* contestant. Walk down any high street these days and it's like passing through the Valley of the Preening Wusses. While women have an impressive variety of 'looks', from Girls Aloud to 1940s vamp, fashionable men only seem to have one: vain prick. Why would anyone want to dress like these see-yoo-enn-tees? This is life, not an audition for *Hollyoaks*.

Anyway, for a show investigating insecurity, this seems ironically insecure itself, throwing about 10 million familiar 'format points' at it in the hope one will stick. So as well as an 'authored documentary' strand in which Shaw hits the gym to see if he can get rid of his 'man boobs', we also get a makeover section in which a bloke from Doncaster is transformed by three 'professionals' – a surgeon, a dentist and a stylist – who've allowed themselves to be filmed in a wanky, swaggering manner guaranteed to make 99% of the audience despise them. On their watch, Mr Doncaster gets sliced up, drilled and tailored until he emerges looking like the sort of man who might host a late-night shopping show demonstrating portable MP3 speakers. And apparently that's a victory.

On top of that, we're given a 'talent show' in which prospective male models compete for the chance to be an anonymous torso on the cover of *Men's Health* (a magazine which might as well call itself Abdominal Grail). This section provides the perfect excuse to whip out yet another essential TV staple: the judging panel. But disappointingly for all concerned there's very little to judge. Just buff blokes taking their shirts off. No crazy blobbos turn up demanding to be seen, waddling into the room with their bellies jiggling around while the producers dub comedy trombone music over it or anything like that.

Then we get some earnest chat about steroid abuse, some footage of Tim Shaw puffing away with a chest expander, a recap on Doncaster Boy, a glimpse of Shaw's dick, and that's it. It's like 10 slightly different shows on the same subject jostling for space in a waiting room. Oh, and male viewers? Unless you're sitting on an exercise bike at the time, do bear in mind that while you're slumped on the sofa watching this, you'll grow slightly fatter, slightly older, and slightly less attractive than you already aren't. Take my advice: give up.

Go Faster Tripe   [9 May 2009]

In 1983, if you wanted to play a videogame, you had to wait five minutes while your Sinclair ZX Spectrum loaded it from a tape. The game would consist of you guiding a crudely animated car mechanic across three screens of irritating peril, collecting magenta spanners and listening to beepy sound effects. You'd die every four seconds, couldn't save your position, and when you got to the end your reward was a stark caption reading 'Well Done', followed by the game starting all over again, except slightly faster.

Eighties games weren't fun at all. But TV wasn't much better. In 1983 the original series of *Knight Rider* hit British TV screens. It was a show about a coiffured berk in a talking car, and it was awful. David Hasselhoff was the berk; the talking car was a Trans Am called 'KITT'. It's fondly remembered today thanks to its cool theme tune and amusingly portentous title sequence, in which a bowel-straining voiceover told us we were about to witness 'a shadowy flight into the dangerous world of a man who does not exist' (presumably because being honest and saying, 'Here's a load of made-up shit about a tit in a car which might help you pass another hour before death,' didn't play as well with the focus groups).

Knight Rider was cancelled in 1986, but TV execs just couldn't let that brilliant berk-in-a-car concept die. In 1991, it returned as a TV movie called *Knight Rider 2000*, which was basically *Knight Rider* in the future (or rather the past, given our current vantage point), in which KITT came equipped with a built-in fax machine. In 1994, they tried again with *Knight Rider 2010*, a sort of Mad Max debacle: it didn't feature KITT or David Hasselhoff at all. 1997 saw the arrival of *Team Knight Rider*: basically Power Rangers on wheels. Died after one season.

For years, things were quiet on the *Knight Rider* front. Now it's back, in a vanilla 'reboot' – i.e. no 'future' nonsense, just the adventures of a new berk (Michael's son) and his talking car. Of course while the show was off-air, thanks to the invention of Sat-Nav, everyone got talking cars in real life, so the 2009 incarnation of KITT has to try extra-hard to impress. It's solar-powered, it can morph into different types of car to confuse the baddies, and it's got an internet connection.

I'd call the new KITT an iPhone with an exhaust pipe, except if it really was like an iPhone then instead of fighting crime, its owner would spend the entire duration of each episode endlessly droning on and on about how brilliant KITT was, and how he can't believe you haven't bought one yourself yet, and every time he passed another KITT driver, they'd feel compelled to pull over and sit there Twittering each other about the latest astounding downloadable KITT 'apps', like the one that makes a shoe appear on the screen, then you tilt it and the shoe rocks around a bit and plays the *Star Wars* theme, and it's amazing really, the things it can do. Actually, you know what I'd watch? A series about a maniac who drives around singling out iPhone owners, slapping their stupid toys out of their hands and stamping on them. That's the first three minutes of each episode; the remaining 57 consist of an unflinching close-up of said iPhone owner's sorrowful face as they scoop all the bits of shattered iPhone off the pavement, clutch it to their bosom, and stagger down the pavement, weeping and lost and alone, unsure whether to carry the remains to the nearest A&E department or drop them in a bin and buy a new one.

Anyway: the new *Knight Rider* is mindless but almost watchable, just like the old *Knight Rider*. Games are infinitely more rewarding than they were in 1983, however. Therefore this series will fail. Its target demographic is busy elsewhere: on Xbox Live, watching blockbusters on their PSPs, playing lightsabers with their iPhones etc.

Knight Rider 2009 could've been a fantastic driving/RPG hybrid videogame. Instead it's a televised quack-fart. Let's use progress properly, people.

Yes, Sir Alan   [16 May 2009]

Something's niggling me about the current run of *The Apprentice*, and it's this: what with this being the fifth series, my notion of what constitutes unacceptable humiliation for the candidates has become skewed beyond measure. The tasks, ostensibly designed to be a measure of their business skills, are really just exercises in making them look stupid – given a day to create a complete rebranding of the seaside resort of Margate, for instance, anyone without prior twatty marketing experience is going to flounder spectacularly. So it made them look like tits. But I scarcely noticed, because they look like tits every week.

Similarly, each episode culminates in Sir Alan hurling insults at all and sundry in the boardroom whether they deserve it or not, like a grouchy stand-up pre-emptively heckling his crowd. And I've developed an alarming immunity to that too. In fact my 'bollocking tolerance' has shot through the roof, to the point where I've started to believe that's how regular conversation between normal human beings should work. Only the other day I told a shopkeeper that the way he'd put the items in my carrier bag was a mess, a shambles, a cock-up so big you could see it from bladdy SPACE, son, and that I was starting to wonder if he was just like one of them balloons with a face drawn on it, an impressive face, yeah, but scratch the surface and there's nothing behind it, just a leaky inflatable full of blummin' arse gas, so he'd better watch his step if he wanted to keep my custom.

This situation will never do. If repeated exposure has left me impervious to *The Apprentice*, then *The Apprentice* has to change – to develop new, meaner twists. More humiliating send-offs. In short, it sorely and surely needs to adopt one of the following three brilliant gimmicks.

1. Uniforms for the candidates. At the moment, they've adopted a uniform of their own – sharp suits for the gents, power bitchwear for the ladies, with the dominant colours being black and charcoal grey. I'm assuming the production team stipulate this (although they made a notable exception for Lucinda last year, who dressed like a mad art teacher with a vision deficiency). Why not force them to wear gaudy bright orange 'fast-food worker' overalls, complete with a name badge and a number of stars? Better yet, if you're one of the final three called into the boardroom, you have to do it next week in your pants.

2. Reject all pretence at testing business skills. The tasks have zilch to do with actual business acumen; we all worked that out ages ago. So why not just see who's best at performing some entirely arbitrary chore? Who's best at writing a children's bedtime story on a laptop computer while sitting in the tiger enclosure at Chester Zoo? Which candidate can permanently cripple themselves the fastest using only one hand and a dowelling rod? The possibilities are endless, and appalling.

3. Make the boardroom a revolting ordeal. The boardroom showdowns are tense, but they're not stomach-churning. *I'm a Celebrity* powers ahead in the ratings each year precisely because it regularly becomes almost too disgusting to watch. *The Apprentice* has to better this. So each week, when the final trio return for the firing ceremony, Sir Alan should suddenly and flatly demand all three of them rim him.

Yes, rim him. And before they rim him, just to make it more humiliating, they each have to describe, in punishing detail, precisely how they're going to tackle it, and just how good they'll be at doing it. The one with the worst technique gets fired. After five minutes of stunned silence, I guarantee they'd set about the task with grim desperation, like poisoned jailbirds frantically licking antidote from a rusted keyhole.

Anyway, there you have it: three sure-fire pathways to ratings gold. If the show doesn't adopt all three of these measures IMMEDIATELY, then absolutely everyone involved in its production – right down to the lowliest runners – is a whimpering pussy. And that's the TRUTH, yeah? Yeah!

Hello Dolly   [23 May 2009]

I've never seen *Buffy the Vampire Slayer*. Not a single episode. Buffy fans are appalled by my negligence. 'You MUST watch it!' they scream. 'It takes about two seasons to get going, but then . . . my God, it's the best show ever made'.

Two seasons to get going? That's a commitment of 34 episodes before even its fans think it becomes worthwhile. And there's a further five seasons after that. Given the fans' sparkly-eyed evangelism, I don't doubt for a moment that there's something of worth there. But I'm not a young man any more. I'm greying. My bones ache. It's too late for me to embark on a quest of that magnitude. Consequently, Buffy's been consigned to the growing list of things I'll never try, like bungee jumping and crystal meth.

Yet I have found time to sit through the first two episodes of *Buffy* creator Joss Whedon's latest creation, *Dollhouse* (Sci-Fi). And it's bloody awful. Perhaps it'll turn into a work of genius in its third season. I won't know, because I'll have either given up or died by then.

The premise is interesting: it's about a young person who has their mind wiped each week and imprinted with the personalities, memories and expertise of a bunch of other people, before being sent on a mission. In other words, it's like *Joe 90*, except you're supposed to want to screw the lead character, because the lead character is the improbably gorgeous Eliza Dushku, not a nine-year-old schoolboy marionette.

In week one, Echo (that's her name) was transformed into an expert in Latin American kidnap negotiations, which meant she donned glasses and wore her hair up in a bun. In week two, she's an outdoor-sports-enthusiast-and-fuck-buddy, which means she gets to dress a bit like Lara Croft and have sex in a tent. Typing this out, I've realised it isn't *Joe 90* at all. It's Mr Benn, except you're supposed to want to screw the lead character, because the lead character is the improbably gorgeous Eliza Dushku, not a two-dimensional paper cutout of a middle-aged businessman.

It's not just *Quantum Leap* week after week, mind. No. There's a whole bunch of other characters walking around overseeing the 'Dollhouse' which Echo gets returned to each week. For instance, there's a black ex-cop who has to oversee her missions by hiding round the corner in a van and tediously getting his cover blown. There's also an irritating nerd who performs the mind-wipe-and-brain-filling ceremonies – one of those implausible, punchable little tits who only exists in TV or movies. Apparently he's a scientific genius, although he looks about 12 years old and everything he says has to pass through about 500 pop culture irony filters before it leaves his smackable wise-cracking mouth. The minute he first popped up on screen, I instinctively knew me and *Dollhouse* would never be friends, in the same way that finding a Scouting for Girls album on someone's iPod would stop you wanting to have sex with them.

The improbably gorgeous Olivia Williams plays an icy boss-type woman who speaks in cool aloof 'mission operative' military code-speak the whole fucking time, and Tahmoh Penikett from *Battlestar Galactica* shows up as Agent Jawbone Hunk, an improbably gorgeous FBI bloke determined to uncover the truth about this 'Dollhouse' thing he's heard about which his colleagues insist is just a wild rumour but he's got this hunch there's more to it than that and blah blah BLAH BLAH OH WHO CARES?

It's just nonsense. And nonsense is fine when it consists of a small kernel of nonsense surrounded by something either plausible or interesting. *Dollhouse* has neither and, crucially, there's too much emphasis on empty prettiness, from the set design to the faces of all involved. Everyone's so improbably gorgeous you won't give a shit whether they live or die. Unless, perhaps, you've had your mind wiped and replaced with the brain of an orange – probably the premise for next week's episode, which I won't tune in for. Someone let me know if this bullshit gets going somewhere round season three, yeah?

Greeks Got Talent [30 May 2009]

Unless the weather's majestically terrible or some new 9/11 magnitude event takes place, there's absolutely no excuse for watching TV on holiday. If you're somewhere sunny, chances are you won't watch anything at all, unless you're such a dull football-liking git you think you'll lose the ability to breathe if you can't see the latest match via satellite in a horrific bar specialising in full English breakfasts and sugary cocktails surrounded by fellow pink-shouldered, cow-brained, hooting, awful wankers.

By the time you read this I'll be back, but right now I'm in Crete, staying in a place whose satellite TV system offers about 10 billion channels, approximately 100% of which aren't in English. OK, so you can pick up the BBC World TV news channel, but no one's ever willingly watched that for longer than nine minutes. It's a channel whose viewer demographic consists exclusively of men sitting on the edge of a hotel bed impatiently waiting for their girlfriend to finish in the shower so they can go and have a shit.

Part of the fun of having so many incomprehensible foreign channels is flicking through them and trying to guess what country they're from. If you're as ignorant as me, this is usually completely impossible. Lots of them look like news broadcasts from the *Star Wars* universe (specifically, the Clone Wars era). The basic visual grammar of news is always the same – host, desk, spinny CGI graphics and so on – but they're often accompanied by national dress codes and entire alphabets I've never seen before. I swear one channel featured a newsreader with a designer lampshade on his head and a headline ticker comprising nothing but triangles and spirals scrolling right to left across the screen. I couldn't tell you precisely what story he was reporting on, but I think it concerned a trade dispute in another dimension.

News aside, there are hundreds of channels promoting phonewank services, usually with an Indian or Middle Eastern flavour. One consisted of a photo of a lady's bum, a phone number, and nothing else. It didn't change once during the six or seven hours I watched it.

Still, every so often you stumble across something that authentically draws you in. The other night it got too windy to venture outside, and I wound up watching an Arabic TV movie (helpfully subtitled in English) about a guy called Majid who kidnapped an Iraqi general who'd killed his parents, and then agonised for ages (and ages and ages) over whether to shoot him or not. There were scenes shot in real bombed-out villages – incredibly disconcerting to my Western eyes – and despite being shot on pretty harsh video, the overall level of visual artistry seemed higher than the average British TV drama. Majid didn't shoot him in the end, incidentally: the general escaped, only to be killed moments later by a land-mine. God moves in predictable ways.

But perhaps the most mesmerising thing I've seen was a few moments of the Greek incarnation of *Britain's Got Talent*. It was instantly recognisable – same format, same logo, same visual grammar and similar acts. This only served to highlight the differences. Instead of young, slim Ant and Dec, there was one middle-aged paunchy bloke standing just off stage giggling to the cameras. The judges, meanwhile, were spectacular. Impossibly, they look even weirder than the British Morgan/Holden/Cowell line-up.

There was a pretty woman, a bloke who resembled a bleached-blond pimp from the year 2049, and a terrifying man who appeared to have undergone extensive plastic surgery at the hands of a demented satirical artist – who'd decided to make him look precisely like David Hasselhoff morphing into Michael Jackson. I didn't see him indoors. I was standing in the night air, watching him for several minutes on a silent plasma TV through the window of a shut hair salon, before snapping out of the trance and getting on with the holiday. Wherever you go, TV ultimately tastes the same. And there's more than enough of it at home.

Attack of the invisible pirates [6 June 2009]

Ross Kemp sits talking to a group of British sailors in the bowels of a Royal Navy ship patrolling off the Somalian coast. 'When you first signed up to the navy, did any of you expect to end up fighting pirates?' he asks. 'I did,' says a guy at the back. 'But then I joined in 1640.' Everyone laughs.

With the possible exception of those who've recently been machine-gunned in the face and tossed overboard by one, everyone loves modern pirates. They've brightened up the news considerably by making it sound more like a swashbuckling adventure movie than a tuneless paean to mankind's perpetual failure.

It's the name. Our brains are hard-wired to find the word 'pirates' thrilling and slightly camp, although modern pirates don't do any of the cool stuff the old, fictional ones used to do, like burying treasure, or making people walk the plank, or hobbling around on one leg with a parrot on their shoulder which keeps butting in to finish their sentences with a squawked rejoinder. Modern pirates are all T-shirts and mobile phones. Not to mention rocket launchers. They're not really much fun at all, but because they're still called 'pirates' we secretly think they're great.

That's evocative brand names for you. If George Bush had called the US military 'The Cowboys', and the Elite Republican Guard 'The Indians', we'd probably have thought the invasion of Iraq was totally justified and brilliant.

Anyway, Ross Kemp. There's another brand name. He's become shorthand for 'macho documentary on the kind of subject Alan Partridge used to fantasise about'. Having tackled gangs and the Taliban, he's moved on to international piracy, in *Ross Kemp: In Search of Pirates*. But do tell your dick not to grow turgid just yet. There's a clue to the amount of actual piracy he encounters hidden in that title. In particular, note how they didn't call it Ross Kemp: Fighting to the Death with Actual Bloodthirsty Pirates on the Listing Deck of a Sinking Ship in a Biblical Thunderstorm.

I could do a documentary called Charlie Brooker: In Search Of Pirates in which I walked around Balham knocking on doors and asking if there's anyone called Bluebeard in, and while it might not rate too well in the Audience Appreciation Index, no one could reasonably complain about the accuracy of the title.

Anyway, Kemp's much harder and tougher than me, so he does actually get reasonably close to some proper pirates, even though most of the first episode consists of him hovering over the ocean in a helicopter as the navy investigates one false alarm after another. What with all the publicity pirates have been getting of late, there are quite a few jittery boats off the African coast, see, and they're likely to report suspicious activity at the merest sight of a fishing boat.

When an act of piracy does occur, the navy finds out too late and consequently doesn't really get to intervene. The helicopter with Ross in it flies quite close but has to keep its distance in case it gets brought down by an RPG (this is the point at which I'd be screaming to go home: like I said, Kemp's harder and tougher than me). Shortly afterwards they find an abandoned skiff that's been used by some pirates, with some weaponry and some petrol on it. Out of sheer frustration the navy crank up a giant machine-gun and spray it with bullets until it explodes, just like it would in a film. This means Ross gets to do a link with a big burning boat in the background. Everyone must have been delighted.

Later in the series Kemp meets a genuine pirate face-to-face, although from what I can gather, instead of standing atop a mainsail, desperately fighting him off with a sword, he's more interested in asking about the political and social problems that have created the phenomenon of modern piracy in the first place. Not fair. Far too sensible. But then Ross Kemp: Calmly Exploring the Topic of Pirates wouldn't have looked so hot on the EPG, I suppose.

Big Brother Q [13 June 2009]

So then, *Big Brother 9*. I mean *Big Brother 10*. Or *Big Brother Q*. When I watched the launch night, I swear I could tell the housemates apart. Then I caught a bit of it a few days later and suddenly they'd all changed . . . except they absolutely hadn't.

It's like that David Lynch movie where all the actors are recast halfway through yet their characters remain the same. Except in this case there aren't any definable characters. Or a plot. Just some people wandering around muttering.

To make things difficult for the casual viewer, two of the housemates quickly changed their names by deed poll as part of a task. Freddie, for instance – a slightly fey posho who always seems to be hesitantly smiling with his mouth open, like someone who's arrived at the end of a joke and suddenly forgotten the punchline – had his name legally changed to 'Halfwit'.

This means Marcus Bentley now has to say 'Halfwit is in the Diary Room' on the voiceover every few minutes. Harmless chuckles, maybe, although I wonder what they'll do if he has some terrible accident while he's in there, a real *Casualty* episode-opener, such as tripping near a kitchen surface and puncturing an eye on a bread knife. How funny would the subsequent news reports sound then? (OK, quite funny, but that's not the point.)

The house also contains two identical booby blondes, one of whom is now called 'Dogface'. This should confuse readers of *Nuts* magazine in a few months' time, when they're trying to masturbate to pictures of her with nothing on. So it's not an entirely futile exercise. It would've been braver to simply rename all of them 'Housemate One', 'Housemate Two', and so on. Or – and here's a far better idea – they could've named them all after characters from *Coronation Street*, then dressed the interior to closely resemble the Rover's Return.

Anyway, apart from Halfwit and Dogface, I'm not really sure who any of the other housemates actually are, even when I look at still photographs of them with their names written down underneath. Having watched and written about reality shows for years, the section of my brain that stores information about new contestants has finally been filled to capacity. It's like trying to pour a quart into a pint jug. It just won't go.

If I squint really hard with my mind's eye I can just about make out Sophia, the tiny shouty one who looks like a June Sarpong action figure. But even there I have doubts, because there's also one called Saffia.

And the two of them don't get on. Sophia shouts at Saffia. Saffia shouts at Sophia. Which is which? I don't know, and before I can work it out, it cuts to Halfwit again. Marcus Bentley calls him Halfwit on the voiceover, but the other housemates still call him Freddie. Dogface (whose real name is Sophie) is telling Halfwit (Freddie) about the argument between Sophia and Saffia. At least that's what I think is happening, until it turns out that it isn't Dogface telling Halfwit this after all: it's Karly. Karly is the girl who looks like Dogface (whose real name is Sophie). Silly me. Maybe they could broadcast a diagram at the start of each episode.

As for the others, there's a three-year-old Brazilian Disney boy, a lesbian in a comedy punk wig circa 1983, a bloke who looks a bit like James Lance playing an Iranian Justin Lee Collins, another woman, some sort of female weirdo who's time in the house is clearly depriving Covent Garden of an annoying mime artist, and a nerdy guy who looks like Lemmy trying to bluff his way into an X-Men convention.

Of this lot, two are currently having to walk around with a moustache and glasses permanently drawn on their face as part of another task. So out of 16 unfamiliar people, two have been given aliases, and another two forced to adopt a disguise. At this rate, by next week they'll be filming the whole thing through a kaleidoscope. Just to alienate the viewer yet further.

Diced Dumbo   [27 June 2009]

If you were to compile a list of 100 things you wouldn't really want to see on TV, 'watching someone methodically dissect the corpse of an elephant' would probably feature somewhere around the mid-30s point, sandwiched between 'Simon Bates investigates naturism' and 'toddler being sick against a butcher's shop window'.

Certainly my initial reaction on hearing about *Inside Nature's Giants* was one of incredulity balls-deep in glee. Once I'd got over the title, I thought: they're ACTUALLY chopping up an elephant? For an HOUR? Bless their sensationalist socks. That'll be fun to write about. Maybe they'll use a chainsaw on the trunk. Maybe there'll be a bit where they get 28 dwarves to climb inside the skin and form a human pachyderm, walking around like a giant pantomime horse while the producers play 'Baby Elephant Walk' on the soundtrack. Maybe they'll pull one of its eyes out and demonstrate how tough it is by asking Vernon Kay to jump up and down on it till it bursts, except it won't burst – it'll be like jumping on a giant squash ball, so he'll slip over and land face-first in its guts.

None of that happens. Make no mistake, they take the poor creature apart. There's not a bit of that elephant you don't get to see. They pull the skin off, drag the intestines out, saw the legs into segments . . . and yet, and yet . . .

And yet the overwhelming sense you're left with is one of towering respect for the wonder of nature, for the excitement of science and its role in explaining the world. This is categorically not an empty freak show, but one of the most remarkable natural history programmes I've ever seen. The gore may sound off-putting but it isn't really. It's fine once you're over the initial shock – like jumping in an unheated swimming pool that feels cold for 10 seconds until your body gets used to it.

The first thing to understand is that the elephant wasn't killed for the sake of the programme. It was dead anyway. Secondly, these dissections take place regularly, for the benefit of trainee veterinary surgeons (there's a large number of them watching proceedings throughout). Thirdly, and perhaps most significantly, the programme takes each segment of the elephant – literally – and uses it as a springboard for a fairly in-depth VT sequence detailing how said part works and why it evolved that way.

So we get an entire section on the digestive system, one on the trunk, another on the feet, and so on, all illustrated with bespoke reports from Africa, archive footage, explanatory CGI animations and even Richard Dawkins, who pops up a couple of times to share his awe of nature (and appears so delighted and enthused by the process of evolution, he manages to talk for several minutes without once calling all organised religion a bastard).

At every turn, you learn new things about elephants – and not just things you didn't know, but things you hadn't even thought of questioning. Take the feet. I always thought of elephants' feet as simply being stumps with toenails. In fact I scarcely thought of them as 'feet' at all, but legs that ended arbitrarily at the point they met the ground. I now know that, inside, the skeletal structure of an elephant's foot is surprisingly human. They're effectively walking around on tip-toes: the rear of each foot is a kind of fatty pad, a shock absorber, like a spongy wedge heel. It evolved to help them cope with their massive weight. That's a small example, but one that's genuinely changed the way I'll look at elephants for ever. And it's precisely the sort of detail that might simply wash over you in a more traditional nature documentary.

This is a rare thing – a hardcore biological science documentary that will both entertain and enlighten almost anyone who watches. It's also strangely moving. Because they chop that elephant to pieces all right – but they do so with palpable love. Watch it. It's amazing.

One small step for (a) man   [4 July 2009]

Neil Armstrong was the first man on the moon. Pretty impressive. So impressive that 40 years later, people still make documentaries wondering what that must've been like. *Being Neil Armstrong* is the latest.

Its premise is this: Neil Armstrong has become a recluse. He never signs autographs and doesn't speak to the press. Why? Why don't you want to come out and talk to us, Neil? Why Neil? Why? Why? Why? What's the matter with you Neil? What's your problem? OI, NEIL! WHY?

Since we're repeatedly told that Neil Armstrong effectively now lives a hermit-like existence in which he scarcely acknowledges the existence of humankind, an interview seems unlikely, so presenter Andrew Smith has to find different ways of discovering what makes him tick. He goes to Neil's home town and talks to a woman who used to be friends with his sister. She reveals that he wasn't a particularly unusual or talkative character.

The woman now runs a model airplane shop, so Smith buys one, goes back to his motel, assembles it, and throws it out of the window. Maybe Neil Armstrong used to do stuff like when he was a kid, he says.

Then he chats to one of Neil's old schoolfriends who reveals that, yes, Neil did play with model planes. Brilliant. We're getting somewhere. When he wasn't making planes, did he like to jump up and down yelping and pointing excitedly at the moon? No. The erstwhile schoolfriend also recalls Neil as fairly subdued person.

We see photos of Neil at school, looking quiet. 'Who would have guessed this quiet boy would one day become one of the most famous men on the planet?' ponders Smith.

Nobody did. Perhaps if he'd spent his childhood bellowing 'I LOVE THE MOON', or 'ONE DAY I'LL GO TO THE MOON', or simply shrieking the word 'MOON!' at passers-by, maybe someone might've guessed. But he didn't, so they didn't.

Next Smith's in his car, thinking. 'Maybe he was just an ordinary, nice man,' he says. As you may have gathered by now, not much is happening in this documentary. He drives to a house in the middle of nowhere where Neil used to live. Can he have a look round? No, because he doesn't have permission. He's not even allowed up the driveway. Someone else is in there, though: a couple being shown round by an estate agent. As they leave, Smith, still standing outside, stops them. Did they know this used to be Neil Armstrong's house?

No they didn't.

Thankfully, before things devolve to the point where Smith is looking at a napkin on the basis that Neil Armstrong probably once looked at a napkin, we get to the part of the story where Neil goes to the moon, and there's lots of thrilling footage of that and some good interviews with other former astronauts. The pressures of fame would overwhelm Neil, they reckon. When you've been an astronaut, everyone asks you to repeat the story of how you walked on the moon again and again until you're not even sure of the details yourself. For Neil, the pioneer, it would be intolerable. We meet a barber who once sold a bag of Neil's hair sweepings for $3,000. Little wonder the poor man became a recluse. Little wonder he lives in a lightless cave, shunning all contact with the world outside. It's a sobering moment.

So imagine my surprise when, after the credits roll, I visit Wikipedia in search of some more facts about this solitary, mankind-dodging loner and quickly discover that as recently as 2005 he approved the release of an official biography called *First Man: The Life of Neil Armstrong*. There's also a photograph of him happily receiving a platinum disc of *Fly Me to the Moon* from Quincy Jones at a Nasa anniversary gala in 2008. He doesn't look like a man crushed by the weight of human expectation, but a normal guy who probably couldn't be arsed talking to the 7,000th film crew to contact him that week. Is that right Neil? Neil? Is it? Is it, Neil? WELL, NEIL? IS IT?

– After this article appeared, an (apparently understandably) irritated Andrew Smith got in touch with the Guardian *to explain that the preview copies of his documentary sent out by the BBC press office had featured a commentary not written or approved by himself, which was subsequently changed prior to broadcast. It's only fair to point that out here. And to redress the balance, I'll throw in a free plug for his book* Moondust, *even though I haven't actually read it yet, on the basis that two friends of mine who HAVE read it tell me it's very, very good indeed.*

Insert plinth pun here   [11 July 2009]

As I type these words I'm periodically switching to another window, in which a chubby woman sits on the fourth plinth in Trafalgar Square, applying make-up. She's occasionally shouting 'morning!' at people. Apart from that, nothing's happening. Yet it's so compelling, I can't stop flipping over to look at it, even though I'm on deadline. Now she's texting. Now she's on the phone to someone. Now she's stood up. This column's never going to get written.

I'm talking, of course, about Antony Gormley's *One & Other*, the 'public art' project in which people take turns standing on the fourth plinth for an hour. It lasts 100 days, so that's 2,400 people, each of whom has their 60 minutes of glory streamed live on the internet. There's also a weekly catch-up 'highlights' show on the Sky Arts channel. It's Big Brother: Tate Modern Edition, essentially.

I say *Big Brother*: it's actually more like the good old days of *Big Brother*, the early ones when we were astounded to watch live footage of people simply pottering around in a kitchen. When the housemates were left to 'get on with it' rather than dress as pirates and play party games every four minutes. The days when nothing happened and we didn't mind. That's what this is like, minus a Geordie voiceover.

Mind you, even though the 'plinthers' have zero opportunity to form holiday romances or start racist arguments (what with being alone up there) they're equally – if not more – attention-seeking than your average BB housemates. Half of them have come in fancy dress. We've already had a man dressed as a town crier bellowing about his pub, a man dressed as a cat fielding texts from the public, and a woman who did the midnight-to-1 a.m. shift disguised as a giant pigeon, occasionally emitting a rather half-hearted 'cooo' noise. (Her costume was particularly rubbish: she looked like the lead in an illegal Turkish version of *Batman* shot on a budget of 25p.)

In other words, it's 'Britain's Got People'. Except no one's judged or voted off. They get their full slot regardless. The comedy writer Dan Maier (a regular *TV Burp* contributor, fact fans) quickly defined a condition called 'Twenty-Minute Sink-In – the point at which plinthers realise their idea will sustain nowhere near an hour'. Andy Warhol was spot on: 15 minutes is just right. After that they start to visibly deflate. A mini-breakdown ensues. The town crier quickly seemed to turn on the passers-by, berating them for not asking any questions. No one's done a shit or started jerking off yet, but that's bound to happen before the 100 days are up. It's like a David Blaine stunt taking place for no discernible point. So just like a David Blaine stunt, then.

There's also no technological 'public interaction' system in place, although you can go down there in person and shout at them. That happened a fair bit last night. Trafalgar Square's pretty rowdy at 1 a.m. No one's thrown a bottle high enough to catch one yet – and hopefully they won't – but that's bound to happen before the 100 days are up too.

Every hour, on the hour, a cherry picker comes in to swap one plinther for another. Right now the chubby woman's now being replaced by – uh oh – a man dressed as a turd carrying a loudhailer. He's protesting that 2.5 billion people don't have a proper toilet. Or clean water. Ah, he's doing it for Water Aid. It's like the London Marathon for people who can't be arsed running.

Fifteen minutes have expired for turd man, so now he's gone a bit quiet. But he does, at least, have some props: a giant fish head, which he'll presumably get to in a few minutes. If you're applying to go on the plinth (which you can do, via their website), I'd recommend taking a good book, or at the very least a Nintendo DS. Or maybe a small video recording of the previous plinther to stare at. Because it's a proper time sponge, this. Dangerously hypnotic. Sod the Angel of the North. This is brilliantly futile.

A nice lie down and a bleed [1 August 2009]

For all its delusions of grandeur, TV drama rarely deals with authentically frightening subjects. Except murder, which has been so overdone it's almost ceased to seem like a real or scary phenomenon. If I died at the hands of a serial killer I'd probably just think, 'Ooh, how exciting, it's like something off the telly', before enjoying a nice lie down and a bleed.

Every so often, however, along comes a drama that takes a long, hard look at something you'd rather blank out altogether, something large and menacing and beyond your control. Take *Threads*, the BBC's profoundly horrifying 1984 nuclear war epic, which brought Armageddon kicking and screaming into the nation's living rooms. You can get it on DVD or find it online: even today, when we spend approximately 98% less time worrying about mushroom clouds, watching it feels like being repeatedly punched in the kidneys during a powerful comedown.

It's hard to know whether shows like this actually do any good. I saw *Threads* when I was about 12 - too young to handle it, frankly - and it left me feeling despairing and helpless. Perhaps if I'd grown up to be a policymaker it would've been a positive influence. But I didn't. I grew up to be a neurotic bell-end.

Threads wasn't the only BBC drama about nuclear war. In 1966 they made *The War Game*, which was judged so terrifying its transmission was postponed for a whopping 19 years. Making shows on touchy subjects is a gamble; there's always a chance real-life events could take an unpalatable turn, leading to your programme being yanked off-air. Of course in the event of nuclear war, you wouldn't have time to moan about the schedulers. You'd be busy turning into a carbonised smudge.

With all this in mind, my vote for Show Most Likely to Be Pulled from the Schedule at the Last Minute this week goes to *Spanish Flu: The Forgotten Fallen*, which I assume (given the lead times for drama) must've been commissioned before the first reports of swine flu started coming in from Mexico. It's a drama-documentary looking at the attempts of Dr James Niven (played by Bill Paterson) to stem the spread of a deadly flu outbreak in Manchester circa 1918. Under normal circumstances the subject matter wouldn't seem too remarkable. Since we're in the middle of a contemporary outbreak, however, it's inherently riveting. Even though our current strain is markedly less lethal than the 1918 lurgy, if you're even slightly jumpy about public health issues it'd probably be best not to tune in. A cheery romp through a valley of saffron daffodils this is not.

In fact, in the present climate, with ministers warning that unnecessary panic could harm the NHS more than the flu virus itself, I'll be downright astonished if the transmission date doesn't change. It's grimly fascinating stuff, all in all, with uniformly excellent performances from the cast, but somewhat undermined by a few unnecessary lurches into sensationalism. The first scene depicts an angelic child dropping dead in the street while watching another group of children playing ring-a-ring-o'-roses (the plague song, geddit?). This is soon followed by an absurdly OTT sequence in which a dying man, staggering around as though infected by an alien disease whose chief symptom is gory melodrama, coughs blood and phlegm all over a window in front of a horrified crowd. Before long Dr Niven's running around trying to convince the doltish, avaricious authorities that there's a killer on the loose, while the bodies start piling up in earnest. It's *Jaws*, essentially, but starring an invisible microbe instead of a rubber shark.

Oh, and just to keep you on your toes, each time you find yourself thinking, 'Yeah, but the 1918 epidemic was far deadlier than ours', the characters discuss the fact that they'd already had a previous, milder outbreak, that this second wave is far more virulent, and that that's how plagues always work. At which point they might as well turn directly to camera, rub their hands together and emit a long, slow, maniacal cackle. Viewer discretion is advised.

When hypotheses attack [8 August 2009]

Good taste is overrated. I ate in a fancy modern Japanese restaurant the other day – like the despicable self-parodying media bastard I am – and the menu was so trendily, minimally written and designed I couldn't tell where the starters were or how many courses to order, or indeed, whether half of it was actually a 'menu' at all. One list of dishes was simply headed 'news'. Were they edible? I would've asked a waiter, but their tasteful uniforms rendered them far too intimidating to question. Instead I ordered at random. My first course resembled a tiny sliced diagram. Again, it was terribly tasteful. So tasteful I felt like shitting in my palms and flinging it around the room while barking like a seal. Hey, it's a standard panic response. Don't judge me.

Bad taste is preferable. Eat somewhere where they hand you a wipe-clean laminated menu slathered with gaudy colour photos and you know exactly what you're getting: something that tastes like it's been retrieved from a murderer's basement and reheated in an electronic armpit. Knowing it'll be bad for you but tucking in regardless – that's inherently glorious.

Which leads us to *Deadliest Warrior*, an astonishing American 'theoretical combat simulation' show that hits our screens this week. Unless you live beside an insane overweight divorcee who regularly shags stray cats to death on his front lawn – and the chances of that are fairly slim – it's easily the least tasteful thing you'll see all year.

At heart, it's a blokey 'who's the hardest' pub debate made flesh. Each week, they take two legendary fighters from history – an Apache and a gladiator in the opening episode – and attempt to work out which is the most effectively violent. Not by, say, interviewing scholars and military historians at punishing length, but by assembling a terrifying arsenal of ancient weapons and getting some 'combat experts' to try them out one by one. What this boils down to is almost an hour of footage of unbelievably angry men performing hideous assaults on worryingly realistic human torsos, wired up to a computer that can work out how

329

loudly a real person would shout 'ow' as its jaw flew off.

Throughout the series, everything gets tested, from terrifying slicing weapons that resemble bits of arcane farming machinery, to present-day funnies such as grenades and assault rifles. Ever wanted to find out precisely how much damage a spiked club could do to a man's face? Here's your chance. Remember that Martin Scorsese cameo in *Taxi Driver* where he invites Travis Bickle to contemplate the horrors a Magnum (the gun, not the ice cream) could inflict upon 'a woman's pussy'? *Deadliest Warrior* could imagine the results and give him a print-out.

But the real fun begins once the arsenal's been assessed. The Top Trumps data is fed into a computer (running 'custom-made software' apparently – Abject Guesswork 4.0, I reckon) and we're treated to a preposterous live-action 'reconstruction' of a theoretical fight between the tough guys; a sort of When Hypotheses Attack. Cue hilariously gory sequences in which Ninjas stab Pirates, William Wallace skewers a Zulu, the Yakuza and the Mafia shoot each other in the knees, and the Taliban take on the IRA.

Yes: the Taliban take on the IRA. In the season finale. Which is better – an Islamic extremist or an Irish republican revolutionary? There's only one way to find out. Fight!

You'll have to wait weeks for that, but if you're a fan of astronomical bad taste, you'll enjoy it. Especially the bit where they watch footage of real IRA operations and go 'woah, that's HARDCORE'. And the bit where they test landmines and nailbombs and flamethrowers. And the bit where the IRA and the Taliban go head-to-head in an American car park for NO REASON WHATSOEVER. It's one of those pieces of television that defies logic, taste, and decency to such an immense degree, it actually ceases to be offensive and teeters on the brink of inadvertent artistic genius instead. Who'd have thought the spectacle of Western civilisation actively collapsing into madness would be this funny? Ha ha! HA HA HA!

CHAPTER SIXTEEN

In which MPs provoke fury, potato crisps appear in appalling new flavours, and the British National Party offends anyone with a basic grasp of human decency and/or graphic design.

The New Media Dictionary

This week, in a break from my traditional self-centred misanthropic festival of whining, here's an abridged version of the *New Media Dictionary*: a useful compendium of terms and definitions for the exciting world of modern mass communication.

abbaration (*abba-rayshun*) n. Inexplicably successful West End musical based on the back catalogue of any once-popular pop act in the vein of *Mamma Mia*; e.g. 'I see *Dancing On the Ceiling*'s opened at the Lyceum. Think it's some sort of Lionel Richie abbaration.'

auntiepathy (*auntee-pathee*) n. Ingrained tabloid hostility towards the BBC.

broverkill (*bro-verr-kill*) n. To be almost, but not quite, as bored of listening to people talk about how they don't watch *Big Brother* as by the continued existence of the programme itself.

carolemalone (*carol-mal-own*) vb. To viciously pontificate about a celebrity's perceived character flaws and imagined motivations while grinning like the dung-fed offspring of Peter Cushing and Zelda from *Terrahawks* channelling Kajagoogoo in your nightmarish byline photo; e.g. 'For God's sake, Jennifer, take off that fright wig and stop carolemaloning about John Cleese's divorce, will you? You're making my soul weep.'

chudge (*chudj*) n. An underqualified judge on an underwhelming TV talent contest.

commentally ill (*com-mental-ly-ill*) adj. To believe that airing one's views in either a newspaper column or the Have Your Say section accompanying the online version of said newspaper column is a meaningful activity when compared to, say, spending eternity masturbating alone in a soundproofed cupboard.

craptitude test (*krap-ti-chewed tessed*) n. A televised talent contest with a panel of chudges (*qv*).

crotchdog (*krotch-dog*) n. Dismal paparazzo whose career consists of lying in the gutter desperately pointing his camera up the skirts of celebrities exiting limousines.

dwindlethink (*dwin-dull-think*) vb. The process by which a member of the public forms an opinion on a subject of national importance after viewing a plebbledashed (*qv*) news report, then finds themselves passing it on to the nation when stopped in the street for another plebbledashed (*qv*) report the following day.

funography (*phun-oh-grafee*) n. Television programme which gleefully revels in its own hideousness. Also funographic (adj); e.g. 'Last night's *I'm a Celebrity* was so funographic I chortled all the shame cells out of my body.'

i-witness (*eyewitness*) n. Any internet messageboard user quoted in a newspaper article in a bid to pad out a weak story; eg: 'Leona Lewis fans were furious last night after the star pulled out of a charity gig at the last minute. An i-witness raged: "We'd queued in the rain for hours . . . Now when I look at my copy of *Spirit* it makes me want to puke."'

inspector Google (*inspector googol*) n. Allegedly 'investigative' reporter who relies solely on the internet.

life-affirminge (*life-affer-minge*) adj. Descriptive of any TV 'makeover' show that purports to boost a participant's confidence in a positive and inspirational manner by encouraging them to weep and strip completely naked on camera, preferably simultaneously.

mock examination (*mokk-eggs-ammy-na-shun*) n. Close-up zoom-lens photograph of vaguely out-of-shape holidaying celebrity accompanied by disdainful copy pouring unwarranted scorn on their physical failings.

mousemob (*mows-mob*) n. Gathering of indignant reality TV viewers on an internet messageboard hellbent on petitioning Ofcom over some illusory injustice perpetrated by their favourite programme; e.g. 'Within minutes of Jeremy Edwards being kicked off *Dancing on Ice* there was a 500-strong mousemob screaming "Fix!" on Digital Spy.'

nowtrage (*nowt-rage*) n. Lame and unconvincing tabloid outrage designed to create a self-perpetuating storm of controversy. Also, nowtrageous (adj); e.g. 'This Jonathan Ross pensioner sex-joke story in the *News of the World* is embarrassingly nowtrageous.'

phwoared escort (*fword-ess-court*) n. Down-on-her-luck vice girl unwittingly captured topless on a hidden camera by an undercover tabloid reporter in order to illustrate a prurient article gleefully belittling her desperately unhappy circumstances.

piersonality (*peers-on-allitee*) n. Self-consciously odious celebrity who trades on their own widely accepted repugnance to infuriatingly lucrative effect, thereby creating an unassailable feedback loop of violent loathing in absolutely everyone other than themselves; e.g. Piers Morgan.

plebbledash (*plebbul-dash*) n. To bulk up a television news report with needless vox-pop soundbites from ill-informed members of the public.

PR-reviewed phindings (*peeyarr-rev-yood-fyne-dings*) n. Light-hearted newspaper article based around any risible 'scientific survey' produced by a marketing agency to promote a product or service; eg: 'It's the BREAST news men have heard in years – Britain's women are set to evolve BIGGER BOOBS in future, according to scientists at Cardiff's Wonderbra Institute of Titology.'

printernot (*pryn-ter-knot*) n. Any example of a newspaper's feeble attempt to appeal to a younger demographic by likening some aspect of itself to the internet, such as re-christening its letters page the 'Messageboard'.

scoffee break (*scoff-ee-brake*) n. Office lunchtime spent sneering pathetically at unflattering snaps of cellulite-peppered thighs in a *Heat* magazine mock examination (*qv*).

twittle-cattle (*twittul-cattul*) n. Hordes of people patiently queuing up to moo aimlessly at each other in the latest online social networking craze.

zerotoleriddance (*zero-toller-riddantz*) n. The moment the public mood finally and irrevocably turns against a hitherto-just-about-tolerable minor celebrity; eg, 'We put Danielle Lloyd on the cover and sales nosedived; looks like she's hit zerotoleriddance.'

Voice of the people [9 February 2009]

What's that? You think it's easy filling a page each week with this gibberish? Well, it is. But some weeks aren't as easy as others. For one thing, pretty much all I've been aware of all week is snow tumbling from the sky, and everyone else has already written about that – and I mean everyone, from Melanie Phillips to the late Roy Kinnear. The only other thing I've noticed is some kind of acute muscular spasm in my neck and left shoulder, and that's hardly entertaining, except maybe for the bit where the doctor rather brilliantly prescribed me diazepam so I necked some and walked very slowly around the Westfield shopping centre listening to Henry Mancini's *Pink Panther* theme on repeat on an MP3 player, smiling eerily at shoppers.

Anyway, being stumped, I decided to ask the people following me on Twitter for some one-word suggestions as to what to write about. For the two or three of you who don't already know, Twitter – which has garnered almost as much coverage as the snow in recent weeks – is a monumentally pointless 'social networking' thingamajig that lets you type 140-word ponderings or questions to an audience of other time-wasters.

The high point in Twittering history appears to be an incident last week in which Stephen Fry got stuck in a lift and passed the time by 'tweeting' about it in real time. Since Fry has about 100,000 followers on Twitter (other users who sign up so they can read about your every move – like benevolent stalkers, basically), this made his ordeal both more entertaining for him and a harmless diversion for everyone else. Like most meaningless indulgences, it sounds fairly nauseating to anyone who hasn't given it a go, but once you've 'got it', there's something strangely compelling about it. It's the online equivalent of popping bubble wrap.

Anyway, the people of Twitter had helped me out once before by explaining how to cook a haggis, which I needed to know in a hurry for reasons too dull to explain. This time I asked them to suggest subjects for this column – and limited them to one word, thinking that might make the selection process easier. In reality, it was like sticking your head out of the window of a moving car and finding the atmosphere was made of words instead of air. Still, having asked for suggestions, it would be churlish not to use some of them. So here's a selection of micro-columns on the most popular suggestions, in order of frequency:

Snow: Every other suggestion, predictably, was 'snow' – thereby giving me an excuse to write about it after all. I'm not a snow fan. It's cold, white mould and nothing more. Still, the worst thing about the snow is all the TV news reports filled with 'Your Pictures' of tittering cretins building snowmen. One after the other, all of them rubbish. Having wasted airtime displaying 10,000 dull family snaps, the anchors still weren't satiated – 'Do keep sending your snow photos to our email address,' they repeatedly pleaded. Jesus Christ, why not abuse your position and ask the audience to send in something genuinely interesting, like close-ups of intimate body parts?

Bale: Another popular suggestion: Christian Bale's shoutburst. It wasn't actually that unreasonable: a director of photography adjusting lights in an actor's eyeline during a take is a huge no-no, especially if they do it repeatedly. Also, if the makers of the film are canny, they'll leave his tantrum in the finished cut and work round it. Might break the fourth wall for a bit, but it's guaranteed box office.

Golliwogs: Should Carol Thatcher have been sacked from *The One Show* on the basis of a private, unaired conversation? No, but then she didn't apologise or clarify what she meant afterwards, so yes. That's that cleared up.

Sex/ Felching/ Nipples etc: A fair proportion of the requests were for 'naughty' subjects, either body parts or unconventional sexual practices, which suggests a public thirst for unnecessary smut which the *Guardian* is spectacularly failing to address. The editors don't like me writing about this sort of thing, but the people have spoken, goddamit – so, for the record, my favourite unconventional sexual practice (to read about, not actually partake in, you understand) is 'docking', which refers to two men facing each other with their penises out; one extends his foreskin and tucks it over the head of the other one's member, thereby 'docking' them together. There. You'll never see that mentioned in the *Daily Telegraph*, which is why this is the greatest newspaper in the world.

Wotsits/ Dirigibles/ Teacakes/ Songsmith etc: See, the problem with asking thousands of people for one-word suggestions is that you're quickly swamped with so many disparate and random entries the exercise becomes less useful than flipping through a dictionary at random. This tallies with my how-to-cook-a-haggis query experience, incidentally: I got so many contradictory responses I was left unsure whether to steam it for 45 minutes or bake it in foil for an hour and a half – which wouldn't matter really, except I was also warned that to cook it incorrectly would result in terrible food poisoning.

To glance back through this list, it would seem that asking Twitter for advice on what to write about isn't a great gambit, full stop. The top three suggestions were either too obvious or have been covered at length elsewhere, and the rest were either too dirty to go into in detail (a shame, in my view), or blended into white noise by dint of sheer volume.

In summary, I've learned nothing and neither have you. But it's passed some time. And that's Twitter all over. Anyway, next week: Israel v Palestine – who's right?

On flavoured potato crisps   [16 February 2009]

In these health-conscious times, potato crisps have a bad reputation. Gone are the days when you could walk down the street cheerfully snuffling through a pack of Smoky Bacon. Try that now and people will stare at you like you're shooting heroin directly into a genital vein.

The standard tuckshop brands of crisps are shameful things, to be eaten in secret on a car journey. Of course, the fey 'gourmet' varieties – thicker, hand-cooked 'artisan' crisps with flavours such as Aged Stilton and Ambassador's Port – are still considered acceptable by the food Nazis, provided they're served in a bowl at a cocktail party, surrounded by organic vol-au-vents and snobs. That's because our food neurosis is actually snootiness in disguise.

Consequently, the cheap end of the crisp market has to pull stunts to distract you from the crushing social disgrace involved in actually purchasing a bag. Walkers' latest wheeze is a fun competition. Stage one: they ran adverts inviting the public to suggest exotic new taste sensations. Stage two: they chose six finalists, released them into the wild, and asked the public to vote for their favourite. Stage three: the votes are counted and the top flavour becomes a permanent member of the Walkers line-up. We're currently in stage two.

To lend the enterprise some gravitas, on the Walkers website you can watch kitchen surrealist Heston Blumenthal discussing the new flavours as though he genuinely believes they're edible. But are they? As the nation's foremost investigative journalist, I decided to find out, by buying a packet of each and sampling them. It was a mission that would take me to the very heart of a newsagent's and back. Here are my capsule reviews of the six competing varieties:

Builder's Breakfast: There's some confusion over the exact contents of the Builder's Breakfast. On the website, Heston claims they taste of 'sausages, bacon, eggs and beans', whereas the packet itself lists 'bacon, buttered toast, eggs and tomato sauce'. This would imply that even Walkers don't know what they've got on their hands, possibly because the crisps themselves taste of stale fried egg and little else. It captures the feeling of sitting in a greasy spoon, being dumped via text while your food repeats on you. Depressing.

Crispy Duck and Hoisin: A fairly accurate rendition, although if you close your eyes they taste like the standard Roast Chicken flavour might if the 'chicken' in them had been killed with a hammer made of compacted sugar. This is probably something Heston actually does in his restaurant.

Fish and Chips: Sounds like a good idea, but think about it: FISH CRISPS. Consequently they smell vaguely infected. Actually eat one and it's like kissing someone who's just eaten a plateful of scampi. Halfway through they belch in your mouth.

Onion Bhaji: The most convincing flavour, but they taste watered-down; as though Heston boiled one tiny bhaji in a swimming pool full of Evian, and then dipped some potatoes in it. It's like a lame TV movie about onion bhajis, starring Adam Woodyatt, with a soundtrack consisting entirely of library music, broadcast directly on to your tastebuds.

Cajun Squirrel: Self-consciously 'wacky' and attention-grabbing entry. Walkers are keen to point out that 'no squirrels were harmed in the making of this crisp', which is a pity because I had chuckle-some visions of thousands of live, screaming squirrels being bull-dozered into an immense bubbling cauldron in front of a party of horrified schoolchildren. The flavour itself is truly vile: if they'd called it Squirrel's Blood, everyone would've believed them. They taste precisely like a tiny cat piping hot farts through a pot-pourri pouch into your mouth.

Chilli and Chocolate: Excreted Battery Acid, more like. A boring lunatic with halitosis explains the smell of charred wood to your tastebuds. It's vaguely like the smell you get when you bleed a radiator, but sharper, more disgusting, and worryingly 'human'. They should've called it 'Dirty Protest' instead.

So there you have it. They're uniformly horrible. Worst of all, none are a patch on, say, standard Salt and Vinegar, which has been around since the Cro-Magnon era. Obviously, they should've chosen more ambitiously. Since the squirrel flavour doesn't actually contain any squirrel, they could unleash other tastes you're vaguely curious about, but would never actually eat, like Cyanide and Lemon, or The Late Marilyn Monroe. If they'd bitten the bullet and genuinely released a flavour called Dirty Protest, people would queue round the block to try it, provided the packet carried a prominent guarantee that it was merely a simulation, not the genuine article. (For the record, according to *The Encyclopedia of Unusual Sex Practices* by Brenda Love [ISBN 0 349 10676 2], 'faeces supposedly has a charred or sour flavour but otherwise tastes similar to whatever was consumed.' So now you know.)

Or maybe they could've worked on flavours that evoked a time and mood instead of mimicking an existing substance. Who could resist Wartime Romance (cigarettes, lipstick, and railway station)? Or Studio 54 (cocaine, sweat, and Bianca Jagger)? Even Medieval Times (mud, gibbet and wet tunic) would be worth trying.

But no. They didn't dare to dream. So in summary: don't vote for any of them. Spoil your ballot paper instead. Because that's what they've done to these innocent potatoes. The bastards. The absolute unconscionable bastards.

– Builder's Breakfast eventually won, proving once again that there is no god.

Show us your bum for ten pence [23 February 2009]

Feeling helpless? Hollow? Futile and joyless? Crushed? Down-trodden? Just plain lousy? I could go on, but the list would only depress you. Depressed? Of course you are. There's an eerie calm in the air as we glide through what feels like a brief 'phoney war' period before the CREDIT CRUNCH (which from now on, according to official guidelines, must be capitalised each time it appears in print, just to make it even more frightening) . . . before the CREDIT CRUNCH starts to bite for real and your local park becomes a shantytown filled with dog-faced people in rags prosti-tuting themselves for a thimbleful of water.

Still, there's no point in despairing. You may feel scared and vul-nerable right now, but all that can be turned around in an instant. You have the power within you! Or rather, slightly outside you! I'm talking about your skin. Your skin isn't simply a handy pliable coat-ing that stops your liver plopping on to the floor like a fat red salmon: it's a magic cloak of empowerment. I've learned this from television: all you have to do is whip your clothes off, show every-one your bum for a few minutes and, bingo, you're empowered. Trinny and Susannah pioneered the idea, encouraging members of the public to pose in front of full-length mirrors in their underwear as part of the makeover process, but it wasn't until Gok Wan began saving women from certain death each week, by making them strip completely naked before projecting their photo up the side of a building, that the idea really took off.

Since then we've had a BBC3 show called, simply, *Naked*, in which each week people from various professions – beauticians one week, nurses the next – are picked apart by psychologists and 'image consultants' for several days, as though they're being inducted into a cult. The show consists of 'a series of challenges designed to help their self-esteem at work and at home' – smashing things up with sledgehammers, primal screaming, bungee jumping and so on – culminating in a full-frontal strip show. It's terribly moving, of course. Plenty of tears and inspiring music. And genitals. Because let's face it, there's no better way to bolster someone's confidence than taking a good long stare at their genitals.

Now Sky have gone one better by announcing a show called *Credit Crunch Monty* (sorry, CREDIT CRUNCH Monty) in which a group of jobless men will be 'laid bare in every sense as they reveal their background stories and their emotional journeys are captured – from overcoming the setback of unemployment to building up the confidence to perform a striptease', i.e. a grand televised performance where you'll presumably get to see their dicks and balls jiggling about, all empowered and that. Excitingly, it's also being broadcast in HD, so if you're still rich enough to afford a sparkly top-of-the-range TV you might just be able to make out the individual hairs bristling on their cringing scrota, thereby empowering them further.

It's a refreshing measure of just how far our society has come. If, during the Great Depression, your great-grandfather had scraped together a living by running a stall at the local docks where he pulled down his trousers and manipulated his testicles in amusing ways while passersby laughed and tossed pennies at him, he'd probably have come away feeling too ashamed to talk about it, let alone give his consent to have the performance filmed for posterity. Whereas now public nudity is feelgood, confidence-boosting fun for all concerned. Provided it's caught on tape. And backed with uplifting indie rock. And prominently displayed in the onscreen listings with a hooky word in the title, like NUDE or NAKED or STRIP or CLICK HERE FOR BUMS.

I don't mean to imply, incidentally, that absolutely everyone who takes their clothes off for a living is desperate, miserable or exploited. That's the cliché, but really – can you name a profession in which there aren't people who are desperate, miserable or exploited? Which would you rather do? Strip for a camera now and then, or work full-time in an office sitting beside a perspiring Coldplay fan who spends each lunchtime getting bits of moist cheese-and-onion crisp in his goatee and chortling over his Facebook messages?

Anyway, these hapless one-night-only TV strippers aren't even making a career out of burlesque performance – they've merely been cajoled into doing it in the name of spiritual fulfilment. There's presumably no substantial or protracted financial reward involved, so unless they get a kick out of sheer physical exhibition-ism, they'd be well advised to keep their pants on until they're offered a share of the proceeds.

Actually, I tell you what would be empowering: they could sell advertising space on their genitals. Get 'CONFUSED.COM' paint-ed down the length of their dickers and the Iceland logo shaved into their pubes. I, for one, would stand and applaud.

Bring on the summer of rage   [2 March 2009]

Any abusive relationship tends to end with a long, slow phase of mounting disappointment followed by a sudden, irreversible snap-ping point. The descent to rock bottom may take years but when you get there, the force of impact still shocks, and it's precisely this shock that gives you the strength to walk away. Take smoking, for instance. You can light up for years, hating yourself and the habit a little bit more with each accumulated puff, yet remain hopelessly locked in nicotine's pointless embrace, until one day you find your-self scrabbling through the kitchen bin, picking potato peelings off a dog end because it's 11 p.m. and the shops are closed and GOD YOU NEED A FAG . . . when you catch sight of your sorry junkie-arsed reflection in the shiny bin lid and undergo an epiphany of self-disgust, vowing to quit there and then.

I bring this up because I suspect that across the country, people are undergoing similar epiphanies every day. Not about cigarettes, but politicians. My personal snapping point was reached last week, at the precise moment Jack Straw announced the government was vetoing the Information Tribunal's order for the release of cabinet minutes relating to that whole invasion-of-Iraq thing. Come on, you remember Iraq: that little foreign policy blip millions of us protested against to absolutely zero avail, because Straw and his pals figured they knew best, even though it turned out they didn't and – oops! – hundreds of thousands of lives were lost as a result. Remember the footage of that screaming little boy with his limbs blown off? Maybe not. Maybe you felt a shiver of guilt when you saw that; guilt that you hadn't personally done enough to prevent it; should've shouted louder, marched further. Or maybe it stunned you into numbness. Because what was the point in protesting any more? These people do what they want.

They do what they want, these people, and you and I are cut out of the conversation. I'm sure they're dimly aware we still exist. They must spot us occasionally, through the window, jumping up and down in the cold with our funny placards . . . although come to think of it, they can't even see us through the window, since they banned peaceful protest within a mile of Parliament.

Instead they pick us up on a monitor, courtesy of one of the 15 billion CCTV cameras that scrutinise our every move in the name of security. On the screen you're nothing but a tiny monochrome blob; two-dimensional and faceless. And that's just how they like it.

Straw and co blocked the release of the minutes, claiming that to actually let us know what was going on would set a dangerous precedent that would harm good government. Ministers wouldn't speak frankly at cabinet meetings if they felt their discussions would be subjected to the sort of scrutiny that, say, our every waking move is. In other words, they'd be more worried about the press coverage they'd get than the strength of their arguments.

Well, boo hoo. Surely craven pussies like that shouldn't be governing anyway?

Having pissed in the public's face, Straw went on to shake the final drips down its nose, writing a defence of the government's civil liberties record in this paper in which he claimed 'talk of Britain sliding into a police state is daft scaremongering, but even were it true there is a mechanism to prevent it – democratic elections . . . People have the power to vote out administrations which they believe are heavy-handed.'

Thanks, Jacksy – can I call you Jacksy? – but who the hell are we supposed to vote in? Despite a bit of grumbling, the Tories supported the veto. Because they wouldn't want cabinet minutes published either.

It's all over. The politicians have finally shut us out of their game for good and we have nowhere left to turn. We're not part of their world any more. We don't even speak the same language. We're the ants in their garden. The bacteria in their stools. They have nothing but contempt for us. They snivel and lie and duck questions on torture – on torture, for Christ's sake – while demanding we respect their authority. They monitor our every belch and fart, and insist it's all for our own good.

Straw wrote, 'If people were angels there would be no need for government . . . But sadly people are not all angels.' That rather makes it sound as though he believes politicians aren't mere people. Maybe they're the gods of Olympus. Maybe that's why they're in charge.

Thing is, they could get away with this bullshit while times were good, while people were comfortable enough to ignore what was happening; when people were focusing on plasma TVs and iPods and celebrity gossip instead of what the politicians were doing – not because they're stupid, but because they know a closed shop when they see one. But now it looks as if those times are at an end, and more and more of us are pulling the dreampipes from the back of our skulls, undergoing a negative epiphany; blinking into the cold light of day.

Consequently the police are preparing for a 'summer of rage'. To the powers that be, that probably just means more tiny monochrome blobs jumping up and down on the long-distance monitor for their amusement. Should it turn out to be more visceral than that, they'll have no one to blame but themselves.

The book(s) I haven't read [9 March 2009]

Congratulations on having read this far. Reading anything whatsoever is apparently a dying art. According to a survey released last week to help promote World Book Day, 65% of respondents admitted lying about which novels they'd read in a desperate bid to impress people. The news was accompanied by a top 10 rundown of the least-read and most-lied-about books. Top of the list: George Orwell's *Nineteen Eighty-Four*. Presumably people don't feel the need to actually read it because they can see the film adaptation taking place all around them every day, yeah? Yeah. In your FACE, Jack Straw.

Nineteen Eighty-Four is the only entry on the list I have actually read. The others include *War and Peace*, *Ulysses*, and the Bible. Apparently people lie about having read all these books because they think it'll make them appear sexier. Which begs the question: who the hell earnestly believes that claiming to have read the Bible from beginning to end is going to get them laid? Mention your love of the New Testament on a date and you might as well stick a fork in your face and start screaming about ghosts. Potential partners who genuinely adore reading the Bible on a daily basis traditionally don't mention it until later, when they've invited you back to their place to unexpectedly nailgun your hand to the wall while loudly reciting a selection of their favourite parables from memory.

Still, the most tragic aspect of the survey is the sheer number of people who lie about the same things. If you assume the respondents are at least vaguely representative of the nation as a whole, almost half of us have pretended to read *Nineteen Eighty-Four*, which means when you're lying about it to impress someone, there's a very good chance they haven't read it either. Both of you are hiding your true selves in order to avoid recrimination, which, ironically enough, is precisely what the citizens in *Nineteen Eighty-Four* wind up doing, not that you'd know. My favourite sequence in the book, incidentally, is the bit where the monkey drives the car.

Of course, whenever two people meet, literary fibs are just the tip of the iceberg. As potential partners initially circle one another, a full 98% of their conversation consists of out-and-out falsehood. The remaining 26% is wild exaggeration. It's an unnecessary game of bluff in which you both claim to be into the same bands, hold the same political viewpoints, harbour the same dark secrets and so on. Assuming it works and the pair of you get together, the rest of the relationship consists of either (a) both of you slowly discovering what the other one's actually like, or (b) one of you grimly maintaining the fiction that, hey, you're really into Bruce Springsteen, fell-walking or sex parties too, until the facade finally crumbles or you die of sheer despair.

The secret, then, is simply to let go: to not give a toss about what anyone else wants or likes or thinks in the first place. That way you won't paint yourself into a corner trying to impress them. In fact, the best strategy of all would be to actively put them off: confess to all your worst traits and guiltiest pleasures at the earliest opportunity. Tell them you don't know about that James Joop and his Ulyssesso pop-up book thingy, but you reckon James Herbert's Nazi-zombie thriller '48 is one of the most exciting books you've ever read (which it is, actually). Not only will this make them feel cleverer than you, and therefore good about themselves – which, let's face it, is a nice present to give to anyone on this cold and awful planet – you'll have set the bar so low there'll be no need to impress them later by packing *Midnight's Children* (number seven on the list) in your carry-on luggage when you eventually zoom off on honeymoon together. Instead you can spend the flight playing Super Mario Shoe Factory on your Nintendo DS. Everyone's happy.

The other irony is that while people lie about having read highbrow novels in order to impress each other, a massive percentage of highbrow novels aren't worth reading anyway because the authors are too busy trying to impress the reader (who, we now know, probably hasn't bothered turning up). That's why so many contemporary novels seem to largely consist of a thinly veiled version of the author discussing politics and art and quantum theory over a carefully selected bottle of wine with the devastatingly beautiful mixed-race wife of an impotent international statesman and/or gangster (delete where applicable) before whisking her off to a swish hotel room to have expert animal sex with her all weekend until a pigeon symbolising the unions or something crashes into the window and blah blah blah blah BLAH. I mean, really, who cares? *Mr Tickle* had 20 times the raw entertainment value – and it came with pictures – so if you can't beat that, don't bother.

In summary: reading is more trouble than it's worth, and lying about reading is even more pointless. Far better to glance at the cover and skip to the end every time. In fact, if you'd done that with this article, you could've got on with your day a bit quicker without listening to me burble on. Sorry about that. Now go away.

Super Mundanity World   [16 March 2009]

Stop picking your backside, you disgusting little pauper; you vile, impoverished speck with your moth-eaten trousers and your brittle, worn-out hair; stop floundering in your own muck for a moment to gawp in humble, awed astonishment at me and my jet-set lifestyle.

Last week, I spent the evening at a glittering Bafta awards ceremony in London's glamorous West End. On the face of it, this sounds like precisely the sort of thing your average *Heat* reader would willingly slice a thumb off (then fry it and eat it) to attend. Except it wasn't honouring movies or soaps or the Top 100 Baked Bean-Coloured Wags or anything like that. It was celebrating the videogames industry. At which point, your average *Heat* reader probably shrugs and turns the page. It might as well be celebrating the UK's foremost curtain rod manufacturers, for all they care.

The glitzy lifestyle mags don't cover the games industry, because there aren't any identifiable personalities to shake a narrative stick at. Sonic the Hedgehog and Lara Croft are never going to go through heartbreak hell together. The Tetris blocks don't get drunk and punch photographers. The most compelling character in any videogame is you, the player. And apart from you, who ultimately gives a toss about you anyway? Even God doesn't care. That's why he gave you that nose.

The resulting lack of mainstream coverage means that, despite being about 10,000 times more successful than the British film and TV industries combined, the British videogames industry continually balances a pathological inferiority complex with a wounded sense of pride. Quite why it still wants validation from these older, fading forms of media is a mystery. It's like a powerful young warrior disgruntled at being ignored by an elderly and irrelevant dying king.

Anyway, outperforming other media is one thing. Widespread affection from the populace is another. And the majority of videogames are still off-puttingly abstruse as far as the average schmoe is concerned. As a lifelong nerd, I often forget this myself, and will excitingly hand over a gamepad to a greenhorn visitor, encouraging them to 'have a quick go' on some new release with the promise that it's 'easy' and 'intuitive', only to spend the next half-hour trying to explain that 'you have to press X to open the door . . . press X . . . that's the blue button with an X on it . . . no, you can't climb that tree in the background, it's just a bit of decoration – look, you just can't, so stop trying – oh . . . you've accessed the inventory now . . . the inventory, that's what you're carrying . . . no, you've gone back to the menu now . . . oh for Christ's sake, just give it here. Just get out and leave me alone . . .'

But things are changing. The biggest growth area in videogames right now is the 'casual gaming' market. For 'casual', read 'mainstream'. Effectively, this means games the average human being can relate to: anyone who's lived in a house can grasp what The Sims is, for instance; anyone who's played tennis knows how to swing a Nintendo Wii remote. Grand Theft Auto might not look like a casual game, but it certainly appeals to a wide demographic, namely anyone who's ever fantasised about going berserk in a city (i.e. 98% of the population).

There are a million similar fantasies people experience on a daily basis that the games industry is yet to exploit. If it really wants to appeal to the population as a whole, I'd suggest some of the following:

Magic Agreement Party: This is simply a game in which you sit at a dinner party table espousing your viewpoints on any subject under the sun, while everyone else slowly comes to agree with everything you're saying. Actually, this gives me an idea for an even better game, which is . . .

Super Squabble Champ IV: This game consists of nothing but petty relationship squabbles in which your character is endowed with the mystical ability to zip back in time and record footage of your partner being a massive bloody hypocrite, then zoom back into the present to play it all back on a giant screen in front of their eyes until they quiver and break down and confess that you were 100% right all along. Then you get a million points and it plays a little song.

Boundless Libertine Plus: Sims-style title in which you build a character that looks exactly like you, living in a house that looks exactly like your own, with a job exactly like yours – basically every detail is as close to your life as possible, except one: there are absolutely no consequences for your actions. So you can walk into the office and have sex with nine co-workers, then go home and eat doughnuts for 200 days without putting on any weight. You can even stamp up and down on your dog's head if you like, and it won't so much as bruise. The day this game comes out is the day the phenomenon of workplace massacres ceases for ever.

Peter Sissons' Tetris: I've included this for my own amusement. It's basically just Tetris, but as played through the eyes and mind of Peter Sissons as he sits in his dressing room at BBC *News 24* waiting to go on air. It's precisely the same as usual, except occasionally you hear him clearing his throat, or someone saying 'need you in the studio in 10, Peter' through an earpiece. And when you clear 100 lines, the viewpoint changes and he stands up in front of the mirror, drops his pants and shows you his bum.

You get the picture. The list could go on. Enough space operas and chainmail. We want more down-to-earth fantasies, and we want them now.

The Brown Minister   [11 May 2009]

If real life were a movie, instead of a cruel and horrifying string of random unfolding events, the mortifying slow-motion car crash that is Gordon Brown's premiership would inspire pity in all but the most stone-hearted audience member. Assailed from all directions, stumbling, bumbling, droning, punch-drunk, hapless, hopeless, and aching with palpable misery, he increasingly resembles a depressed elephant, slowly being felled by a thousand pin-sized arrows fired into his hide by a million tiny natives, still somehow moving forward, trudging wearily toward its allotted graveyard-slot with morose resignation.

Here is a man apparently allergic to luck. Nothing goes right for the Brown minister. He can't even pop onto YouTube and attempt a smile without everyone laughing and calling him creepy. And they're right. The smiles were creepy: they made him look like the long-dead corpse of a gameshow host resurrected by a crazed scientist in some satirical horror movie. It's Saturday night, live from Television Centre! The theme tune plays on a church organ. Your children shriek when he bounds on to the screen. As he descends the glittering staircase, one decomposing arm drops off at the shoulder socket, hitting the studio floor with a damp thud. Oblivious, he steps over it to approach camera one, gazing down the lens with frozen eyes, intermittently twitching that smile. Your screen cracks. Hot plasma leaks out. This broadcast is over.

In fact Brown's extended drubbing has gone far beyond mere eeriness, and now teeters on the verge of harrowing spectacle – a protracted humiliation so total, so crushing, that merely witnessing it feels almost as terrible as being the man on its receiving end. It's like someone's dropped an indignity bomb directly on his head, and we're all caught up in the blast.

Normally, to experience this sort of shared mutual shame, you would have to stumble unannounced into a room and unexpectedly catch someone doing something acutely embarrassing, such as masturbating or miming to Kaiser Chiefs in front of a mirror. Following 10 crushed aeons of infinite silence, both parties would stare at the ground for a few moments, you'd mutter a dented apology about knocking first next time, inch your way backwards through the door as though quietly observing a religious ceremony, and spend the next half hour standing in the corridor cringing your skin inside out. From then on you'd share your painful-yet-private little circle of grief in silence, the pair of you implicitly understanding that The Incident Must Never Be Referred to Again.

That's what would happen on a personal level. This is different. This is national. We're all witnesses to The Incident. And I don't know about you, but I'm finding the tension unbearable. I can't wait for the general election – not because I want to see Prime Minister Wormface Cameron smugging his way into Downing Street, because I don't – but just because I don't think I can bear this mishap-strewn landscape a moment longer. It's like being trapped in a hot room filled with an overpowering fart smell, waiting for someone outside to come along and open the window.

In the meantime, is there anything Brown can do? On Friday, Simon Jenkins suggested in this paper that a hastily orchestrated overseas war might save the prime minister's bacon, although, given his track record for bumbling calamity, picking a fight with an entire country seems ridiculously ambitious. Maybe he could declare war on a small town – something the size of Newbury or Ashby de la Zouch. Don't worry about the motive – just make something up. Claim the inhabitants were illegally stockpiling Tamiflu or something, then pound them for a fortnight using all the murderous technology the Ministry of Defence can muster. Use something exotic. Something you have to drop from a Super Huey.

Something that whooshes and goes bang and looks cool in widescreen. Dish out a medal each time one of the residents gets a leg shot off. And when everyone's dead, or at least they've stopped twitching, plant a flag in the council offices, pop up some 'Mission Accomplished' bunting and plough through the market square in a whopping great tank for a photo opportunity and press conference.

Failing that, simply bursting into tears on live TV might be a good move. Pay a visit to *This Morning* for an ostensibly upbeat chat about how this whole government thing's been working out for you, then suddenly go quiet and well up. Wait till Phillip Schofield puts a hand on your shoulder before letting rip – but when you let rip, really LET RIP. Wail. Howl. Punch the cushions. Quake with sobs. Say you're sorry for all the mistakes and beg for a chance to put it all right. Make stuff up if necessary.

Pretend you've been a heroin addict or something like that. Weep 16 litres right there on the sofa if you have to.

Or tell a joke! A bad one! Anything! Do anything! Please – just do something to clear the air. Because the public still has a few pity cells left. Many will forgive you. I'm not sure everyone believes the current mess is entirely your fault. It's just the tragi-comic misery and embarrassment of it all. It's too much for our embattled nation to bear. It's awful. Truly awful.

On the BNP [18 May 2009]

I was born in the 70s and grew up in a tiny rural village. There was, I think, only one black kid in my primary school. One day, someone pushed him over and called him 'blackjack'. The headmaster called an impromptu assembly. It involved the entire school, and took place outdoors. No doubt: this was unusual.

We stood in military rows in the playground. I must have been about six, so I can't remember the words he used, but the substance stuck. He spoke with eerie, measured anger. He'd fought in the Second World War, he told us. Our village had a memorial commemorating friends of his who had died. Many were relatives of ours. These villagers gave their lives fighting a regime that looked down on anyone 'different', that tried to blame others for any problem they could find; a bullying, racist regime called 'the Nazis'. Millions of people had died thanks to their bigotry and prejudice. And he told us that anyone who picked on anyone else because they were 'different' wasn't merely insulting the object of their derision, but insulting the headmaster himself, and his dead friends, and our dead relatives, the ones on the war memorial. And if he heard of anyone – anyone – using racist language again, they'd immediately get the slipper.

Corporal punishment was still alive and well, see. The slipper was his nuclear bomb.

It was the first time I was explicitly told that racism was unpleasant and it was a lesson served with a side order of patriot fries. Or rather, chips. Our headmaster had fought for his country, and for tolerance, all at once. That's what I understood it meant to be truly 'British': to be polite, and civil and fair of mind. (And to occasionally wallop schoolkids with slippers, admittedly, but we'll overlook that, OK? We've moved on.)

But according to the BNP, I'm wrong. Being British is actually about feeling aggressed, mistrustful, overlooked, isolated, powerless, and petrified of 'losing my identity'. Britishness incorporates a propensity to look around me with jealous eyes, fuming over imaginary sums of money being doled out to child-molesting asylum-seekers by corrupt PC politicians who've lost touch with the common man – a common man who, coincidentally, happens to be white.

They're wrong, obviously. None of these qualities has anything whatsoever to do with being British, but everything to do with ugly nationalist politics. And ugly nationalist politics are popular all over the world. Just like Pringles. Every country has its own tiny enclave of frightened, disenfranchised, misguided souls clinging to their national flag, claiming they're the REAL patriots, saying everyone's out to get them. It's an international weakness. For the BNP to claim to be more British than the other British parties is as nonsensical as your dad suddenly claiming to have invented the beard.

The other day, the BNP had a political broadcast on the box. I wasn't in my beloved homeland at the time, but I heard about it, via internet chuckles of derision. Fellow geeky types tweeting about the poor production values. I looked it up on YouTube. Sure enough, it was badly made. No surprise there. Extremist material of any kind always looks gaudy and cheap, like a bad pizza menu. Not because they can't afford decent computers – these days you can knock up a professional CD cover on a pay-as-you-go mobile – but because anyone who's good at graphic design is likely to be a thoughtful, inquisitive sort by nature. And thoughtful, inquisitive sorts tend to think fascism is a bit shit, to be honest. If the BNP really were the greatest British party, they'd have the greatest British designer working for them – Jonathan Ive, perhaps, the man who designed the iPod. But they haven't got Jonathan Ive. They've got someone who tries to stab your eyes out with primary colours.

But there's more to the advert's failure than its hideous use of colour schemes. Every aspect of it is bad. The framing is bad. The sound is bad. The script is bad. For all their talk about representing the Great British Worker, when it comes to promotional material, the BNP can't even represent the most basic British craftsmanship.

Nick Griffin's first line is 'Don't turn it off!', which in terms of opening gambits is about as enticing as hearing someone shout 'Try not to be sick!' immediately prior to intercourse. He goes on to claim that, 'We're all angry about professional politicians with their snouts in the public trough.' He's right, we are: so angry we're prepared to instantly forget all the occasions we've fiddled our own expenses, thereby enabling us to add a dash of undeserved self-righteousness to our existing justified anger.

But by referring to 'professional politicians', Griffin is presumably suggesting we should elect amateurs instead. Maybe that's why the advert's so amateurish. Maybe that's why all the BNP representatives in the ad read their lines so clumsily, like DFS employees in a bank holiday sale commercial circa 1986, or recently revived chemical coma patients being forced to recite barcode numbers at gunpoint. It's deliberate incompetence. Don't vote for those nasty slick parties. Vote for a shoddy one! Never mind the extremism, feel the ineptitude.

Here's a fantasy. We – the decent British majority – spend years toiling in secret, creating a lifesize replica of Britain in the middle of the Pacific. It's identical down to the tiniest blade of grass, or branch of Gregg's. And one night, while every member of the BNP is asleep, we whisk them via helicopter to this replica UK, this Backup Britain. Put them in replica beds in replica homes. Then we fly back home to watch the fun on CCTV.

For several weeks, they walk around, confused, but pleased. The weather's nice! More importantly, there are no black faces! Then the infrastructure breaks down and they start to starve, and there's no one to blame but themselves. And then someone with GPS on their phone works out what's happened, realises they've all become immigrants in their own land. Half of them go mad and start attacking each other. The rest desperately apply for asylum in Britain. The real Britain. The decent, tolerant Britain. The country you can be proud of.

Paranoia island   [25 May 2009]

I'm not really here. That is, I'm not really here in Britain, because I'm on holiday at the moment. In Crete, to be precise, where everything's considerably warmer and sunnier and more congenial than jolly old London which, from my current perspective, consists almost entirely of looming grey building-shaped objects constructed from bin lids and misery.

Still, don't be jealous. It's not like I'm lolling around in the sun doing nothing. I'm sitting indoors typing this. Then I'm going to loll around in the sun doing nothing. Before you hurl your newspaper across your dingy tube carriage in disgust, remember I'm allowed to do nothing because I'm on holiday – under doctor's orders to relax, no less – but still, it makes me uncomfortable.

I guess I'm supposed to lie back and let go, but in the absence of anything to fret about I quickly start to lose all sense of my own identity, like a lumberjack waking up to discover all the trees in the world built a space rocket and left for another galaxy during the night. Worries hold me together. Worries form my exoskeleton. But the sky's blue, the sea's clear and the sun's beating down: worries are hard to find and even harder to hold on to.

I tried worrying about tanning, for starters. I don't tan. Different bits of my body react to the sun in different ways, none of them conventionally sexy. My forehead gets vaguely darker, but my arms merely freckle a bit before giving up, and my stomach sizzles itself pink within three minutes. Consequently, I have to apply a dizzyingly high-factor sunscreen, slopping it on like Persil-white emulsion until I out-gleam the sun itself. As you might imagine, I look and feel out of place on a beach, but then again I look and feel out of place almost everywhere. I've been badly Photoshopped into this world. So there's no point in worrying about tans. Damn.

I could worry about stepping on a sea urchin. I was flipping through the guide book on the plane, and apparently sea urchins are (a) everywhere and (b) painful. Tread on one and you'll need a doctor to tease out the spikes. Never mind that I'm less likely to step on a sea urchin and get a spike in my foot in Crete than trip over a dead neigbour and get a syringe in my eye in London: it's an exotic new threat, and I'm alert to it. Or rather I was. For the first few days I watched my step, dipping my toe into the surf as though the sea itself might bite me. Now I've forgotten all about it.

Driving. Now I can definitely worry about that. I don't drive, but throughout my stay I've been accompanied by friends who can, so I've seen my fair share of Cretan driving at close quarters. And it's fair to say faith plays an important role in everyday life here. I've lost count of the number of times I've watched people overtaking one another on blind cliff-side corners. It's like a Bond movie. Either Cretan drivers have a far better appreciation of the realities of blind chance I have, or they're crazy. Thing is, it actually gets quite funny after a while, chuckling over each near miss. So even that doesn't feel like a real concern.

Last night I barbecued some freshly caught fish beneath the night sky. Textbook poncy *Guardian* holiday stuff which ought to be outrageously relaxing, not to mention delicious. Fortunately, I managed to imbue the entire experience with needless anxiety. It was a gas-operated barbecue for one thing, so I kicked off by worrying about the canister suddenly exploding and blasting the entire front of my body off, so I'd spend the rest of my life looking like a surprised, cauterised medical diagram. Then there was the fish itself: an unidentified pointy, sharky sort of creature with accusing eyes and tiny rows of sharpened doll's teeth. It was so long it wouldn't fit properly over the coals, which was absolutely brilliant since it meant I got to worry about whether it was properly cooked or not. Maybe I'd end up poisoned, clutching at my throat and trying to explain to a Greek doctor who didn't speak a word of English that I'd fallen victim to some underdone poisonous barracuda. Sadly, that didn't happen. Didn't even choke on any bones. Instead I ate the fish, and the fish was nice. This will never do.

My first bit of holiday reading was a book called *Risk* by the

357

journalist Dan Gardner, about all the scary things in the world and what degree of hazard they actually pose. I was secretly hoping it'd frighten the shit out of me. It did the opposite. It patiently explains that there's never been a better time to be alive. It even makes potentially horrifying future threats such as nuclear terrorism seem less inevitably ominous and more soothingly unlikely. It cheered me up immensely. I almost hurled it in the pool in disgust.

In summary, try as I might, for the time being I've managed to successfully get away from it all. And that's just not me. It makes me feel like an optical illusion in my own mind's eye. Which is why, as I said at the start, I'm not really here. At least I can think of all those delicious worries I can tuck into on my return. That's the only thing keeping me going through this current ordeal.

The worm that turned?   [1 June 2009]

Women – why aren't you running the world yet? Frankly I'm disappointed in you. Men are still far too dominant for their own good, and consequently we've made a testosterone-sodden pig's ear of just about everything: politics, the economy, religion, the environment . . . you name it, it's in a gigantic man-wrought mess. The world's been one big dick-swinging contest, and we've caught our collective glans in a nearby desk fan. By rights we should be squealing for your help, but we're not, because we're too damn stupid and too damn proud. We swagger convincingly, and that's about it. And swaggering's fine for scraping by in primitive times, but the world we've built is altogether more complex now. We've got stock exchanges and nuclear warheads. It's too easy to swagger your way into big trouble without even realising. Well, we've had our turn. It's time for the Rise of the Ladies.

We don't need a few women in conspicuous positions of power scattered here and there – we need a 10-year prohibition on all forms of male power. Seriously: a decade in which men don't get to control anything, from the remote control upwards. Imagine the consequences. For one thing, there would be an instant and massive reduction in armed conflict around the globe. Sure, nations would routinely bitch about each other in secret (and with a new, hair-curling viciousness), but there'd be fewer intercontinental punch-ups and a far smaller bodycount.

The economy should clearly be run by women. City boys are dicks, plain and simple. Look at them. Listen to them. Consider the carnage of the past 10 years. What the hell were these idiots thinking? Even now they're still at it. In any sane world they'd all be herded into a shed and blasted with hoses until they promised to stop. Everything they say, think, do, watch, read and fill up their iPods with is awful. Even their girlfriends are awful. Straight women, reading this: if your partner is a City boy, leave him. Leave him now. Dump him with a text message, right this very second. It'll hurt for about six days, then your life will improve beyond measure. Sod that little number-swapping dick who dares call himself a man. Lob him in the shed with the other squeaking fakes and train the cold jets on the bastards. Shut the door and let them shiver.

Men love machines, because machines remind them of themselves. As a result, men quickly became very very good at building machines and then driving them round rather too quickly, shouting 'Toot toot! Look at me in my brilliant car!' This was cute for a while, but the novelty's worn off now that the planet's teetering on the brink of becoming an inhospitable cinder. Please, women, for all our sakes: just lock us in a room with some Lego or something. I'm sorry, but we're just too bloody stupid to save the planet. Looks like you'll have to clean up our mess once again. Mankind's depending on you.

'This is all very well, but none too realistic,' thinks the female reader. 'Men aren't just going to hand over the reins that easily. I know what men are like. They're self-righteous and stubborn – just like women, but worse.'

Oh, you. Pretty, silly you. We've got you brainwashed. See, that's what our incessant, ruinous swaggering was all about: pretending to be more complex and dangerous than we actually are. In truth your suspicions are correct: we're very, very simple. We're lazy and we like blowjobs. That's all there is to us. Literally: that's it. From

Sir John Betjeman to Barack Obama, from Copernicus to Liam Gallagher. The core software we run on could fit in the memory of a digital watch circa 1985 without even scraping the sides.

And you know this, you women. You know this of course, but it's so dazzlingly obvious you actually doubt it's true. Most of my friends are women. I often find myself counselling them as they agonise for hours, trying to fathom what men are thinking, what men want. Yet no matter who they're talking about, or what the circumstance, from my perspective the answer always seems so glaringly basic it could be scratched on the back of a button. This one wants a shag. That one wants a biscuit. Every time: the butler did it.

The only mistake women make is crediting men with far more mystery than they're capable of. We're impulsive yet thuddingly predictable, and you'd better learn to love us for it because that's just about all we can muster. That's why we bollocksed the planet up. We didn't mean to. We're men, that's all.

And now, surely now, it's time for you to shunt us off the podium and take charge for a decade. If only as an experiment to see what happens. I for one welcome our titted overlords. Give us our toys and our daily bread and permit us to lie on the sofa for 10 whole years, like snoozy, spluttering pigs. We get to loll around contentedly, you get to save the world. Sound good? Do we have a deal? Well do we, you wonderful bitches?

Aural contraceptive   [8 June 2009]

Apologies if I sound like a fusty old colonel randomly dribbling memories on his way to the graveyard, but I remember the days when carefully compiling a C90 cassette of personally selected tunes for a friend was a key bonding moment in almost any relationship.

You'd assemble a collection of your favourite tunes (interspersed with a few ironic flourishes or comedy tracks), then spend an hour painstakingly inking the titles and artist names on the inlay card, which never had enough room on it unless you scratched away in tiny capitals, as though manually typesetting a newspaper aimed at squinty-faced ants in a dollhouse. It took effort and patience. It was a tailored gift. It showed you cared.

Making a compilation for a friend was one thing. Assembling a tape for someone you wanted to see naked was something else entirely; a real high-wire act. Open with something earnestly romantic and you'd mark yourself out as a sexless drip. Go the other way, spicing up the playlist with an explicit rap in which the protagonist lists 5,000 assorted and sobering tricks he can perform with his penis, and you'd fail twice as quickly. And if you somehow avoided sex entirely, and concentrated instead on showcasing how eclectic your musical tastes were by segueing from the Jackson Five into a self-consciously difficult 19-minute electronic epic which sounded like someone hitting a gigantic metal pig with a damp phonebook while a broken synthesizer slowly asks for directions to the kettle factory, you'd alienate them completely.

Nonetheless, compilation tapes were a joy. The best had a quirky theme, such as Surprising Lyrics, or Appalling Covers, or Music to Slay Co-Workers By. That last one opened with 'Xanadu' by ELO, which works better than you'd think.

But then progress jiggered it all up. First CDs smothered cassettes. Then 50% of 18-to-34-year-olds started running their own DJ night, which was just like compiling a tape minus the faffing around with the inlay card, except you had to take it more seriously and pretend you were cool.

Boring. And then finally everyone got iPods, effectively granting their existing musical collection a monopoly over their own ears. Compilation tapes were dead.

Or not. The other week I was tinkering around with a bit of software called Spotify. If you're not familiar with it, it's effectively a cross between iTunes and a customisable online radio station. I'd heard people raving about it and didn't grasp why, until suddenly I realised you could compile a playlist, then generate a URL for it that others can click on. It's like being able to mass-produce a compilation tape in minutes. OK, so it's broken up with irritating adverts now and then, but hey, it's easy to use and it seems to work.

What this means is I'm suddenly in a position to offer you, dear reader, a free compilation tape. But rather than any old tape, I've rustled up a specialist challenge.

Summer's here. Consequently many of you will be embarking upon thrilling new romances. Others will be cementing existing ones. But passion can be fleeting.

Today's heart-fluttering sexpot is tomorrow's irritant. How can you be sure the pair of you really like each other? By trying to have sex while listening to a deliberately off-putting musical playlist, of course. After all, in moments like that, what goes in your ears makes a big difference. Once, in my early 20s, I was enjoying an impromptu eruption of mid-afternoon 'adult fun' with a girlfriend while a radio blasted away merrily in the background. Suddenly the music was replaced with a news bulletin – specifically a live police press conference in which two parents tearfully begged for the return of their missing son. As mood-killers go, it was on a par with looking down to discover your own genitals had suddenly and impossibly sprouted the face of Alan Titchmarsh, and he was look- ing back up at you and licking his lips and grinning and reciting limericks in a high-pitched voice. We broke up five years later. I blame the radio.

My playlist, while tasteless in parts, doesn't contain anything quite that horrifying, but it should prove one heck of an obstacle course. All you have to do is download and install Spotify, then go to this URL: tinyurl.com/moodkill. Click around a bit and it should open the compilation. Don't read the tracklisting, it'll spoil it (that's why I'm not divulging it here). Beckon over your beloved. Dim the lights. Get yourselves in the mood, press play, and prepare to test your ardour to its very limits. The first couple to successfully slog their way through the entire list wins a trophy or something. It's a hefty running time, so don't expect to conquer it all on your first go. There's no set order; you can put it on shuffle if you like. And you're allowed tackle it in chunks over the course of a few weeks if need be. But no declaring victory until you've managed the lot. If that's too much, total respect will still be accorded to anyone who man- ages to kiss with earnest animal passion for the entire duration of the St Christopher Ensemble's Gregorian Chant version of 'I Guess That's Why They Call it the Blues', then upload the evidence to YouTube.

It won't be easy. But if you make it to the end, then congratulations: you've proved your love will abide through the ages. Oh, and as a bonus, pick one of the entries for a wedding song. Then watch all your guests throw up.

Heavy petting   [15 June 2009]

Sorry to brag, sorry to lord it over you like this, but I've got a cat flap. Yeah. A little feline-sized door-within-a-door for a cat to walk through. A cat flap! Beat that. I didn't even have to install it. It came with the flat, courtesy of the previous owners. As a child I never dared to dream that one day I'd own my own cat flap, and even now that I do, I sometimes have to pinch myself and remember that yes: this is real. This is my cat flap. And it lives in my door. I don't have a cat though.

I don't have any pets. Yet people keep telling me to get one, just like they keep telling me to get a wife. (Incidentally, before Alison Donnell from the department of English and American literature at the University of Reading writes another impenetrable article for Comment is Free in which she humourlessly over-analyses one of my throwaway sentences, I should perhaps point out that I'm not equating wives with pets. For one thing, you can't bury a wife in a shoebox. In several shoeboxes, sliced thinly, maybe – but not one. I should also clarify that when I mention 'burying a wife in a shoebox' I'm not making light of murder or anything like that; I'm talking about a hypothetical wife who died of natural causes – and that furthermore, said hypothetical wife was a postoperative transsexual who'd been born a man, and that her dying wish was to be sliced thinly and lovingly placed in a series of shoeboxes. Finally, I'd like to point out that in her will, she bequeathed everything she owned to an institute of gender studies run by a team of hermaphrodites. It's actually a bloody inspiring story, OK?)

Anyway, back to pets, and people telling me to get one. Assuming the stone's being thrown by a powerful robot, I live a stone's throw from Battersea Dogs and Cats Home, a building full of lonely-looking furry creatures with gigantic pleading eyes. I could go in there and walk out with armfuls of puppies and kittens. But I won't. Or rather can't. I just can't. Why?

Because animals die, that's why. And they die too soon. They've got short lifespans. I had a cat once. And I loved that cat. But eventually the cat died, and I don't know if I want to go through that again. Literally every time I stroke someone else's cat or dog, all I can think is, 'Yes, it's lovely, but it'll die'. Every time I envisage myself owning a pet, my mind immediately floods with pre-emptive grief. What if it got run over? Or it choked on something? What if I tripped and fell and dropped a Yellow Pages on its head? I just couldn't bear it.

Yes, I know humans die too, and usually leave even sharper grief in their wake when they do so. But you can't go through life without becoming at least vaguely attached to at least one or two humans in some form or another. The pain they'll cause is unavoidable. Whereas pets seem easier to cut out.

I know, pet lovers, I know. The joy your pets give while alive far outweighs the grief of their passing. You might even argue that foreknowledge of your pet's future death actually lends your delight in their comparatively fleeting existence even more reso-nance. That's all very well. I still don't want to come home one night to find a dead cat on the floor.

When I asked the internet whether I should get a pet, I got a vari-ety of responses. One person suggested buying something danger-ous, like a scorpion or a tiger. That way, rather than worrying about its death, I'd be worrying about my own. Our day-to-day existence would turn into a nail-biting contest in which only one of us would make it out alive. But I live in London. My stress levels peaked some time ago, thanks.

Someone else suggested a virtual pet, like a Tamagotchi. I had one of those years ago: accidentally put it through the washing machine in a jeans pocket and felt like a murderer. Taxidermy also got a mention. True, a stuffed pet wouldn't die. But it would stand around in a glass box, advertising death. And that's what I see when I look in the mirror. I see death. The ageing process and death. And a mop. The mop's often propped up against that wall at the back I can see from the mirror. It's not relevant to the discussion. I just threw it in to lighten the mood.

I suppose what I'm getting at here is I'm just too damn angsty to own a pet. Which is a pity because, like I say, I've got a cat flap. And whenever people see it they go, 'Ooh, have you got a cat?' and I have to explain that I don't, because of death and everything, and it's a bit of a conversation-killer to be honest. And it's happened so many times now that every time I see the cat flap, I think about the cat I don't have, and how much I'd like one if only it wouldn't die, and then I realise I'm mourning a theoretical cat, which in turn leads me to contemplate how little time I have in my own life, and how I shouldn't really waste it in morbid mental cul-de-sacs, and that makes me sad. The cat flap makes me sad.

Which is why I'm going to stop typing now and brick the bastard up. Who's laughing now, cat flap? WHO'S LAUGHING NOW?

Hobby or not hobby? [22 June 2009]

I'm a jammy little bastard, because as time's gone by I've somehow managed to convert each of my interests into a job. There's been a chain of good fortune. As a child I idly doodled cartoons; as a teenager I drew comic strips for a kids' comic. Since cartooning was now my job, I needed a new hobby. Luckily I had one: videogames. In my 20s I began reviewing games for a living. That put food on the table, but in my spare time, for a laugh, I built a website taking the piss out of TV shows. This led to a column in the *Guardian* Guide and so on and so forth and blah de blah. Lucky, lucky, lucky all the way.

The only trouble is that when your hobby becomes your job, it immediately ceases, by default, to be your hobby any more. And now I've run out of hobbies. I'm not into theatre or chess or steam trains or any of that. Films are too similar to TV shows to really offer relaxation, and there's no way I'm taking up a sport. Spare time is dead time. What I really need is to develop a deep interest in a subject deep enough to absorb decades of my life.

Take history. You can read thousands of books about it, or go to museums, or form little local societies where you all go on organised excursions to Sutton Hoo or whatever. I wish I was into history, but I'm not. Besides robbing me of hours of potential hobby time, this lack of historical interest leaves me feeling guilty and uninformed. Those who forget the past are condemned to repeat it, after all. What if I accidentally kickstart the First World War all over again through sheer ignorance? That wouldn't look good on anyone's CV.

And interest can't be faked. Every now and then I'll try to force myself to suddenly find history fascinating. I'll buy a popular history paperback peppered with glowing review quotes, open it up and stare earnestly at the words within. It's like dangling a toy in front of an uninterested cat. My eyes may be locked on the page, but my brain simply glanced with mock curiosity for the first 10 minutes before wandering off somewhere else. And there's nothing I can do to tempt it back.

Recently, on holiday, I visited some ancient ruins, to shuffle around alongside some other random tourists. Everyone was being quiet and reverential, because that's what's expected of you by the International Thought Police. It's quite stressful and eerie. Say you find yourself staring at an old pot. Your brain, being an incredibly sophisticated computer, immediately assesses that it's an old pot, and that old pots are boring. It's not going to dance, or sing heartbreaking songs of yesteryear. It won't even rock gently in the breeze. It's just going to sit there being a pot. Probably a broken one at that. If it was on television, they'd at least have the decency to back it with some upbeat techno while zooming in and out, and even then you'd immediately switch over. But instead, because you've got the misfortune of actually being there in front of it, surrounded by other people, you have to stand and look at the poxy thing for a minimum of 30 seconds before moving on to gawp at the next bit of old shit, or everyone's going to think you're a philistine. The same principle applies in art galleries and museums.

They're full of secretly bored people pulling falsely contemplative faces. It's a weird mass public mime.

Obviously I'm not saying all history and culture is rubbish, or indeed that everyone's as shallow as me. But I strongly suspect that unless you're a hobbyist or expert – and most of the visitors won't be – then the average museum or gallery probably contains four or five fascinating items sprinkled among a whole lot of filler. In other words, you'll spend 10 minutes being interested for every 50 minutes of boredom. Yet if you dare shrug or yawn, everyone'll call you a bastard. To your face. Or at least that's how it feels.

All of which makes it difficult to envisage developing a deep interest in history or art, at least from a standing start. So they're out as hobbies.

Perhaps 'starting a collection' would do the trick – although I've never quite understood how collectors pass the time. Technology has presumably muted the thrill of the chase somewhat; thanks to eBay, I could probably assemble a championship-level thimble collection in less than a fortnight if I put my mind to it. What do you do with a collection, apart from look at it? You can clean it, I suppose. You can build a display cabinet. You can bore other people by pointing at bits of it and saying, 'Guess how much that one's worth, go on'. But apart from that, what's the point? Essentially you're just accumulating atoms. Well, whoopie doo. How pointless.

Tell you what else I don't get: breathing. Every day, all day. Breathing. No let-up. It's relentless. And that's just a load of atoms too. They go in, they come out, they go back in. Bo-r-ing. When you break it down, it's as futile as collecting stamps or staring at bits of old pot.

In which case, I might as well start nurturing it as a hobby. At least it's one I'll definitely stick to till the day I die.

The King is Dead [29 June 2009]

I was at Glastonbury when Jacko died. That's not a factual statement, but a T-shirt slogan. The day after his death, souvenir tops with 'I was at Glastonbury when Jacko died' printed on them were already on sale around the site. In fact, when Jacko died, I was at home playing Grand Theft Auto: Chinatown Wars on a Nintendo DSi. I am 38 years old.

Many festival-goers apparently discovered the news when DJs around the site began playing Michael Jackson records simultaneously. Music combined with word of mouth. That's a nice way to find out. I learned it via a harsh electric beep, bringing my attention to a text message that simply proclaimed 'Jackson's dead' in stark pixelated lettering. Clearly it's the sort of information you have to mindlessly share with the rest of the herd the moment you hear about it. But first I needed confirmation. I occasionally text people to say there's been a massive nuclear explosion in Canada, or David Cameron's gone mad and launched his own breakfast cereal shaped like little swastikas or whatever, in the hope they'll pass it on without checking. I didn't want to fall for my own jape.

I switched on the TV. Jackson was still alive on BBC *News 24*, where they seemed to be reporting he was in hospital following a heart attack. That wasn't good enough, so I flicked over to Sky News, which tends to blab stuff out while the Beeb drags its feet tediously checking the facts. He was bound to be dead on Sky. But he wasn't; he was possibly in a coma. In desperation, I turned to Fox. They would already be attempting to communicate with him via the spirit realm, surely. But they weren't. If anything, they were being more cautious than the Beeb. Boo.

Back to Sky, which was now reporting that a website was announcing his death. That'd do for now. I beamed a few texts out: 'Michael Jackson apparently dead'. 'Piss off' came the reply. It was my own fault. I'd texted a few weeks earlier to say Huw Edwards had just vomited live on the news.

Confirmation of his death gradually spread across the news networks, but the main terrestrial channels were still obliviously broadcasting their scheduled programmes. ITV won the newsflash race, diving straight in after *Trial and Retribution*. Alastair Stewart abruptly shouted 'MICHAEL JACKSON HAS DIED' down the lens like a man standing on the shoreline trying to get the attention of someone on the deck of a passing ferry during gale-force winds.

Fair enough. Whenever I hear the phrase, 'And now a special news report', I automatically start scanning the room for blunt objects to club myself to death with in case they're about to announce nuclear war. Since this wasn't the apocalypse, but an unexpected celebrity death – sad, but not worth killing yourself with a paper-weight over – Stewart was right to blurt it out as fast as he could.

After watching the news long enough to assess that, yes, he was dead, and the circumstances all seemed rather tragic, long enough for them to play a bit of 'Billie Jean' and 'Beat It' and 'Smooth Criminal' and 'Blame it on the Boogie' and so on, reminding me that he was a bona fide musical genius, I went to bed.

The next day he was still dead, but somehow deader than the day before. He was all over the radio and papers. The TV had clips of *Thriller* on heavy rotation, which seemed a tad inappropriate, what with him playing a decomposing corpse in it. If Bruce Willis died falling from a skyscraper, I doubt they'd illustrate his life story by repeatedly showing that bit from *Die Hard* where he ties a fire-hose round his waist and jumps off the building.

Across all the networks, a million talking heads shared their thoughts and feelings on his death. They had rung everyone in the universe and invited them on the show. On *This Morning*, a *Coronation Street* actor revealed he had once had tickets for a Michael Jackson concert but couldn't go because of the traffic. It was a sad day indeed. At 3 p.m., his death was still 'BREAKING NEWS' according to Sky, which has to be some kind of record. Even 9/11 didn't 'break' that long.

Next day, the news was apparently still sinking in around the globe. The BBC went live to Emily Maitlis as she stood on Holly-wood Boulevard (at 1 a.m. local time) waiting for two young Latinos to perform a breakdance tribute to the King of Pop. Something went wrong with the iPod hooked up to their speakers so she had to stand there for a full two minutes, awkwardly filling in while they fiddled with the settings. Sky had flown Kay Burley out to LA too, to hear the fans' pain and pull concerned faces. This contin-ued into the following day. It's probably still going on now.

But the news is not the place to 'celebrate' Jackson's music. The

Glastonbury stage, the pub, the club, the office stereo, the arts documentary: that's the place. The news should report his death, then piss off out of the way, leaving people to moonwalk and raise a toast in peace.

If I was God, here's what I'd do now. I'd force all the rolling networks to cover nothing but the death of Michael Jackson, 24 hours a day, for the next seven years. Glue up the studio doors and keep everyone inside, endlessly 'reporting' it, until they start going mad and developing their own language – not just verbal, but visual. And I'd encourage viewers to place bets on which anchor would be the first to physically end it all live on air.

And while that was happening, I'd create some other stations that covered other stuff. Current affairs type stuff. I think I'd call them 'news channels'. They might catch on.

'Crowdsourcing' [6 July 2009]

So there I was, a few minutes ago, all set to write about the anniversary of the moon landings when I opened the paper only to discover everyone else in the world has written about the anniversary of the moon landings. Seriously. There were articles written by Englishmen, Scotsmen, Irishmen and women. Unending spools of text composed by Capricorns, octogenarians, sailors, bison, foetuses still in the womb, individual gas molecules, you name it. Even the odd astronaut chipped in. There hasn't been this much talk about moonwalking since Michael Jackson died.

Clearly I couldn't go to the moon. Others had got there before me. I was stuck between a rock and a hard place; specifically between now and the deadline. What to do? In days of yore, I'd have been forced to use my imagination. Now I can simply crowdsource. In case you don't know what CROWDSOURCING is, it's a stomach-churning new media term obviously invented by a bastard made of piss. In this case, it means going online and asking passersby to suggest subjects for me to write a smattering of short pieces about, in order to fill up this page and send you away happy.

So that's precisely what I've just done: it's like pulling random subjects from a hat, but with even less preparation. The following 'search terms' came from people on Twitter. I limited them to three words and no more. I've done my best to answer their 'queries', stream-of-consciousness style. I've done something similar on this page before, and make absolutely no apology for doing so again. Splutter all you want. Splutter till your lungs pop and run down your T-shirt. It's my page and I'll do what I like with it. Off we go.

Who invented meringue? Someone bloody lucky because they got to eat the first one and come up with the name. In fact, it sounds as if they initially uttered the name during the first mouthful.

Which would make a good blanket law: all new food inventions must be named immediately by the inventor while they're experiencing the inaugural gobful, to give a more accurate impression of what it actually tastes and feels like. After all, 'biscuit' doesn't really describe the sensation of a biscuit. In any properly run universe, a biscuit would be called an 'umch'.

Sky+ killed adverts: No, it changed them. Many ads now contain bold captions that you can see even on fast forward. It's DIY subliminal blipvertising, basically. Probably causes brain haemorrhages. It'll all come out in the wash in a few years' time, when we're striding about like Cybermen, reciting the URL for confused.com like a flat mantra while blood dribbles out of our ears.

Greggs' sausage rolls: I once mentioned them in print and the next day their PR company sent a van containing stacks of freshly baked sausage rolls to my office as a surprise gift. The following week I prominently name-dropped Blaupunkt stereos and Sony televisions. Not a sausage. HA HA. NOT A SAUSAGE HA HA. Oh sod off, you're probably reading this column for free anyway.

Smurf sexual reproduction: The mating rituals of Smurfs were never fully explored in any of the novelty records or cartoon serials in which they featured, because the reality of Smurf sexual activity is too sudden and ugly to lend itself easily to either amusing high-pitched songs or light-hearted animation. Their playful characteristic twinkle in the eye is quickly replaced by the dull shine of brute instinct. They go at it like foxes, jack-hammering and shrieking behind the bins for around 45 seconds, before mopping themselves clean with their distinctive hats and going their separate ways.

God/no God?: No God. We're all freelancers. Some of us may choose to sit in imaginary offices from time to time, pretending to receive memos from our made-up boss, or enjoying watercooler conversations about the loving/vengeful/forgiving nature of our fictional chief with our colleagues, but no matter how many hours we clock up, it doesn't alter the fact that no one's actually running things on the top floor. This is good news. We own the company!

Bastard mouth ulcers: Yes, they are. The worst thing about mouth ulcers is that when you've got a nasty one it's simultaneously too trivial to complain about and too annoying not to complain about. That's why each time you open your mouth to complain about it, it hurts a little bit more, just to teach you a lesson. The CIA forced Guantánamo detainees with mouth ulcers to eat salt and vinegar crisps in order to get them to talk.

All they could say was 'ow'. As in 'Ow-Qaida', presumably. Christ, I'm spewing some gibberish today. Someone punch me in the kidneys.

Unwise column request: Yes, OK, agreed. Maybe it was. Crowdsourcing overrated. But it was this or a continuous low hum for 850 words. Normal service resumes next week.

National breakdown recovery [13 July 2009]

It's all gone wrong. Our belief in everything has been shattered by a series of shock revelations that have shaken our core to its core. You can't move for toppling institutions. Television, the economy, the police, the House of Commons, and, most recently, the press . . . all revealed to be jam-packed with liars and bastards and graspers and bullies and turds.

And we knew. We knew. But we were deep in denial, like a cuckolded partner who knows the sorry truth but tries their best to ignore it. Over the last 18 months the spotlight of truth has swung this way and that, and one institution after another was suddenly exposed as being precisely as rotten as we always thought it was. What's that? Phone-in TV quizzes might a bit of con? The economic boom is an unsustainable fantasy? Riot police can be a little 'handy'? MPs are greedy? The *News of the World* might have used underhand tactics to get a story? What next? Oxygen is flavourless? Cows stink at water polo? Children are overrated? We knew all this stuff. We just didn't have the details.

After all their histrionic shrieking about standards in television, it was only a matter of time before the tabloids got it in the neck. Last Monday even the Press Complaints Commission, which is generally about as much use as a Disprin canoe, finally puffed up its chest and criticised the *Scottish Sunday Express* for its part in the Dunblane survivors' story scandal. You remember that, don't you? Back in March? When the *Scottish Sunday Express* ran a story about survivors of the Dunblane massacre who'd just turned 18? It fearlessly investigated their Facebook profiles and discovered that some of them enjoyed going to pubs and getting off with other teenagers, then ran these startling revelations on its front page, with the headline ANNIVERSARY SHAME OF DUNBLANE SURVIVORS.

'The *Sunday Express* can reveal how, on their social networking sites, some of them have boasted about alcoholic binges and fights,' crowed the paper. 'For instance, [one of them] – who was hit by a single bullet and watched in horror as his classmates died – makes rude gestures in pictures he posted on his Bebo site, and boasts of drunken nights out.'

Nice, yeah?

As I'm sure you recall, there was an immediate outcry, which was covered at length in all the papers. You remember their outraged front pages, right? All their cries of SICK and FOUL and VILE in huge black text? Remember that? No? Of course you don't. Because the papers largely kept mum about the whole thing. Instead, the outrage blew up online. Bloggers kicked up a stink; 11,000 people signed a petition and delivered it to the PCC. The paper printed a mealy-mouthed apology that apologised for the general tenor of the article, while whining that they hadn't printed anything that wasn't publicly accessible online. All it had done was gather it up and disseminate it in the most humiliating and revolting way possible. Last Monday's PCC ruling got next to zero coverage. Maybe if it had happened after the *News of the World phone*-hacking story broke it would have gathered more. Or maybe not. Either way, the spotlight of truth is, for now, pointing at the press.

But this is just one small part of the ongoing, almighty detox of everything. There's been such an immense purge, such an exhaustive ethical audit, no one's come out clean. There's muck round every arse. But if the media's rotten and the government's rotten and the police are rotten and the city's rotten and the church is rotten – if life as we know it really is fundamentally rotten – what the hell is there left to believe in? Alton Towers? Greggs the bakers? The WI?

The internet. Can we trust in that? Of course not. Give it six months and we'll probably discover Google's sewn together by orphans in sweatshops. Or that Wi-Fi does something horrible to your brain, like eating your fondest memories and replacing them with drawings of cross-eyed bats and a strong smell of puke. There's surely a great dystopian sci-fi novel yet to be written about a world in which it's suddenly discovered that wireless broadband signals deaden the human brain, slowly robbing us of all emotion, until after 10 years of exposure we're all either rutting in stairwells or listlessly reversing our cars over our own offspring with nary the merest glimmer of sympathy or pain on our faces. It'll be set in Basingstoke and called, 'Cuh, Typical'.

What about each other? Society? Can we trust us? Doubt it. We're probably not even real, as was revealed in the popular documentary *The Matrix*. That bloke next door? Made of pixels. Your co-workers? Pixels. You? One pixel. One measly pixel. You haven't even got shoes, for Christ's sake.

As the very fabric of life breaks down around us, even language itself seems unreliable. These words don't make sense. The vowels and consonants you're hearing in your mind's ear right now are being generated by mere squiggles on a page or screen. Pointless hieroglyphics. Shapes. You're staring at shapes and hearing them in your head. When you see the word 'trust', can you even trust that? Why? It's just shapes!

Right now all our faith has poured out of the old institutions, and there's nowhere left to put it. We need new institutions to believe in, and fast. Doesn't matter what they're made of. Knit them out of string, wool, anything. Quickly, quickly. Before we start worshipping insects.

Learn, Hollywood, learn   [3 August 2009]

It's summer, so the cinemas are cluttered with films unfit for human consumption. CGI has ruined everything. Don't get me wrong: I love computer graphics. I thought *Wall-E* was brilliant. I'm even excited by the prospect of next year's *Tron* sequel. CGI is great when it has earned the right to be there. Kneejerk CGI action, however, is the single most tiresome development of the 21st century.

In 2007 I saw *Die Hard 4.0* on the big screen. It was the 3,000-foot computer-generated straw that broke the 3D camel's back. Towards the end of the film there's a lengthy sequence in which antediluvian tough guy Bruce Willis (played by Touché Turtle) hurtles along in an articulated lorry while a fighter jet tries to stop him by machine-gunning the entire world to pieces. The scene grows steadily more outlandish: huge sections of highway buckle and collapse; the truck swerves and tumbles and is literally shredded by bullets; Bruce leaps on to the back of the jet and leaps off just as it explodes in a massive fireball.

And it's boring. Unbelievably boring. At any given moment, only 17% of what you're watching is real, and you know it. You're not immersed in the slightest. At best you're impressed by the rendering of the smoke plumes. It would genuinely have been more exciting to replace the entire chase with a scene in which the bad guy made Bruce stand at one end of a bar and threatened to shoot him unless he successfully tossed a dried pea into a novelty Charlie Brown eggcup down by the toilet door before the alarm went off on his iPhone.

The second *Transformers* movie came out this year. I didn't fight for a ticket. I'd caught the first one by accident. It was like being pinned to the ground while an angry dishwasher shat in your face for two hours. Any human dumb enough to voluntarily sit through a second helping of that unremitting fecal spew really ought to just get up and leave the planet via the nearest window before their continued presence does lasting damage to the gene pool.

CGI isn't the only villain. On Friday, a remake of *The Taking of Pelham One Two Three* opened in British cinemas. The 1974 original is a brilliant, grubby little thriller; the perfect heist movie. The remake is directed by Tony Scott and stars Denzel Washington and John Travolta. Merely reading that sentence should be enough to give even the most blasé film buff cancer of the enthusiasm. Obviously, these are desperate times. With that in mind, here are three deceptively great movie ideas for Hollywood to pinch at its leisure:

Title: *Come Alive!*
Synopsis: God decides to grant evangelical preacher Will Ferrell the power to heal the sick with his fingertips. But the almighty's lightning bolt misses its target, hitting Will's penis instead. Now Will is cursed with the miraculous ability to cure any disease or fix any injury – but only if he has full sexual intercourse with the patient. Since Will is also a 45-year-old unmarried virgin with strong views on sex outside marriage, it won't be an easy ride!
Review: What starts as a regulation gross-out comedy soon takes an unsettling turn as Will faces an agonising decision at his father's deathbed, before building to a frankly unbelievable conclusion in which a terrorist cell releases the Ebola virus in a nearby donkey sanctuary . . . and only one man can save the day.

Title: *Hollywood Mosquito 3D*
Synopsis: Seizing on the current vogue for 3D Imax releases, *Hollywood Mosquito 3D* is a cinematic spectacle shot entirely from the point of view of a hungry mosquito flying around Los Angeles during a heatwave. Filmed with microscopic high-definition cameras, the action consists of eye-popping and shockingly frank sequences in which the naked, breathing bodies of your favourite Hollywood

stars are transformed into immense, surreal landscapes: living canyons of flesh for you to fly over, around . . . even inside.
Review: No blemish is left secret, no crevice goes unexplored, and absolutely no blushes are spared in this bluntly explicit thrill ride starring Harvey Keitel, Megan Fox, Philip Seymour Hoffman, Anjelica Huston, Mickey Rourke and Zac Efron.

Title: *Nic Cage: My Life as John Lennon the Cow*
Synopsis: In this groundbreaking experimental documentary and extreme 'method acting' challenge Nicolas Cage spends an entire year living life as a cow – standing in fields, eating grass, crapping on all fours, with no human contact whatsoever. Having spent 365 days becoming fully immersed in the cow mindset, he is unceremoniously whisked to New York's Dakota building where he must simulate the last eight weeks of John Lennon's life while retaining his bovine perspective and continuing to wear his prosthetic hooves.
Review: Cage's brave attempt to experience Lennon's final days through a cow's eyes offers a refreshing insight into the ex-Beatle's musical genius, as well as a hilarious scene in which, frustrated by his inability to play the chords to 'Jealous Guy' thanks to his hooves, he angrily butts his head against the sideboard and drops a manpat on the carpet.

There you go, dream factory: yours for the taking. And all I ask in return is an onscreen credit, an embroidered baseball cap, and 750 million dollars.

GAMING APPENDIX

Pixel kingdom   [12 May 2008]

In a previous life, I reviewed videogames for a living. As jobs go, it was a curate's egg. On the one hand, I could legitimately sit around playing games until three in the morning without feeling guilty – even if I wasn't specifically reviewing whatever I was currently playing, it all provided useful background knowledge. It never felt like work.

But on the other hand, whenever I told people what I did, they pulled pained, sympathetic expressions and automatically began treating me like some kind of adult baby, as though I'd suddenly started wheeling myself around the room on an undersized tricycle, gurgling and suckling on a dummy. Because games are for kids, right? So I was essentially a grown man reviewing *Mr Men* books, yeah?

And when I wasn't viewed as a child, I was viewed as a nerd. How sad my little interests were. How dorky. It was bad enough enjoying the damn things but, being a games journalist, I took things one stage further by developing some understanding of how they were actually constructed. I might look at a new release and be impressed by the polygon count or the draw distance. Apparently this made me a tedious loser, because society decrees anyone who knows anything whatsoever about computers to be a boring idiot, while those possessing a similar level of nerd-knowledge of football or cinema or food are well-informed and sophisticated and sexually attractive and cool.

I didn't realise it at the time, but being a games journo in the 1990s meant I was on hand to witness the birth of several landmark cultural icons first-hand. For instance, back in 1995 I visited the studios of Core Design in Derby to report on the development of a new game starring a female explorer called Lara Croft. Tomb Raider was still in a rough-and-ready state – Lara was running through a grey landscape of textureless polygons – but it was clear this was going to be massive; she already had character.

A year later, I travelled to Dundee to drop in on a company called DMA Design, previously responsible for the popular strategy/puzzle game Lemmings. They were working on a new title partly inspired by a ZX Spectrum game called Turbo Esprit. Turbo Esprit came out when I was 15; I loved it. You had to drive around a city (in a Lotus Esprit Turbo, naturally) seeking out criminals. What made it unique was the sense that the city you were driving through actually 'worked'. There were traffic lights and petrol stations, roadworks and one-way streets. It was way ahead of its time.

DMA Design's new game featured an even more sophisticated city, with pedestrians and fire engines and its own police force. You could walk around it on foot, committing crimes, pinching vehicles and trying to evade the law. It was called Grand Theft Auto.

It looked very different to the GTA millions know and love/hate today: it was all viewed from overhead, and featured simple 'retro' graphics. But it was great. I gave it a rave review, calling it 'the gaming equivalent of a smack in the mouth'. 'Give us a sequel with polygons and cars that flip over,' I squealed. Years later, they did.

GTA IV is its latest incarnation. In its first week of release, it made around $500m. It's been rightly, and widely, proclaimed a masterpiece. And it is – at least technically. As far as the script and storyline goes, it tries so hard to appear 'adult', it winds up looking downright adolescent. The bad guys are implausibly amoral, everyone shouts 'fuck' every two seconds, and the women are little more than haircuts and orifices. In other words, it's like almost any Hollywood action film you care to mention.

But if you can ignore that, there's a wealth of incredible detail and some surprising moments of satire. For example, Liberty City has its own TV networks, which you can sit down and watch if the mood takes you. One channel, Weazel, is a thinly-veiled parody of Fox that features shows such as *Republican Space Rangers* (a fascistic cartoon in which dimwitted right-wing hicks roam the galaxy exterminating peaceful life forms) and the brashly titled *Vinewood Cunts* (a reality show about Paris Hilton types). And yes, they use the C-word right there in the game, in the gravelly voiceover for the virtual trailer you watch on the virtual TV in your virtual apartment in the virtual city teeming with virtual life. I don't know quite why, but this really leapt out at me. I don't think I've ever heard the word in a game before. Never mind the polygon count – that's genuine progress.

The one thing everyone knows about Grand Theft Auto is that you can kill prostitutes in it. That's because it's a 'sandbox' game in which you can kill anyone you like. Or you can not kill them. Or you can simply drive around slowly, obeying the traffic lights. If you break the law and the in-game police spot you, they'll hunt you down and nab you. Murdering innocent people is neither (a) encouraged, (b) free of consequence, or (c) any more realistic than a Tex Avery cartoon. Nonetheless, Keith Vaz MP is probably standing on his roof screaming for a ban right now, confidently telling the world's press that Grand Theft Auto IV is a dedicated, ultra-realistic prostitute-murdering simulator aimed exclusively at easily corruptible three-year-olds.

He means well, possibly. But he's ignorant. The irony is that every time I read some dumb anti-gaming proclamation by Vaz and co, I get so angry I have to fire up GTA IV and shoot 29 pedestrians in the face just to vent the frustration they've caused. Thank God these games exist, or I'd be taking it out on real people.

The best videogames of all time [5 April 2008]

Originally written for the Guardian Weekend'*s 'Dork Talk' segment.*

Write a thing about the best videogames of all time, the *Guardian* commands me. And I obey. But space is short, so I've done it briefly. Bear in mind that these aren't the best videogames of all time, just a personal and possibly perverse selection, listed in order of release, not merit. Anyway: insert coin. Hit start button.

Asteroids (1979, Atari): Of all the early monochrome classics, Asteroids was my favourite, because it's truly bleak. Rather than aliens or robots, your enemies are unthinking lumps of rock that are hurtling through space. Twirling somewhere in the middle of this cluttered void is your tiny, heartbreakingly fragile spaceship, armed only with a feeble electric peashooter. If Asteroids has a message, it's this: you are insignificant, the universe doesn't care about you, and you are definitely going to die. Brilliant.

Pac-Man (1980, Namco): Pac-Man himself may be an ultimately unknowable yellow disc, but his spectral pursuers had proper googly eyes and everything. And nicknames. And blood types. OK, not blood types. But this was one of the first games with identifiable characters, which goes a long way to explaining its success.

3D Deathchase (1983, Micromega): A Spectrum game in which all you had to do was avoid trees and shoot fellow motorcyclists. Simple, speedy pseudo-3D graphics meant suddenly you were starring in the bike section from *Return of the Jedi*. Yes. You really bloody were.

Stop the Express (1983, Hudson Soft): A rare Japanese Spectrum game, this was an insanely breakneck combat/platformer in which you had to scamper along the top of a runaway train, fighting assassins and dodging obstacles. Best of all, when you beat it, your sole reward was a caption reading 'Congraturation! You sucsess!'

Elite (1984, Acornsoft): Most home computer games were simplistic, flick-screen affairs in which you played a fat mayor jumping over a nettle or something like that. Then Elite came along and took the piss. A groundbreaking 3D space combat-and-trading simulator that managed to convince me my computer could, when programmed correctly, house an entire alternative universe.

Jet Set Willy (1984, Software Projects): Back in the day, you needed only a single programmer to create a game – and since said programmers were often geeked-out stoners, said games were often weird. Jet Set Willy's blend of flying pigs, in-jokes, *Python* and *Freak Brothers* references encapsulates the homebrew quirkiness of the cottage industry software scene of the early 80s. We shall not see their like again.

The Hitchhiker's Guide to the Galaxy (1984, Infocom): Still one of the only games to contain proper, structured jokes, H2G2 was a text adventure co-written by Douglas Adams himself. It was also the first postmodern game, since it knew it was a game, and also knew you knew, so sometimes it would refer to you as Arthur Dent (star of the game) and other times simply as you (the player controlling him) – whichever seemed funniest at the time.

The Sentinel (1986, Firebird): You played a nomadic consciousness that had to absorb parts of the 3D landscape, then transfer itself inside a series of motionless avatars in order to travel – your goal being to ascend the highest peak before the ominous Sentinel stared you to death with his huge, cycloptic eye. In other words, it makes sense only when you play it.

Kato Chan and Ken Chan (1988, Hudson Soft): An import-only title for the PC Engine (a tiny Japanese console), Chan And Chan was a below-average platform game – but one that revolved, startlingly, around shitting, farting and pissing. The point at which I first grasped the illicit joy of off-kilter Japanese imports. (Also for the PC Engine: Toilet Kids, a shoot-'em-up in which you fired turds at flying penises.)

Tetris (1989): There can't be a human being on Earth who doesn't love Tetris. Perpetual order from perpetual chaos. The most inherently satisfying video game ever created.

Road Rash (1991, EA): Road Rash was a Mega Drive motorbikin' game with a twist: you could swerve across the road to punch the other riders in the head, simply because you didn't like them. All your opponents had irritating names, which made developing pointless vendettas a breeze. Few things in life have satisfied me as much as repeatedly smacking preppy, clean-cut Biff in the face until he hurtled into an oncoming taxi at 100mph.

Doom (1993, id software): The king of all first-person shooters. Doom represented a huge technological leap forward, with graphics and multiplayer gameplay options that were way ahead of their time. But, most of all, Doom was scary. Really bloody scary. Flickering lights, horrifying monsters, pitch-black rooms and blood-curdling sound design. The snarling, bull-like 'pinky' beasts that galloped over and bit your face off without warning are the most unsettling enemy in videogame history.

UFO: Enemy Unknown (1993, Microprose): It runs on the PC. It's a turn-based strategy game. It's got a 'suburban alien invasion' vibe straight out of the X-Files. Bored already? Your own yawning mouth is lying to you. UFO (also known as X-COM) was one of the creepiest, most addictive and absorbing games of the 90s. Today, turn-based games are out of favour and UFO itself is a forgotten relic – a shame, because if it was released next week on Nintendo DS, it would be a bestseller. Someone needs to resurrect it.

Tekken 2 (1996, Namco): In 1996 I spent weeks sitting hunched over a PlayStation controller in my living room, fighting flatmates and friends in an uninterrupted Tekken trance. It's a hypnotic orgy of violence in which martial artists, thugs, robots, wrestlers and pandas knock 10 bells out of each other for no good reason; cue punches, kicks and harrowing acts of cartilage-grinding chiropractic violence that almost made you pity your opponent. Wonderful.

The Grand Theft Auto series (1997–2008, DMA/Rockstar): Controversial series of 'sandbox' games that gift the player an entire city in which to misbehave. It began in 1997 as a cheeky mayhem simulator with a top-down, 2D viewpoint and a ZX Spectrum vibe. In 2001, it graduated to 3D and became an unstoppable blockbuster. The sun-kissed San Andreas is my favourite GTA, at least until the next-gen GTA IV arrives in a few weeks. Few Brits realise these games are made in Scotland: we should be far prouder of this stuff than we are.

The Orange Box (2007, Valve): Must-have compilation containing both Half-Life 2 (the best first-person shooter since Doom) and Portal (one of the most inventive brain-ticklers ever conceived). Playing Half-Life 2 is a bit like starring in a sci-fi horror remake of Die Hard, but better, while Portal is a description-defying 3D puzzle that folds your sense of spatial awareness in on itself. Utterly fantastic.

The Burnout series (2001–8, Criterion) Another great British creation. Forget the stuffy gearstick-porn of Gran Turismo, Burnout provides the most thrilling racing experience around. Not in the slightest bit realistic, and better for it, it's the spiritual successor to Road Rash – ramming your opponent off the road at mind-mangling speed. The most recent entry, the free-roaming Burnout Paradise, is fun, but punishes the player at every turn with an abysmal navigation system; 2004's Burnout Takedown remains the high water mark.

Super Mario Galaxy (2007, Nintendo): All the Mario platformers are superb: Galaxy happens to be the most recent. A dizzying, challenging, ingenious romp, it's like having liquid joy poured into your head via the eyeholes. Anyone who believes videogames to be a mindless waste of time should play this. As surreal and inventive as *Python*; as much pure entertainment as 100 *Tom and Jerry* cartoons, it's a bona fide work of modern genius.

In September 2008, I wrote a one-off review for the 200th edition of PC Zone *magazine, the place where I started my 'career' in 'journalism'. Since I'd been away for a while, they gave me a rubbish title to review.*

Euro Truck Simulator: Thanks, *PC Zone*. You bring me back from the dead for one last review and what do you give me to look at? A game in which you drive a lorry full of tomatoes to Lyon. I thought the whole appeal of games was that they let you do things you can't do in real life, like shooting a Nazi or jumping over a daffodil and landing on a cloud. Not so here. As glamorous exercises in escapism go, Euro Truck Simulator is on a par with fishing hair from a plughole.

The gameplay: pick a truck, pick a cargo (Sugar! Electronics! Frozen food! It could be literally any pedestrian item you can think of!), then drive it from one location to another. Along the way, you have to fill up at petrol stations and take the occasional nap. You also have to obey red lights and avoid crashing into things. You don't get to do any of the other things truck drivers are famous for, like wanking over pornography in lay-bys or murdering attractive 19-year-old hitchhikers, so the tedium quotient remains fairly constant. Most of the time you're just trundling slowly down a not-very-interesting motorway. While you're driving you can look around the cab by sliding the mouse about. That's quite interesting, and when your eyes alight on the empty passenger seat beside you, it can get downright poignant. The road is lonely and monotonous, and there's so little to do, you wind up staving off the boredom by holding negotiations with God in your head, just like a real truck driver.

Then you arrive at your destination, at which point there's an infuriatingly fiddly bit where you have to reverse your trailer into a docking bay. I left the experience feeling slightly more resentful of humankind than when I started, which would indicate that this sort of thing really isn't aimed at me. The score reflects my personal take on the damn thing. Add 50 points if you really, really want to drive a truck through some dull sections of Europe, like a cunt, with your cuntish hands and your cuntish truck-liking head. Fuck off.

Score: 40%

Dictionary corner   [6 August 2007]

Don't kick your own teeth out with excitement or anything, but I've been playing Scrabble. Virtual Scrabble. Or 'Scrabulous' as it's known. It's a plug-in for Facebook: you challenge a friend, then play turn-by-turn; casually, languidly, via email, which means games often last a week or more – like Test match cricket, but faintly more interesting.

And it's brightened my life considerably – except that there's a glaring flaw, which is that because (a) you're not playing in the same room, and (b) you have as much time as necessary to take your turn, it's subsequently far too easy – and tempting – to cheat.

Cheating comes in two main forms – 'soft' and 'hard'. Soft cheating involves looking stuff up in the dictionary before placing your tiles on the board. Hard to get away with in real life, but not on Scrabulous, where it's actively encouraged: an interactive dictionary lurks beside the board.

Thus tempted, I became a habitual soft cheater: trying out all my letters in various combinations, tile-by-tile, desperately hoping I could 'wish' a word into existence; preferably one that would let me use up both the X and the J and still hit that treble-word-score square.

How about JOGHEXY? Does that mean anything? Something medical? Please? Well, what about just JOXEY? That sounds like a proper word. Almost. Come on, you bastard dictionary. Throw me a sodding bone here.

(Incidentally, I surely can't be the first person to have thought of this, but isn't it time someone released a bogus novelty dictionary containing nothing but made-up, joxey-esque words, with the definition for every entry reading 'a word commonly used for cheating at Scrabble'?)

Anyway, soft cheating might not be full-blown hard cheating, but it still leaves you feeling rather cheap. Who knew GIVED was a valid word? Not me, until I looked it up. As I slid the final D into position, I felt hollow inside. Numb.

Inevitably, I soon began hard cheating. It started slowly, with an online anagram generator. I could justify this to myself: hell, if I squinted at my letters I could almost make out a proper word – it was just on the tip of my mind, and the anagram software was only giving me a gentle nudge, which isn't really cheating, right? Besides, a deft Scrabble move is a beautiful thing, and who am I to deprive the world of beauty?

Then I discovered scrabblesolver.co.uk, a site where you simply input the entire layout of the board, and leave it to work out the best possible options. In cheating terms, this was as hard as it gets – so just to keep things plausible, rather than use the No. 1 suggestion (generally a what-the-hell word like OREXIS), I'd scan the list and pick a suggestion I might have conceivably come up with myself. This was now the only genuine skill I was exercising – choosing a plausible lie. But what the heck? I won every time.

But then my opponents started catching up, placing seven-letter bingos, plus plentiful two- and three-letter branching bonus words such as AA and JO – sneaky words only a computer might know.

Then it hit me: they were using Scrabble Solver, too. We'd

rendered ourselves obsolete. It was 100% uncensored computer-on-computer action, with two meat puppets pulling the levers, fooling no one but themselves.

Worst of all, it was hard work. As a game progressed, with ever-more-obscure words snaking hither and thither, it took longer each time to input the entire board layout into the Scrabble Solver engine. What had started as a fun diversion had become an arduous job in which I received regular instructions (the layout of the board), inputted them into the system (Scrabble Solver) and then fed the results back into the machine, ready for regurgitation. It was duller than working in a call centre, and I wasn't even getting paid. I couldn't even enjoy the dull thrill of a pathetic, ill-gotten, vicarious win any more, because with cheats prospering on every side, the outcome was entirely arbitrary.

Eventually I rebelled. Threw off the yoke of my new robot overlords, stopped cheating and started losing honestly. Not because of some kind of ethical awakening, but because I'd discovered the ultimate truth about cheating: it's boring. Grindingly boring.

All those famous cheats – Milli Vanilli, the coughing *Who Wants to be a Millionaire* major, and about 50% of the riders in this year's Tour de France . . . they must feel this hollow and despondent all the time. We shouldn't vilify them: we should pity them.

Anyway, I'm still crap at Scrabble. My one-man mission to redefine ineptitude continues apace. But now at least I'm honest. Or should that be SCRUPULOUS (4H across, 72 points).

INDEX